Building Thinking Skills®

LEVEL 2

Critical Thinking Skills for Reading · Writing · Math · Science

SERIES TITLES

Building Thinking Skills®

Beginning ▪ Primary

Level 1 ▪ Level 2

Level 3 Figural

Level 3 Verbal

Written By

Sandra Parks

Howard Black

© 2006, 1998, 1984
THE CRITICAL THINKING CO.™
(Bright Minds™)
www.CriticalThinking.com
Phone: 800-458-4849 • Fax: 831-393-3277
P.O. Box 1610 • Seaside • CA 93955-1610
ISBN 978-1-60144-150-8

Table of Contents

CHAPTER SEVEN—VERBAL SIMILARITIES AND DIFFERENCES

CHAPTER EIGHT—VERBAL SEQUENCES

CHAPTER NINE—VERBAL CLASSIFICATIONS

CHAPTER TEN—VERBAL ANALOGIES

ANSWER GUIDE

CHAPTER ONE

Describing Shapes → **Describing Things**

Figural Similarities and Differences → **Verbal Similarities and Differences**

Figural Sequences → **Verbal Sequences**

Figural Classifications → **Verbal Classifications**

Figural Analogies → **Verbal Analogies**

DESCRIBING SHAPES—SELECT

DIRECTIONS: Look at each shape. Read the words in the choice box. Complete each sentence with the correct words from the choice box.

CHOICE BOX: narrow, short, tall, wide

EXAMPLE: This shape is _____*short*_____ and _____*wide*_____.

A-1

This parallelogram is _____ and _____.

A-2

This parallelogram is _____ and _____.

A-3

This trapezoid is _____ and _____.

A-4

This trapezoid is _____ and _____.

DESCRIBING SHAPES—SELECT

DIRECTIONS: Look at each shape. Read the words in the choice box. Complete each sentence with the correct words from the choice box.

CHOICE BOX: no, one, two, three, four, five, six

EXAMPLE

This parallelogram has _____four_____ sides and _____four_____ angles.

A-5

This quadrilateral has _____ sides and _____ angles.

A-6

This triangle has _____ sides and _____ angles.

A-7

This pentagon has _____ sides and _____ angles.

A-8

This hexagon has _____ sides and _____ angles.

DESCRIBING SHAPES—SELECT

DIRECTIONS: Look at each shape. Read the words in the choice box. Complete each sentence with the correct words from the choice box.

CHOICE BOX: all, none, one, two, three, four, five, six

EXAMPLE:
This triangle has _____*three*_____ sides and
_____*three*_____ angles.
_____*One*_____ of the angles is square.

A-9
This rectangle has _____ sides
and _____ angles.
_____ of the angles are square

A-10
This square has _____ sides and
_____ angles.
_____ of the angles are square.

A-11
This irregular pentagon has _____
sides and _____ angles.
_____ of the angles are square.

A-12
This hexagon has _____ sides and
_____ angles.
_____ of the angles are square.

DESCRIBING SHAPES—SELECT

DIRECTIONS: Look at each shape. Read the words in the choice box. Complete each sentence with the correct words from the choice box.

CHOICE BOX: all, none, two, three, four, five, six, hexagon, pentagon, rectangle, square, trapezoid, triangle

A-13

This _____ has _____
              shape name

sides and _____ are the same length.

A-14

This _____ has _____
              shape name

sides and _____ are the same length.

A-15

This _____ has _____
              shape name

sides and _____ are the same length.

A-16

This _____ has _____
              shape name

sides and _____ are the same length.

A-17

This _____ has _____
              shape name

sides and _____ are the same length.

DESCRIBING SHAPES—SELECT

DIRECTIONS: Look at each shape. Read the words in the choice box. Complete each sentence with the correct words from the choice box. Use the most specific name for each shape.

CHOICE BOX: all, none, two, three, four, five, six, hexagon, parallelogram, pentagon, quadrilateral, rectangle, square, triangle

A-18

This _____ has _____
shape name

sides and _____ are the same length.

A-19

This _____ has _____
shape name

sides and _____ are the same length.

A-20

This _____ has _____
shape name

sides and _____ are the same length.

A-21

This _____ has _____
shape name

sides and _____ are the same length.

A-22

This _____ has _____
shape name

sides and _____ are the same length.

DESCRIBING SHAPES—EXPLAIN

DIRECTIONS: In each description box, describe the shape in the picture at the left. Use complete sentences in your descriptions.

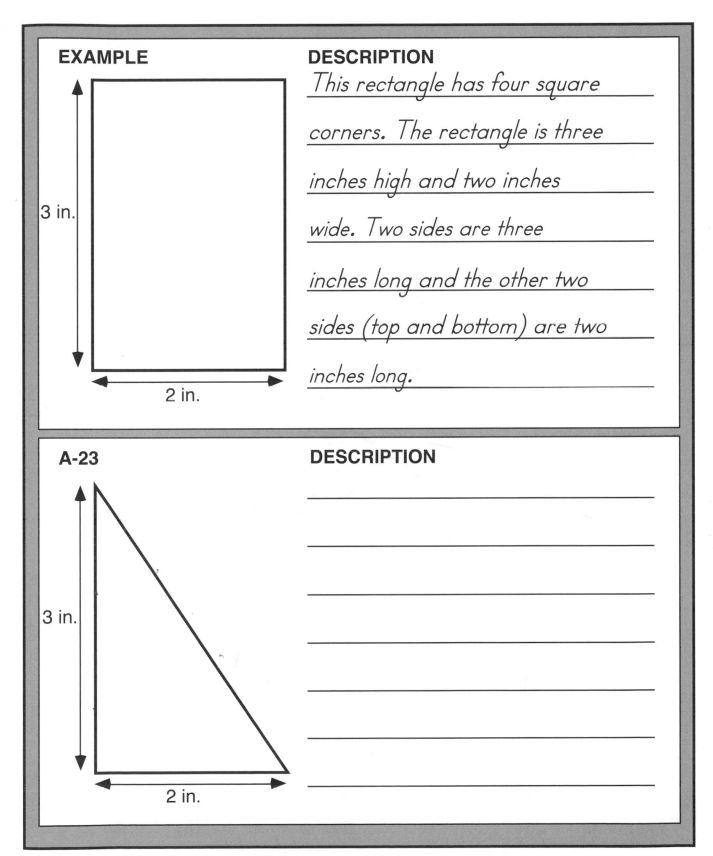

EXAMPLE

3 in.

2 in.

DESCRIPTION

This rectangle has four square corners. The rectangle is three inches high and two inches wide. Two sides are three inches long and the other two sides (top and bottom) are two inches long.

A-23

3 in.

2 in.

DESCRIPTION

DESCRIBING SHAPES—EXPLAIN

DIRECTIONS: In each description box, describe the shape in the picture at the left. Use complete sentences in your descriptions.

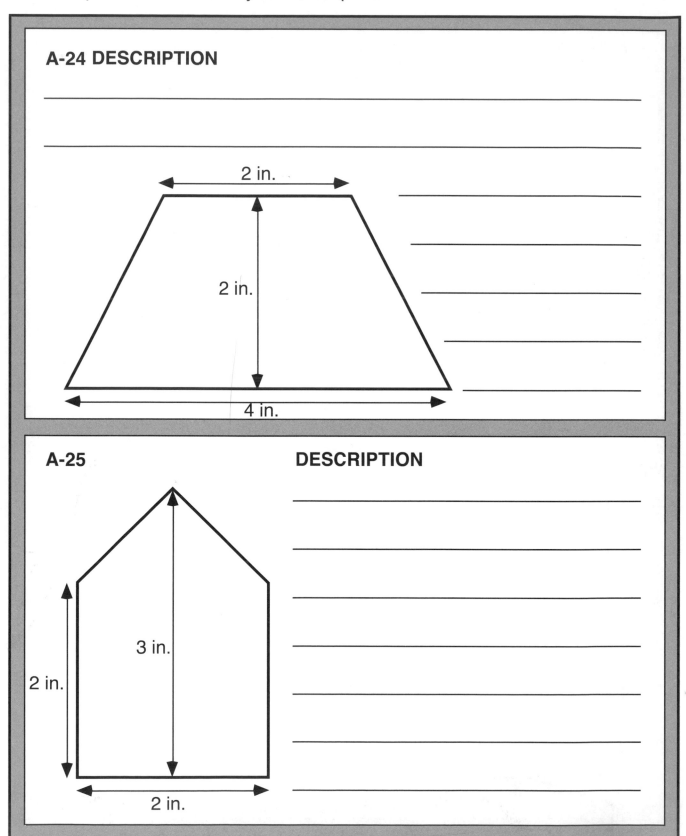

A-24 DESCRIPTION

2 in.

2 in.

4 in.

A-25   **DESCRIPTION**

3 in.

2 in.

2 in.

DESCRIBING POSITION—SELECT

DIRECTIONS: Write the words from the choice box that correctly complete the sentences. Draw a figure as directed.

CHOICE BOX

above, below, center, circle, left, right, square, triangle

A-26

The square is _____ the circle. The circle is _____ the square.

Draw a triangle below the circle.

A-27

The triangle is _____ the square. The circle is on the _____ side of the square.

Draw a black triangle to the right of the square.

DESCRIBING POSITION—SELECT

DIRECTIONS: Write the words from the choice box that correctly complete the sentences. Draw a figure as directed.

CHOICE BOX

above, below, center, circle, left, right, square, triangle

A-28

The triangle is _____ the circle and to the _____ of the square.

Draw a black circle near the lower left corner. The black circle will be _____ the square.

A-29

The triangle is near the upper _____ corner. The circle is in the _____.

Draw a black square directly below the circle. The black square will be to the _____ of the gray square.

DESCRIBING POSITION—SELECT

DIRECTIONS: Write the words from the choice box that correctly complete the sentences in the directions. Draw a figure as directed.

CHOICE BOX

above, below, larger, left, right, smaller

A-30

The _____ square is in the center. The _____ square is near the upper left corner. The large circle is near the lower _____ corner.

Draw a small circle near the upper right corner.

A-31

The circle in the center is _____ than the circle directly above it. The large square is to the _____ of the small circle.

Draw a small square directly to the right of the large circle. The small square will be _____ the large square.

DESCRIBING POSITION—EXPLAIN

DIRECTIONS: Describe the color, shape, and position of the figures in each drawing.

EXAMPLE

DESCRIPTION

The gray square is above the

white circle.

OR

The white circle is below the

gray square.

A-32

DESCRIPTION

DESCRIBING POSITION—EXPLAIN

DIRECTIONS: Describe the color, shape, and position of the figures in each drawing.

A-33

DESCRIPTION

_____

_____

_____

_____

_____

_____

A-34

DESCRIPTION

_____

_____

_____

_____

_____

_____

DESCRIBING POSITION—SELECT

DIRECTIONS: Describe the color, shape, and position of the shapes in each drawing.

A-35

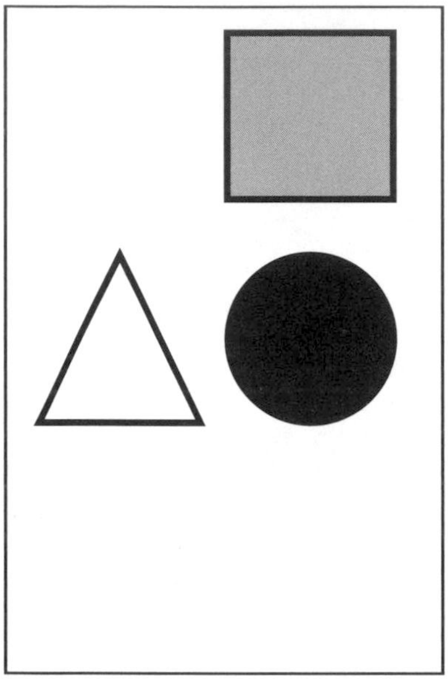

DESCRIPTION

_____

_____

_____

_____

_____

_____

A-36

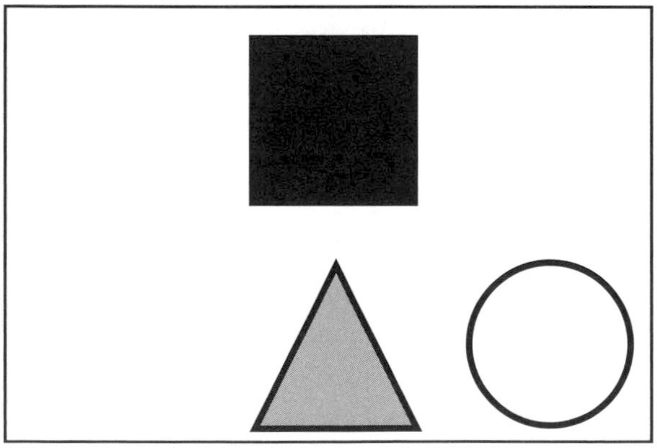

DESCRIPTION

_____

_____

_____

_____

_____

_____

CHARACTERISTICS OF A SHAPE

DIRECTIONS: Look at the pentagon in the center of the diagram. Write a characteristic of the pentagon in each of the four boxes. Use these characteristics to write a description of the pentagon in the description box.

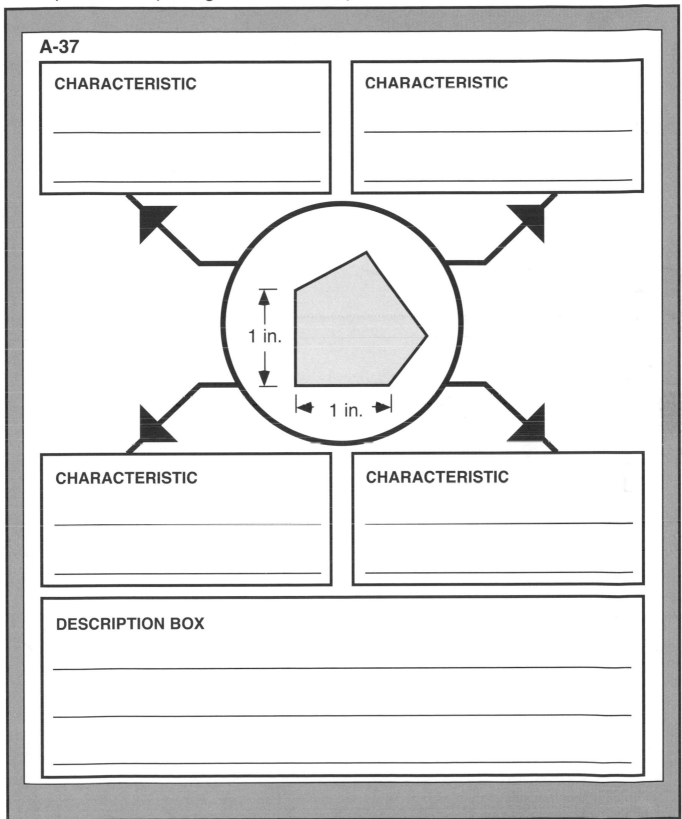

A-37

CHARACTERISTIC

_____

CHARACTERISTIC

_____

1 in.

1 in.

CHARACTERISTIC

_____

CHARACTERISTIC

_____

DESCRIPTION BOX

_____

_____

_____

CHARACTERISTICS OF A SHAPE

DIRECTIONS: Look at the hexagon in the center of the diagram. Write a characteristic of the hexagon in each of the four boxes. Use these characteristics to write a description of the hexagon in the description box.

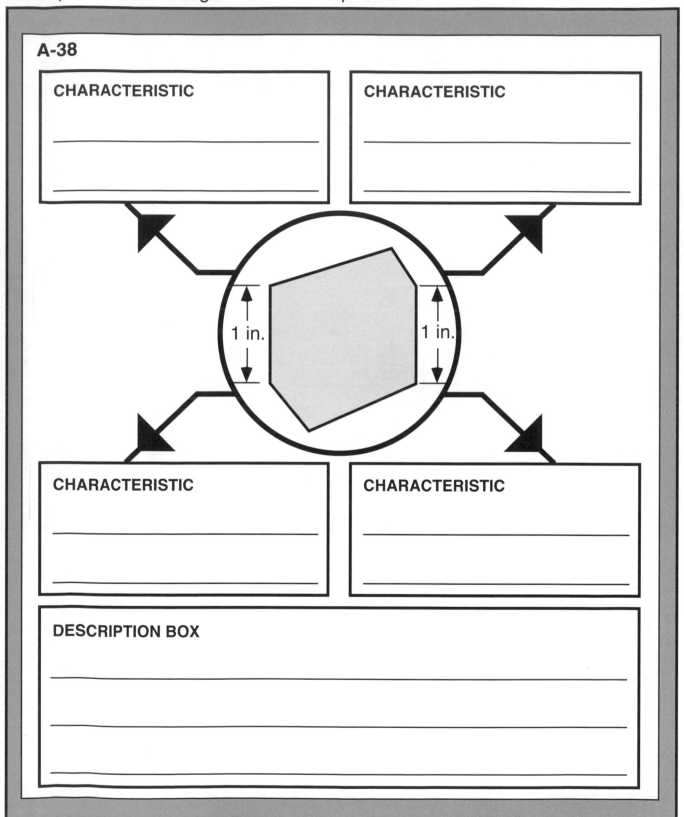

A-38

CHARACTERISTIC

CHARACTERISTIC

1 in.   1 in.

CHARACTERISTIC

CHARACTERISTIC

DESCRIPTION BOX

CHAPTER TWO

Describing Shapes	→	Describing Things
Figural Similarities and Differences	→	Verbal Similarities and Differences
Figural Sequences	→	Verbal Sequences
Figural Classifications	→	Verbal Classifications
Figural Analogies	→	Verbal Analogies

MATCHING FIGURES

DIRECTIONS: In each row, circle the figure that matches the one in the box on the left.

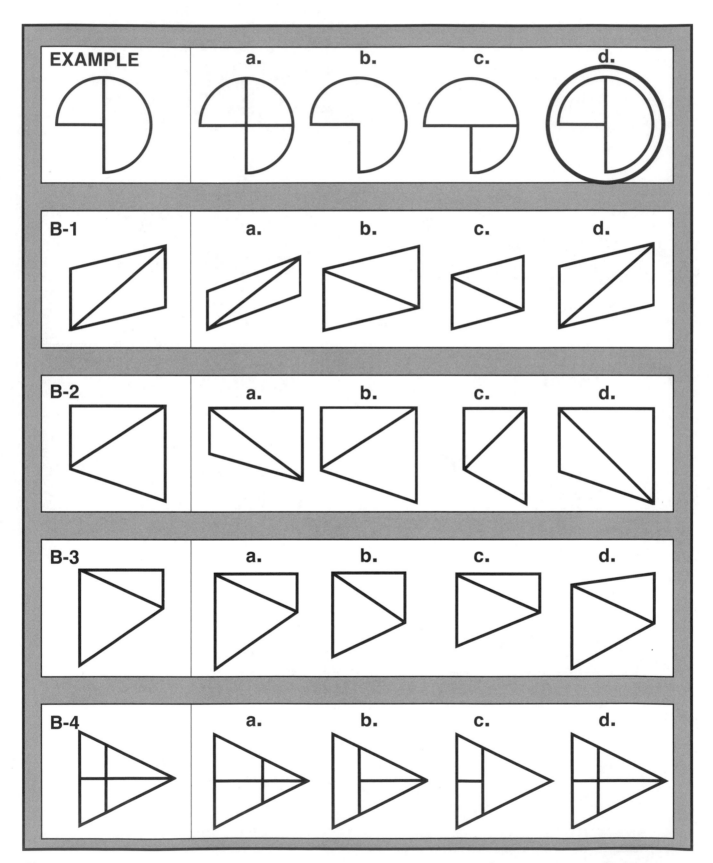

MATCHING FIGURES

DIRECTIONS: In each row, circle the figure that matches the one in the box on the left.

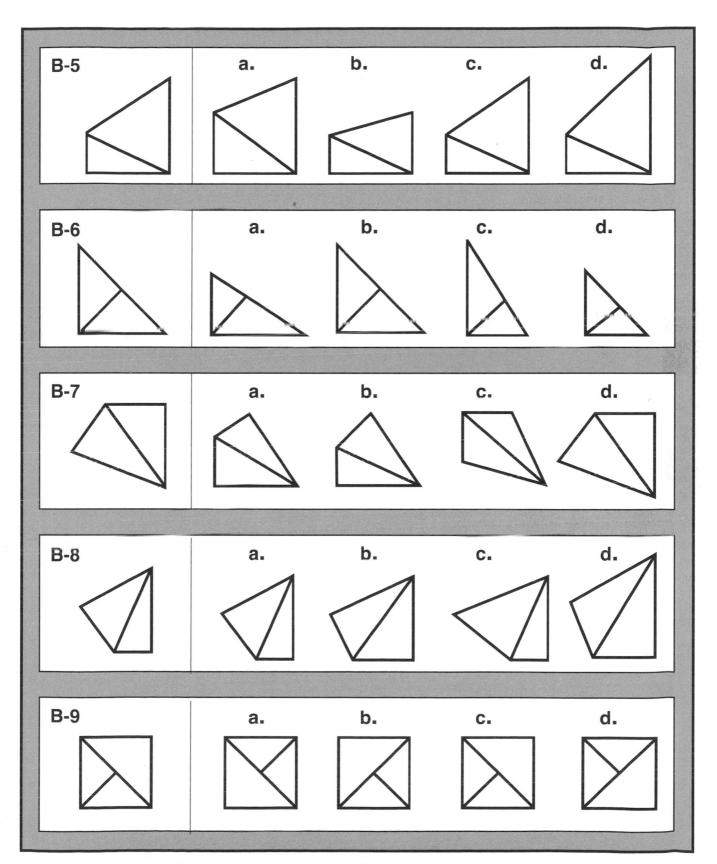

MATCHING FIGURES

DIRECTIONS: In each row, circle the figure that matches the one in the box on the left.

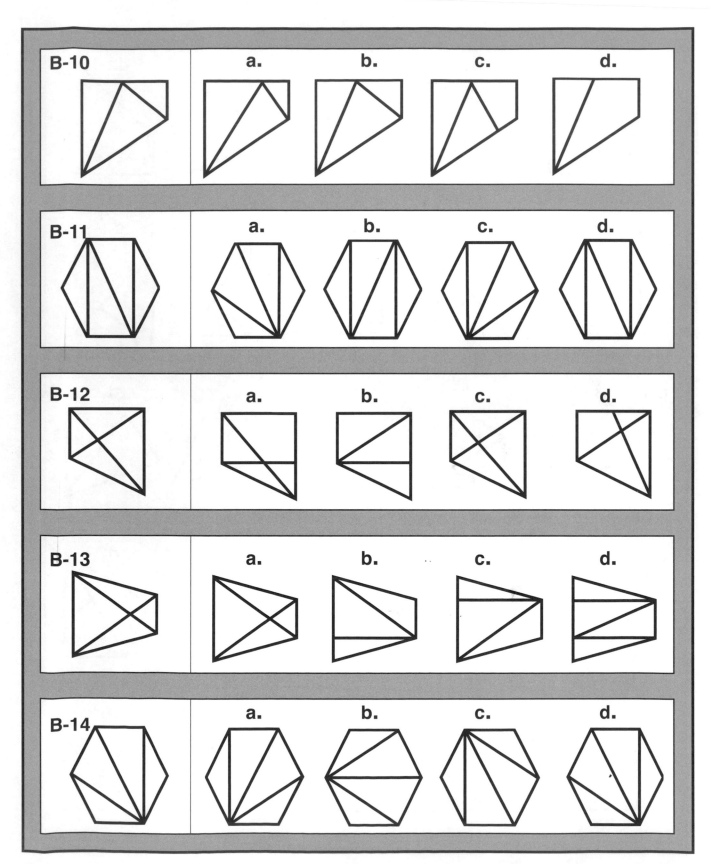

MATCHING SHAPES

DIRECTIONS: Circle the shapes that match the one on the left. The matching shapes must face the same direction as the shape on the left.

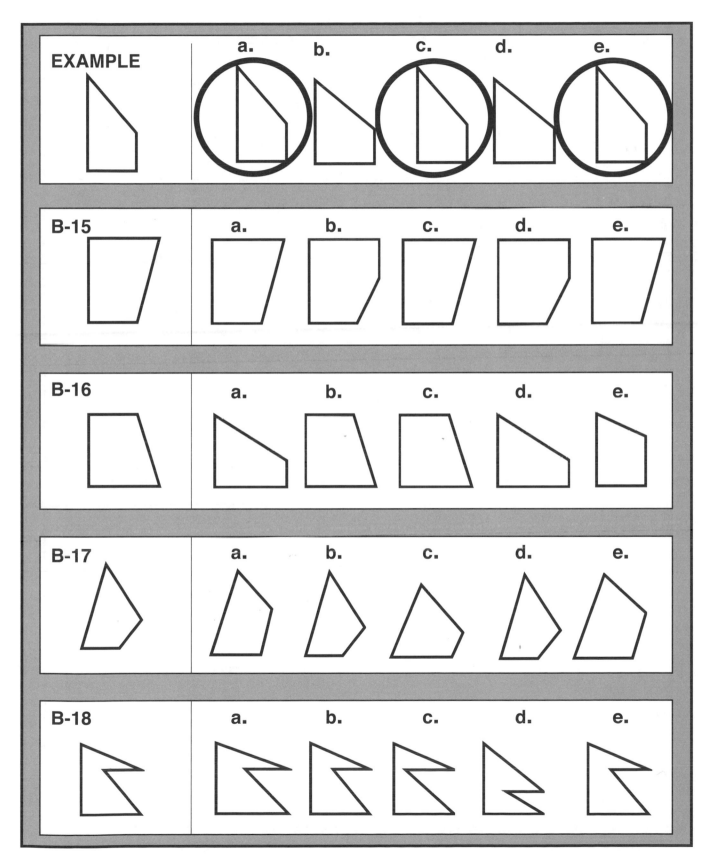

MATCHING SHAPES

DIRECTIONS: Circle the shapes that match the one on the left. The matching shapes must face the same direction as the shape in the box.

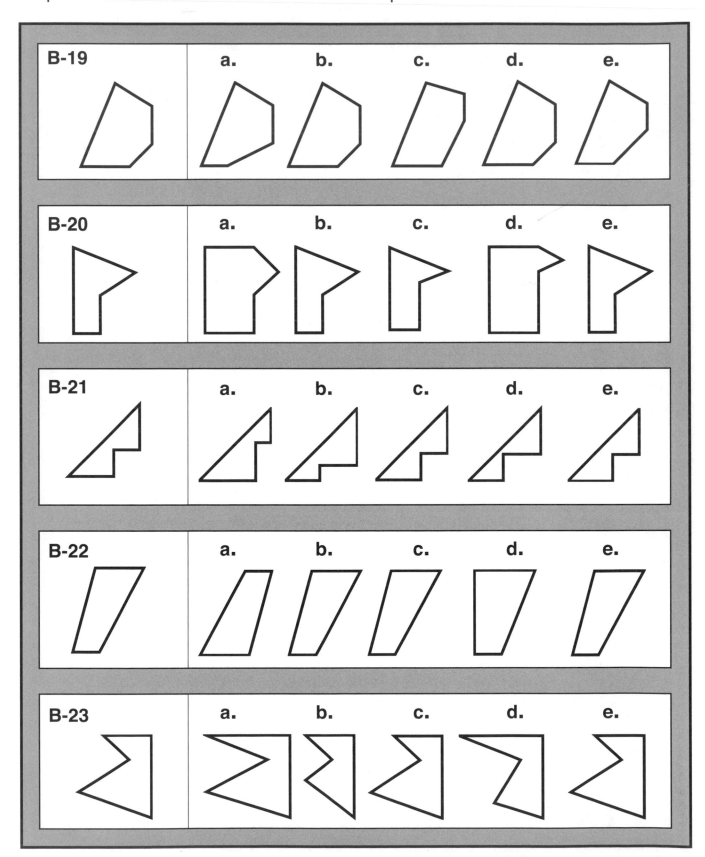

MATCHING FIGURES

DIRECTIONS: Circle the figures that are the same in each row.

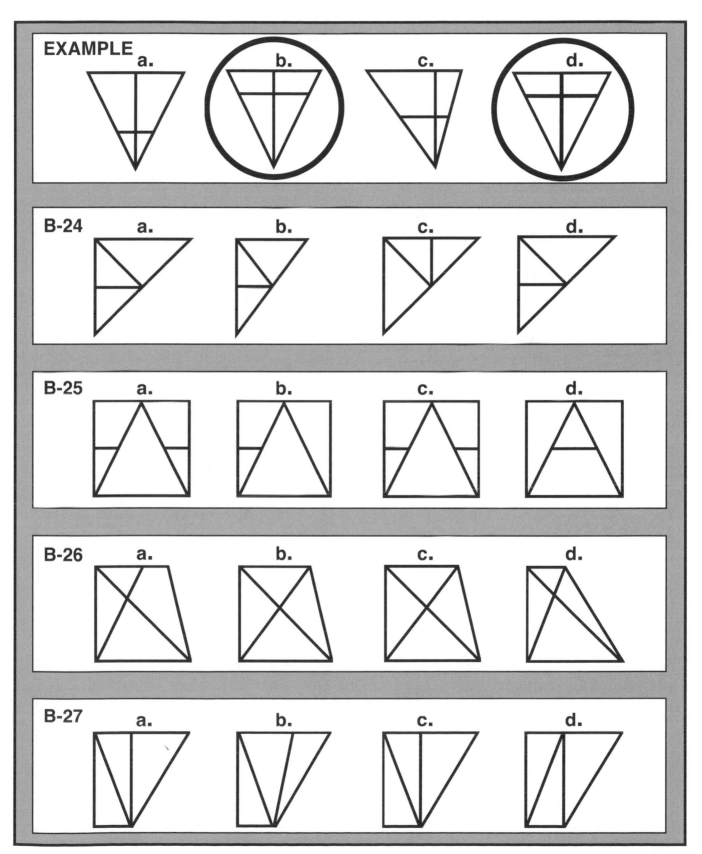

MATCHING FIGURES

DIRECTIONS: Circle the figures that are the same in each row.

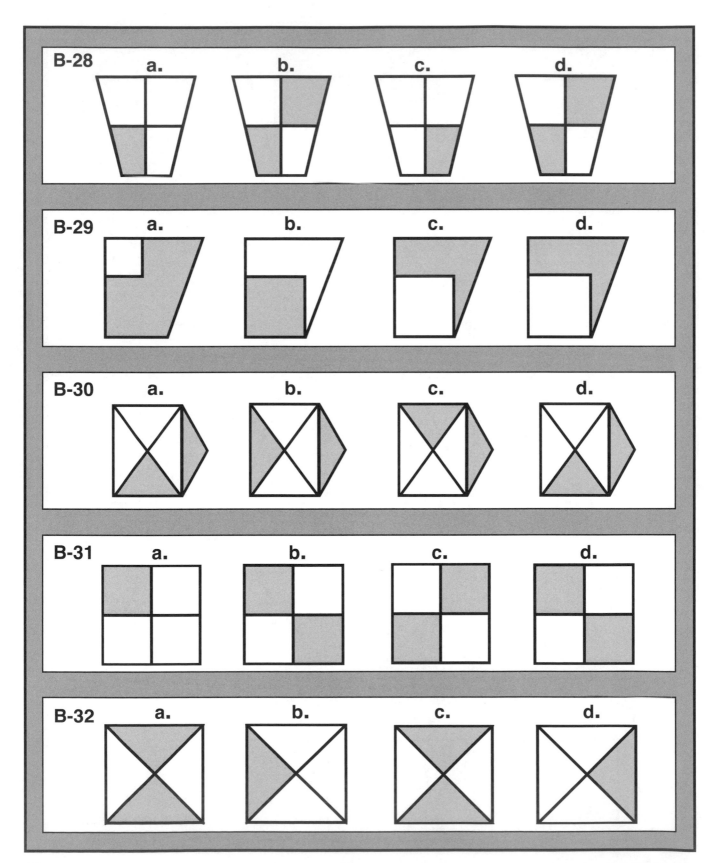

WHICH SHAPES DO NOT MATCH?

DIRECTIONS: Cross out the shapes that DO NOT match the shape on the left. The matching shapes must all face in the same direction.

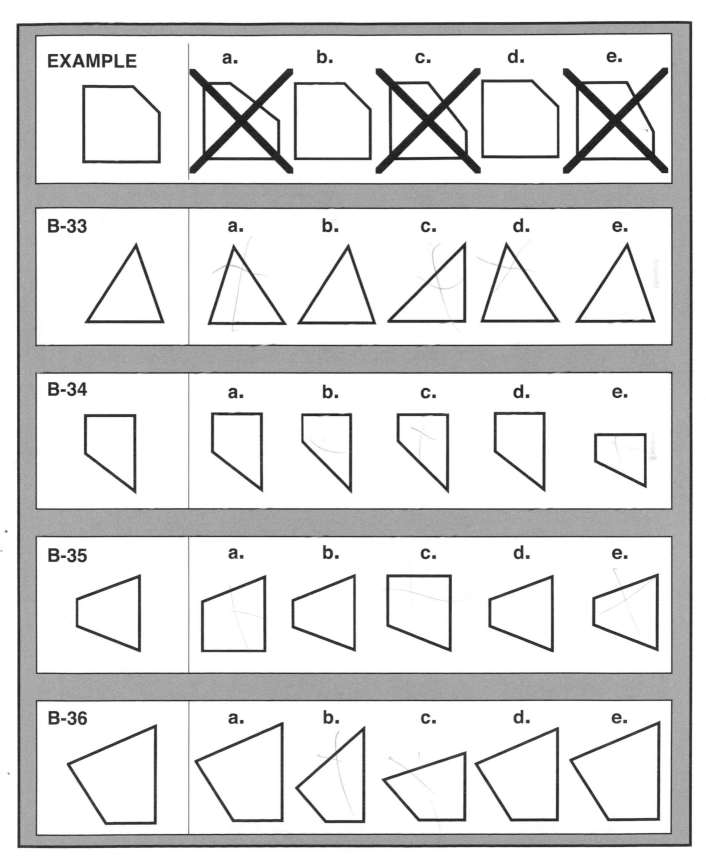

WHICH SHAPE DOES NOT MATCH?

DIRECTIONS: In each row, cross out the shape or figure that does not match the other four figures.

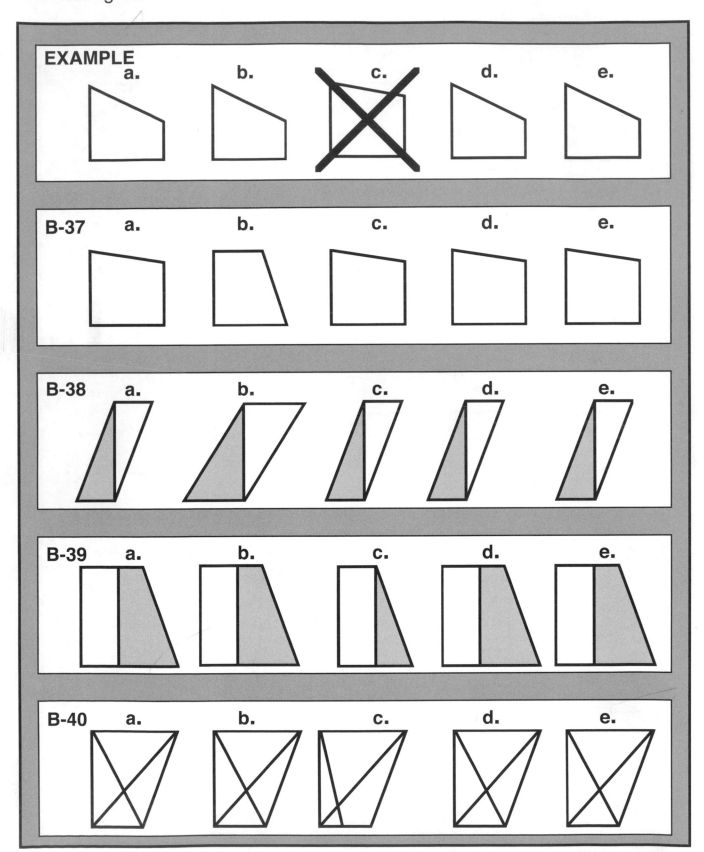

WHICH FIGURE DOES NOT MATCH?

DIRECTIONS: In each row, cross out the figure that does not match the other four figures.

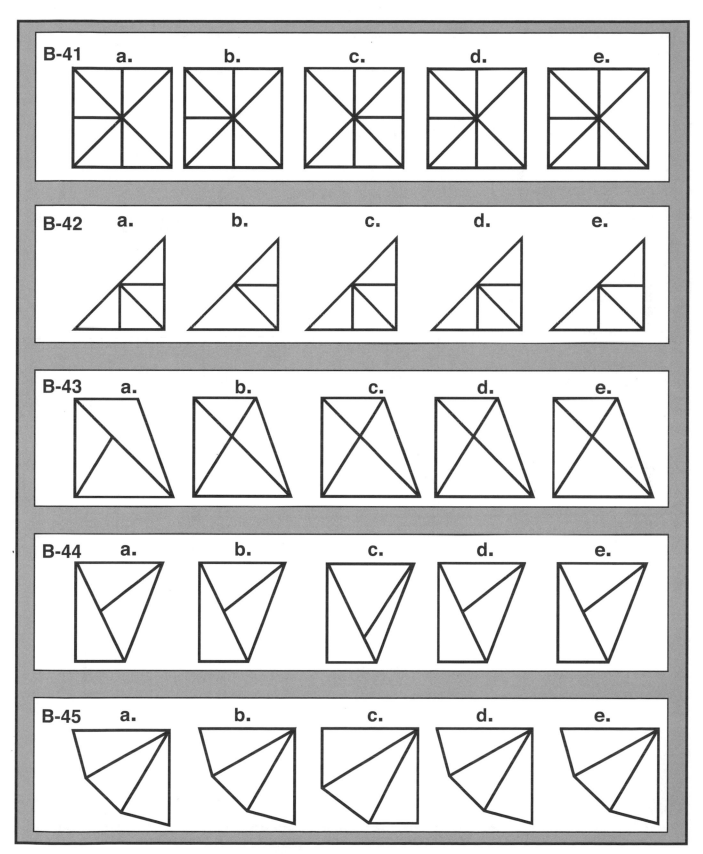

FINDING SHAPES

DIRECTIONS: Circle any shape that exactly matches one of the shapes in the figure on the left.

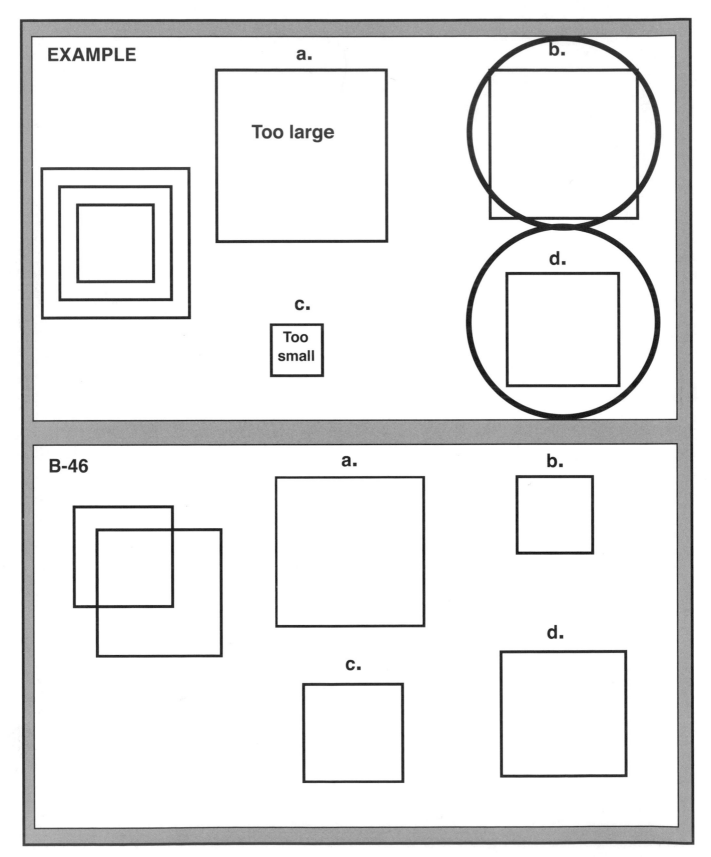

FINDING SHAPES

DIRECTIONS: Circle any shape that exactly matches one of the overlapping shapes in the figure on the left.

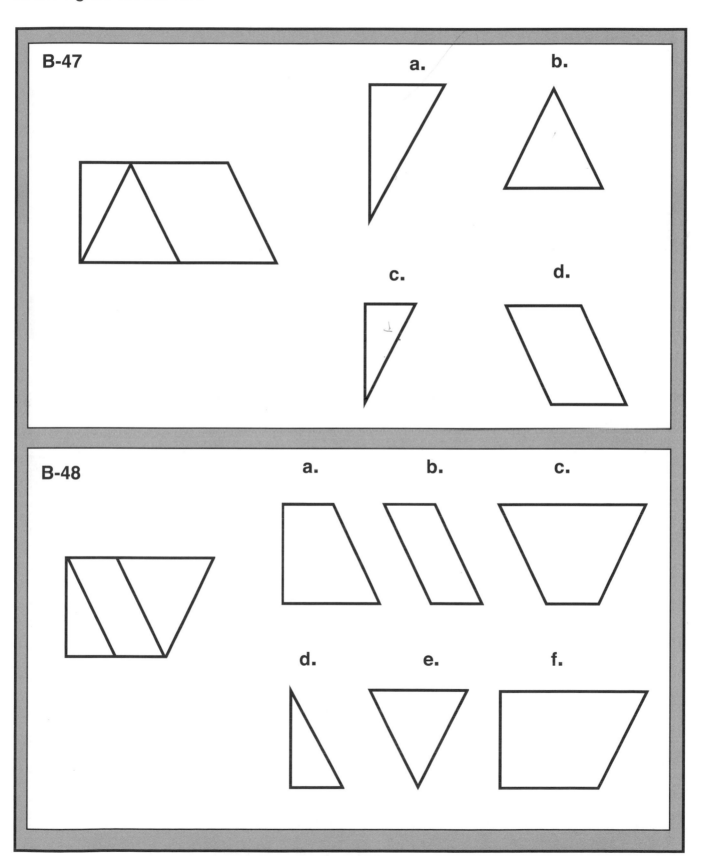

FINDING SHAPES

DIRECTIONS: Circle any shape that exactly matches one of the overlapping shapes in the figure on the left.

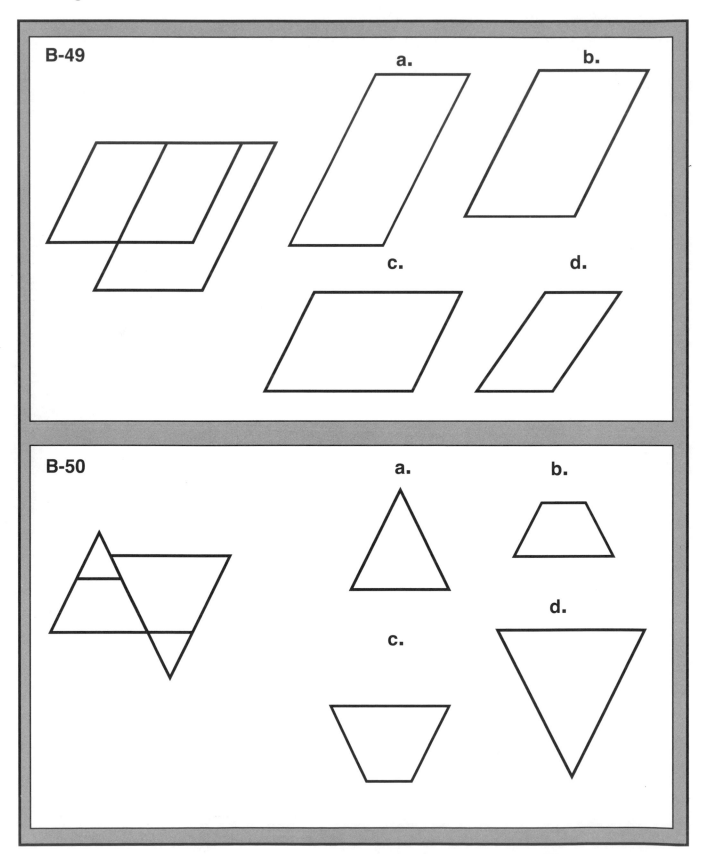

FINDING AND TRACING PATTERNS

DIRECTIONS: Circle any figure that contains the figure on the left. The figure must be in the same position but may have extra lines. Trace over the matching figure to make sure you are right.

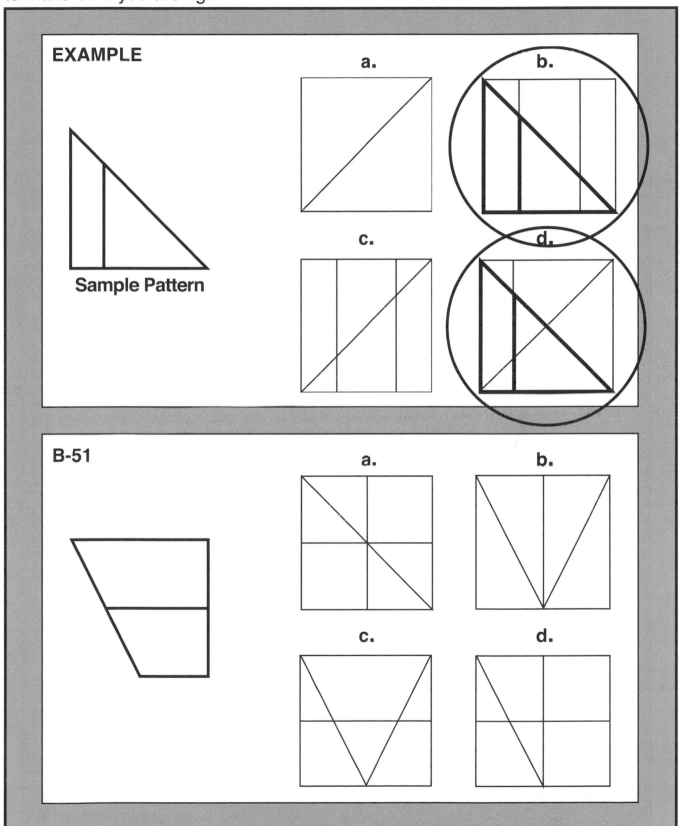

FINDING AND TRACING PATTERNS

DIRECTIONS: Circle any figure that contains the shape on the left. The shape must be in the same position but may have extra lines. Trace over the matching figure to make sure you are right.

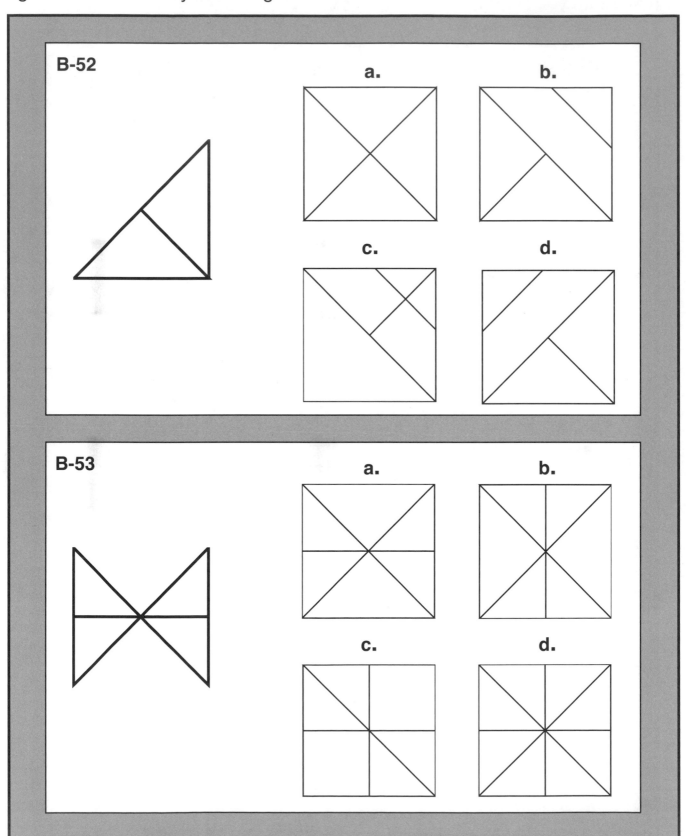

FINDING AND TRACING PATTERNS

DIRECTIONS: Circle any figure that contains the figure on the left. The figure must be in the same position but may have extra lines. Trace over the matching figure to make sure you are right.

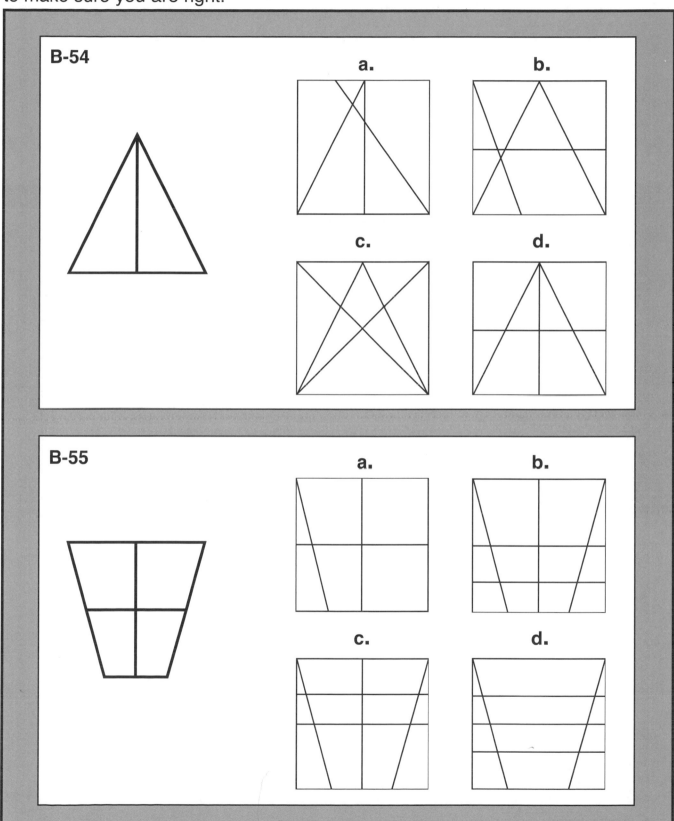

COMBINING SHAPES

DIRECTIONS: Check the figures that can be formed by joining the three shapes in the box. Shapes may be turned or flipped.

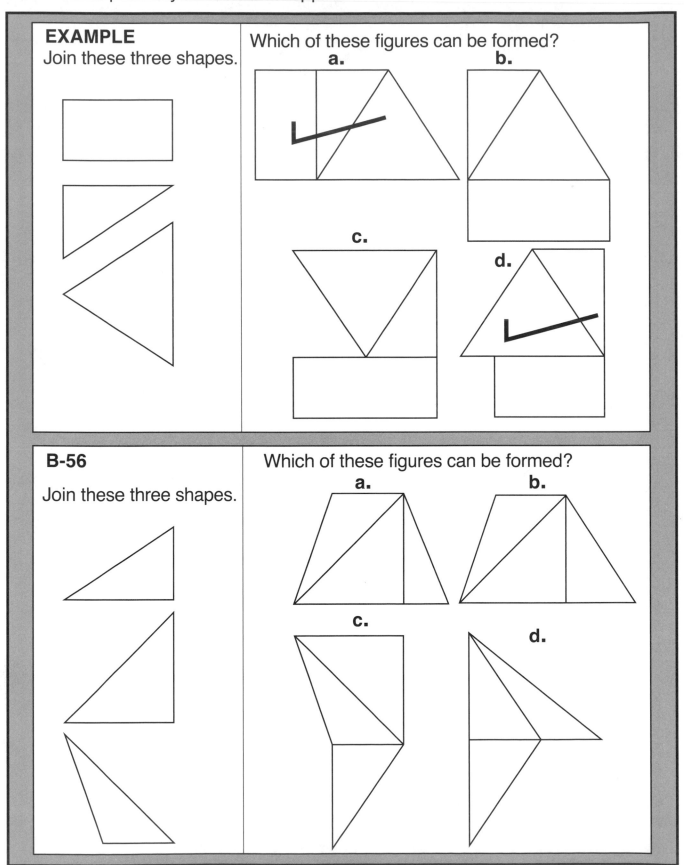

COMBINING SHAPES

DIRECTIONS: Check the figures that can be formed by joining the three shapes in the box. Shapes may be turned or flipped.

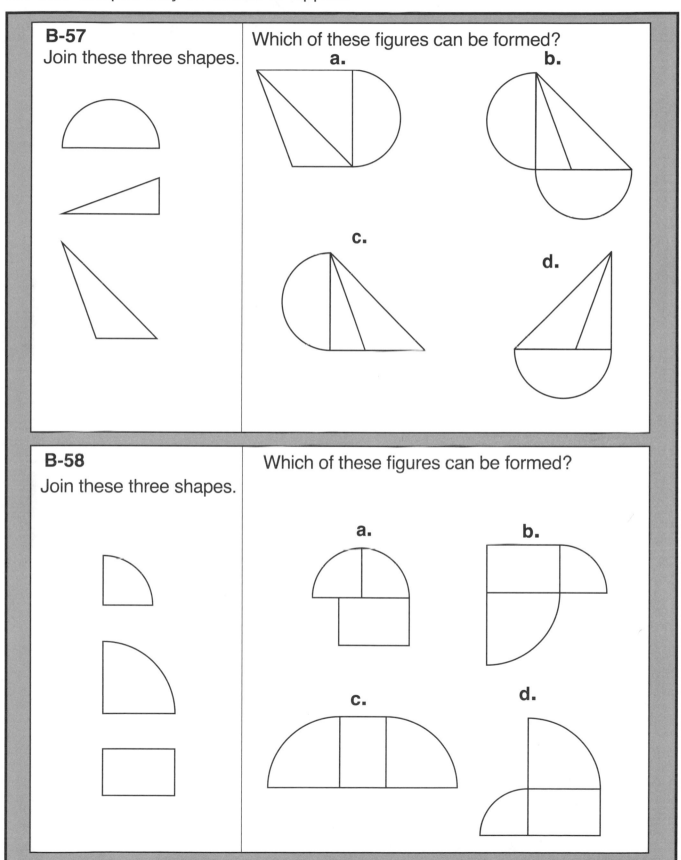

B-57
Join these three shapes.

Which of these figures can be formed?

a.

b.

c.

d.

B-58
Join these three shapes.

Which of these figures can be formed?

a.

b.

c.

d.

COMBINING SHAPES

DIRECTIONS: If each square was cut into three parts, check the figures that could be formed by joining those parts.

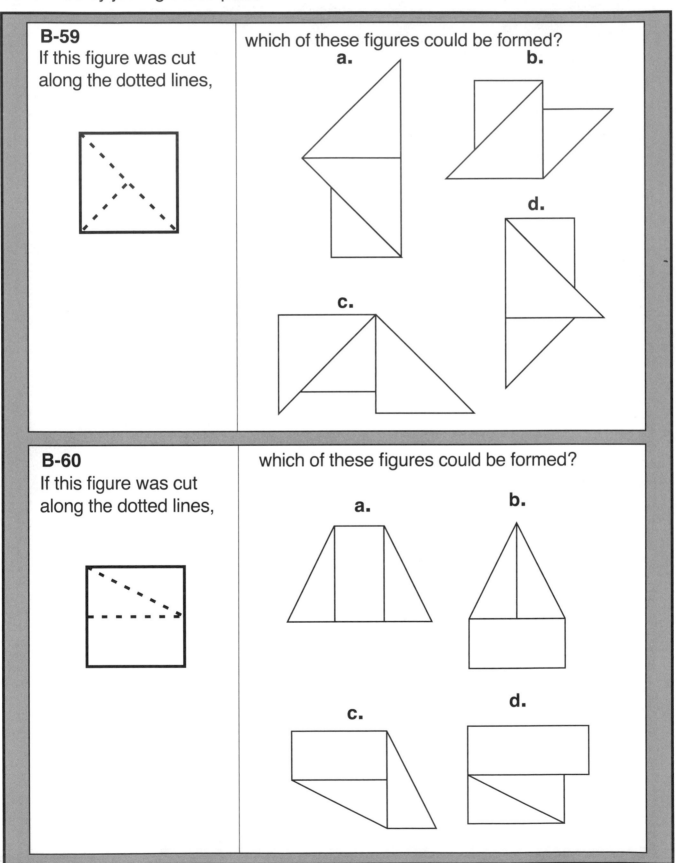

B-59
If this figure was cut along the dotted lines,

which of these figures could be formed?

a.

b.

c.

d.

B-60
If this figure was cut along the dotted lines,

which of these figures could be formed?

a.

b.

c.

d.

DIVIDING SHAPES INTO EQUAL PARTS—A

DIRECTIONS: Look at the two parts of the square. Answer the question, "Are the parts exactly alike?" Write *yes* or *no* in the blank below each question.

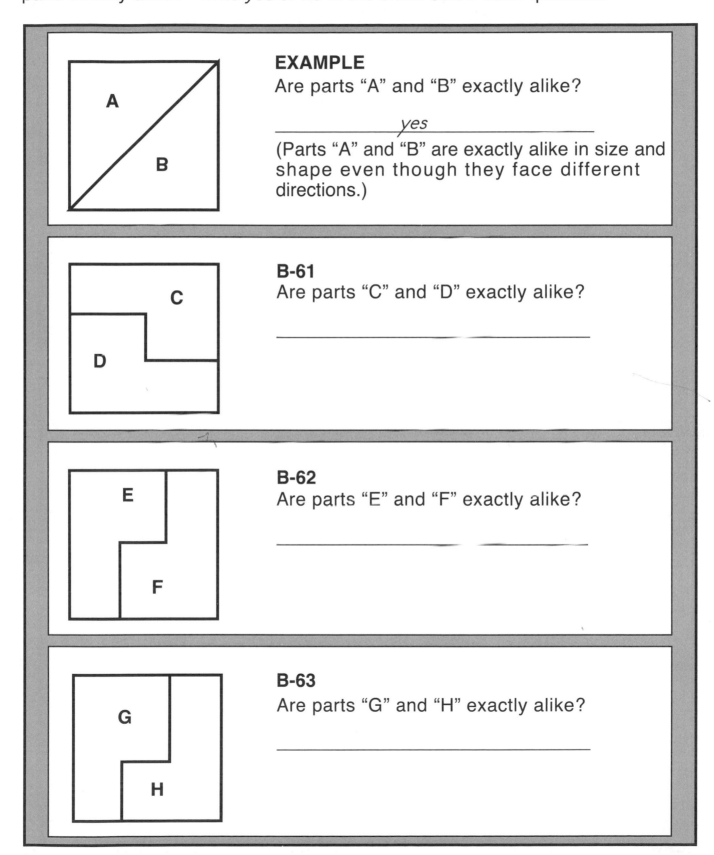

EXAMPLE

Are parts "A" and "B" exactly alike?

_____*yes*_____

(Parts "A" and "B" are exactly alike in size and shape even though they face different directions.)

B-61

Are parts "C" and "D" exactly alike?

_____

B-62

Are parts "E" and "F" exactly alike?

_____

B-63

Are parts "G" and "H" exactly alike?

_____

DIVIDING SHAPES INTO EQUAL PARTS—A

DIRECTIONS: Look at the two parts of the square. Answer the question, "Are the parts exactly alike?" Write *yes* or *no* in the blank below each question.

B-64
Are parts "I" and "J" exactly alike?

_____

B-65
Are parts "K" and "L" exactly alike?

_____

B-66
Are parts "M" and "N" exactly alike?

_____

B-67
Are parts "O" and "P" exactly alike?

_____

DIVIDING SHAPES INTO EQUAL PARTS—A

DIRECTIONS: Look at the two parts of the square. Answer the question, "Are the parts exactly alike?" Write *yes* or *no* in the blank below each question.

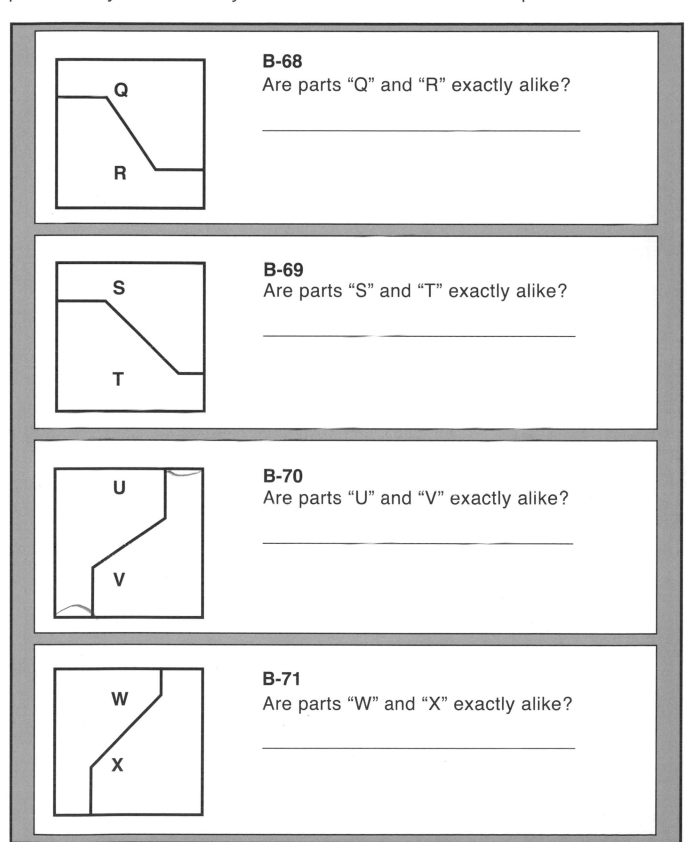

B-68

Are parts "Q" and "R" exactly alike?

_____

B-69

Are parts "S" and "T" exactly alike?

_____

B-70

Are parts "U" and "V" exactly alike?

_____

B-71

Are parts "W" and "X" exactly alike?

_____

DIVIDING SHAPES INTO EQUAL PARTS—B

DIRECTIONS: Divide each shape into equal parts as directed below.

B-72 Divide each of the two rectangles into four equal rectangles. There are three ways to do this. Divide each rectangle differently.

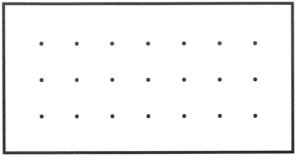

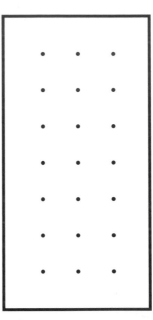

B-73 Divide each of the following shapes into two shapes that are exactly alike. (The parts do not have to face in the same direction.) The shape on the right is to be divided into two equal shapes that are exactly like those of the divided shape on the left.

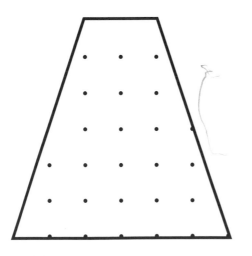

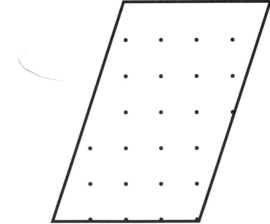

DIVIDING SHAPES INTO EQUAL PARTS—B

DIRECTIONS: Divide each of the rectangles into two equal parts. Do not draw squares or rectangles. Divide each rectangle differently.

B-74

DIVIDING SHAPES INTO EQUAL PARTS—B

DIRECTIONS: Divide each of the triangles into equal parts as directed below.

B-75 Divide this triangle into two equal triangles.

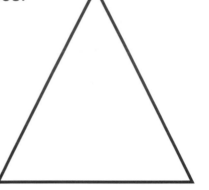

B-76 Divide this triangle into four equal triangles.

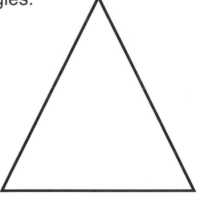

B-77 Divide this triangle into nine equal triangles.

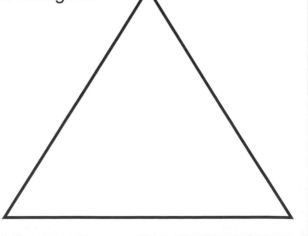

PAPER FOLDING—SELECT

DIRECTIONS: The left side of each exercise shows an unfolded sheet of paper with holes punched in it. One of the drawings in the choice box shows how the paper will look when folded. Circle the correct answer.

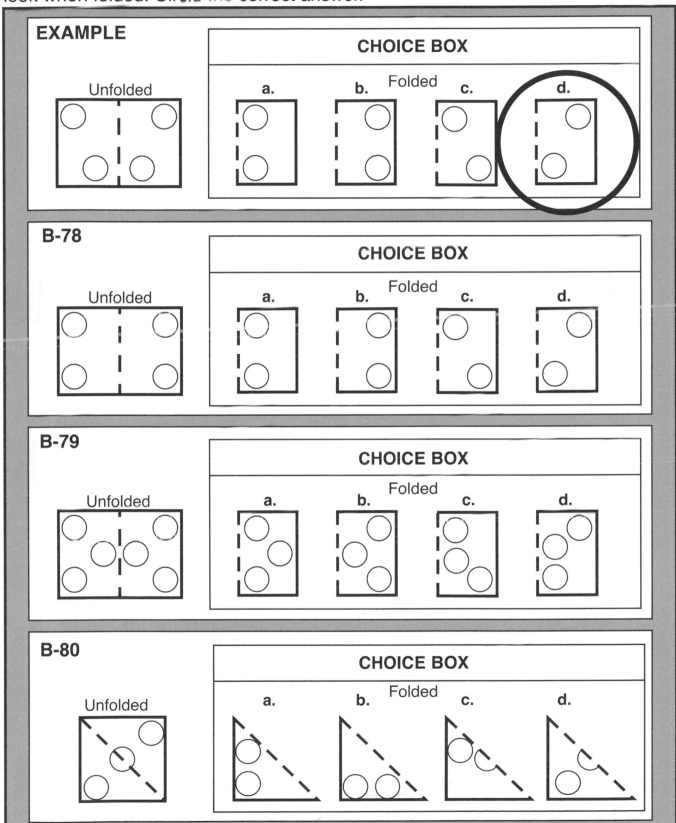

PAPER FOLDING—SELECT

DIRECTIONS: The left side of each exercise shows a folded sheet of paper with holes punched in it. One of the drawings in the choice box shows how the paper will look when unfolded. Circle the correct answer.

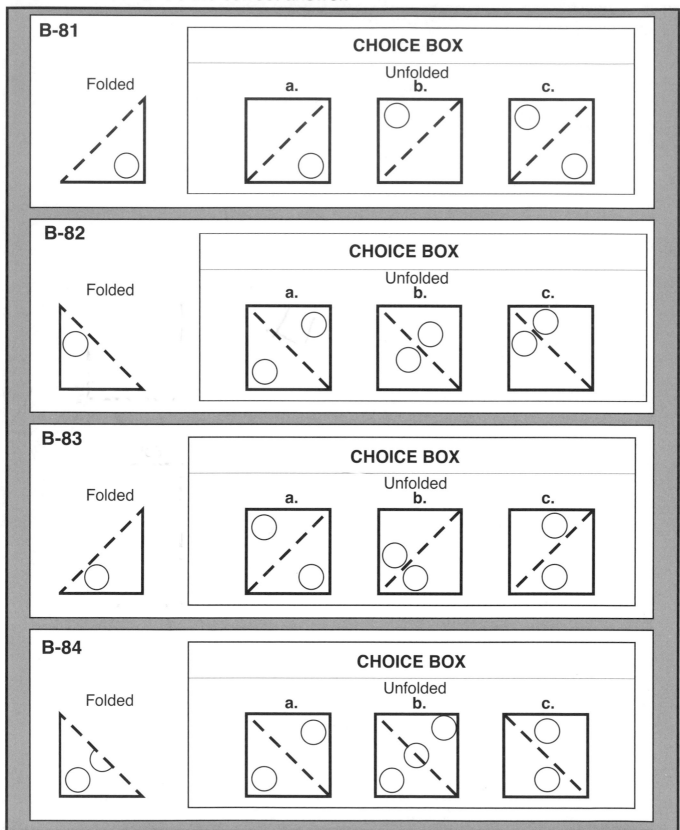

PAPER FOLDING—SUPPLY

DIRECTIONS: Here are four sheets of paper with holes punched in them. They are to be folded along the dotted line. Draw how each sheet will look after it is folded.

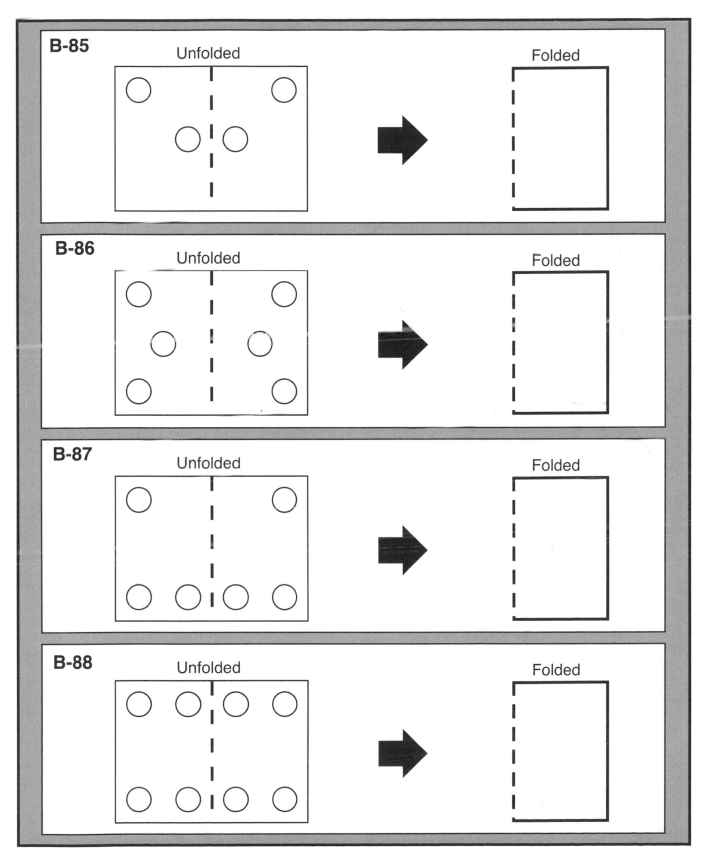

PAPER FOLDING—SUPPLY

DIRECTIONS: Here are four sheets of paper with holes punched in them. They are folded along the dotted line. Draw how each sheet will look when unfolded.

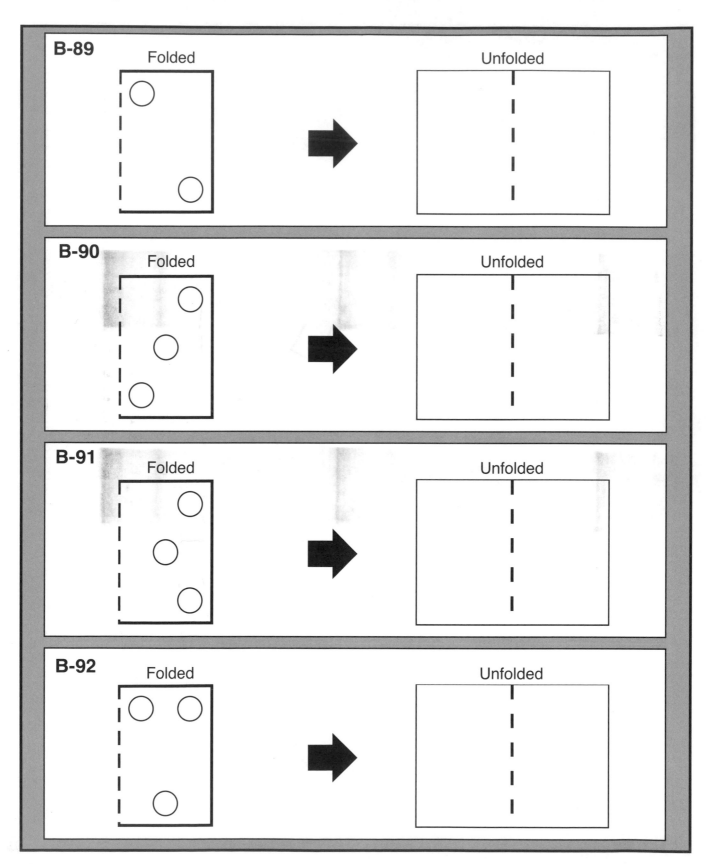

SYMMETRICAL PATTERNS—SUPPLY

DIRECTIONS: Here are four symmetrical patterns. They are to be folded along the dotted line of symmetry. Draw how each pattern will look when folded.

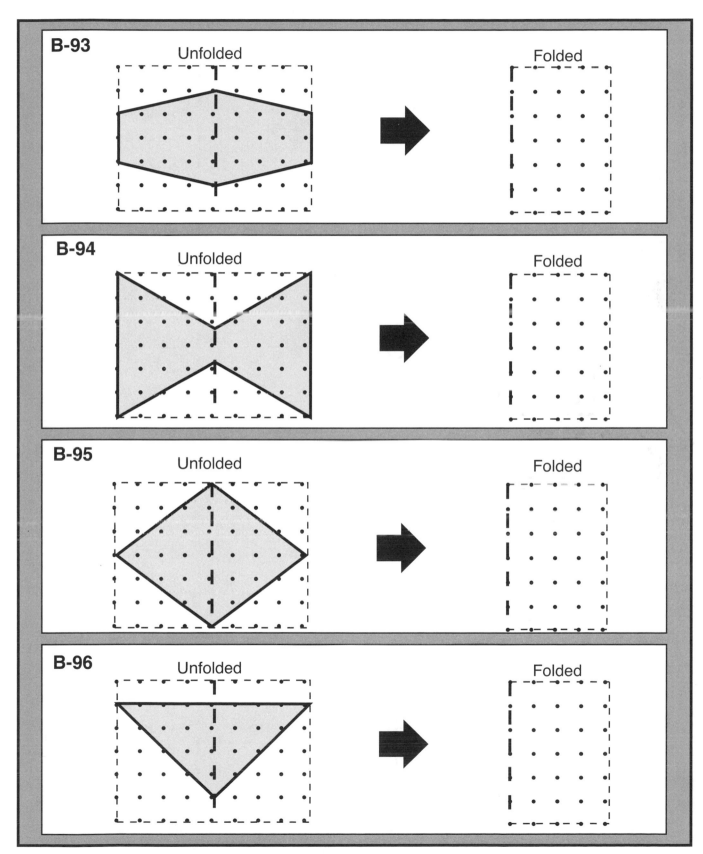

SYMMETRICAL PATTERNS—SUPPLY

DIRECTIONS: Here are four symmetrical patterns. They are to be folded along the dotted line of symmetry. Draw how each pattern will look when folded.

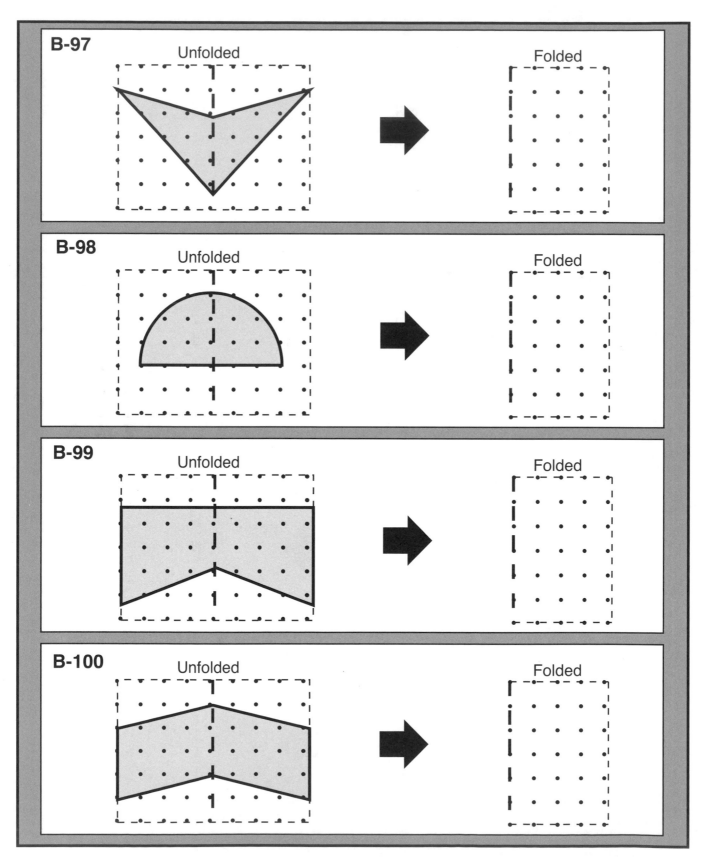

SYMMETRICAL PATTERNS—SUPPLY

DIRECTIONS: Here are four folded patterns. They are to be unfolded along the dotted line of symmetry. Draw how each unfolded symmetrical pattern will look.

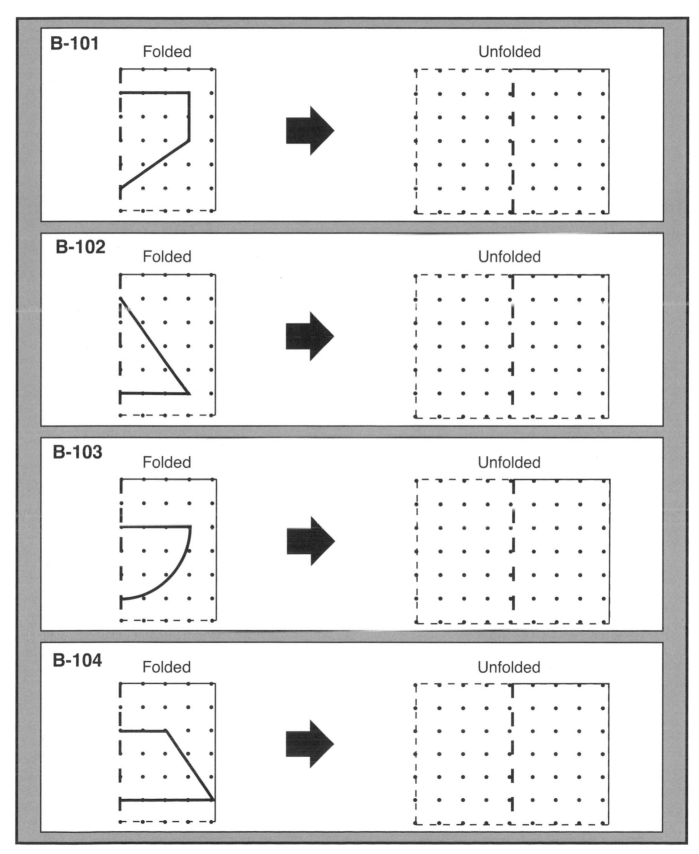

SYMMETRICAL PATTERNS—SUPPLY

DIRECTIONS: Here are four folded patterns. They are to be unfolded along the dotted line of symmetry. Draw how each unfolded symmetrical pattern will look.

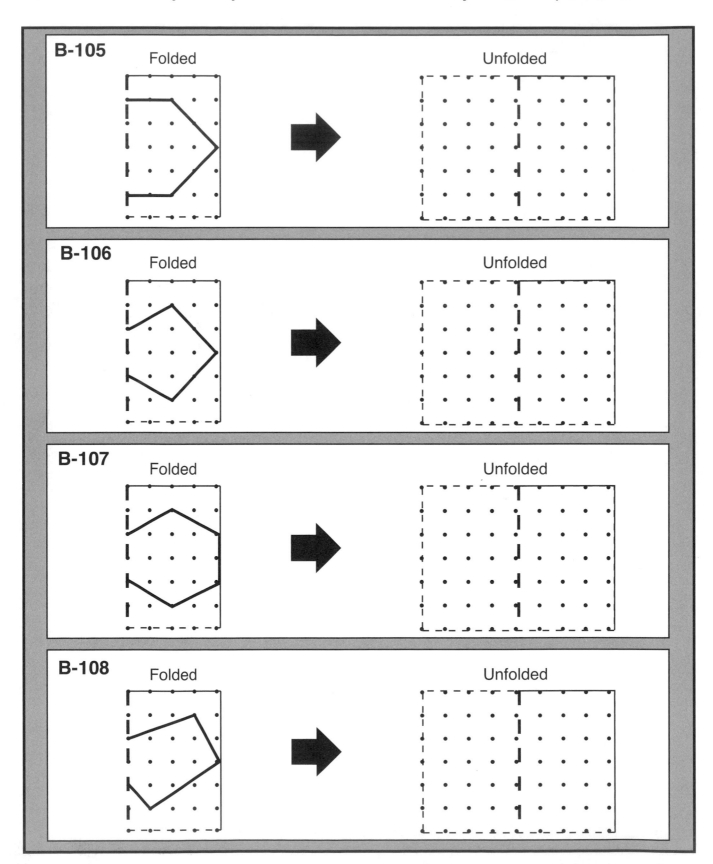

SYMMETRICAL PATTERNS—SUPPLY

DIRECTIONS: Complete each of the six patterns below so that each is symmetrical about the dashed line of symmetry.

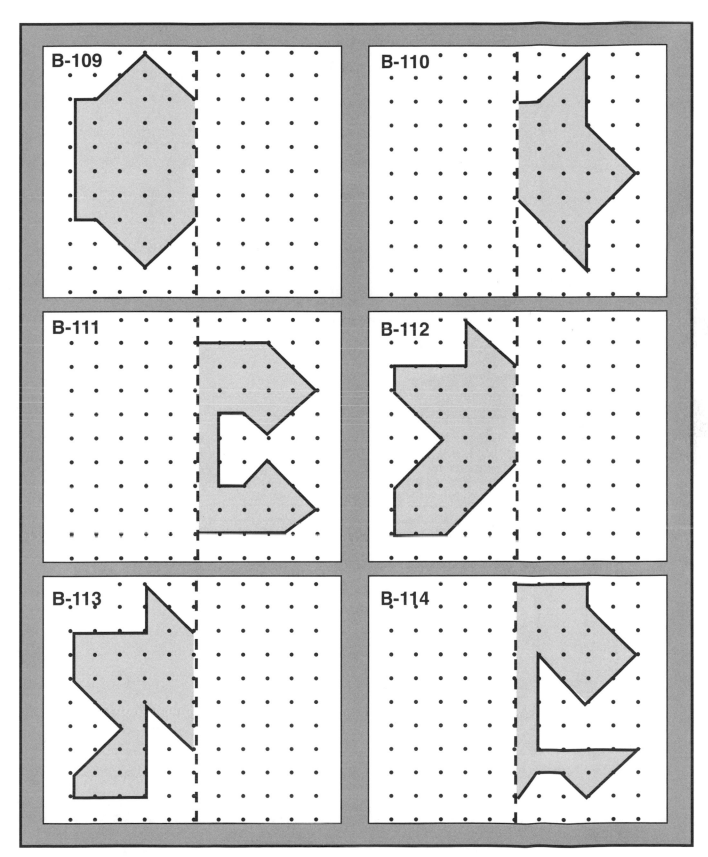

AXIS OF SYMMETRY—SUPPLY

DIRECTIONS: An axis of symmetry is a line which divides a design into two equal parts. Draw an axis of symmetry on each of the drawings below.

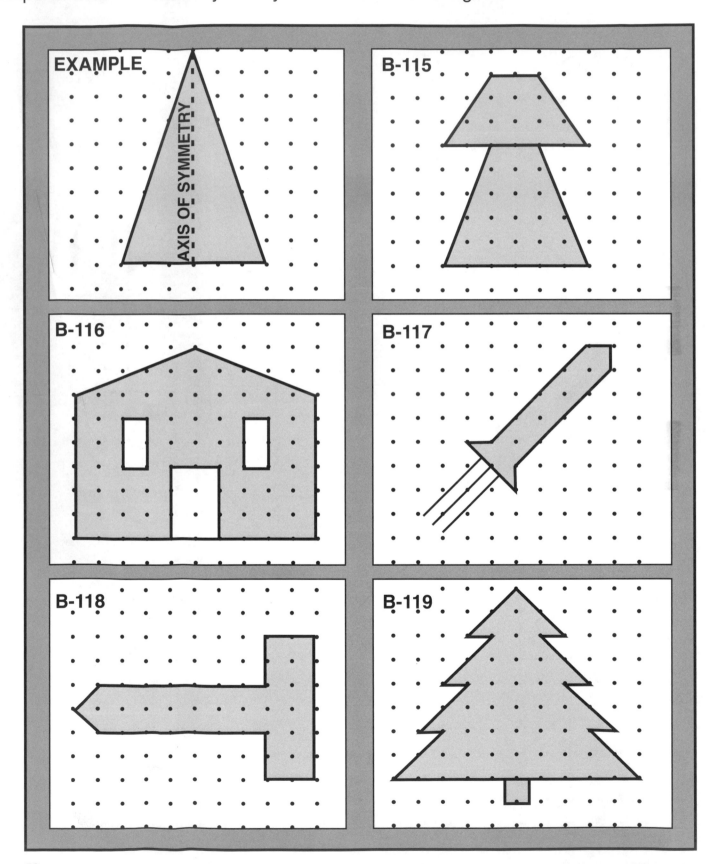

EXAMPLE

AXIS OF SYMMETRY

B-115

B-116

B-117

B-118

B-119

AXIS OF SYMMETRY—SUPPLY

DIRECTIONS: An axis of symmetry is a line which divides a design into two equal parts. Draw an axis of symmetry on each of the drawings below.

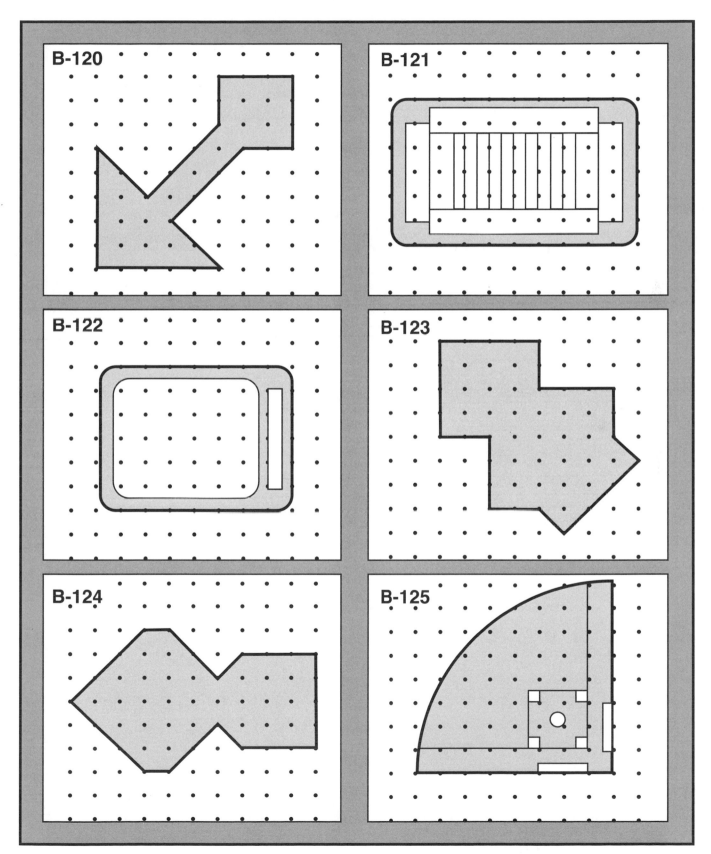

COVERING A SURFACE

DIRECTIONS: Draw the top rectangle on the lower grid of dots as many times as needed to cover the whole grid. There should be no empty space left on the grid.

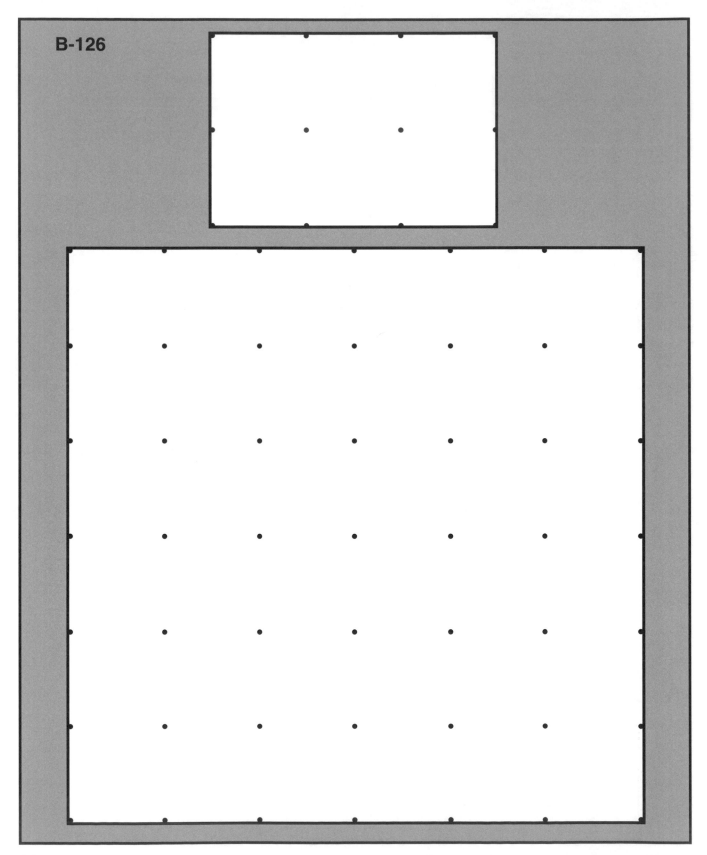

B-126

COVERING A SURFACE

DIRECTIONS: Draw the top triangle on the lower grid of dots as many times as needed to cover the whole grid. There should be no empty space left on the grid.

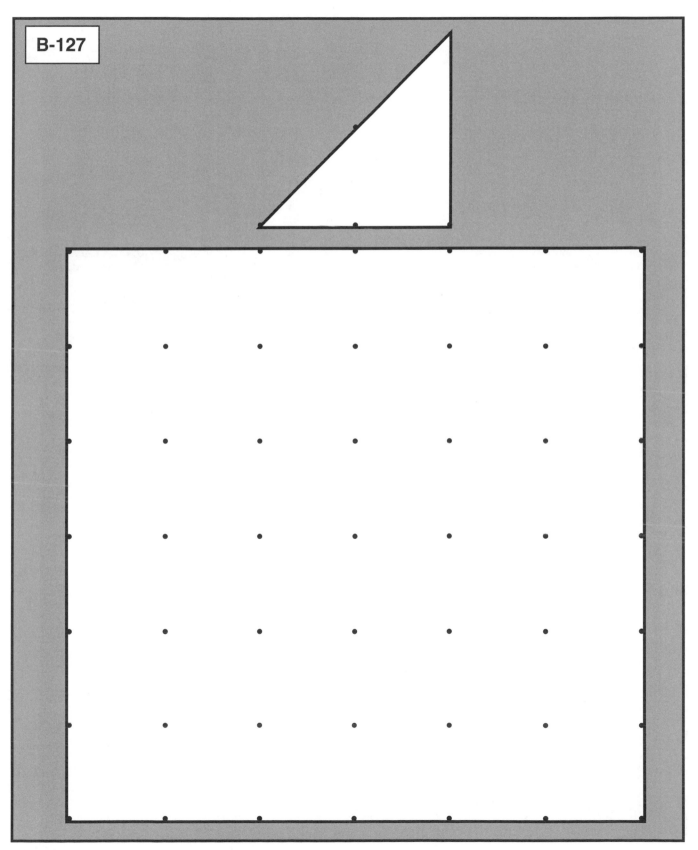

B-127

COVERING A SURFACE

DIRECTIONS: Draw the top figure on the lower grid of dots as many times as needed to cover the whole grid. There should be no empty space left on the grid.

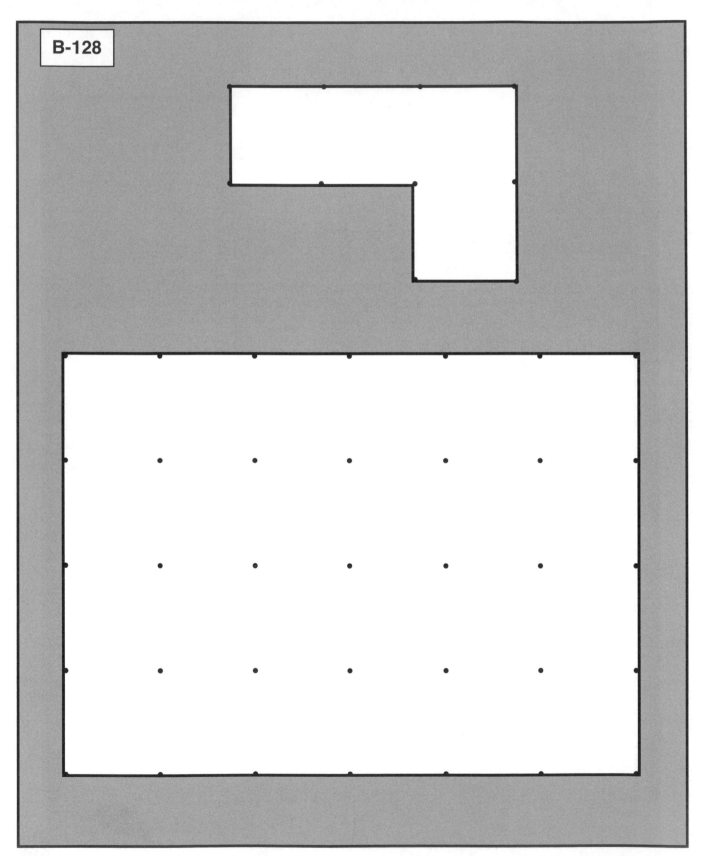

B-128

WHICH SHAPE COMPLETES THE SQUARE?

DIRECTIONS: Circle the shape that completes the big square.

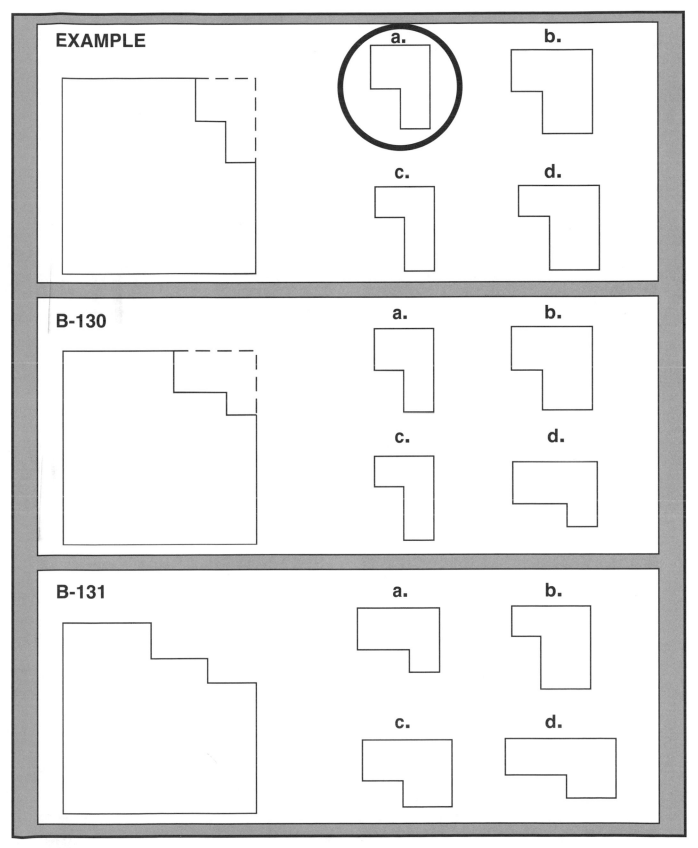

COVERING A SURFACE

DIRECTIONS: Draw the top figure on the lower grid of dots as many times as needed to cover the whole grid. There should be no empty space left on the grid.

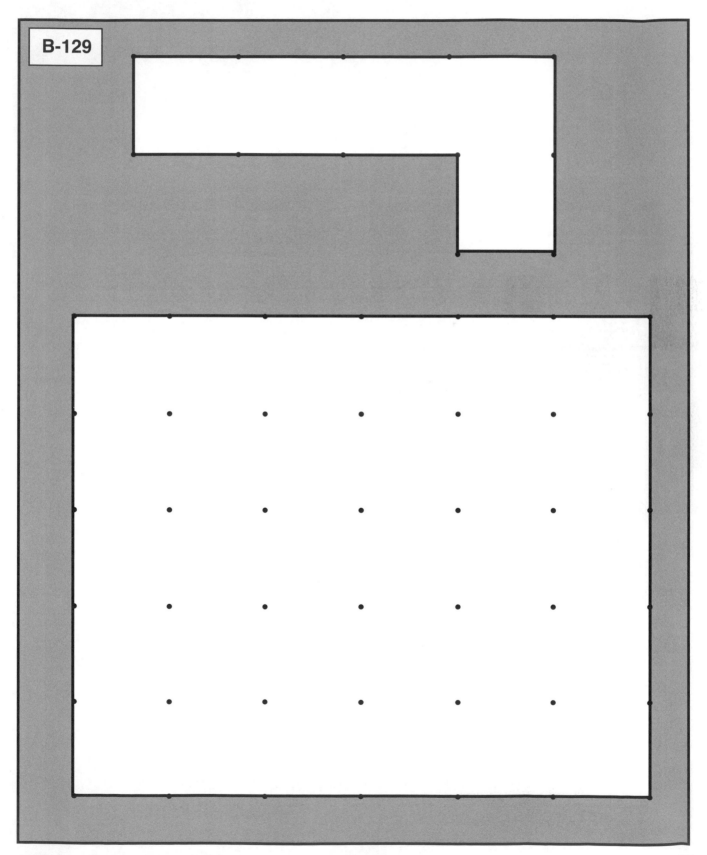

B-129

WHICH SHAPE COMPLETES THE SQUARE?

DIRECTIONS: Circle the shape that completes the big square.

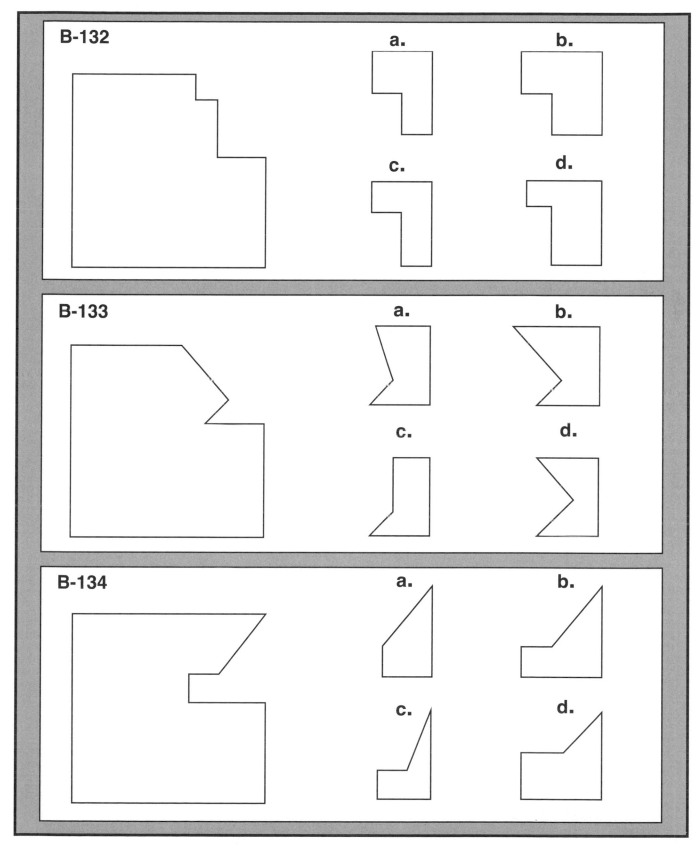

WHICH SHAPE COMPLETES THE SQUARE?

DIRECTIONS: Circle the shape that completes the big square.

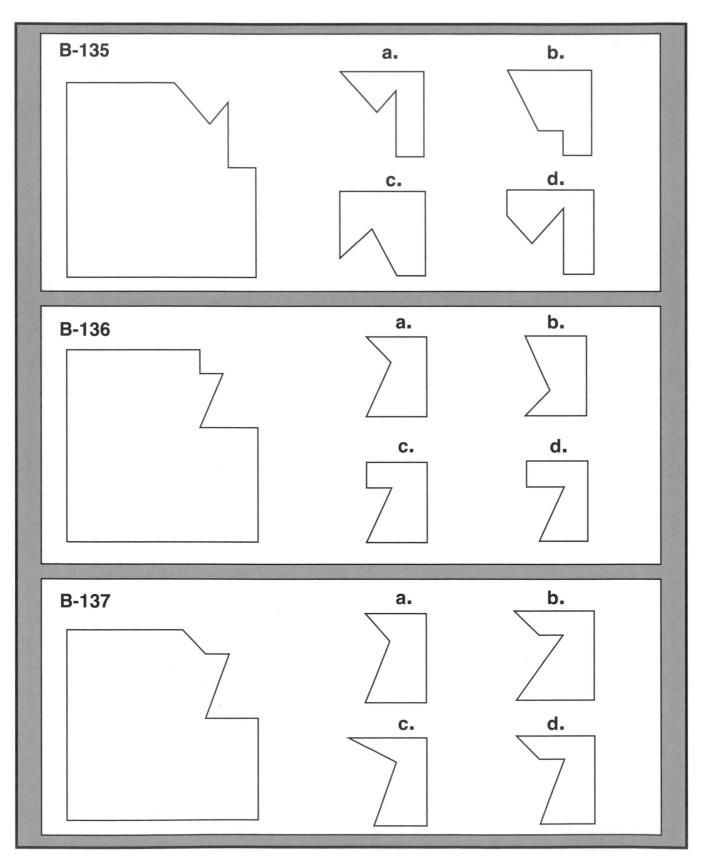

B-135   a.   b.   c.   d.

B-136   a.   b.   c.   d.

B-137   a.   b.   c.   d.

WHICH SHAPES COMPLETE THE SQUARE?

DIRECTIONS: Circle the two shapes that, together, complete the big square. Imagine rotating the shapes as necessary.

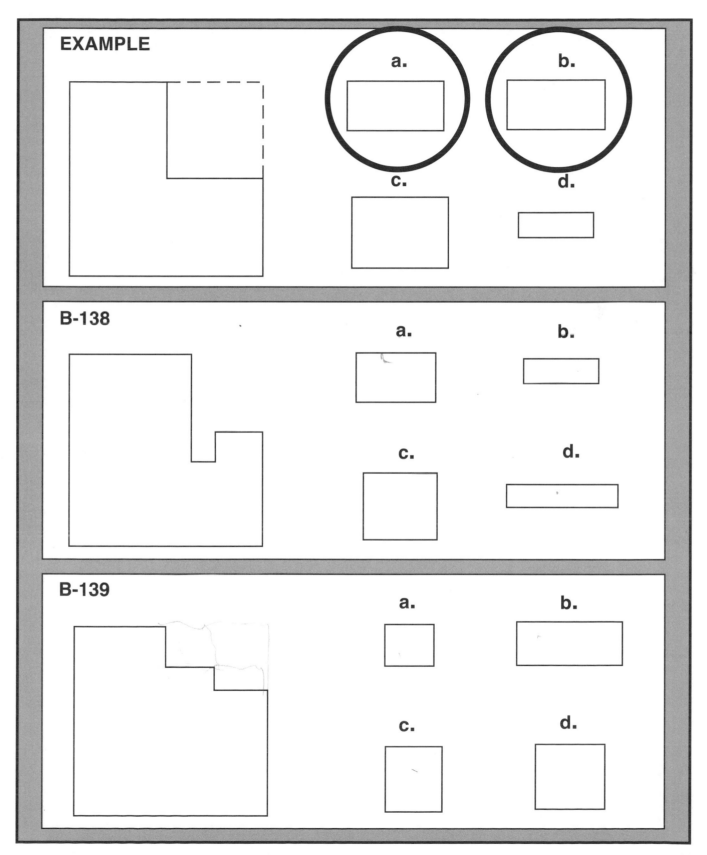

WHICH SHAPES COMPLETE THE SQUARE?

DIRECTIONS: Circle the two shapes that, together, complete the big square. Imagine rotating the shapes as necessary.

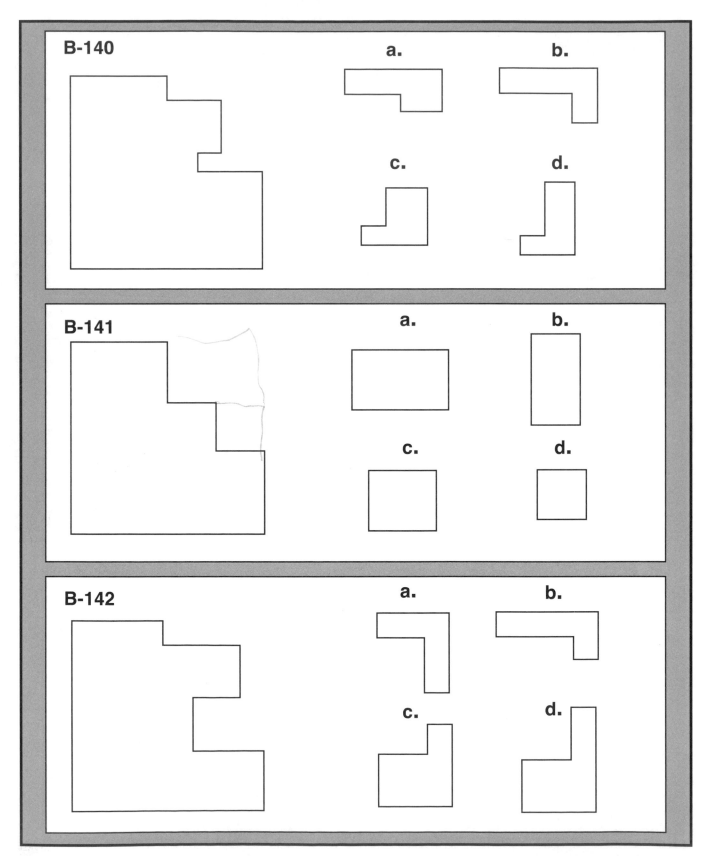

WHICH SHAPES COMPLETE THE SQUARE?

DIRECTIONS: Circle the two shapes that, together, complete the big square. Imagine rotating the shapes as necessary. More than one set of shapes may work.

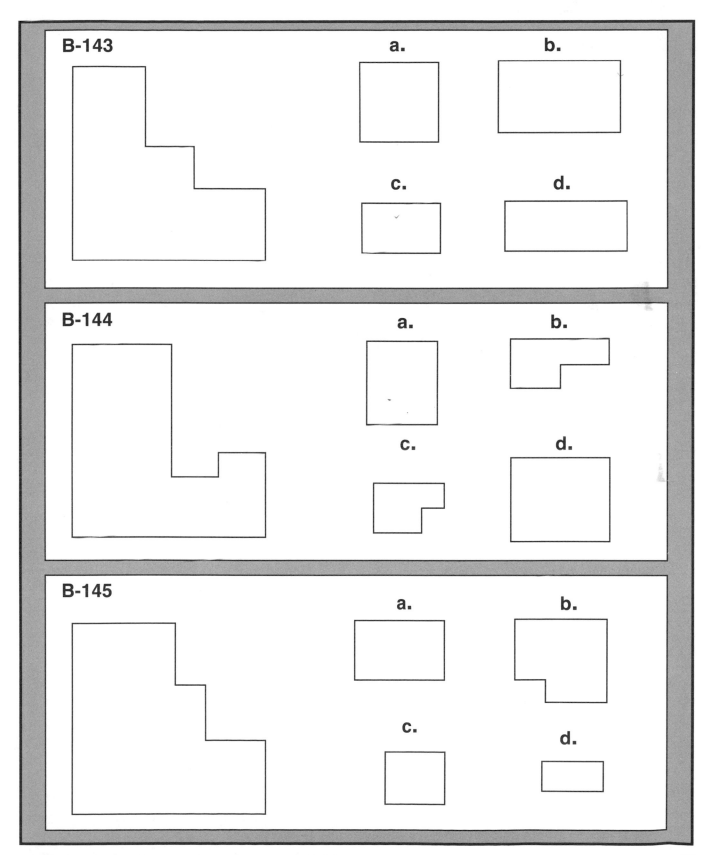

COPYING A FIGURE

DIRECTIONS: To copy a figure, count the number of spaces between the dots on each side of the figure. Count the spaces, not the dots. Use the dot grid to mark off the length of each side.

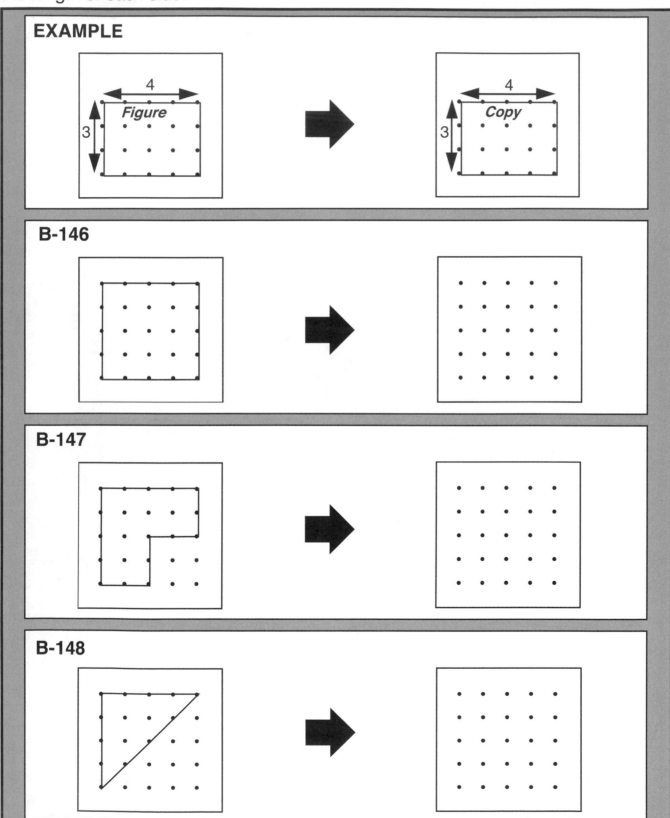

WHICH SHAPES COMPLETE THE SQUARE?

DIRECTIONS: Circle the two shapes that, together, complete the big square. Imagine rotating the shapes as necessary.

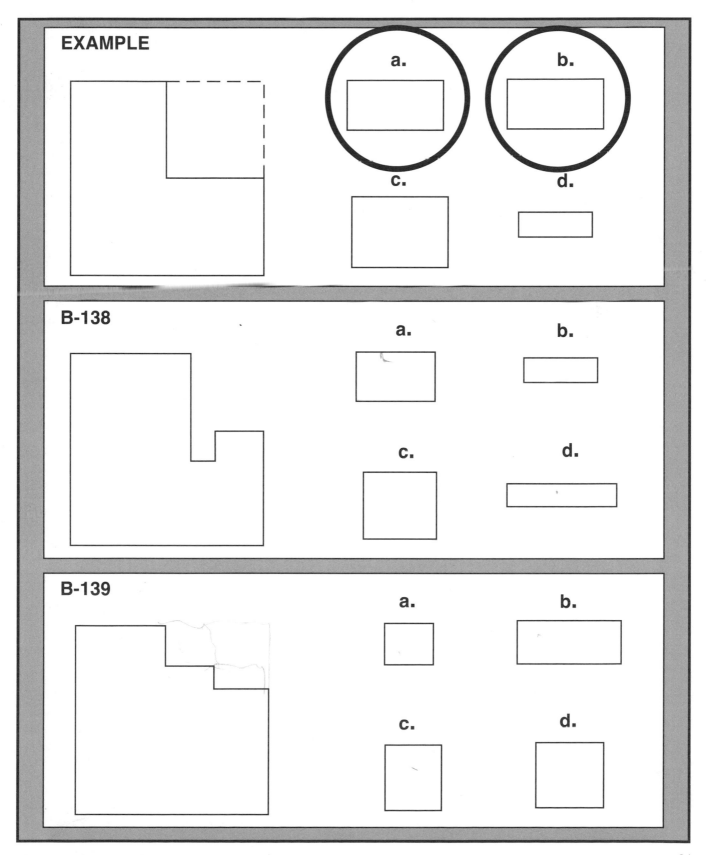

WHICH SHAPES COMPLETE THE SQUARE?

DIRECTIONS: Circle the two shapes that, together, complete the big square. Imagine rotating the shapes as necessary.

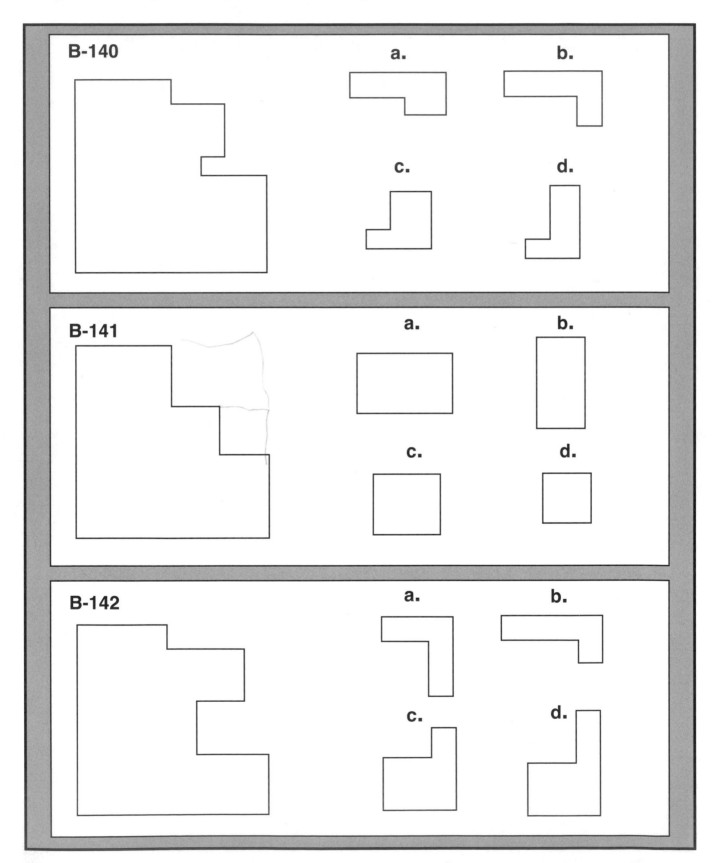

WHICH SHAPES COMPLETE THE SQUARE?

DIRECTIONS: Circle the two shapes that, together, complete the big square. Imagine rotating the shapes as necessary. More than one set of shapes may work.

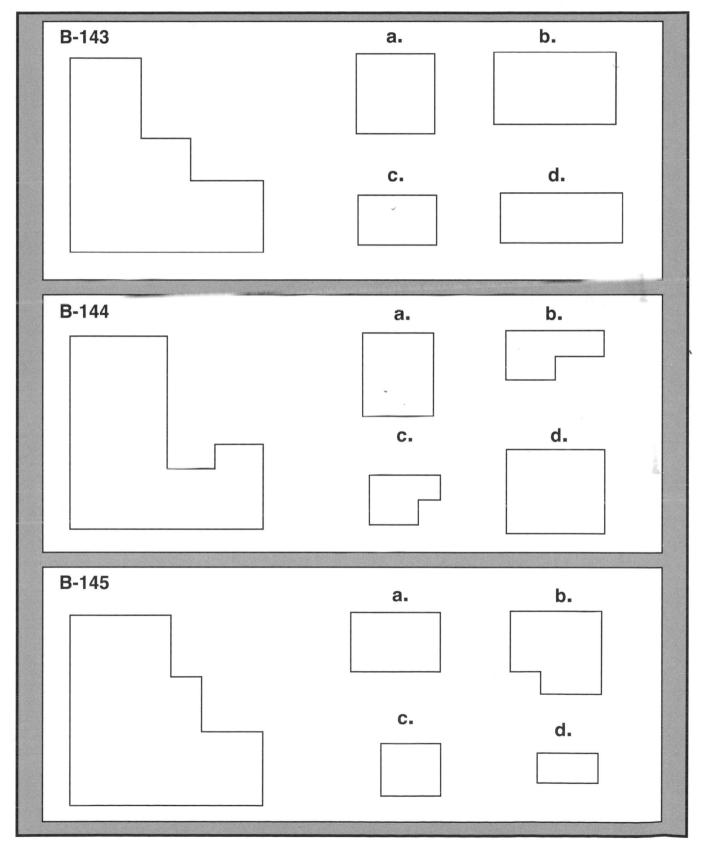

COPYING A FIGURE

DIRECTIONS: To copy a figure, count the number of spaces between the dots on each side of the figure. Count the spaces, not the dots. Use the dot grid to mark off the length of each side.

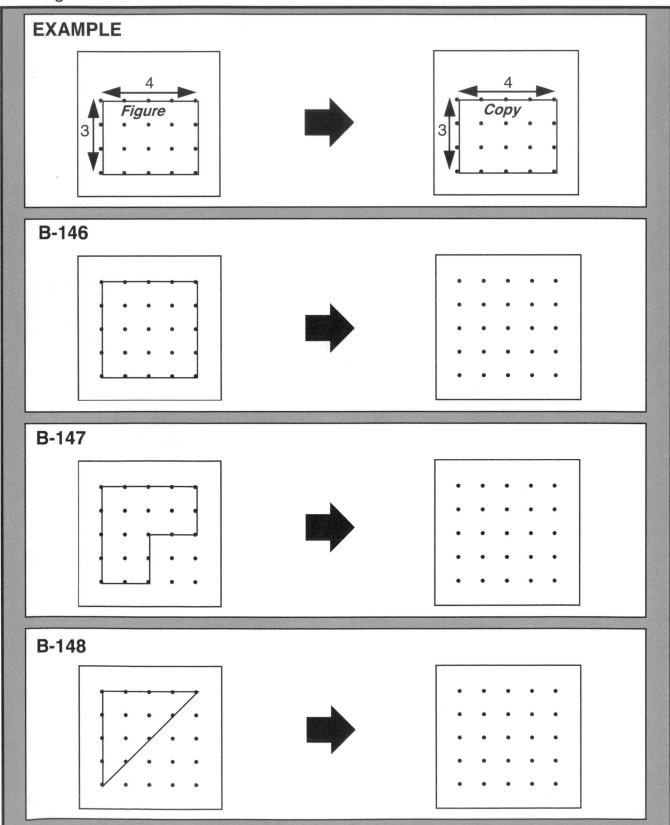

EXAMPLE

4

Figure

3

4

Copy

3

B-146

B-147

B-148

ENLARGING FIGURES

DIRECTIONS: To enlarge a figure so that each side is twice as long, count the number of spaces between the dots on each side of the figure and multiply by two. Count the spaces, not the dots. Use the dot grid to mark off the length of each side of the enlarged figure.
Enlarging a rectangle:

Original Figure

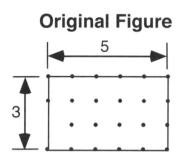

Enlarged Figure

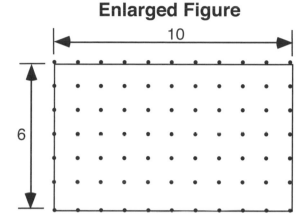

If the pattern is not a rectangle, then it is difficult to count the spaces directly. For example, the line from point A to point B does not pass through dots exactly.

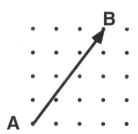

The path from A to B can be replaced with lines AC and CB. Lines AC and CB do go through dots exactly; therefore, the dots can be used as a guide for measuring the lengths AC and CB. Count the spaces to measure the lengths. If the lengths of lines AC and CB are doubled, then line A'B' will be twice the length of line AB. This "triangle rule" will help you enlarge more complicated patterns.

3 spaces over

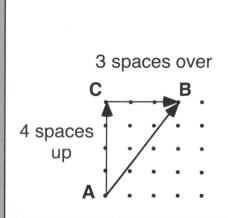

4 spaces up

when doubled, it becomes

6 spaces over

8 spaces up

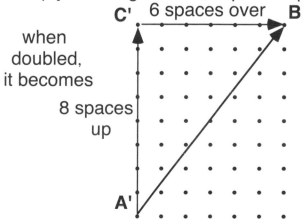

ENLARGING FIGURES

DIRECTIONS: Use the dot grid to draw a figure with sides twice as long as the figure on the left.

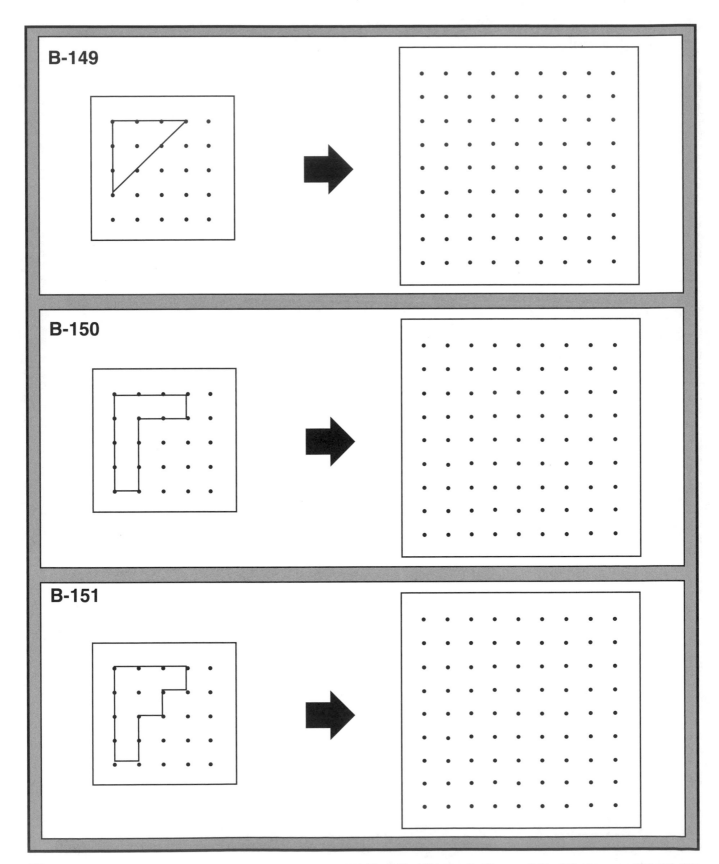

B-149

B-150

B-151

ENLARGING FIGURES

DIRECTIONS: Use the dot grid to draw a figure with sides twice as long as the figure on the left.

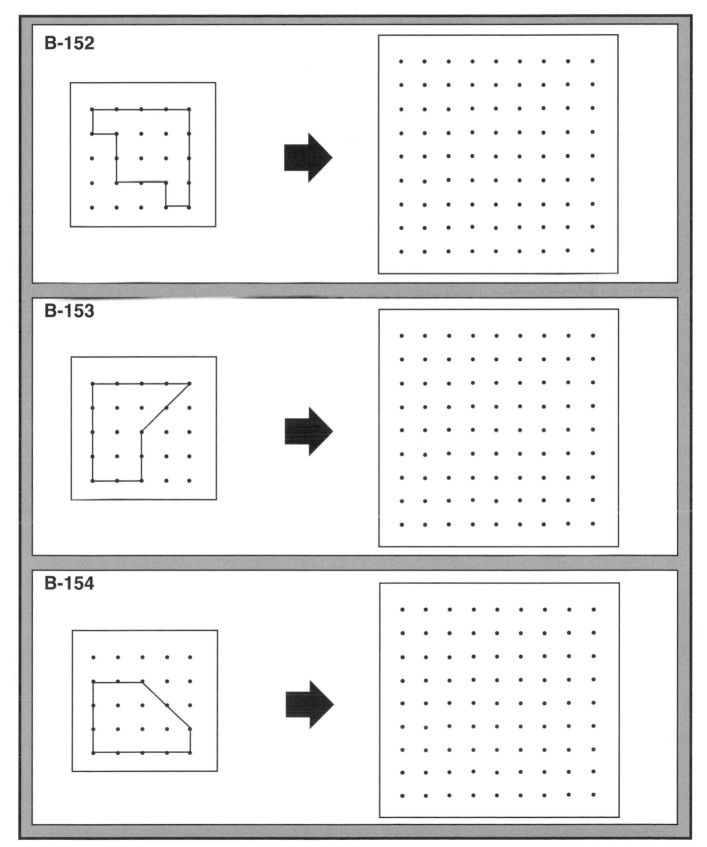

B-152

B-153

B-154

REDUCING FIGURES

DIRECTIONS: To reduce a figure so that each side is half as long, count the number of spaces between the dots on each side of the figure and divide by two. Count the spaces, not the dots. Use the dot grid to mark off the length of each side of the reduced figure.

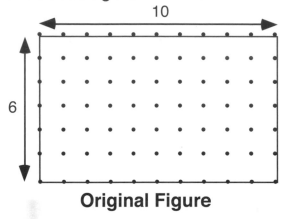

Original Figure

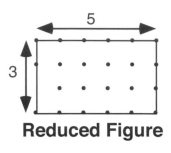

Reduced Figure

If the pattern is not a rectangle, then the "triangle rule" may be used to reduce the size of a line drawn at an angle. Here is an example of the "triangle rule". Start at point A and go upward until your pencil is in line with point B. Then go over until your pencil is on point B. Next, count the spaces between the dots and divide by two. Finally, draw a reduced figure as shown.

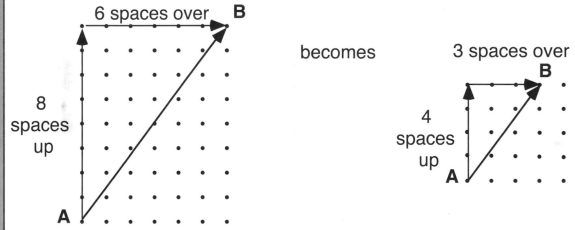

becomes

B-155 Try the "triangle rule" on line CD.

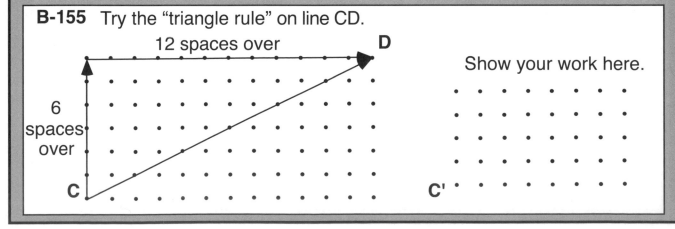

Show your work here.

REDUCING FIGURES

DIRECTIONS: Use the dot grid to draw a figure with sides half as long as the figure on the left.

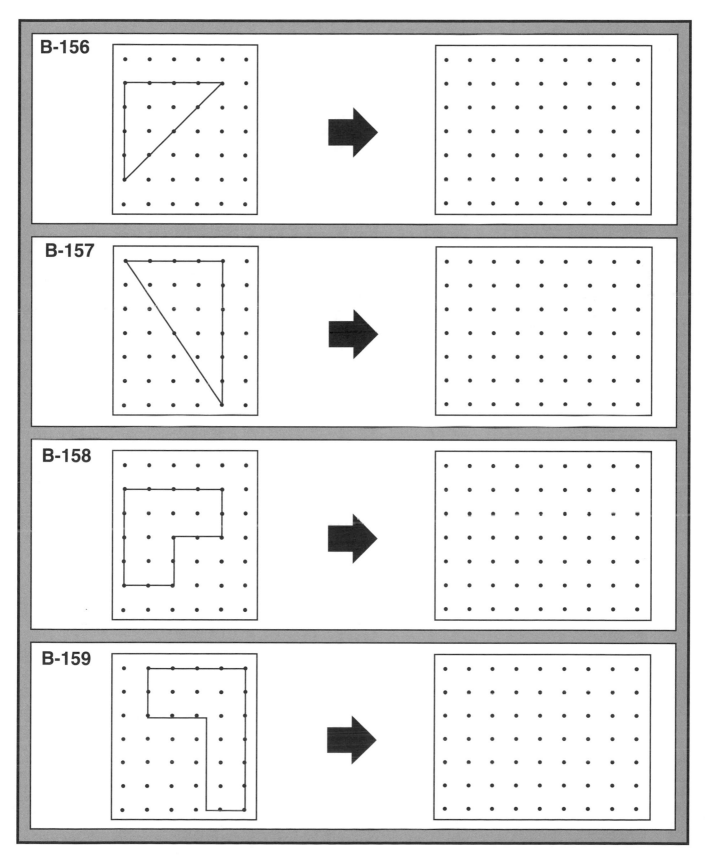

REDUCING FIGURES

DIRECTIONS: Use the dot grid to draw a figure with sides half as long as the figure on the left.

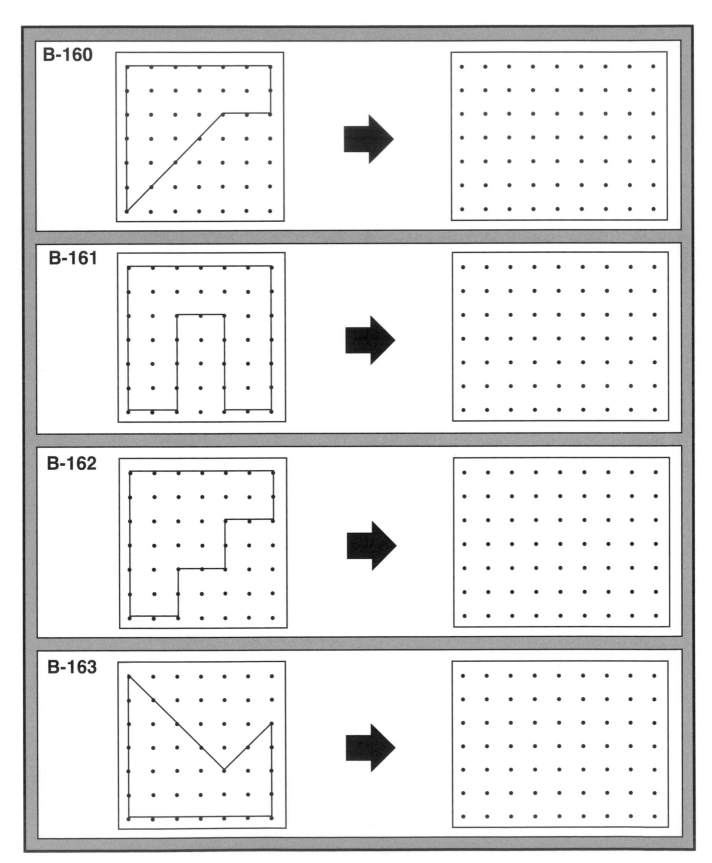

B-160

B-161

B-162

B-163

COMPARING SHAPES—EXPLAIN

DIRECTIONS: Use this diagram to organize your thinking about how a triangle and a trapezoid are alike and how they are different.

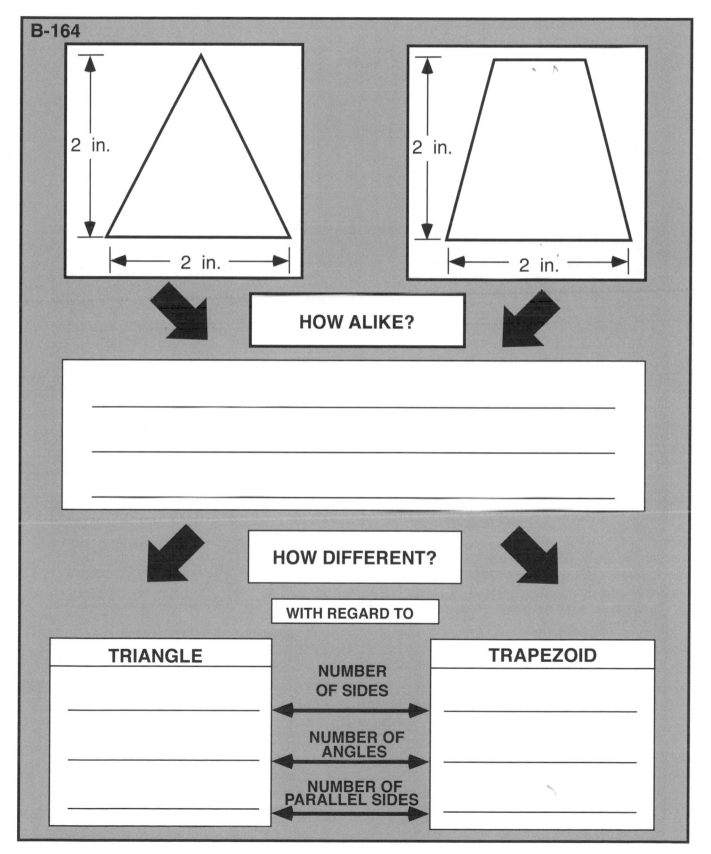

COMPARING SHAPES—EXPLAIN

DIRECTIONS: Use this diagram to organize your thinking about how a square and a parallelogram are alike and how they are different.

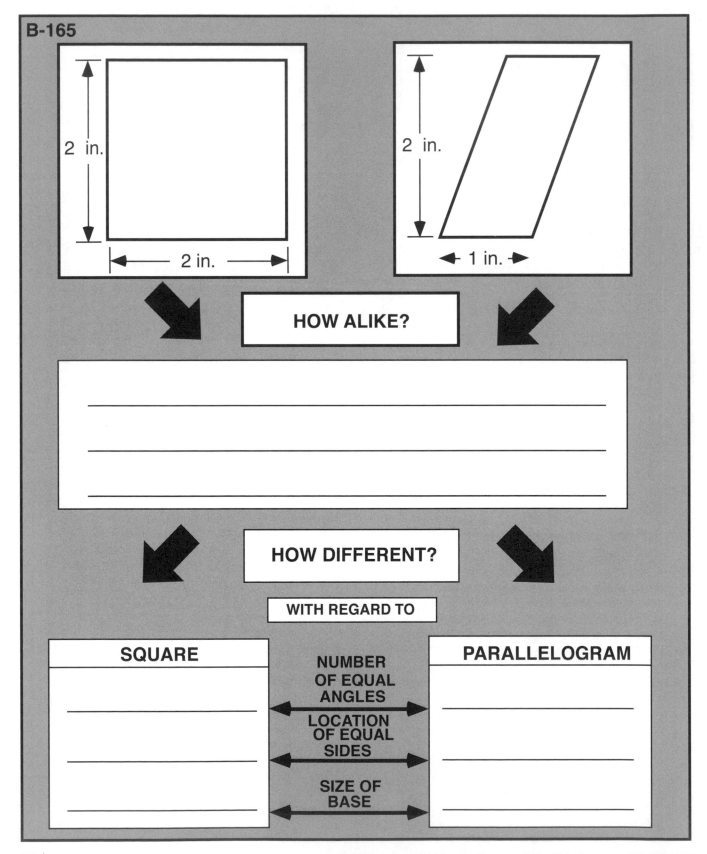

COMPARING SHAPES—EXPLAIN

DIRECTIONS: Use this diagram to organize your thinking about how a rectangle and a parallelogram are alike and how they are different.

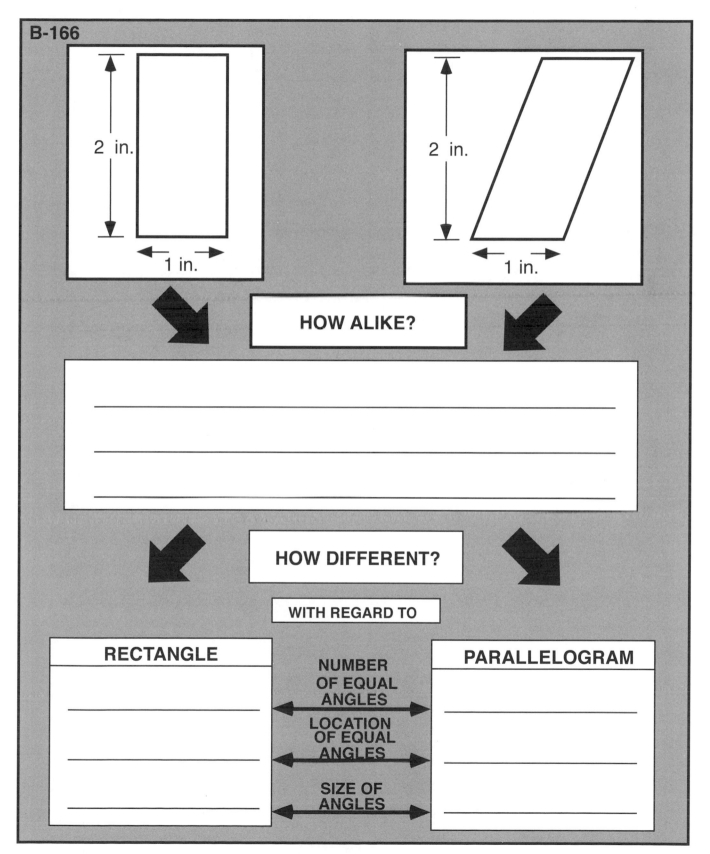

CHAPTER THREE

Describing Shapes	Describing Things
Figural Similarities and Differences	Verbal Similarities and Differences
Figural Sequences	Verbal Sequences
Figural Classifications	Verbal Classifications
Figural Analogies	Verbal Analogies

SEQUENCE OF FIGURES—SELECT

DIRECTIONS: Here are examples of three sequences. The correct figure that completes each sequence is circled and a description of the kind of sequence is given.

EXAMPLE

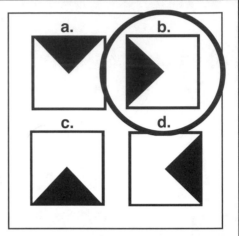

This sequence shows "flipping" horizontally, like the pages of a book.

EXAMPLE

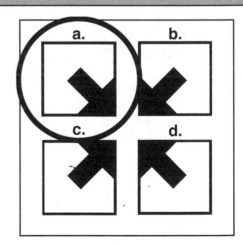

This sequence shows "turning." The arrow is turning to the left.

EXAMPLE

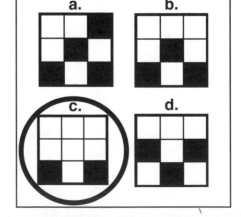

This sequence shows "subtracting detail."

SEQUENCE OF FIGURES—SELECT

DIRECTIONS: Circle the figure that best continues the sequence.

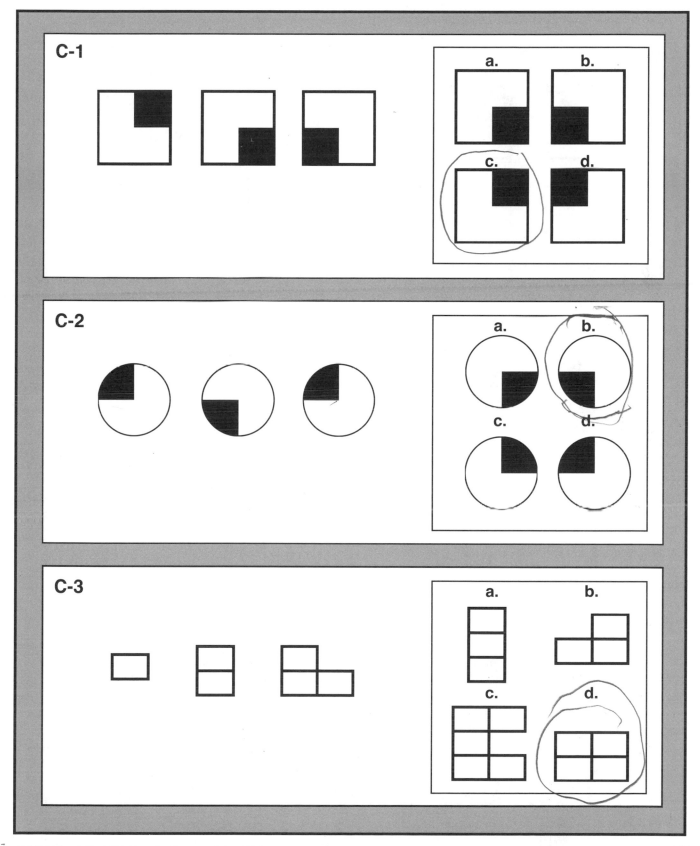

SEQUENCE OF FIGURES—SELECT

DIRECTIONS: Circle the figure that best continues the sequence.

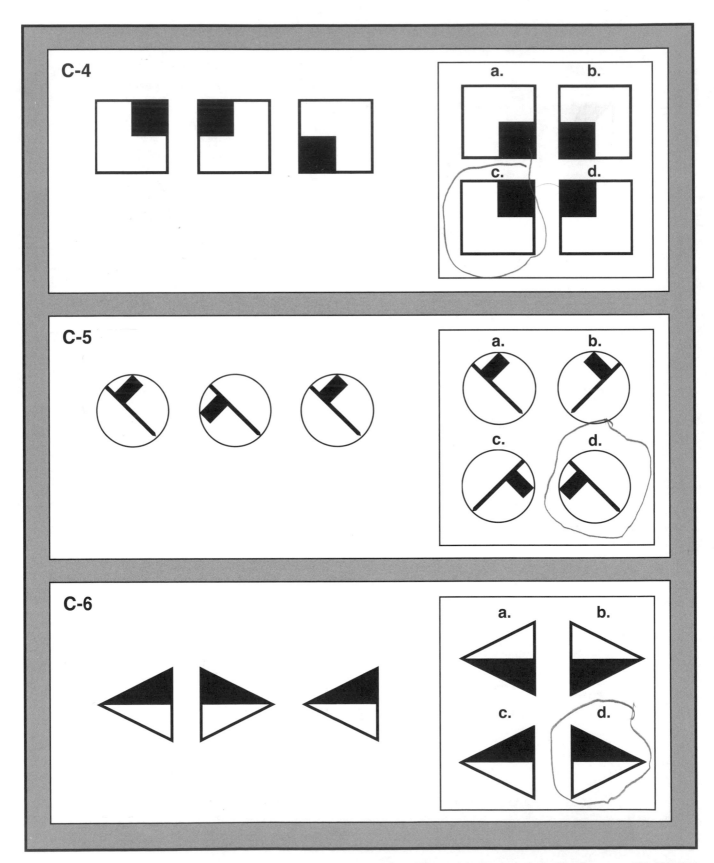

SEQUENCE OF FIGURES—SELECT

DIRECTIONS: Circle the figure that best continues the sequence.

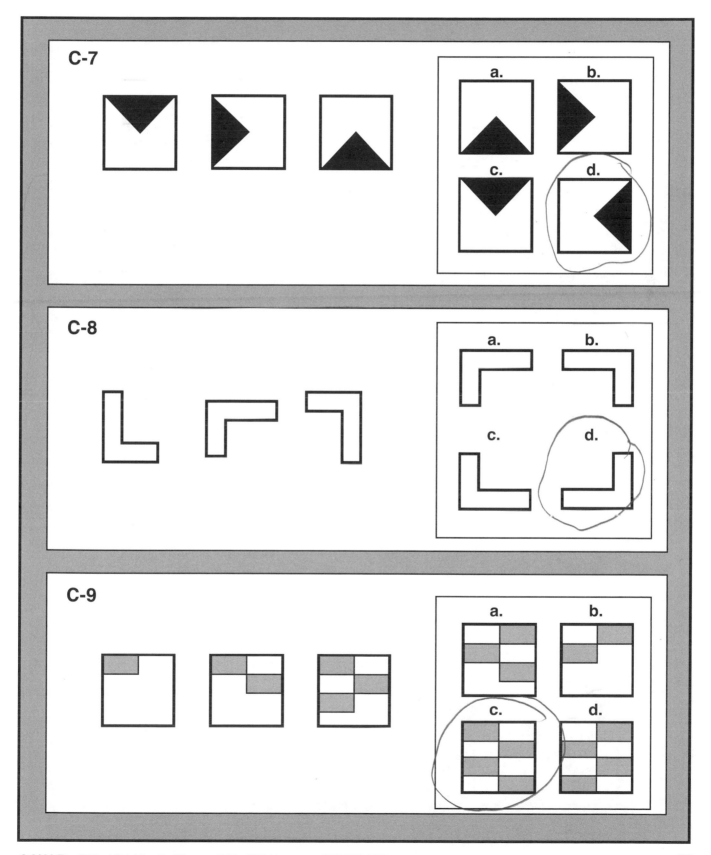

SEQUENCE OF FIGURES—SUPPLY

DIRECTIONS: Shade in the fourth shape in each row to continue each sequence.

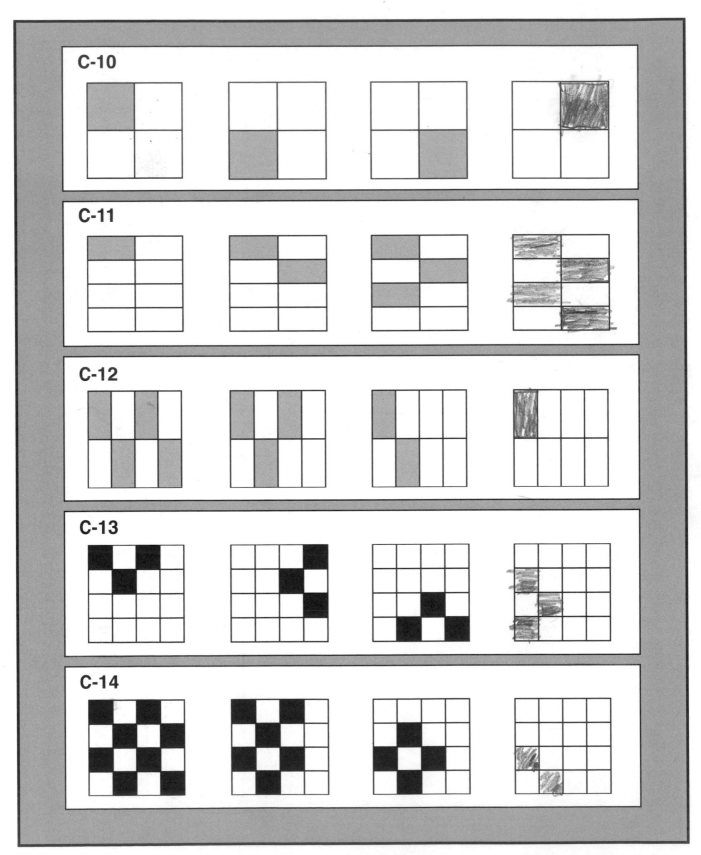

SEQUENCE OF FIGURES—SUPPLY

DIRECTIONS: Shade in the fourth shape in each row to continue each sequence.

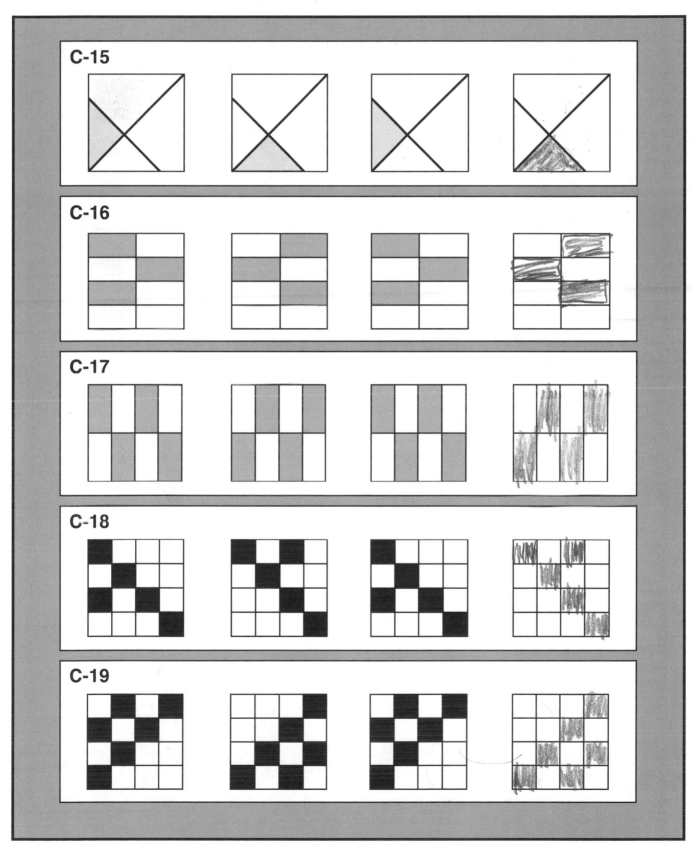

C-15

C-16

C-17

C-18

C-19

TUMBLING—SHADING

DIRECTIONS: As a shape tumbles along, the side that is on the ground changes. Darken the following figures to show how they look as they tumble across the page.

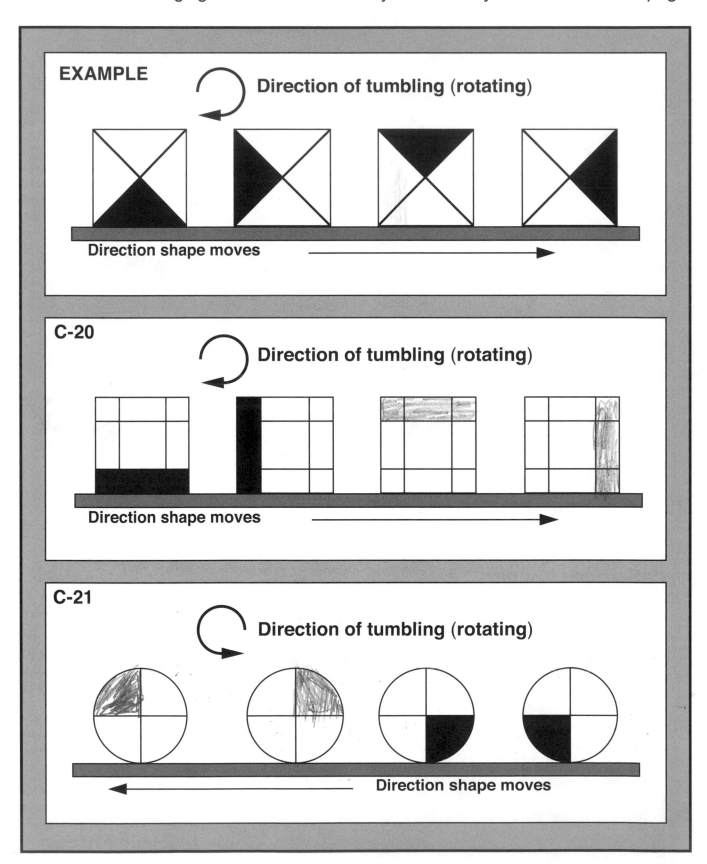

TUMBLING—SHADING

DIRECTIONS: As a shape tumbles along, the side that is on the ground changes. Darken the following figures to show how they look as they tumble across the page. You may not need to fill in all the shapes.

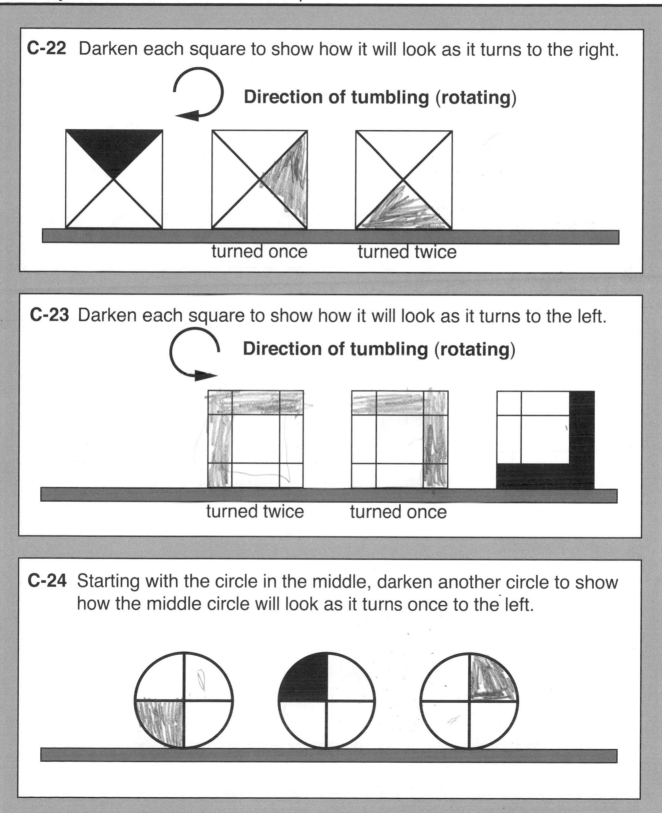

C-22 Darken each square to show how it will look as it turns to the right.

Direction of tumbling (rotating)

turned once   turned twice

C-23 Darken each square to show how it will look as it turns to the left.

Direction of tumbling (rotating)

turned twice   turned once

C-24 Starting with the circle in the middle, darken another circle to show how the middle circle will look as it turns once to the left.

TUMBLING—SHADING

DIRECTIONS: As a shape tumbles along, the side that is on the ground changes. Darken the following figures to show how they look as they tumble across the page. You may not need to fill in all the shapes.

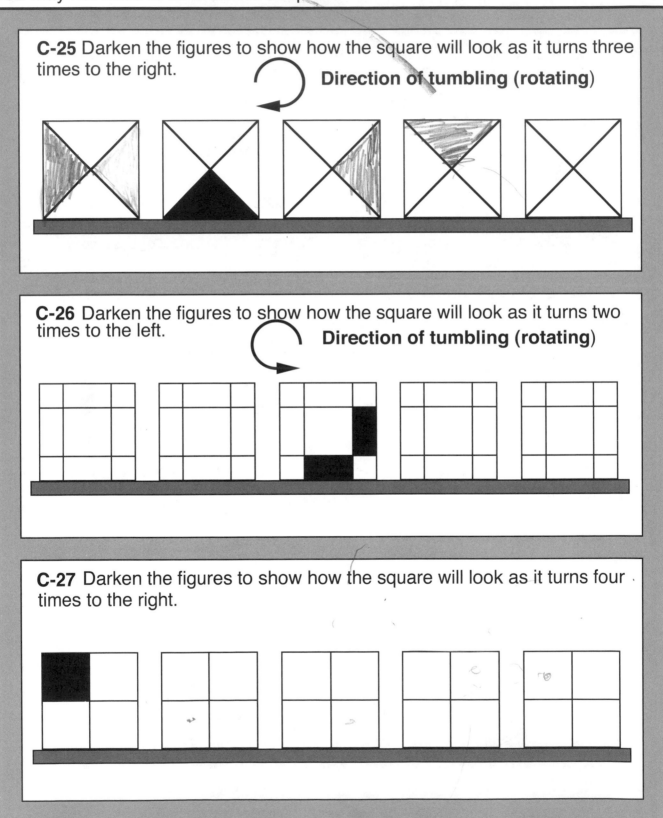

C-25 Darken the figures to show how the square will look as it turns three times to the right.

Direction of tumbling (rotating)

C-26 Darken the figures to show how the square will look as it turns two times to the left.

Direction of tumbling (rotating)

C-27 Darken the figures to show how the square will look as it turns four times to the right.

TURNING (ROTATING) FIGURES

DIRECTIONS: Explain how the first figure has been turned to produce the second by filling in the number of position changes and the direction of change.

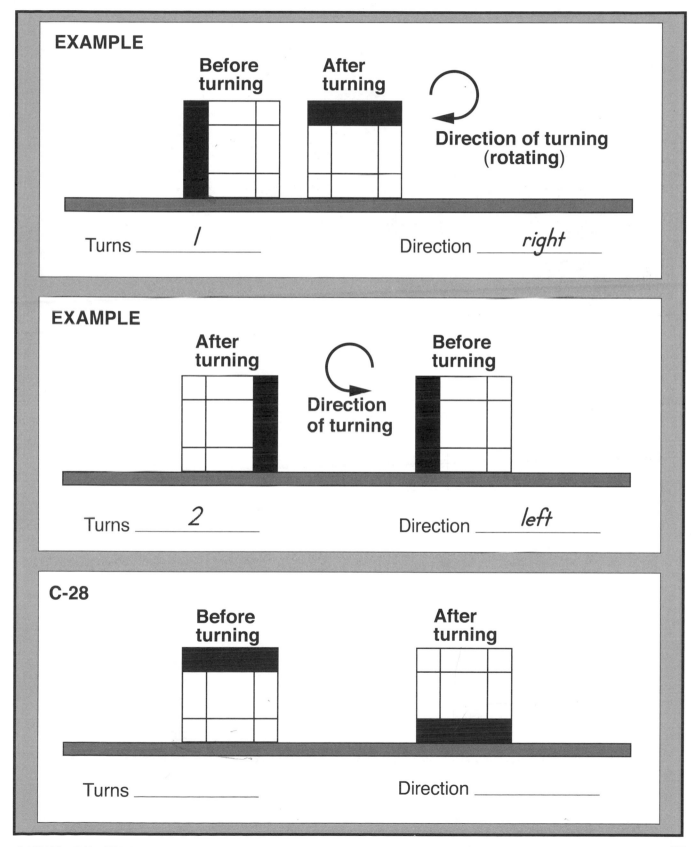

EXAMPLE

Before turning   **After turning**

Direction of turning (rotating)

Turns _____*1*_____   Direction _____*right*_____

EXAMPLE

After turning   **Direction of turning**   **Before turning**

Turns _____*2*_____   Direction _____*left*_____

C-28

Before turning   **After turning**

Turns _____   Direction _____

TURNING (ROTATING) FIGURES

DIRECTIONS: Explain how the first figure has been turned to produce the second by filling in the number of position changes and the direction of change.

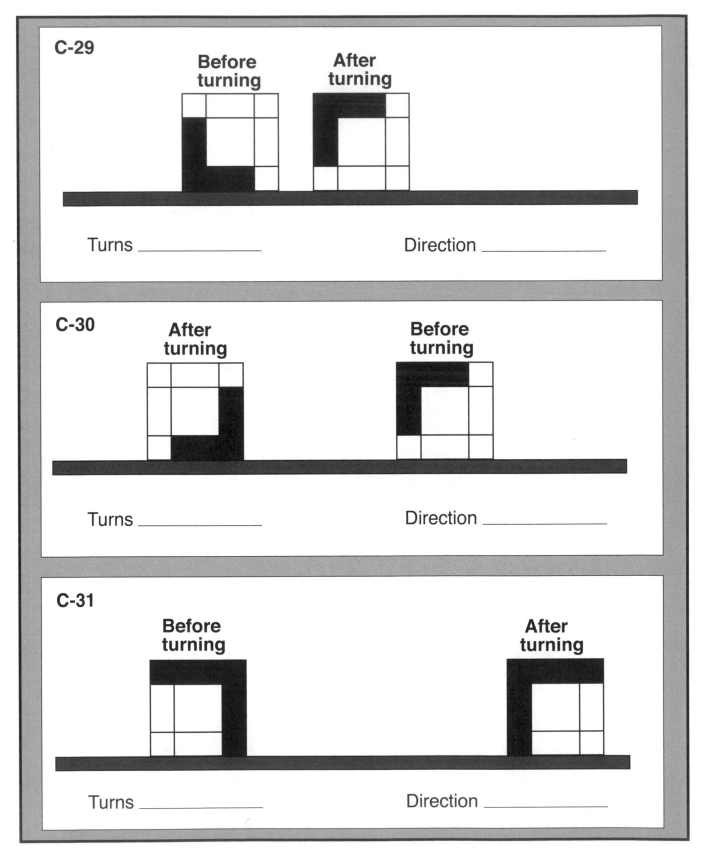

C-29

Before turning   After turning

Turns _____   Direction _____

C-30

After turning   Before turning

Turns _____   Direction _____

C-31

Before turning   After turning

Turns _____   Direction _____

PATTERN FOLDING—SELECT

DIRECTIONS: The pattern on the left is a wrapper for one of the solids on the right. Draw a circle around the correct solid.

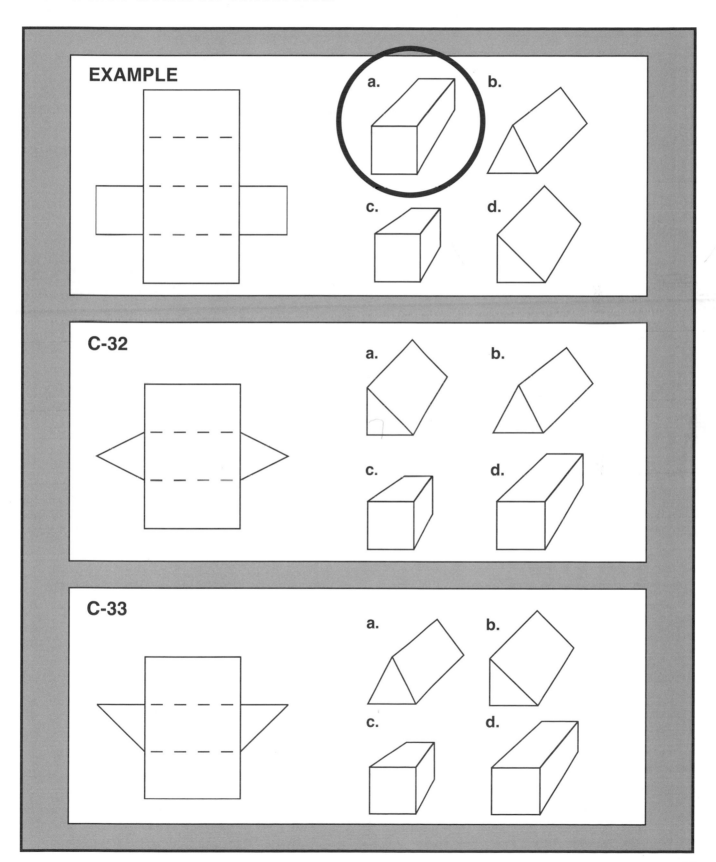

PATTERN FOLDING—SUPPLY

DIRECTIONS: The patterns at the bottom of the page, when folded, produce the cube at the top of the page. Fill in the blanks on the pattern with the correct position number for that face of the cube.

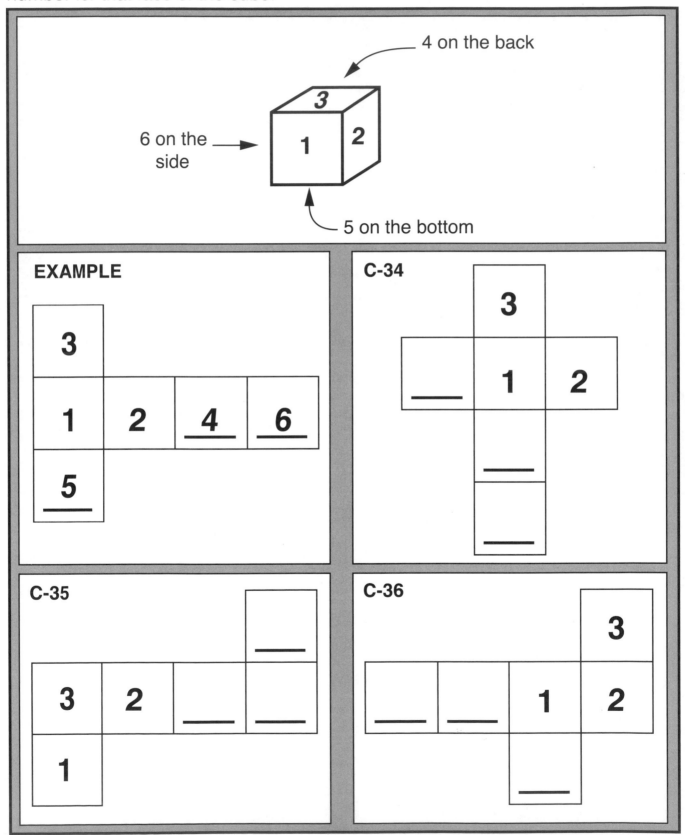

PATTERN FOLDING—SUPPLY

DIRECTIONS: The patterns at the bottom of the page, when folded, produce the cube at the top of the page. Fill in the blanks on the pattern with the correct position number for that face of the cube.

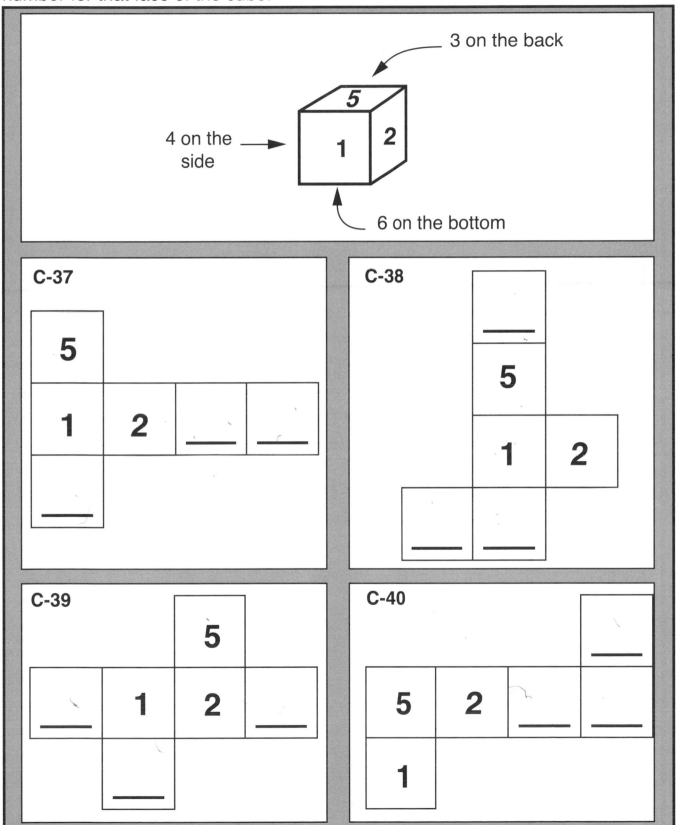

PATTERN FOLDING—SUPPLY

DIRECTIONS: The patterns at the bottom of the page, when folded, produce the cube at the top of the page. Fill in the blanks on the pattern with the correct position number for that face of the cube.

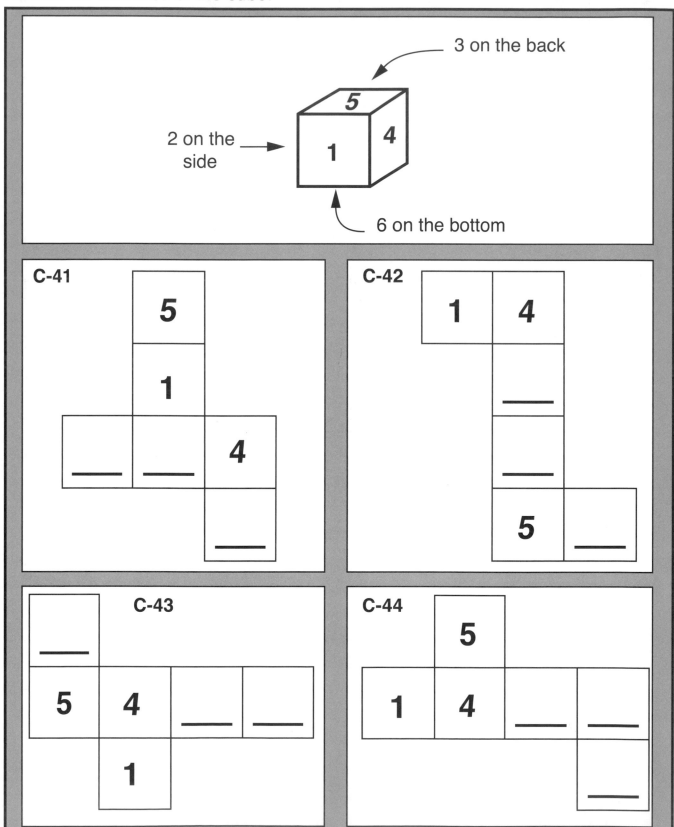

STACKING SHAPES—SELECT

DIRECTIONS: Look at the four shapes in the top box. At the bottom of the page are six combinations formed by placing one shape on another. Select the stack that fits each description.

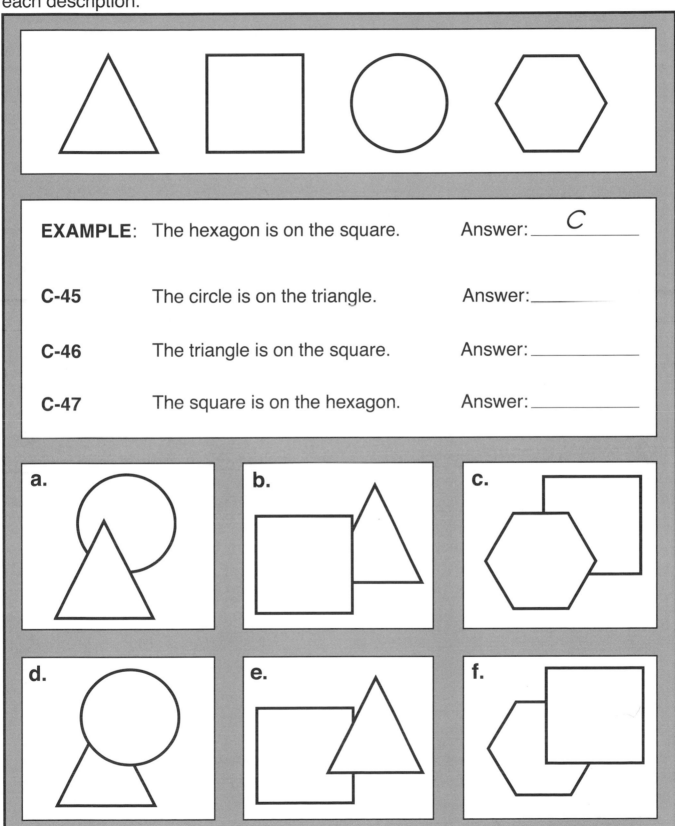

EXAMPLE: The hexagon is on the square.   Answer: _____C_____

C-45   The circle is on the triangle.   Answer: _____

C-46   The triangle is on the square.   Answer: _____

C-47   The square is on the hexagon.   Answer: _____

a.   b.   c.

d.   e.   f.

STACKING SHAPES—SELECT

DIRECTIONS: Look at the four shapes in the top box. At the bottom of the page are eight combinations formed by placing one shape on another. Select the stack that fits each description.

C-48	The circle is on the square.	Answer: _____
C-49	The triangle is on the rectangle.	Answer: _____
C-50	The rectangle is on the square.	Answer: _____
C-51	The square is on the circle.	Answer: _____
C-52	The circle is on the rectangle.	Answer: _____

STACKING SHAPES—SUPPLY

DIRECTIONS: Shade in the shapes to show how each pair of shapes will look after they are stacked according to the directions.

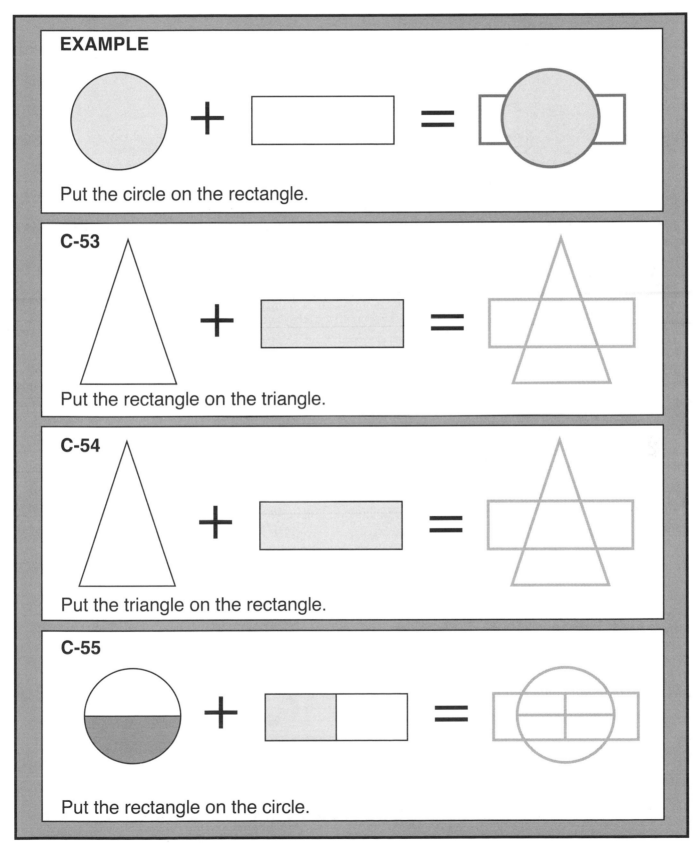

EXAMPLE

Put the circle on the rectangle.

C-53

Put the rectangle on the triangle.

C-54

Put the triangle on the rectangle.

C-55

Put the rectangle on the circle.

STACKING SHAPES—SUPPLY

DIRECTIONS: Shade in the shapes to show how each pair of shapes will look after they are stacked according to the directions.

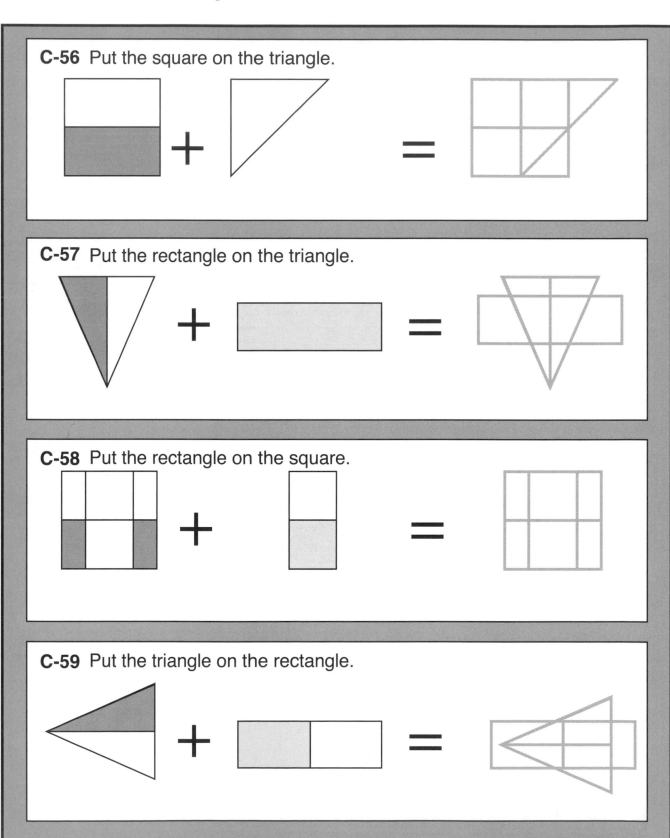

C-56 Put the square on the triangle.

C-57 Put the rectangle on the triangle.

C-58 Put the rectangle on the square.

C-59 Put the triangle on the rectangle.

STACKING SHAPES—SUPPLY

DIRECTIONS: Draw how each group of three shapes will look after they are stacked according to the directions.

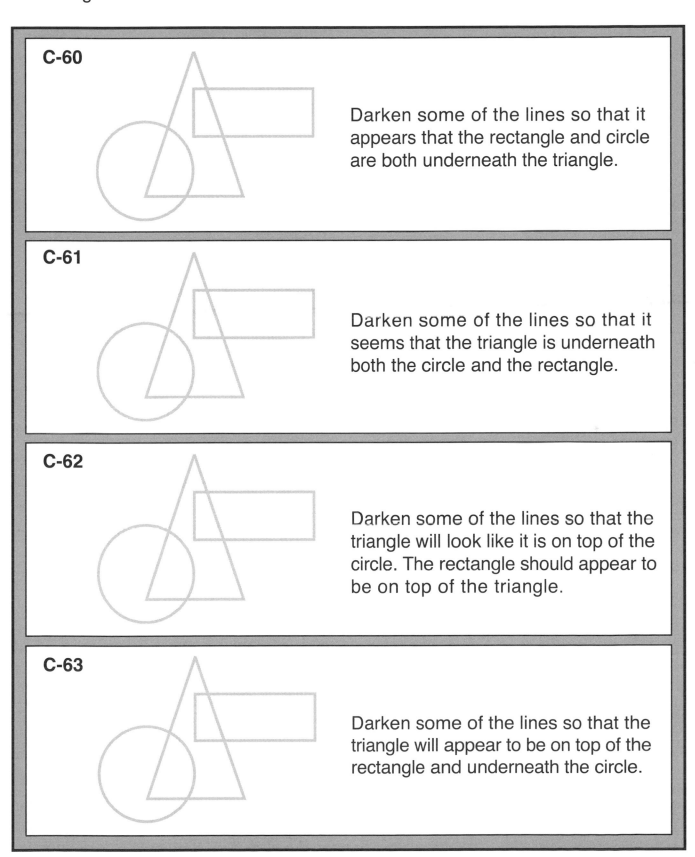

C-60

Darken some of the lines so that it appears that the rectangle and circle are both underneath the triangle.

C-61

Darken some of the lines so that it seems that the triangle is underneath both the circle and the rectangle.

C-62

Darken some of the lines so that the triangle will look like it is on top of the circle. The rectangle should appear to be on top of the triangle.

C-63

Darken some of the lines so that the triangle will appear to be on top of the rectangle and underneath the circle.

STACKING SHAPES—SUPPLY

DIRECTIONS: Draw how each group of four shapes will look after they are stacked according to the directions.

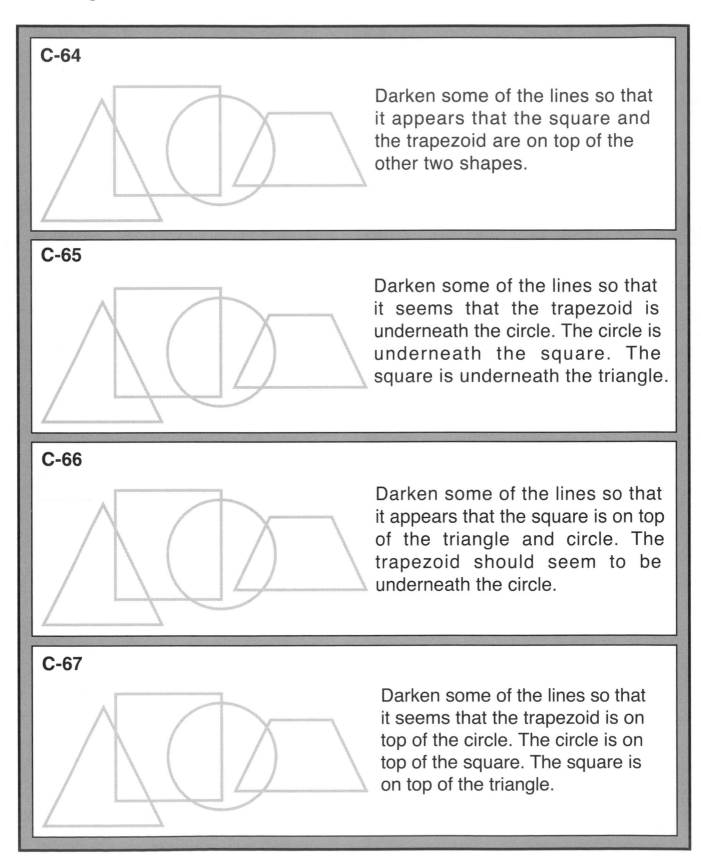

C-64

Darken some of the lines so that it appears that the square and the trapezoid are on top of the other two shapes.

C-65

Darken some of the lines so that it seems that the trapezoid is underneath the circle. The circle is underneath the square. The square is underneath the triangle.

C-66

Darken some of the lines so that it appears that the square is on top of the triangle and circle. The trapezoid should seem to be underneath the circle.

C-67

Darken some of the lines so that it seems that the trapezoid is on top of the circle. The circle is on top of the square. The square is on top of the triangle.

STACKING SHAPES—EXPLAIN

DIRECTIONS: Supply the directions for stacking the shapes to make the figure on the right. If you need help with spelling, use the words in the word box at the bottom of the page.

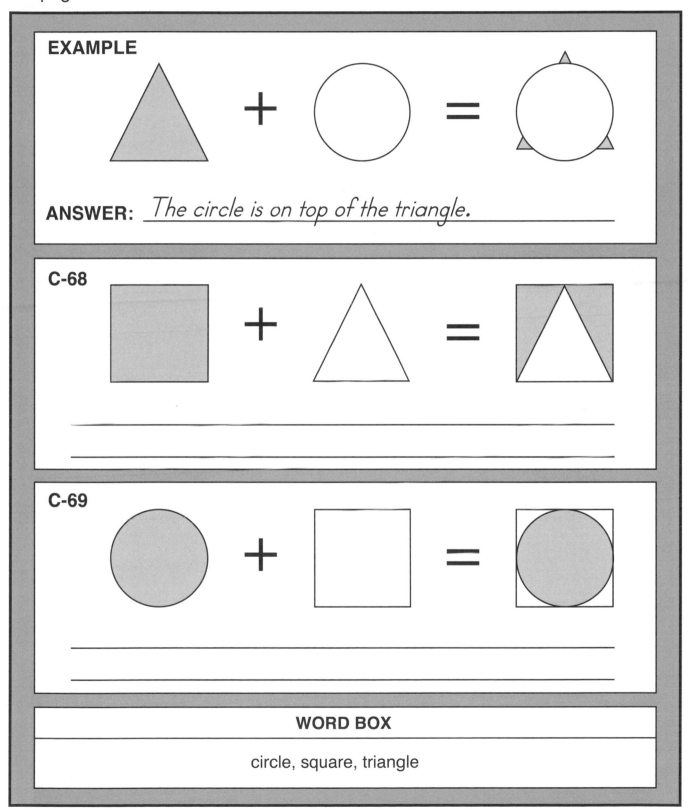

EXAMPLE

ANSWER: *The circle is on top of the triangle.*

C-68

C-69

WORD BOX

circle, square, triangle

STACKING SHAPES—EXPLAIN

DIRECTIONS: Supply the directions for stacking the shapes to make the figure on the right. If you need help with spelling, use the words in the word box at the bottom of the page.

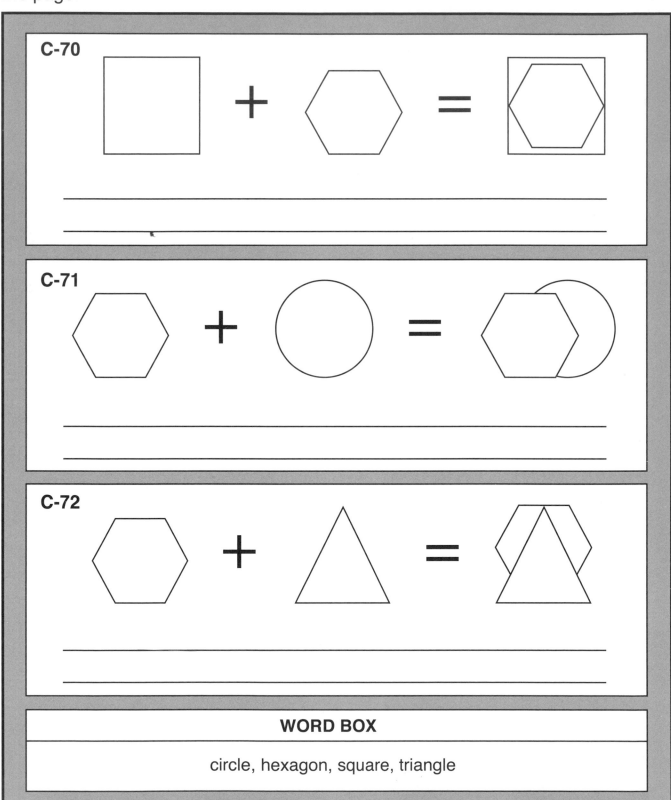

C-70

C-71

C-72

WORD BOX

circle, hexagon, square, triangle

STACKING SHAPES—EXPLAIN

DIRECTIONS: Supply the directions for stacking the shapes to make the figure on the left. If you need help with spelling, use the words in the word box at the bottom of the page.

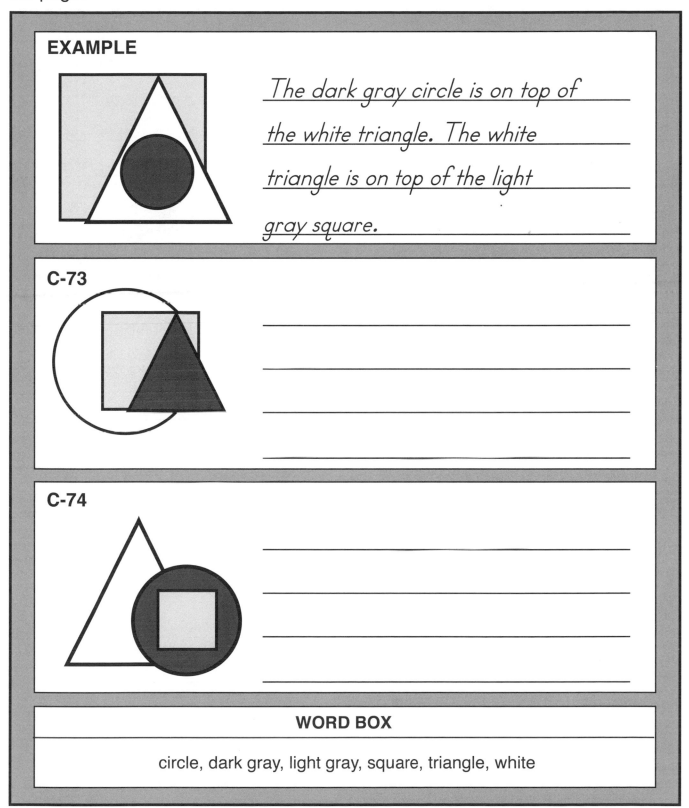

EXAMPLE

The dark gray circle is on top of the white triangle. The white triangle is on top of the light gray square.

C-73

_____

_____

_____

_____

C-74

_____

_____

_____

_____

WORD BOX

circle, dark gray, light gray, square, triangle, white

STACKING SHAPES—EXPLAIN

DIRECTIONS: Supply the directions for stacking the shapes to make the figure on the left. If you need help with spelling, use the words in the word box at the bottom of the page.

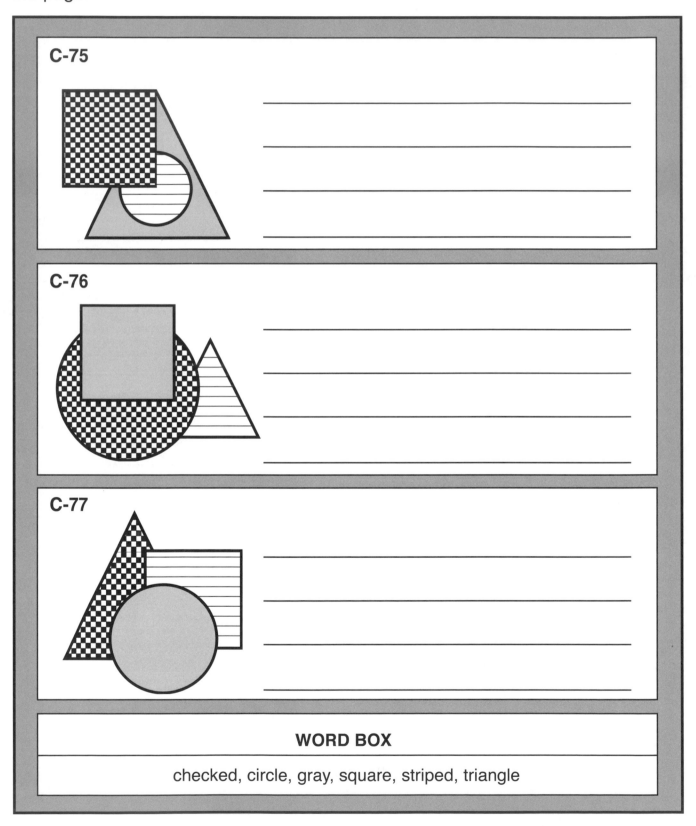

WORD BOX

checked, circle, gray, square, striped, triangle

CHAPTER FOUR

Describing Shapes →	Describing Things
Figural Similarities and Differences	Verbal Similarities and Differences
Figural Sequences	Verbal Sequences
Figural Classifications →	Verbal Classifications
Figural Analogies	Verbal Analogies

DESCRIBING CLASSES

DIRECTIONS: Circle the letter in front of each statement that is true.

EXAMPLE

All the figures
(a.) are squares
b. are the same size
c. are striped
(d.) are black

"a" should be circled (all the shapes are square)
"b" should not be circled (some of the shapes are large
and others are small)
"c" should not be circled (the shapes are not striped)
"d" should be circled (all the shapes are black)

D-1

All the figures
a. are triangles
b. are black
c. are striped
d. have a square corner

D-2

All the figures
a. are squares
b. are half black
c. are the same size
d. are half white

D-3

All the figures
a. are half circles
b. are black
c. are the same size
d. are white

DESCRIBING CLASSES

DIRECTIONS: Circle the letter in front of each true statement.

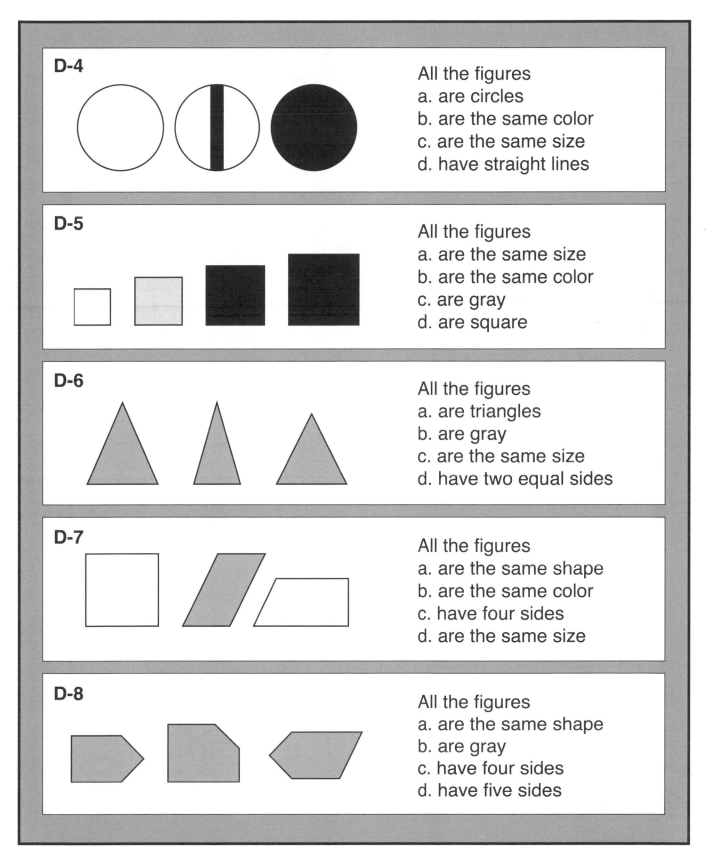

D-4

All the figures
a. are circles
b. are the same color
c. are the same size
d. have straight lines

D-5

All the figures
a. are the same size
b. are the same color
c. are gray
d. are square

D-6

All the figures
a. are triangles
b. are gray
c. are the same size
d. have two equal sides

D-7

All the figures
a. are the same shape
b. are the same color
c. have four sides
d. are the same size

D-8

All the figures
a. are the same shape
b. are gray
c. have four sides
d. have five sides

MATCHING CLASSES BY SHAPE

DIRECTIONS: Draw a line from each group of shapes on the left to a group on the right that belongs to the same class.

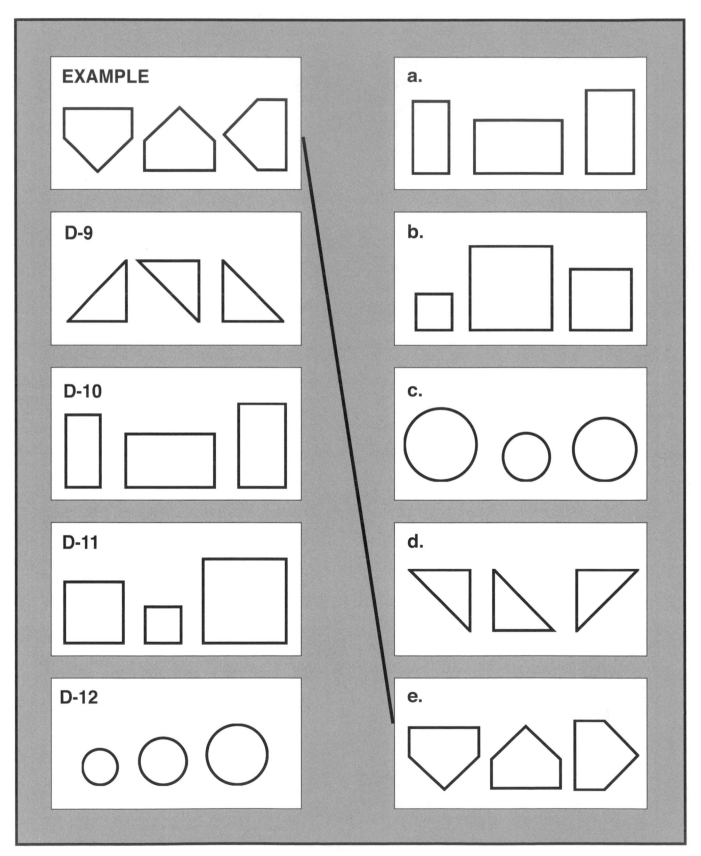

EXAMPLE

D-9

D-10

D-11

D-12

a.

b.

c.

d.

e.

MATCHING CLASSES BY SHAPE

DIRECTIONS: Draw a line from each group on the left to a group on the right that belongs to the same class.

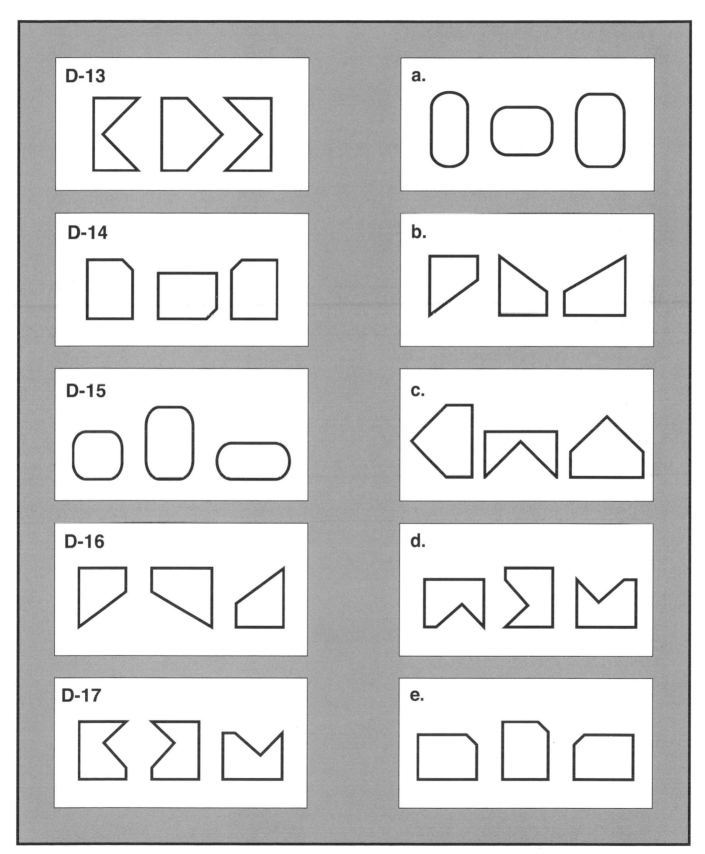

D-13

a.

D-14

b.

D-15

c.

D-16

d.

D-17

e.

MATCHING CLASSES BY PATTERN

DIRECTIONS: Draw a line from each group on the left to a group on the right that belongs to the same class.

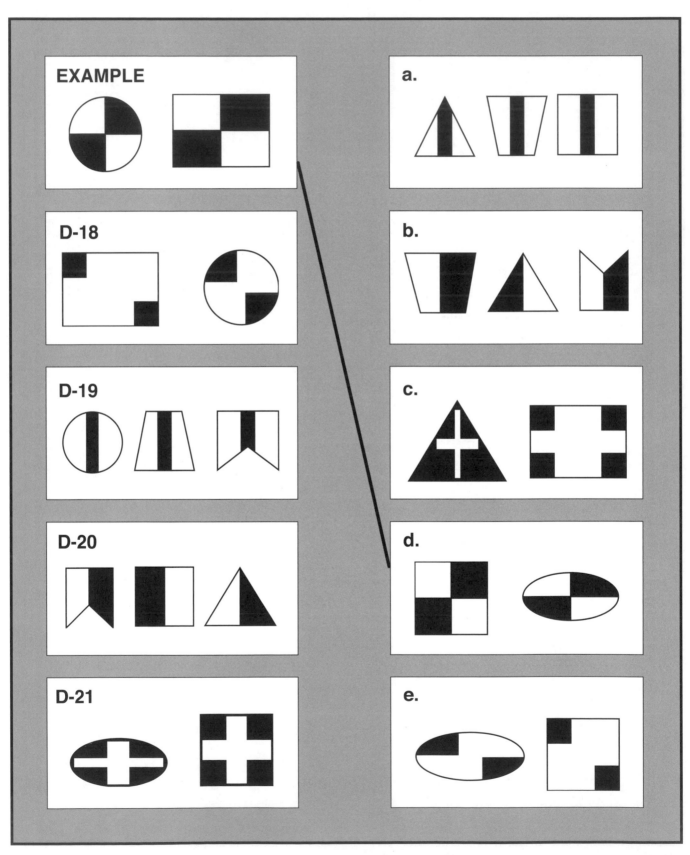

CLASSIFYING MORE THAN ONE WAY—MATCHING

DIRECTIONS: Match the figure in each box on the left to all the classes on the right to which it can belong. Write the letters of the correct classes on the line next to the figure. For example, the triangle in the example belongs to both class *c* (the white class) and class *f* (the triangle class).

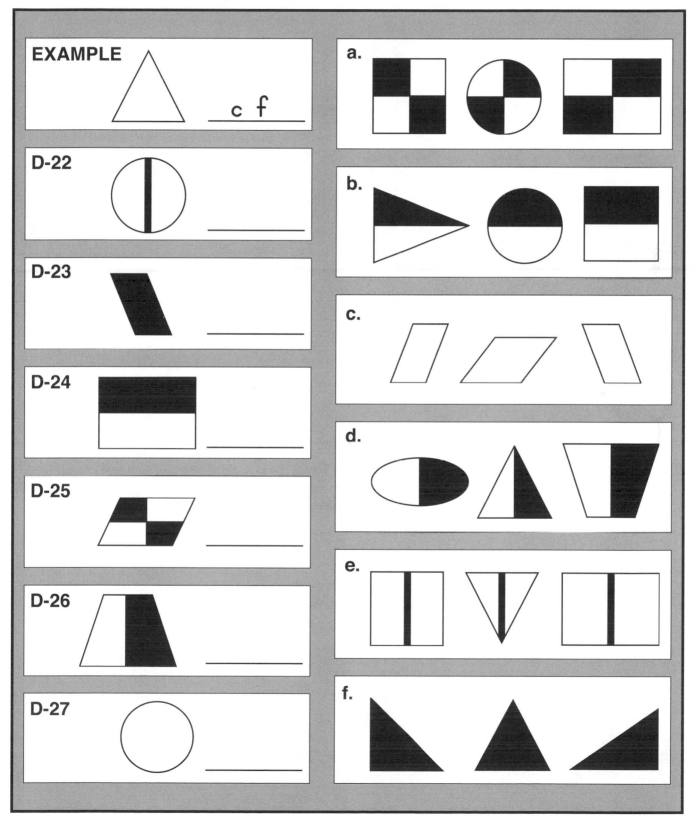

CLASSIFYING MORE THAN ONE WAY—MATCHING

DIRECTIONS: Match the figure in each box to all the classes on the right to which it can belong. You can match the figure by one or more characteristics. Write the letters of all the classes to which it can belong.

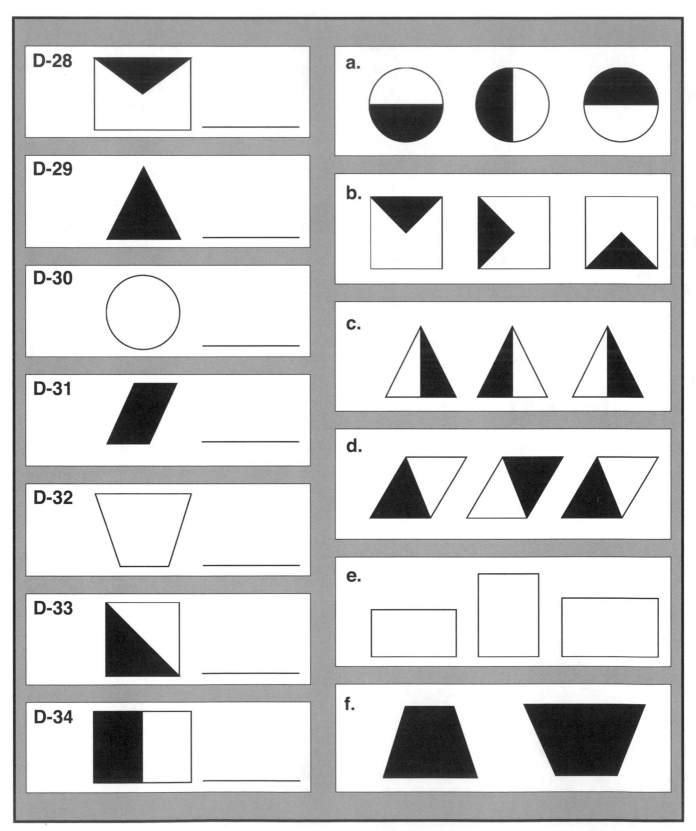

D-28 _____

D-29 _____

D-30 _____

D-31 _____

D-32 _____

D-33 _____

D-34 _____

a.

b.

c.

d.

e.

f.

CHANGING CHARACTERISTICS—SELECT

DIRECTIONS: Look at each pair of figures below. In the answer column, circle "S" if the characteristic is the same for both figures. Circle "D" if the characteristic is different.

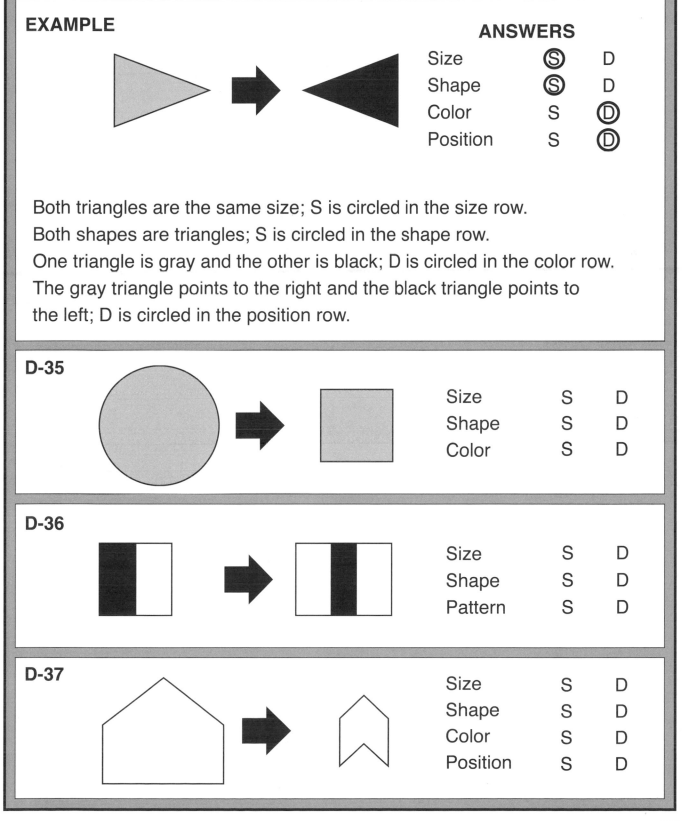

EXAMPLE

ANSWERS

Size	Ⓢ	D
Shape	Ⓢ	D
Color	S	Ⓓ
Position	S	Ⓓ

Both triangles are the same size; S is circled in the size row.

Both shapes are triangles; S is circled in the shape row.

One triangle is gray and the other is black; D is circled in the color row.

The gray triangle points to the right and the black triangle points to the left; D is circled in the position row.

D-35

Size	S	D
Shape	S	D
Color	S	D

D-36

Size	S	D
Shape	S	D
Pattern	S	D

D-37

Size	S	D
Shape	S	D
Color	S	D
Position	S	D

CHANGING CHARACTERISTICS—SELECT

DIRECTIONS: Look at each pair of figures below. In the answer column, circle "S" if the characteristic is the same for both figures. Circle "D" if the characteristic is different.

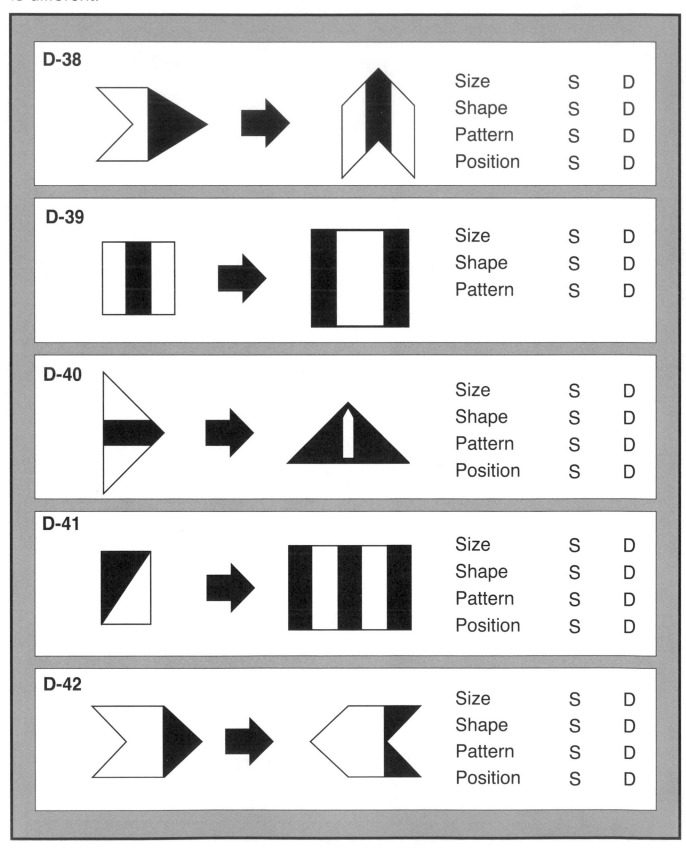

D-38

Size	S	D
Shape	S	D
Pattern	S	D
Position	S	D

D-39

Size	S	D
Shape	S	D
Pattern	S	D

D-40

Size	S	D
Shape	S	D
Pattern	S	D
Position	S	D

D-41

Size	S	D
Shape	S	D
Pattern	S	D
Position	S	D

D-42

Size	S	D
Shape	S	D
Pattern	S	D
Position	S	D

CHANGING CHARACTERISTICS—SUPPLY

DIRECTIONS: Look at the figure on the left. Read the directions and then draw another figure with the characteristics described in the instructions.

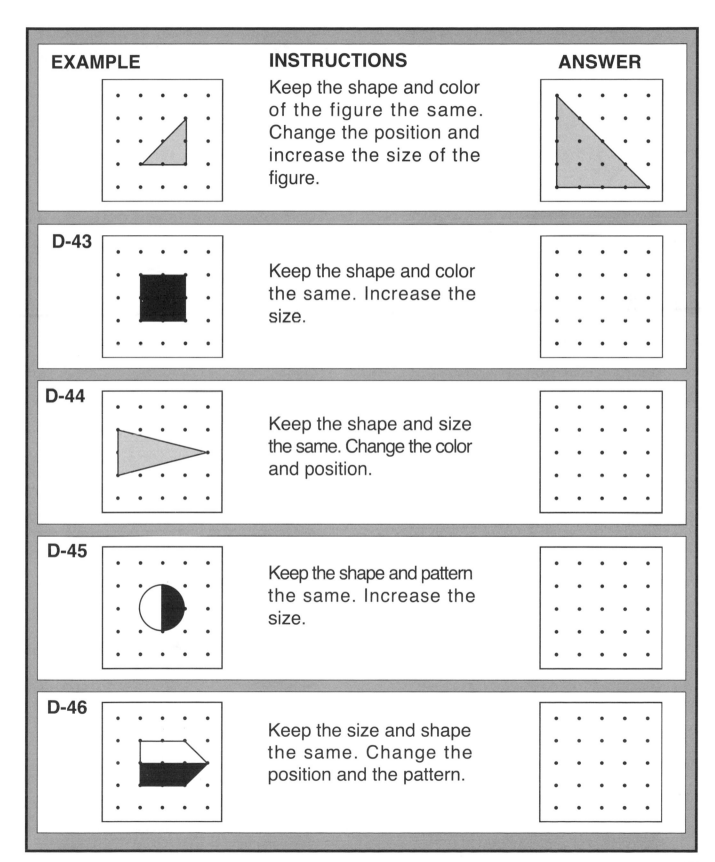

EXAMPLE   **INSTRUCTIONS**   **ANSWER**

Keep the shape and color of the figure the same. Change the position and increase the size of the figure.

D-43

Keep the shape and color the same. Increase the size.

D-44

Keep the shape and size the same. Change the color and position.

D-45

Keep the shape and pattern the same. Increase the size.

D-46

Keep the size and shape the same. Change the position and the pattern.

CHANGING CHARACTERISTICS—SUPPLY

DIRECTIONS: Look at the figure on the left. Read the directions and then draw another figure with the characteristics described in the instructions.

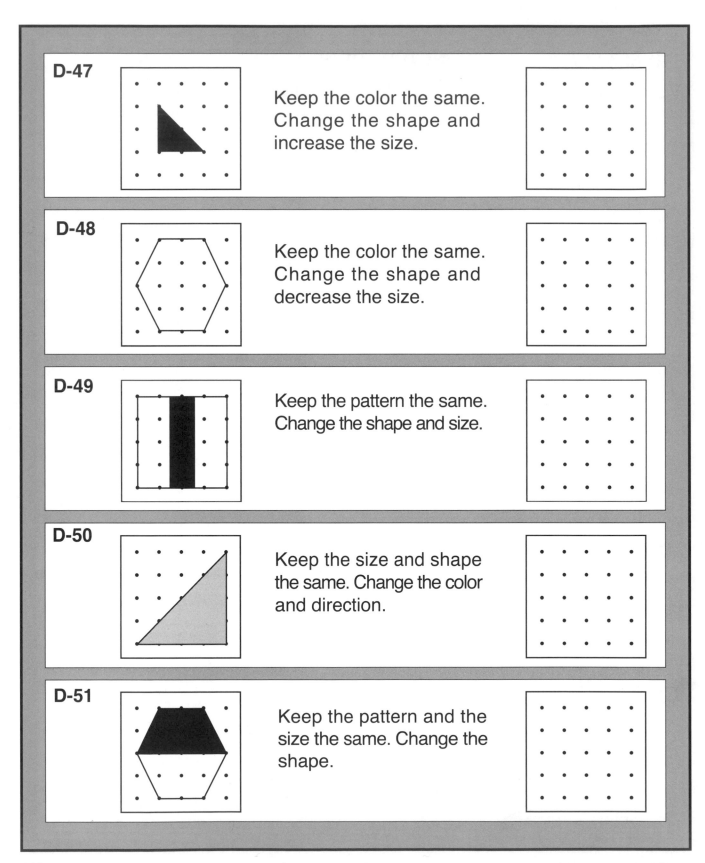

D-47 Keep the color the same. Change the shape and increase the size.

D-48 Keep the color the same. Change the shape and decrease the size.

D-49 Keep the pattern the same. Change the shape and size.

D-50 Keep the size and shape the same. Change the color and direction.

D-51 Keep the pattern and the size the same. Change the shape.

DRAW ANOTHER

DIRECTIONS: In the box on the right, draw another figure that belongs to the group on the left.

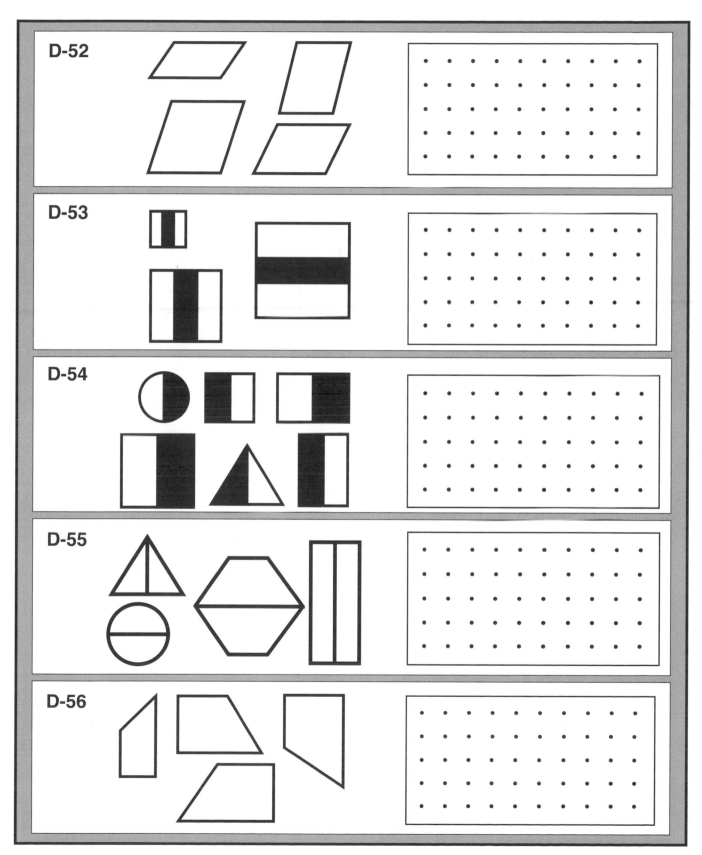

DRAW ANOTHER

DIRECTIONS: In the box on the right, draw another figure that belongs to the group on the left.

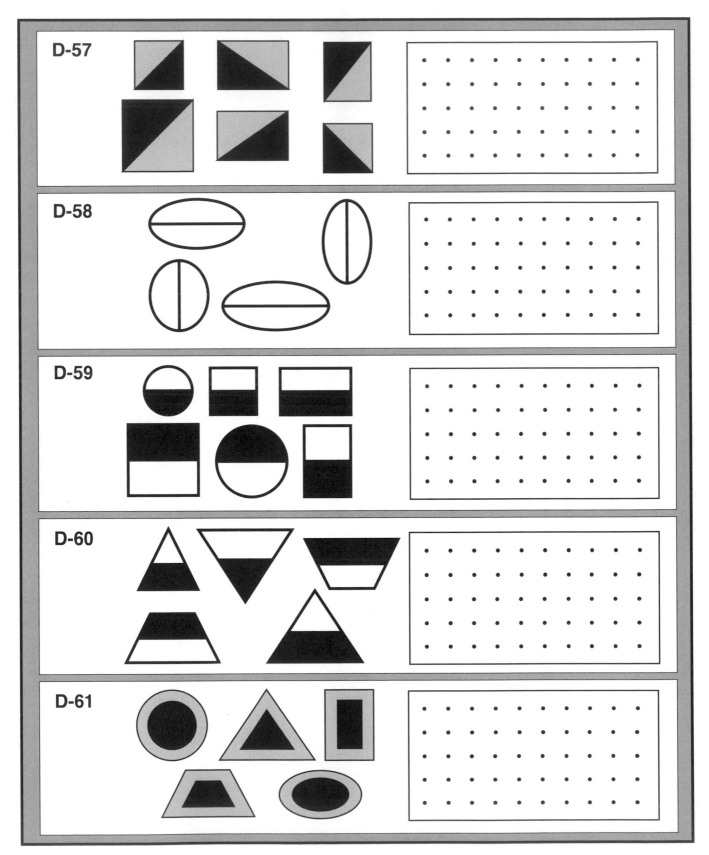

D-57

D-58

D-59

D-60

D-61

CLASSIFYING BY SHAPE—SORTING

DIRECTIONS: Sort this group of shapes according to the number of sides each shape has. Copy the shapes in the correct boxes; use the dot grid to help you draw them accurately.

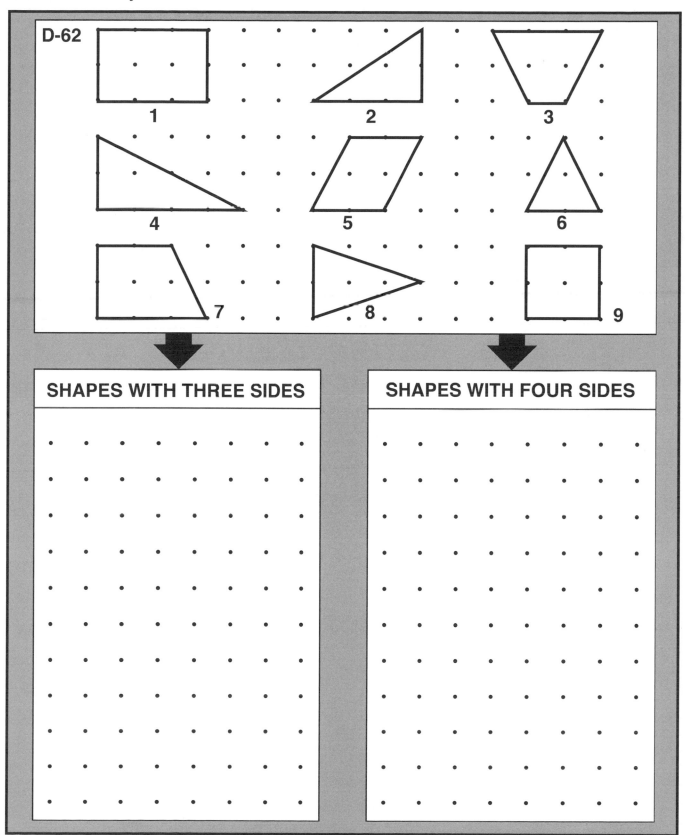

D-62

1 2 3

4 5 6

7 8 9

SHAPES WITH THREE SIDES

SHAPES WITH FOUR SIDES

CLASSIFYING BY SHAPE—SORTING

DIRECTIONS: Sort this group of shapes according to the number of sides each shape has. Below each shape is a number. Put the number of each shape in the correct box.

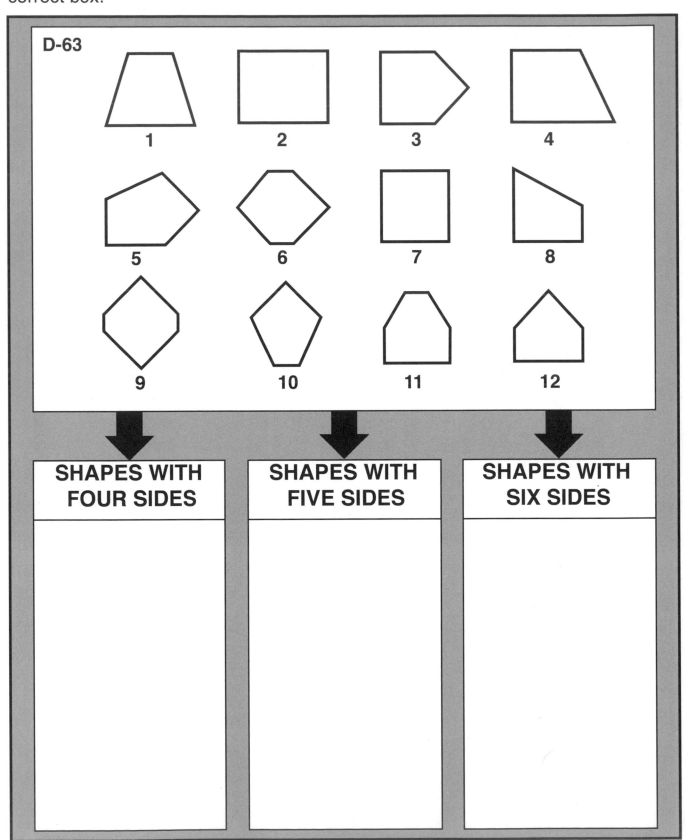

D-63

1   2   3   4

5   6   7   8

9   10   11   12

SHAPES WITH FOUR SIDES	SHAPES WITH FIVE SIDES	SHAPES WITH SIX SIDES

CLASSIFYING BY PATTERN—SORTING

DIRECTIONS: Sort this group of shapes according to the patterns drawn on the shapes. Below each shape is a number. Put the number for each shape in the box with the correct matching pattern.

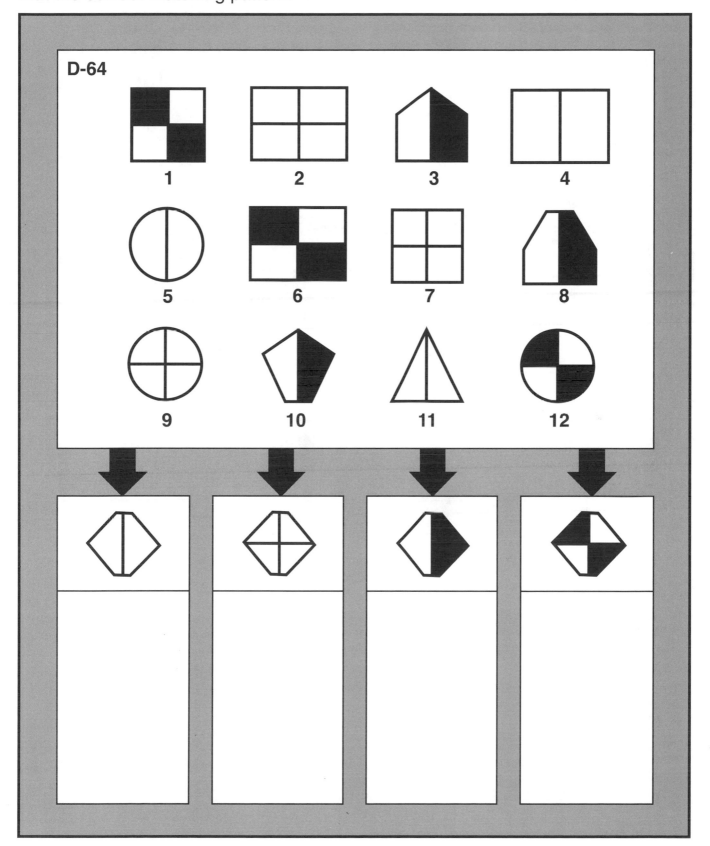

CLASSIFYING MORE THAN ONE WAY—SORTING

DIRECTIONS: Sort this group of shapes according to the size, pattern, or number of sides each shape has. On each shape is a number. Put the number for each shape in the correct sorting boxes; each shape number may go in more than one box.

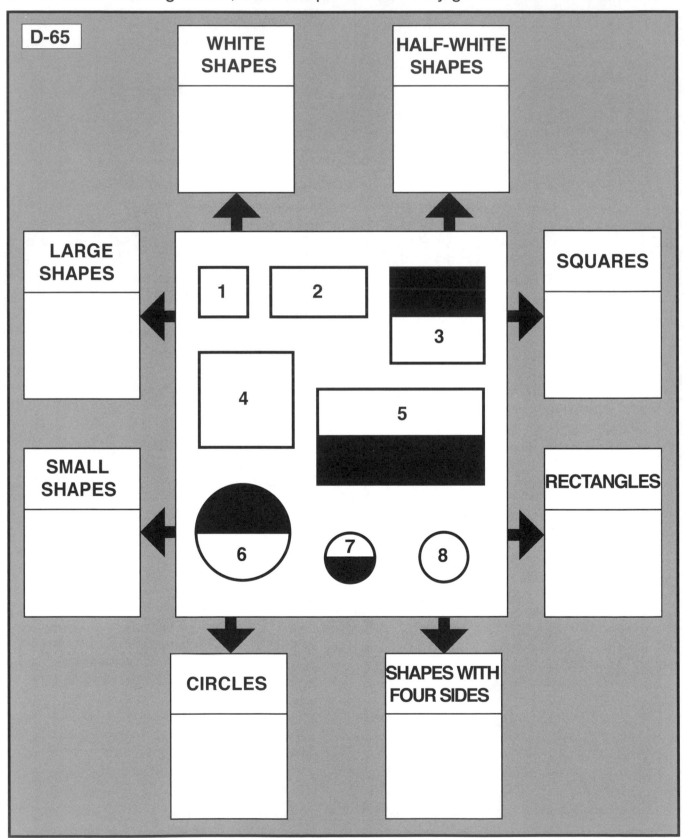

OVERLAPPING CLASSES—INTERSECTIONS

DIRECTIONS: Read the explanation of overlapping classes before going on to the next page.

This group of squares can be sorted by color and size.

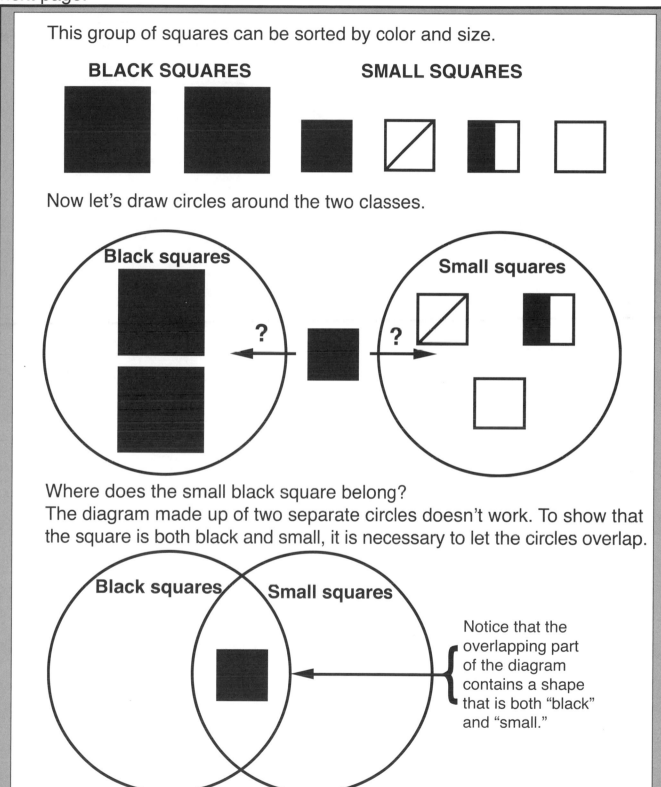

Where does the small black square belong?
The diagram made up of two separate circles doesn't work. To show that the square is both black and small, it is necessary to let the circles overlap.

The small black square belongs in the overlapping part of the diagram. Any shape in that area should have the characteristics of both circles.

OVERLAPPING CLASSES—INTERSECTIONS

DIRECTIONS: Using the information in the top diagram, darken part of the small, overlapping circles diagram next to each figure to show where that figure would belong.

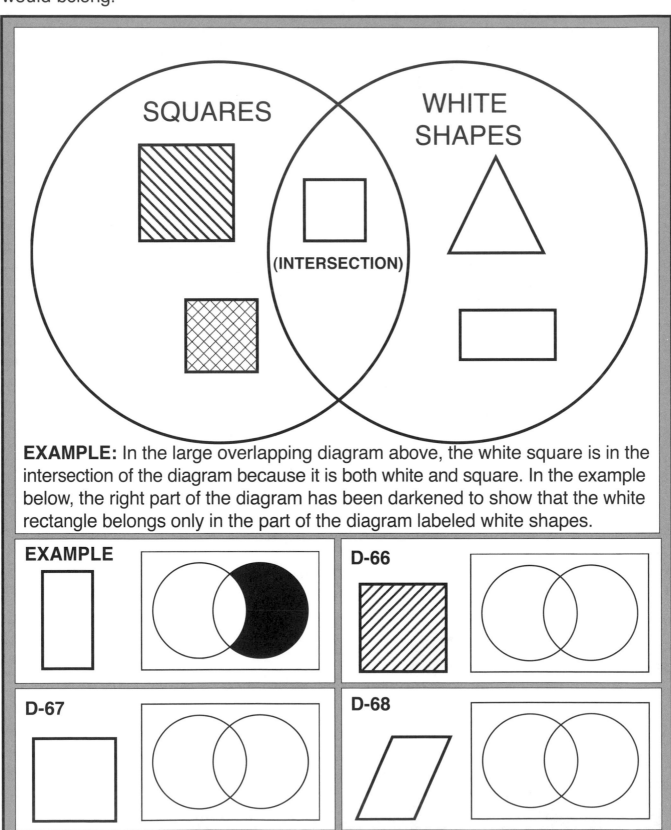

EXAMPLE: In the large overlapping diagram above, the white square is in the intersection of the diagram because it is both white and square. In the example below, the right part of the diagram has been darkened to show that the white rectangle belongs only in the part of the diagram labeled white shapes.

OVERLAPPING CLASSES—INTERSECTIONS

DIRECTIONS: Three regions are labeled on the large overlapping classes diagram. "I" is the overlapping part or intersection. On the line next to each small shape below, write an "A," "B," or "I" to indicate where the shape belongs. In the example, the striped triangle belongs in the left ("A") region of the diagram.

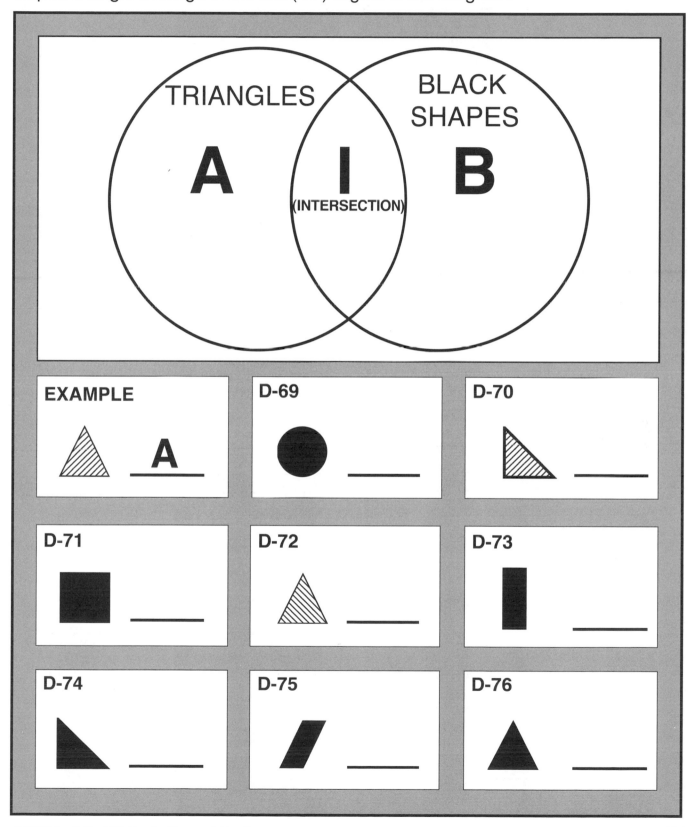

OVERLAPPING CLASSES—INTERSECTIONS

DIRECTIONS: Four regions are labeled on the large overlapping classes diagram. "O" is outside the overlapping circles. On the line next to each small shape below, write an "A," "B," "I," or "O" to indicate where the shape belongs. In the example, the black triangle belongs in the outside ("O") region of the diagram because it is not striped and has three sides, not four.

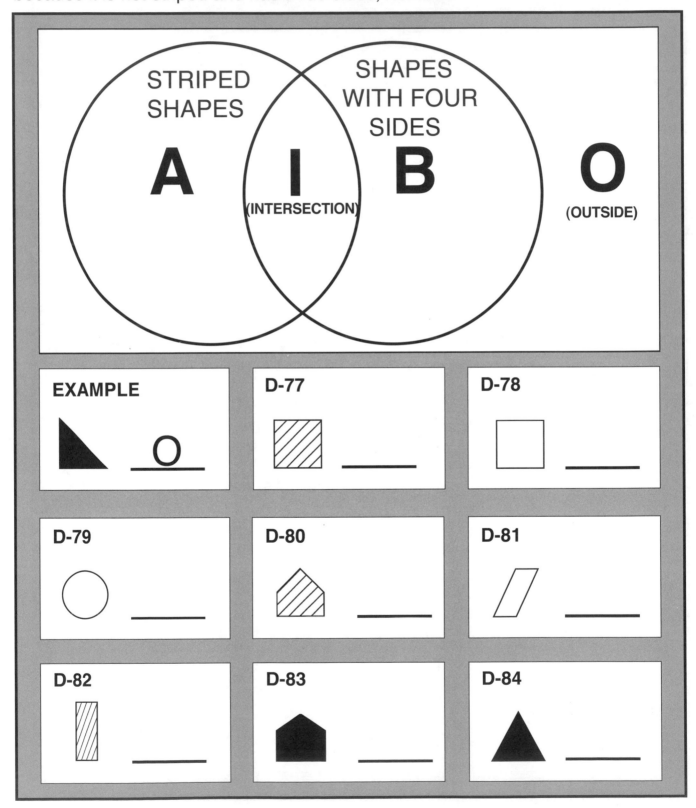

OVERLAPPING CLASSES—INTERSECTIONS

DIRECTIONS: Look at the shapes in circles 1 and 2 to answer questions **D-85** through **D-87**. In exercises **D-88** to **D-93**, write an "A," "B," "I," or "O" on the line to indicate where each shape belongs.

D-85 Circle 1 contains the class_____.

D-86 Circle 2 contains the class_____.

D-87 The intersection contains the class_____.

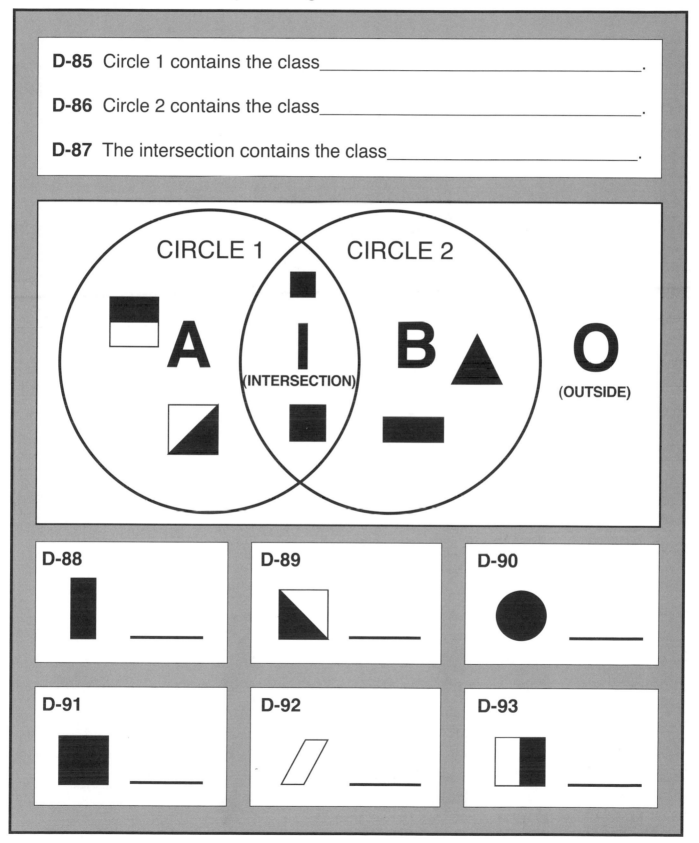

OVERLAPPING CLASSES—INTERSECTIONS

DIRECTIONS: Look at the shapes in the intersection (I) and Circle 2 to answer questions **D-94** through **D-96**. In exercises **D-97** to **D-102**, write an "A," "B," "I," or "O" on the line to indicate where each shape belongs.

D-94 Circle 1 contains the class_____.

D-95 Circle 2 contains the class_____.

D-96 The intersection contains the class_____.

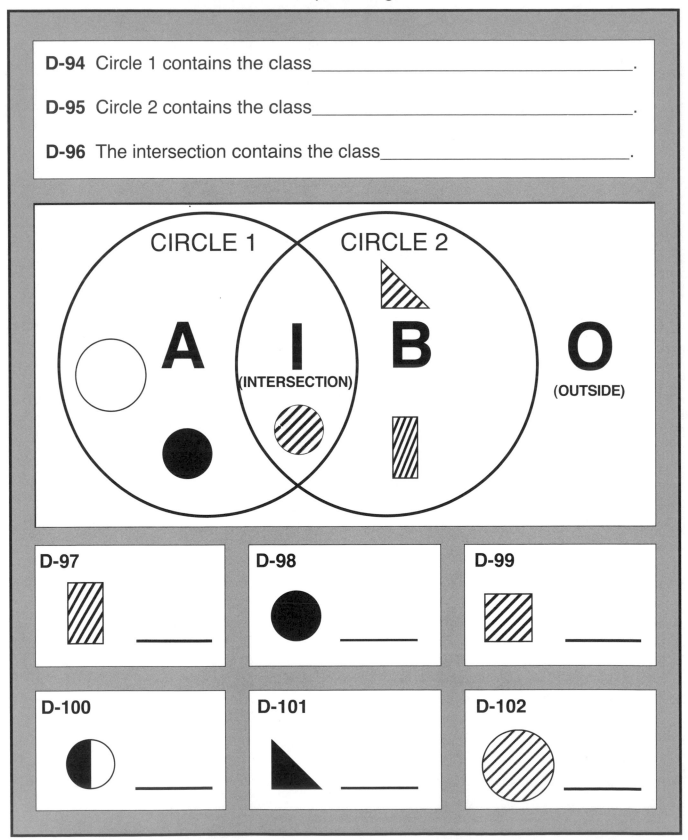

CIRCLE 1   CIRCLE 2

A   I   B   O
(INTERSECTION)   (OUTSIDE)

D-97 _____

D-98 _____

D-99 _____

D-100 _____

D-101 _____

D-102 _____

OVERLAPPING CLASSES—INTERSECTIONS

DIRECTIONS: Look at the shapes in the intersection (I) and Circle 2 to answer questions **D-103** through **D-105**. In exercises **D-106** to **D-111**, write an "A," "B," "I," or "O" on the line to indicate where each shape belongs.

D-103 Circle 1 contains the class_____.

D-104 Circle 2 contains the class_____.

D-105 The intersection contains the class_____.

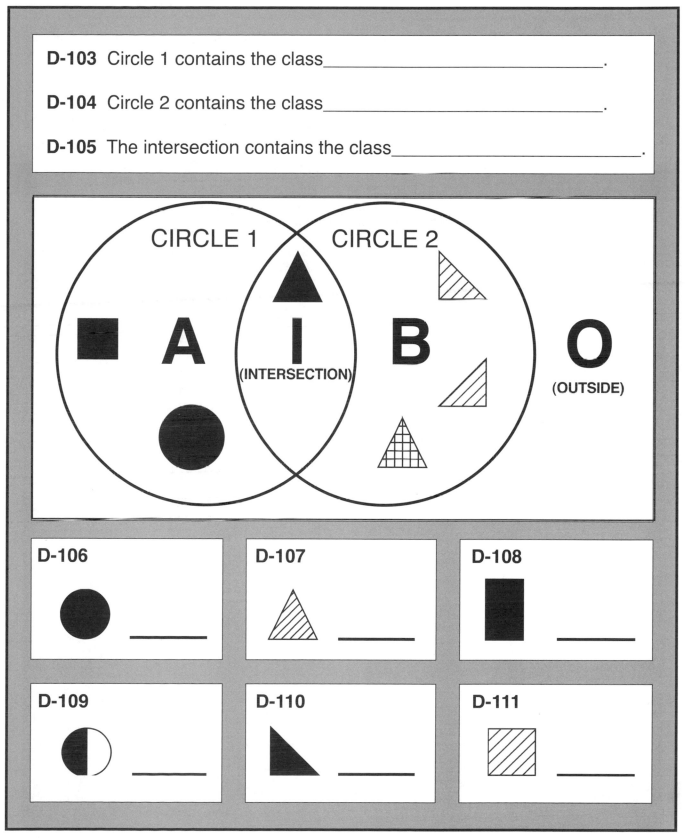

OVERLAPPING CLASSES—MATRIX

DIRECTIONS: Using the given figures as clues, decide which characteristic is true for each row and which characteristic is true for each column. Draw in the missing figures.

A matrix diagram can be used to organize a group of objects to describe their characteristics in more than one way. All the objects in a row must have the same characteristic, and all the objects in a column must share another characteristic. (Note: Rows go across and columns go up and down.)

Each figure has two characteristics. For example, in the first matrix the figure in the top corner is square and black. The figures in each row share a common characteristic, as do the figures in each column. So the figures in the top row of the first matrix will be either all black or all squares.

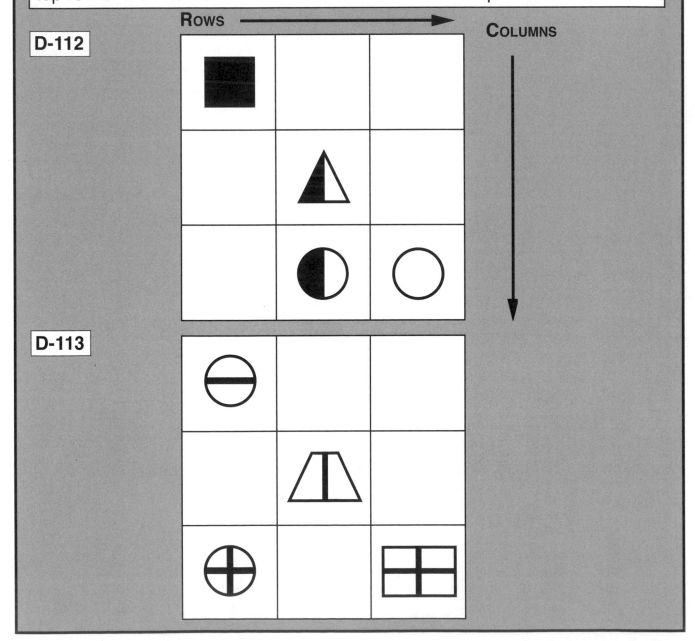

OVERLAPPING CLASSES—MATRIX

DIRECTIONS: Complete each matrix.

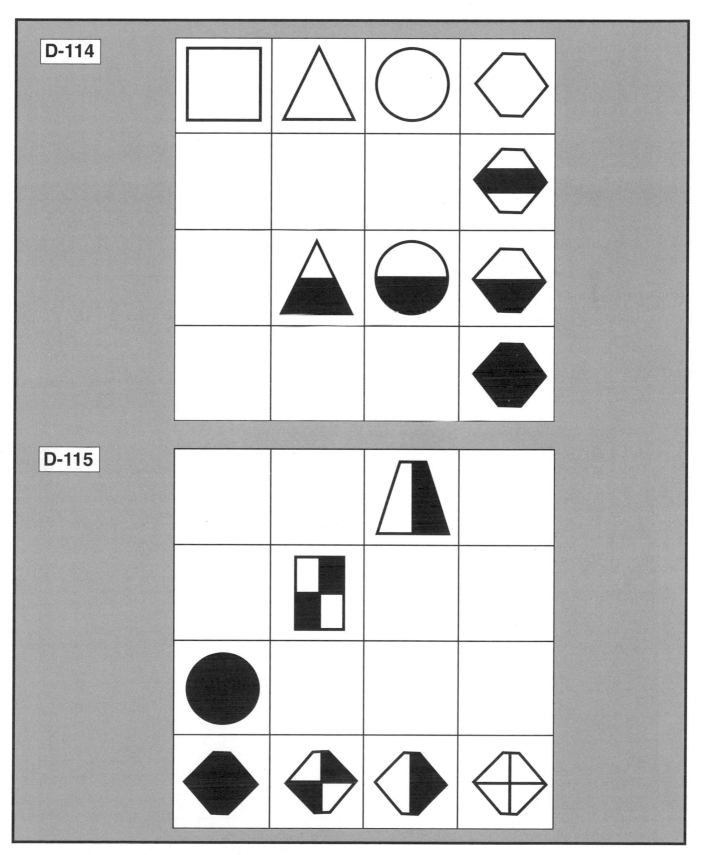

OVERLAPPING CLASSES—MATRIX

DIRECTIONS: Complete each matrix.

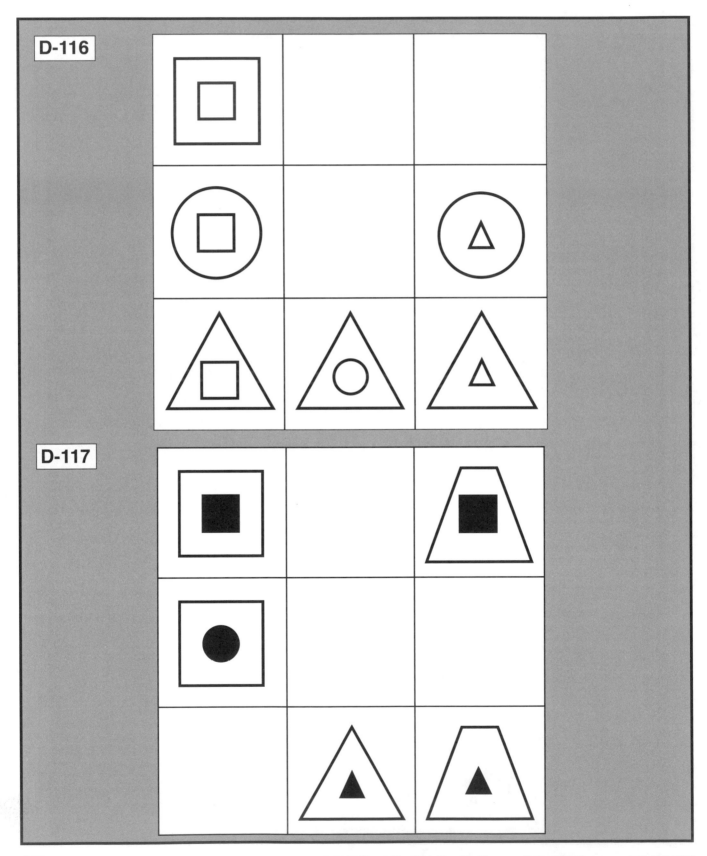

DEDUCE THE CLASS

DIRECTIONS: In the next group of exercises, you will continue to classify figures, but now you must determine the characteristics of the class. Look at the figures that belong to the class. Then look at the figures that do **not** belong to that class.

By looking at the clue figures, decide what is true of the members of the group or class. You may wish to look at the number of straight lines and the number of curved lines in each figure.

After you have decided (deduced) the characteristics of the class, you will decide which of the given figures belong to that class.

HERE ARE THE STEPS:

1. Carefully study the "clue" figures.

2. Decide (deduce) the characteristics of the "clue figures" by asking yourself:

    a. How are the clue figures alike?

    b. How are the clue figures different?

3. Look at the figures in the questions and decide if they belong in the class.

DEDUCE THE CLASS

DIRECTIONS: Use the five clue figures to deduce what a quad is. Then answer the questions yes or no.

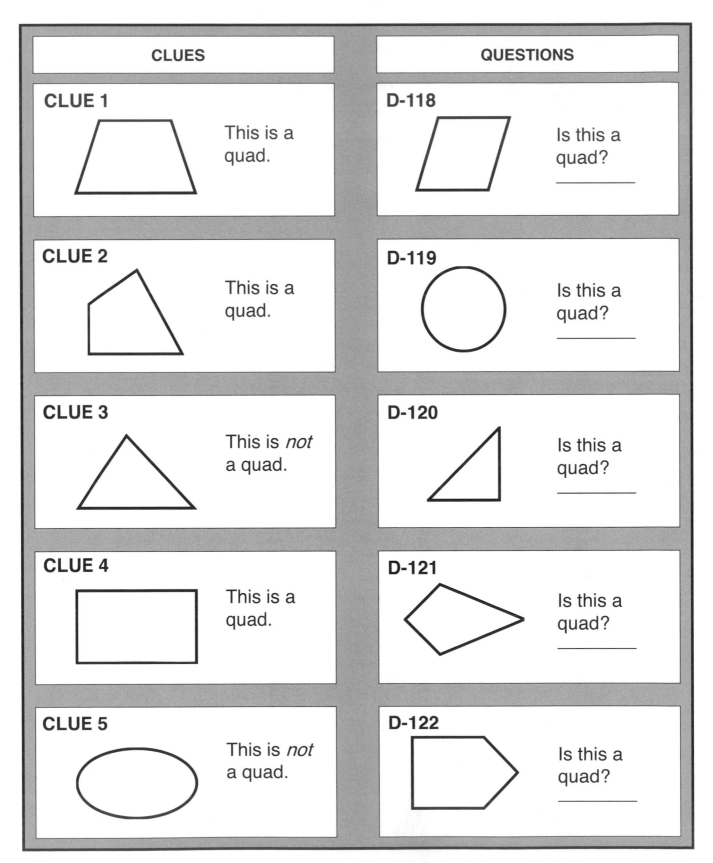

CLUES	QUESTIONS
CLUE 1 — This is a quad.	**D-118** — Is this a quad? _____
CLUE 2 — This is a quad.	**D-119** — Is this a quad? _____
CLUE 3 — This is *not* a quad.	**D-120** — Is this a quad? _____
CLUE 4 — This is a quad.	**D-121** — Is this a quad? _____
CLUE 5 — This is *not* a quad.	**D-122** — Is this a quad? _____

DEDUCE THE CLASS

DIRECTIONS: Use the five clue figures to deduce what a penta is. Then answer the questions yes or no.

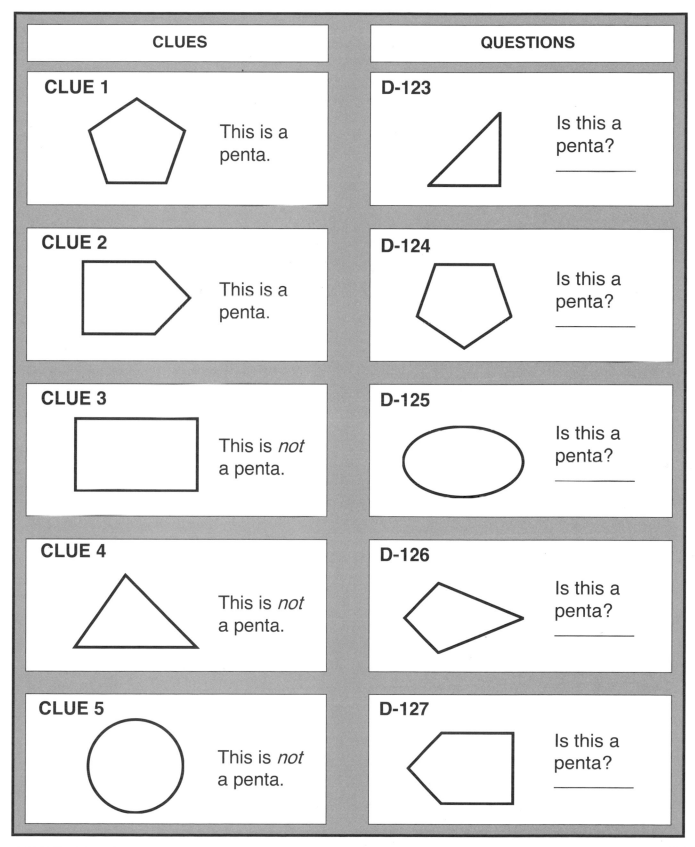

CLUES	QUESTIONS
CLUE 1 — This is a penta.	**D-123** — Is this a penta? _____
CLUE 2 — This is a penta.	**D-124** — Is this a penta? _____
CLUE 3 — This is *not* a penta.	**D-125** — Is this a penta? _____
CLUE 4 — This is *not* a penta.	**D-126** — Is this a penta? _____
CLUE 5 — This is *not* a penta.	**D-127** — Is this a penta? _____

CHAPTER FIVE

Describing Shapes	→	Describing Things
↓		↓
Figural Similarities and Differences	→	Verbal Similarities and Differences
↓		↓
Figural Sequences	→	Verbal Sequences
↓		↓
Figural Classifications	→	Verbal Classifications
↓		↓
Figural Analogies	→	Verbal Analogies

FIGURAL ANALOGIES—SELECT

DIRECTIONS: Circle the figure that completes the analogy.

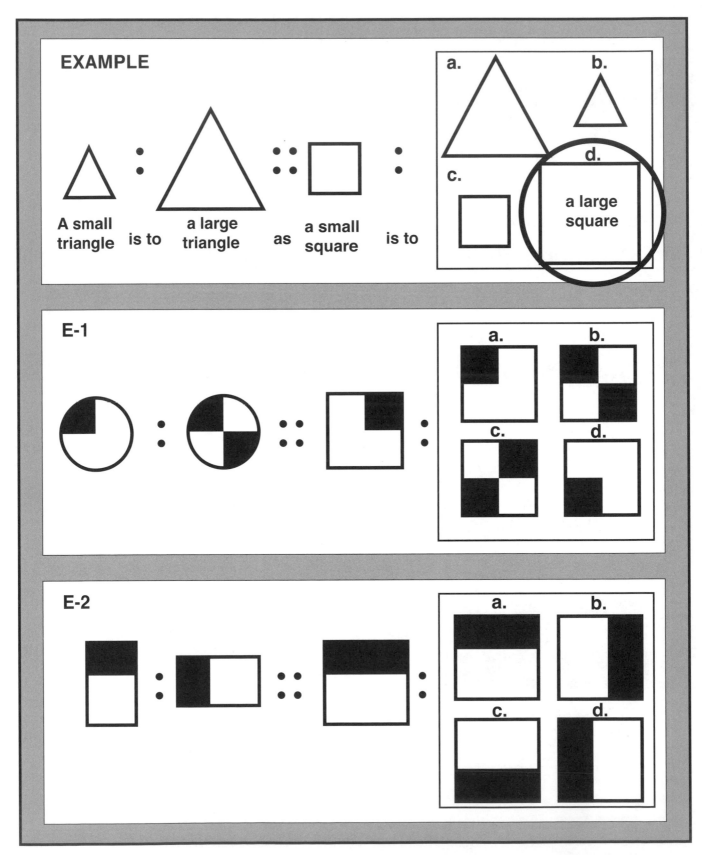

FIGURAL ANALOGIES—SELECT

DIRECTIONS: Circle the figure that completes the analogy.

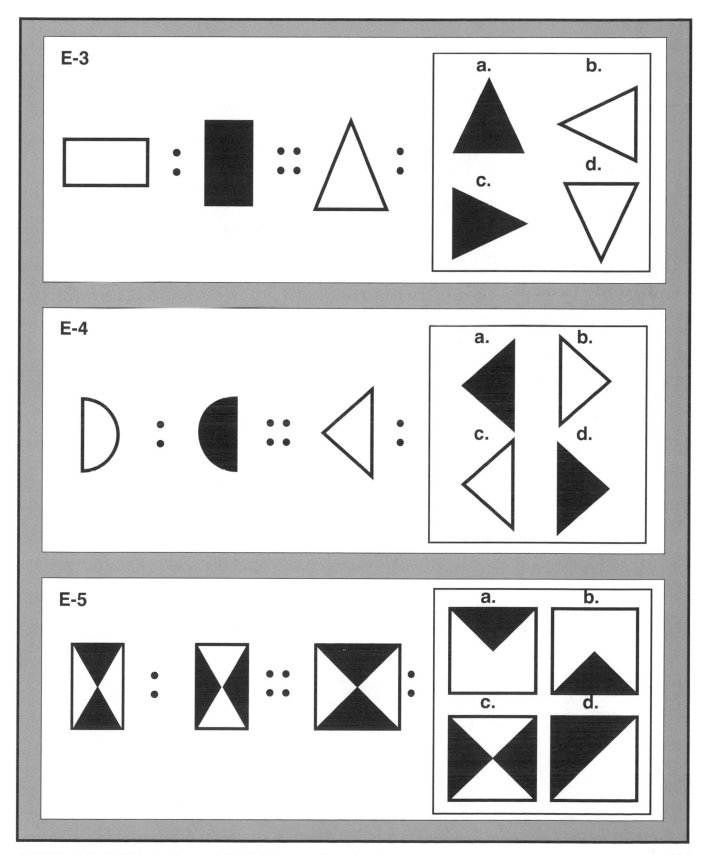

FIGURAL ANALOGIES—SELECT

DIRECTIONS: Circle the figure that completes the analogy.

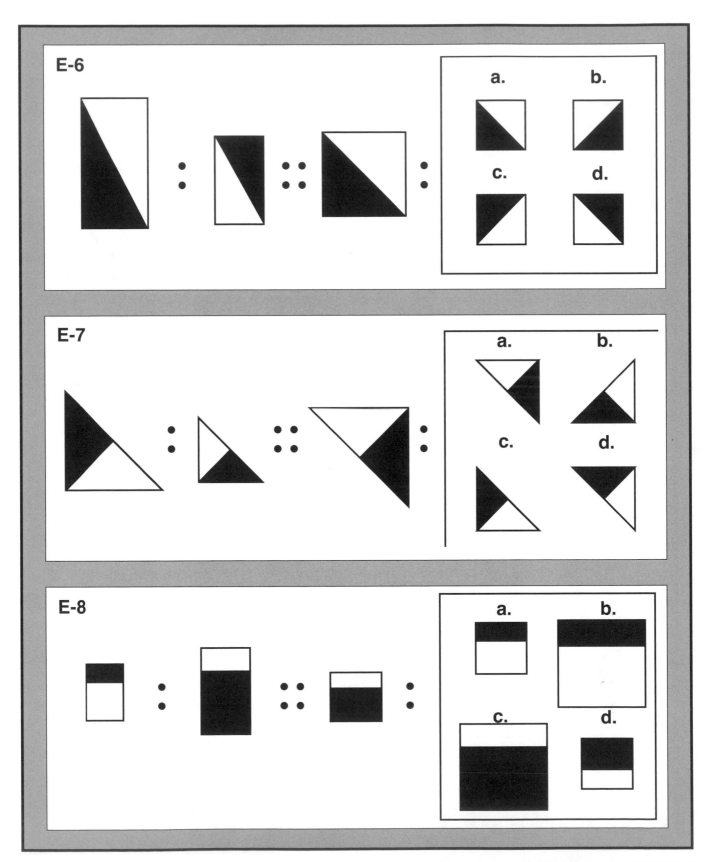

FIGURAL ANALOGIES—SELECT

DIRECTIONS: Circle the figure that completes the analogy.

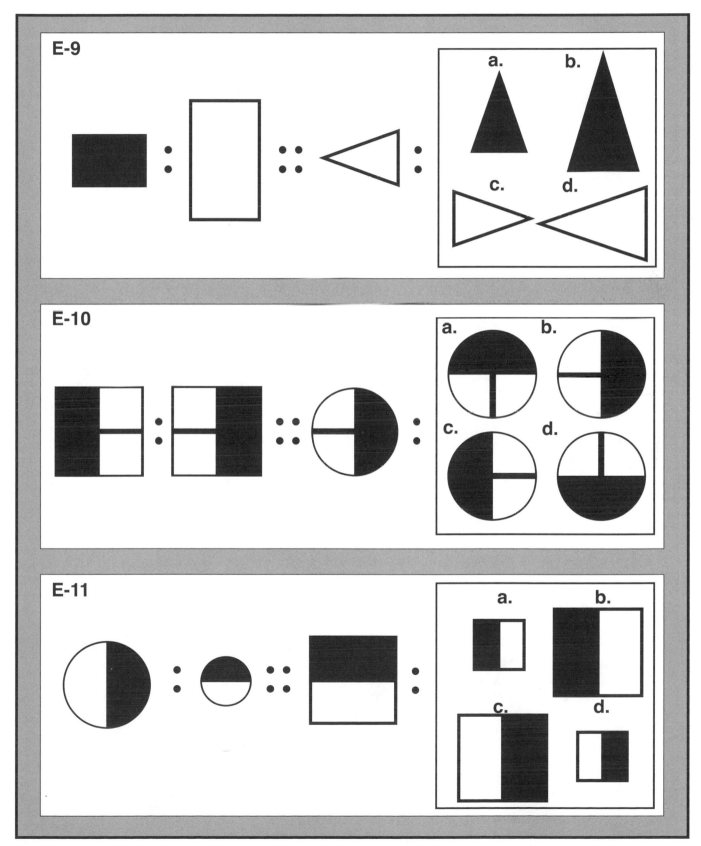

FIGURAL ANALOGIES—SELECT

DIRECTIONS: Circle the figure that completes the analogy.

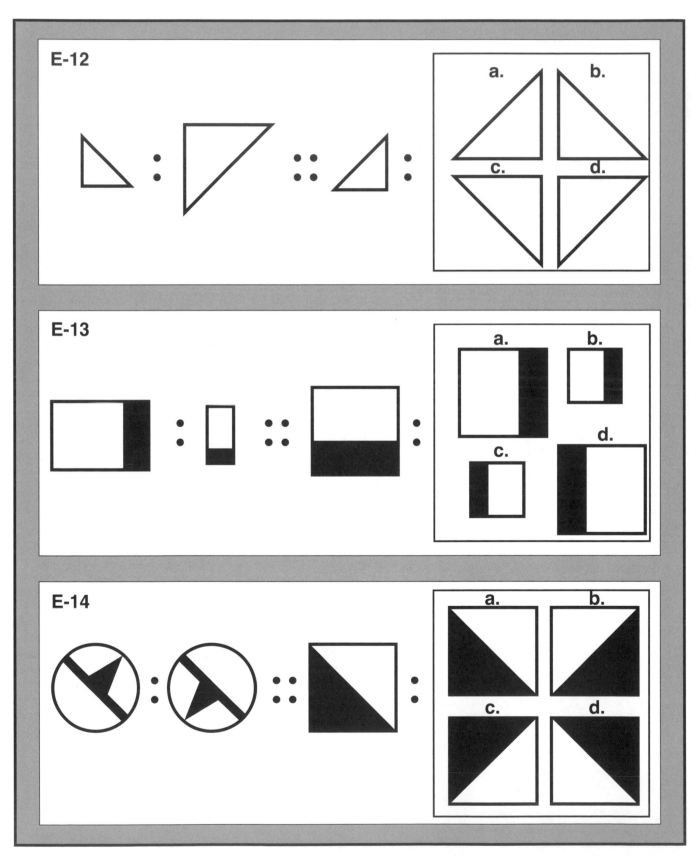

FIGURAL ANALOGIES—SELECT A PAIR

DIRECTIONS: Draw a line between the pairs that correctly form an analogy, A : B :: C : D. Remember, in an analogy, both pairs must be related in the same way.

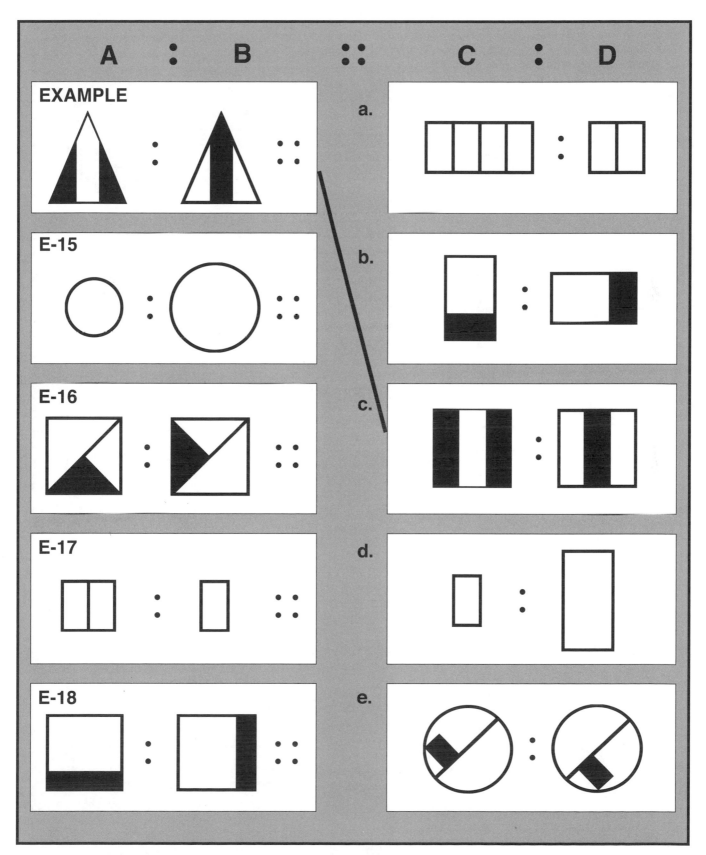

FIGURAL ANALOGIES—SELECT A PAIR

DIRECTIONS: Draw a line between the pairs that correctly form an analogy, A : B :: C : D. Remember, in an analogy, both pairs must be related in the same way.

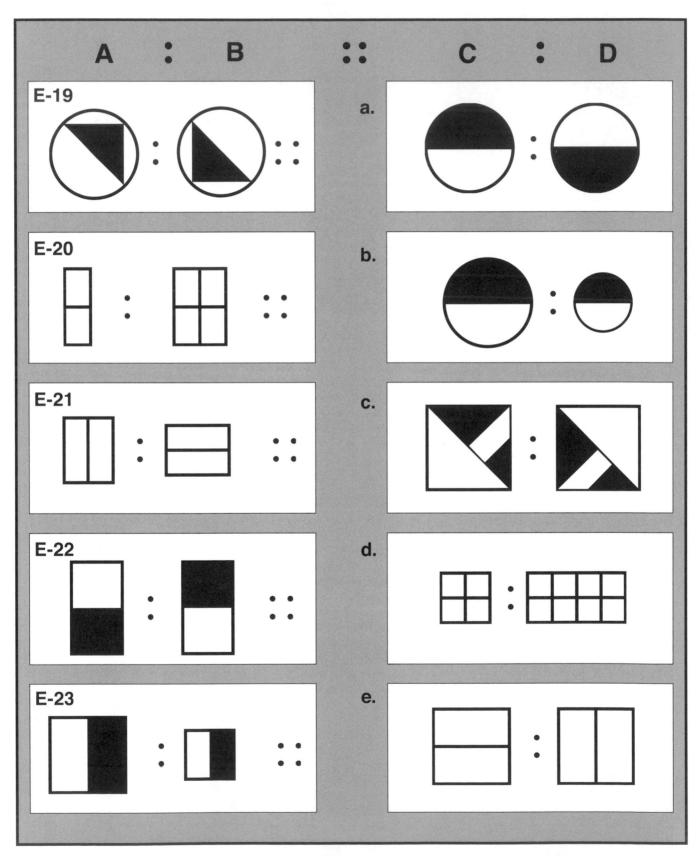

DESCRIBING TYPES OF FIGURAL ANALOGIES

DIRECTIONS: In the exercises you have just done, there are several types of analogous relationships. These relationships can be described as follows:

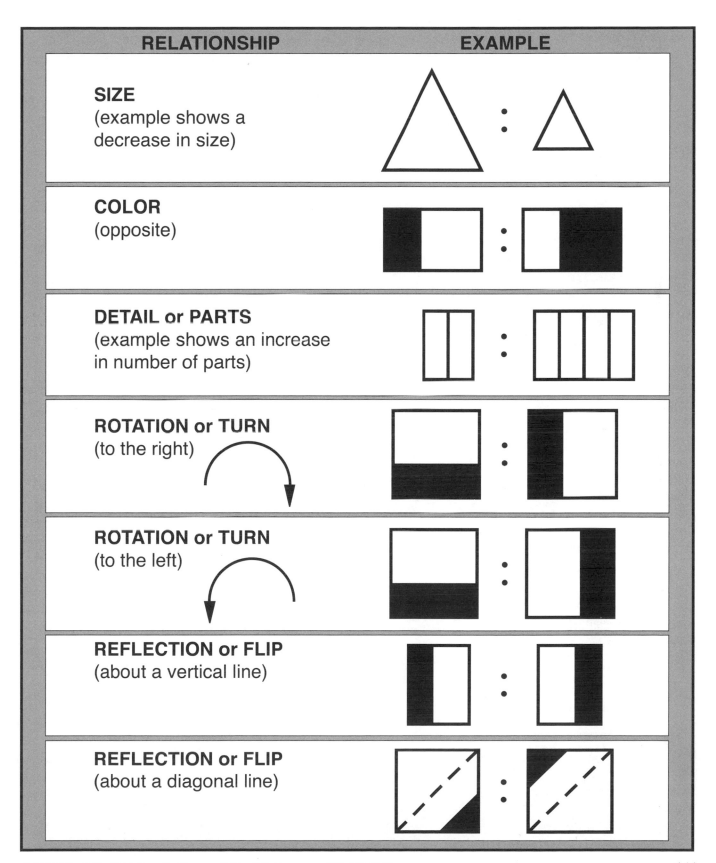

RELATIONSHIP	EXAMPLE
SIZE (example shows a decrease in size)	
COLOR (opposite)	
DETAIL or PARTS (example shows an increase in number of parts)	
ROTATION or TURN (to the right)	
ROTATION or TURN (to the left)	
REFLECTION or FLIP (about a vertical line)	
REFLECTION or FLIP (about a diagonal line)	

COMPLETE THE PAIR

DIRECTIONS: Using the grid as a guideline, draw a figure which illustrates the relationship written below each box.

EXAMPLE

Color—opposite

E-24

Add parts—double the number

E-25

Rotate to the right

E-26

Reflect about a vertical line

E-27

Increase size

E-28

Color—opposite

E-29

Reflect about a diagonal

E-30

Rotate to the left

E-31

Take away half the parts

E-32

Decrease the size

FIGURAL ANALOGIES—COMPLETE

DIRECTIONS: Shade in the last figure in each row so that the figural analogies are complete.

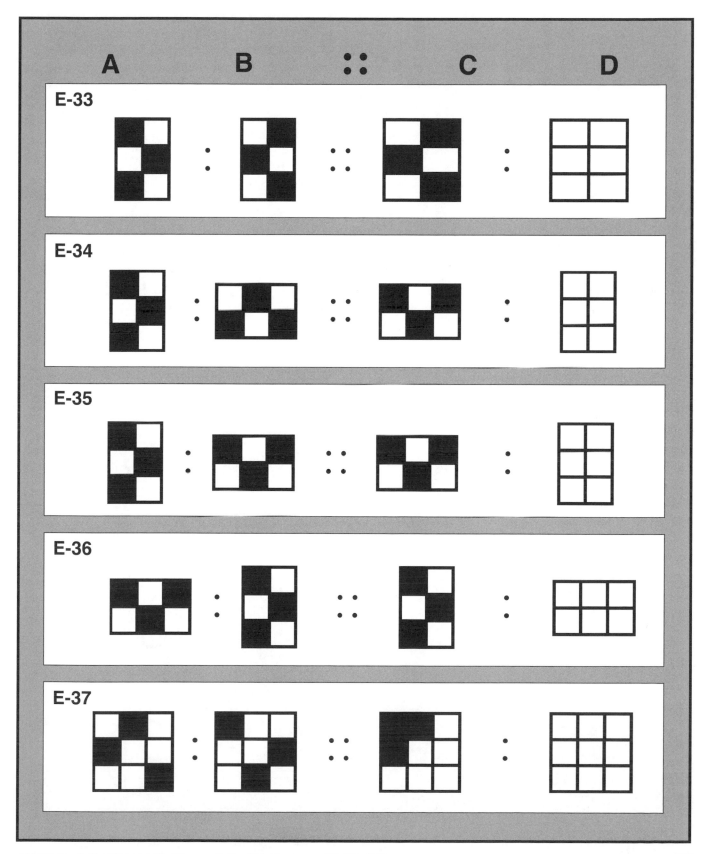

FIGURAL ANALOGIES—COMPLETE

DIRECTIONS: Shade in the last figure in each row so that the analogies are complete.

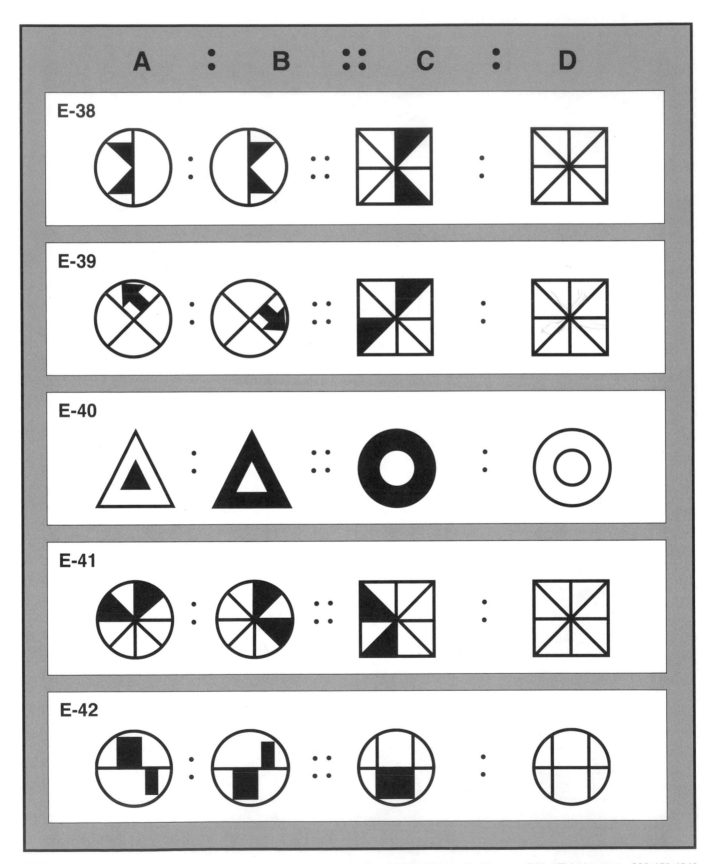

FIGURAL ANALOGIES—COMPLETE

DIRECTIONS: Shade in the last figure in each row so that the figural analogies are complete.

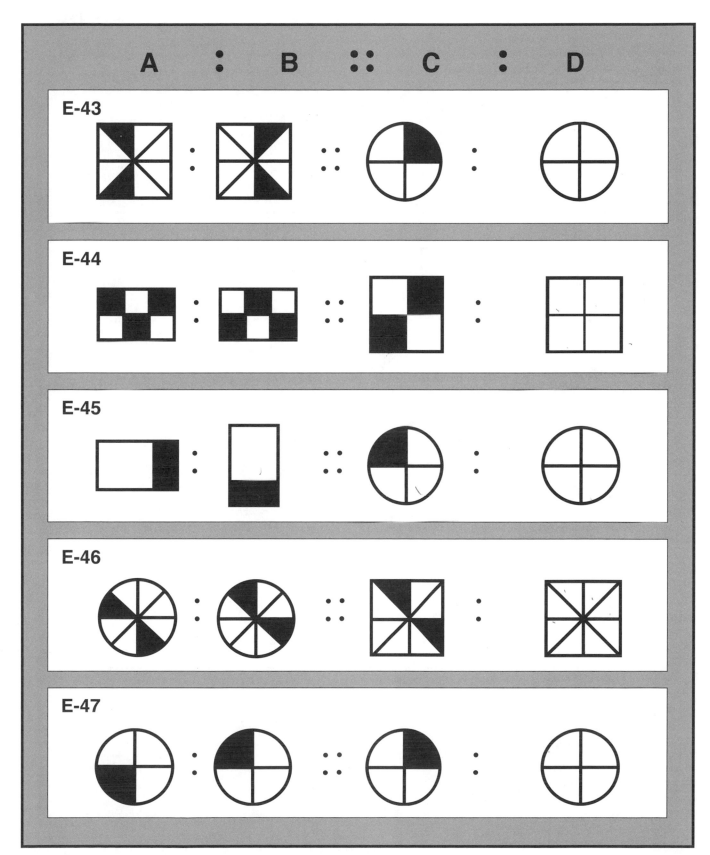

FIGURAL ANALOGIES—SUPPLY

DIRECTIONS: Using the dot grid, draw in a figure to complete each analogy.

E-48

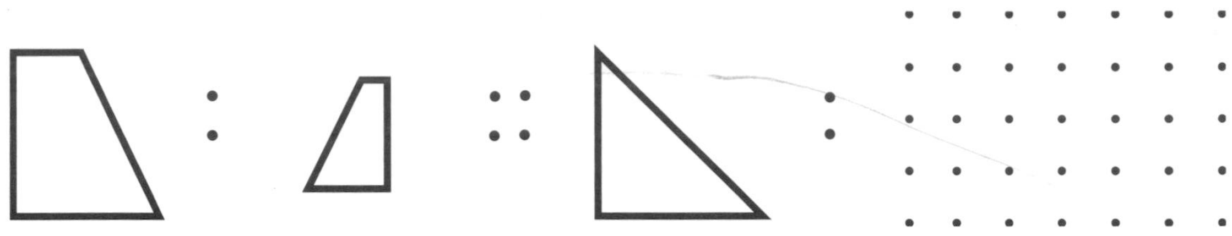

E-49

E-50

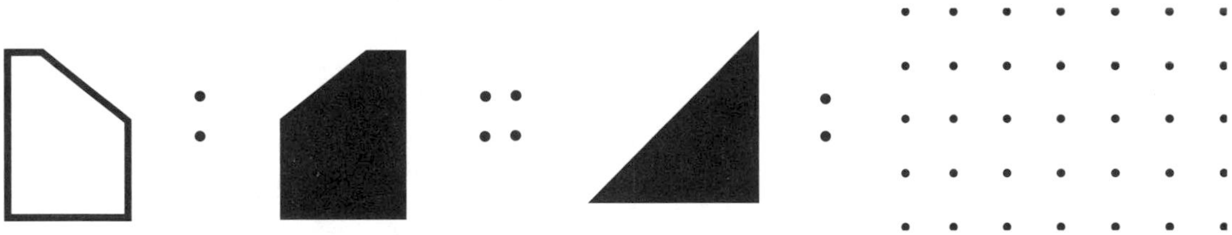

E-51

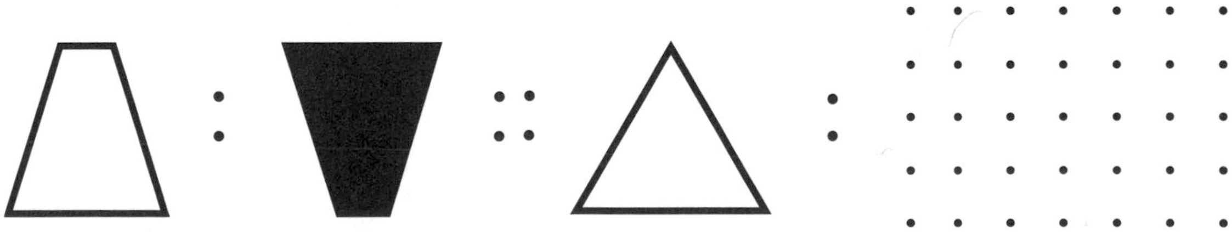

E-52

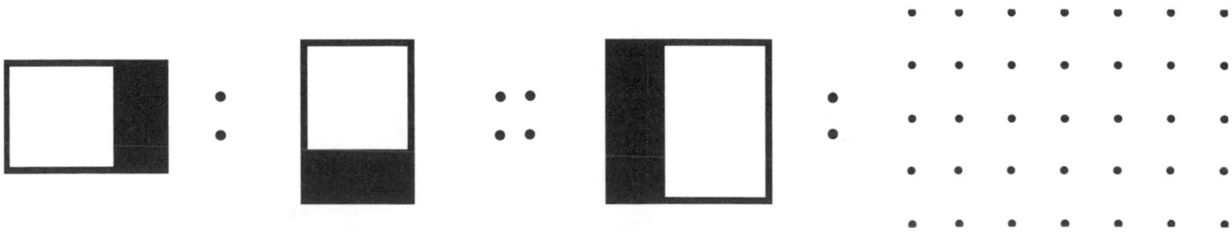

FIGURAL ANALOGIES—SUPPLY

DIRECTIONS: Using the dot grid, draw in a figure to complete each analogy.

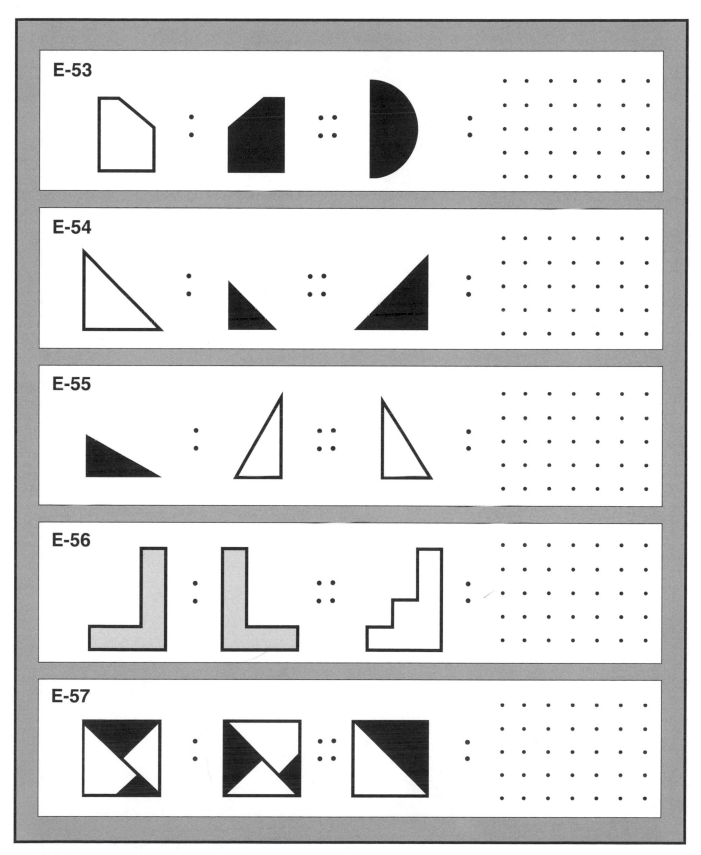

FIGURAL ANALOGIES—SUPPLY

DIRECTIONS: Using the dot grid, draw in a figure to comlete each analogy.

E-58

E-59

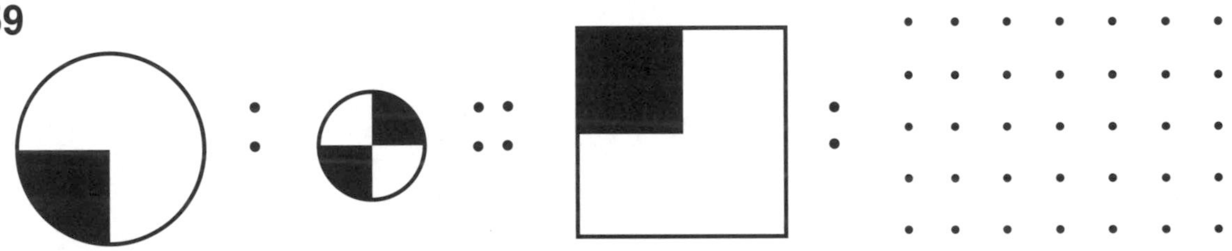

E-60

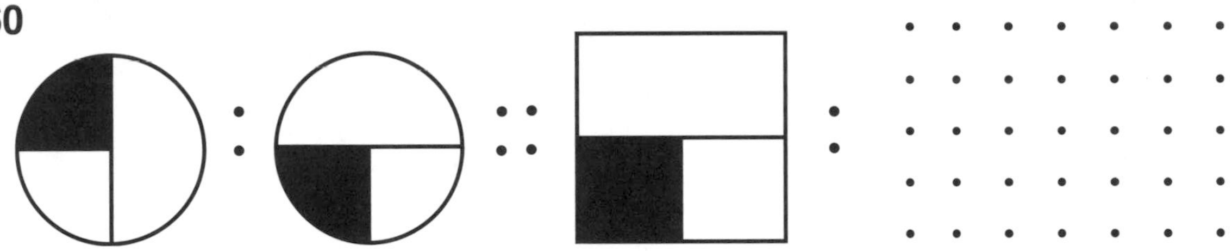

E-61

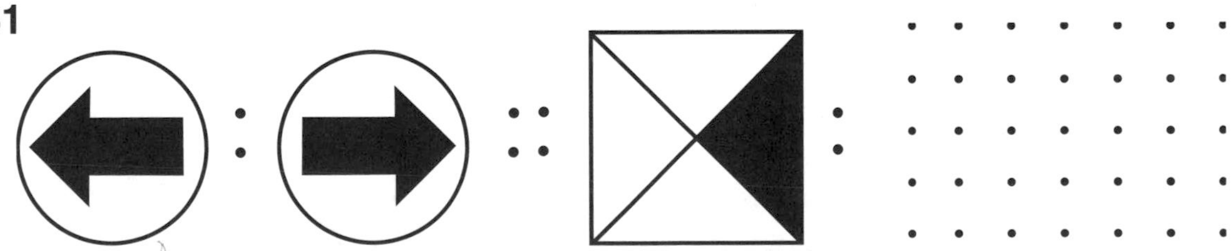

E-62

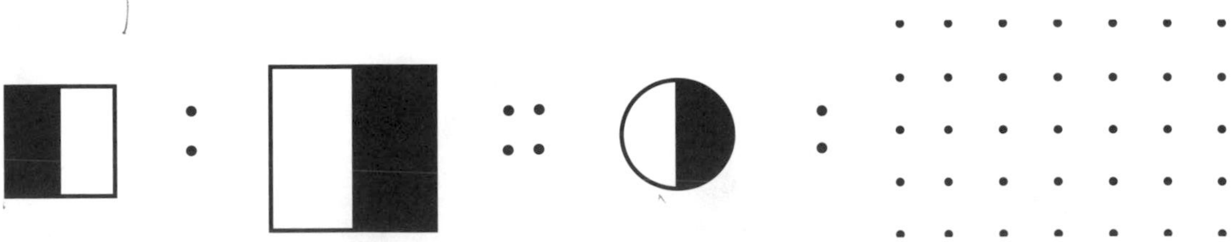

FIGURAL ANALOGIES—SUPPLY A PAIR

DIRECTIONS: Using the dot grid, draw the last two figures, "C" and "D," to complete the analogy. Figures "C" and "D" should be related to each other in the same way that the first two figures, "A" and "B," are related.

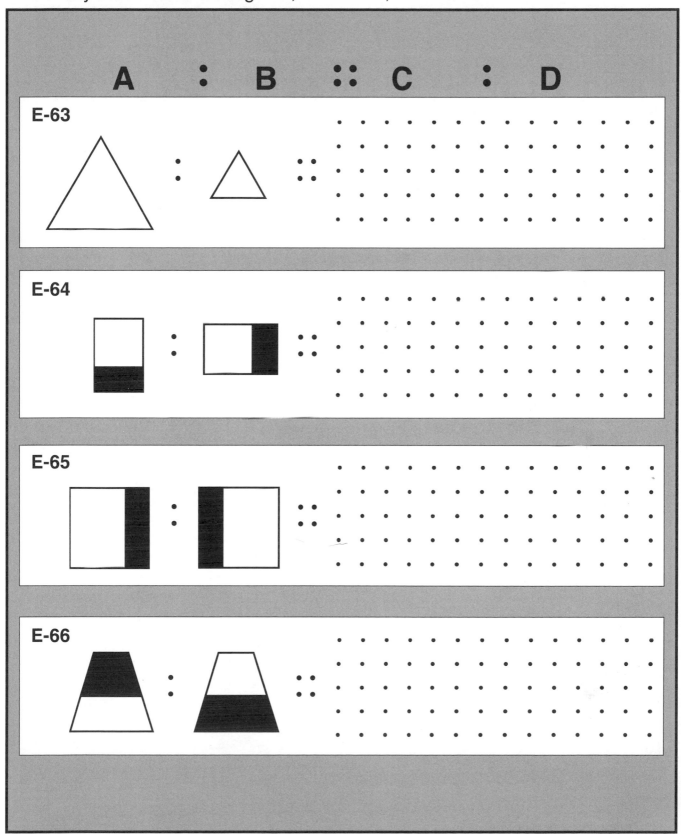

FIGURAL ANALOGIES—SUPPLY A PAIR

DIRECTIONS: Using the dot grid, draw the last two figures, "C" and "D," to complete the analogy. Figures "C" and "D" should be related to each other in the same way that the first two figures, "A" and "B," are related.

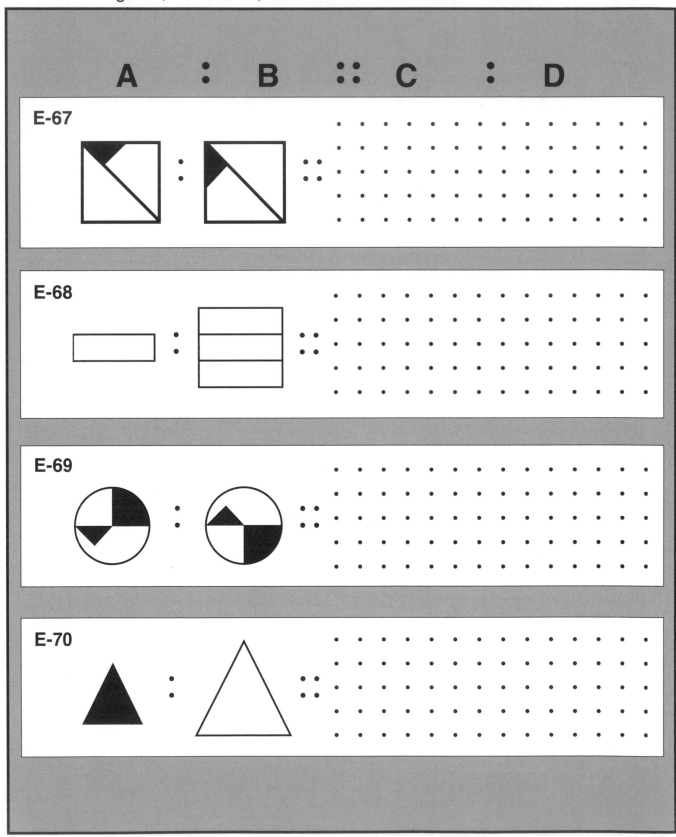

© 2006 The Critical Thinking Co.™ • www.CriticalThinking.com • 800-458-4849

FIGURAL ANALOGIES—FOLLOW THE RULE

DIRECTIONS: Read the rule in each box. Complete each pair in these analogies by drawing shapes which follow that rule.

E-71 Increase detail by doubling the number of parts.

E-72 Illustrate color-opposites.

E-73 Reflect about an up-down (vertical) line.

E-74 Rotate in the direction of the arrow (counterclockwise).

FIGURAL ANALOGIES—FOLLOW THE RULE

DIRECTIONS: Read the rule in each box. Complete each pair in these analogies by drawing shapes which follow that rule.

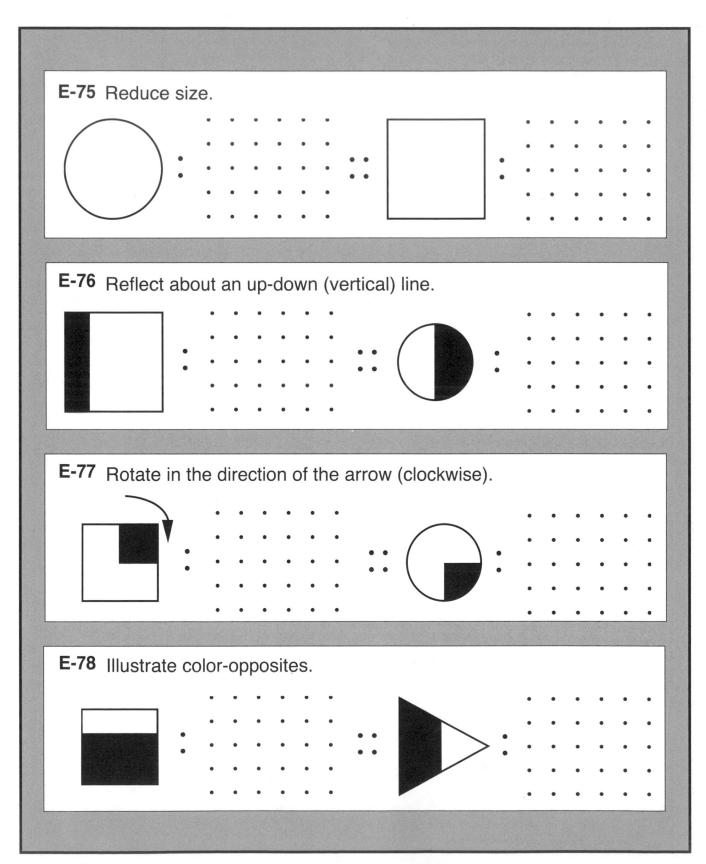

E-75 Reduce size.

E-76 Reflect about an up-down (vertical) line.

E-77 Rotate in the direction of the arrow (clockwise).

E-78 Illustrate color-opposites.

FIGURAL ANALOGIES—FOLLOW THE RULE

DIRECTIONS: Read the rule in each box. Complete each pair in these analogies by drawing shapes which follow that rule.

E-79 Rotate clockwise.

E-80 Reflect about a vertical line.

E-81 Reduce detail or number of parts.

E-82 Increase size.

CHAPTER SIX

Describing Shapes	Describing Things
Figural Similarities and Differences	Verbal Similarities and Differences
Figural Sequences	Verbal Sequences
Figural Classifications	Verbal Classifications
Figural Analogies	Verbal Analogies

DESCRIBING FOODS—SELECT

DIRECTIONS: Each exercise contains the names of three foods, followed by descriptions of two of the words. Choose the word that fits each description and write it in the blank.

EXAMPLE

WORD CHOICES: corn, rice, wheat

A. We eat the seeds of this yellow vegetable. The seeds are protected by husks that grow on a tall stalk.

corn

B. We eat the seeds of this grain, which grows as a tall grass. The seeds are often ground into flour to make bread.

wheat

F-1 WORD CHOICES: cucumber, yellow squash, zucchini

A. This long, round, green salad vegetable is often made into pickles.

_____

B. This squash looks like a cucumber and is eaten boiled or fried.

_____

F-2 WORD CHOICES: lemonade, milk, water

A. This liquid has no nutritional value, but we need to drink 6 to 8 glasses of it each day. It makes up most of our body.

_____

B. This liquid is an important source of calcium to build strong teeth and bones. You can drink it or pour it on your cereal.

_____

DESCRIBING ANIMALS—SELECT

DIRECTIONS: Each exercise contains the names of three animals, followed by descriptions of two of the words. Choose the word that fits each description and write it in the blank.

F-3 WORD CHOICES: deer, elk, moose

A. The largest member of the deer family, this animal has a very large head and a long flap of skin, called a bell, that hangs under its throat. The males have large, broad, spoon-shaped antlers.

_____

B. A medium-sized member of the deer family, this animal's coat is grayish brown with a white patch on its rump. In the United States, it is only found in the Rocky Mountains and in the Central Valley of California.

_____

F-4 WORD CHOICES: butterfly, moth, wasp

A. This insect is dull in color, has large wings, and flies at night.

_____

B. Groups of these stinging insects build large, paperlike, "woven" nests.

_____

F-5 WORD CHOICES: seal, sea lion, walrus

A. This member of the seal family has ears and flippers that are larger than those of true seals. Its long, tapered body is covered with thin, short, coarse hair. This animal can turn its hind flippers forward to move about on land.

_____

B. This large marine mammal lives in the open water at the edge of the Arctic ice pack. It lacks external ears, has long tusks and thick, nearly hairless, skin, except for long bristles on the cheek pads. It has reversible hind flippers for moving over ice.

_____

DESCRIBING VEHICLES—SELECT

DIRECTIONS: Each exercise contains the names of three vehicles followed by descriptions of two of the words. Choose the word that fits each description and write it in the blank.

F-6 WORD CHOICES: bicycle, moped, motorcycle

A. This two-wheeled vehicle can be pedaled or driven by a small engine. Its top speed is about 30 miles per hour.

_____

B. This two-wheeled vehicle is powered by a gasoline engine that can propel it at speeds up to 100 miles per hour. Because it is often driven at high speeds, it is a very dangerous vehicle, and accidents on it often result in injuries or death.

_____

F-7 WORD CHOICES: backhoe, bulldozer, crane

A. This very large vehicle moves short distances on rolling tracks. A motor-driven cable runs over the end of a long, necklike boom. A hook at the end of the cable is used to lift heavy objects.

_____

B. This large vehicle has a large, movable scoop shovel on the back that is used to dig ditches and trenches.

_____

F-8 WORD CHOICES: all-terrain vehicle, motocross bicycle, snowmobile

A. This vehicle has large, fat tires that allow it to move over almost any land or marshy area.

_____

B. This two-wheeled vehicle is small and tough. It is built to fly over dirt jumps and race around tracks. It has special tires and a rugged frame.

_____

DESCRIBING GEOGRAPHIC TERMS—SELECT

DIRECTIONS: Each exercise contains the names of three landforms or bodies of water, followed by descriptions of two of the words. Choose the word that fits each description and write it in the blank.

F-9 WORD CHOICES: canal, channel, stream

A. A natural, narrow waterway connecting two bodies of water.

_____

B. A manmade, narrow waterway connecting two bodies of water.

_____

F-10 WORD CHOICES: basin, canyon, mesa

A. A flat-topped hill with steep sides, common in deserts.

_____

B. A broad flat area surrounded by hills or mountains.

_____

F-11 WORD CHOICES: island, isthmus, peninsula

A. A narrow strip of land connecting two larger land areas.

_____

B. Land surrounded by water on three sides.

_____

DESCRIBING OCCUPATIONS—SELECT

DIRECTIONS: Each exercise contains the names of three occupations, followed by descriptions of two of the jobs. Choose the word that fits each description and write it in the blank.

F-12 WORD CHOICES: dental hygienist, dental assistant, dentist

A. This person gives dental examinations and cleans patients' teeth but does not fill or cap teeth.

_____

B. This person prepares a patient to see the dentist. He or she hands instruments and materials to the dentist during dental procedures, takes X-rays, takes impressions of the teeth, and performs other dental tasks.

_____

F-13 WORD CHOICES: inhalation therapist, nurse, physical therapist

A. This person helps hospitalized patients regain their ability to breathe.

_____

B. This person helps injured people learn to walk and/or use their arms and hands again.

_____

F-14 WORD CHOICES: computer engineer, data clerk, programmer

A. This person is responsible for entering the correct information into a computer.

_____

B. This person is responsible for designing and building computers.

_____

DESCRIBING COMPUTER DEVICES—SELECT

DIRECTIONS: Each exercise contains three computer terms, followed by descriptions of two of the terms. Choose the word that fits each description and write it in the blank.

F-15 WORD CHOICES: computer processing unit, computer memory, compact disk

A. This computer component allows processed data to be stored within the computer.

_____

B. This computer component allows the operator to perform complex tasks such as calculations, word processing, drawing, and bookkeeping.

_____

F-16 WORD CHOICES: e-mail, Internet, modem

A. This device connects a computer to the World Wide Web.

_____

B. This system of interconnections between computers allows a computer operator to send and receive information (drawings, messages, or files) from other computer users.

_____

F-17 WORD CHOICES: CD ROM, Random Access Memory (RAM), Read Only Memory (ROM)

A. This integrated circuit allows a computer to access (find) and use the instructions (programs) stored or fed into a computer.

_____

B. This computer component allows a computer to read and store (remember) the calculations, written documents, and drawings produced by the computer operator.

_____

IDENTIFYING CHARACTERISTICS OF FOOD

DIRECTIONS: Read each passage about a food. Identify the characteristics of the food and write them in the blanks.

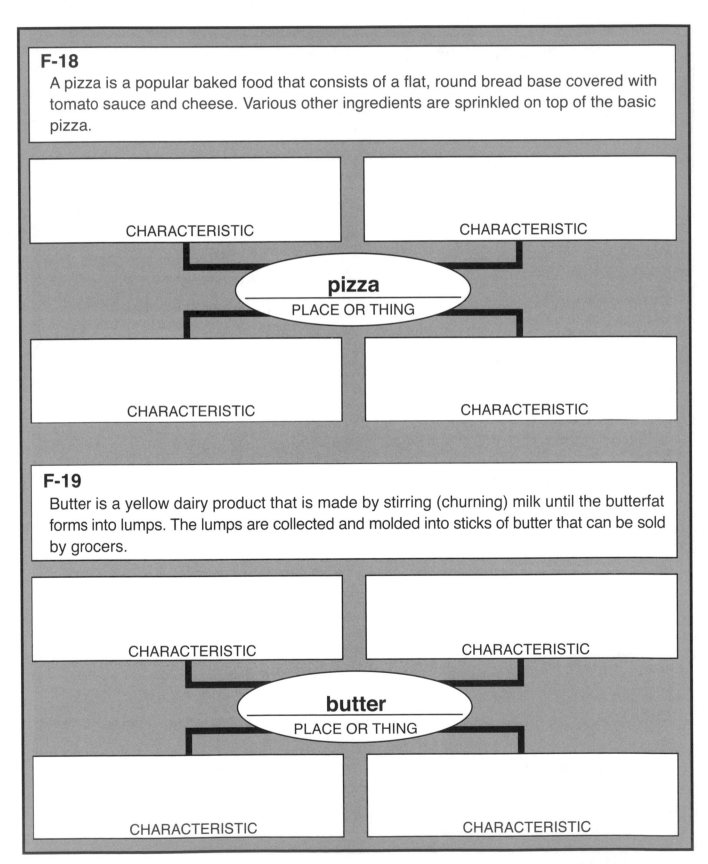

F-18
A pizza is a popular baked food that consists of a flat, round bread base covered with tomato sauce and cheese. Various other ingredients are sprinkled on top of the basic pizza.

CHARACTERISTIC

CHARACTERISTIC

pizza
PLACE OR THING

CHARACTERISTIC

CHARACTERISTIC

F-19
Butter is a yellow dairy product that is made by stirring (churning) milk until the butterfat forms into lumps. The lumps are collected and molded into sticks of butter that can be sold by grocers.

CHARACTERISTIC

CHARACTERISTIC

butter
PLACE OR THING

CHARACTERISTIC

CHARACTERISTIC

IDENTIFYING CHARACTERISTICS OF ANIMALS

DIRECTIONS: Read each passage about an animal. Identify the characteristics of the animal and write them in the blanks.

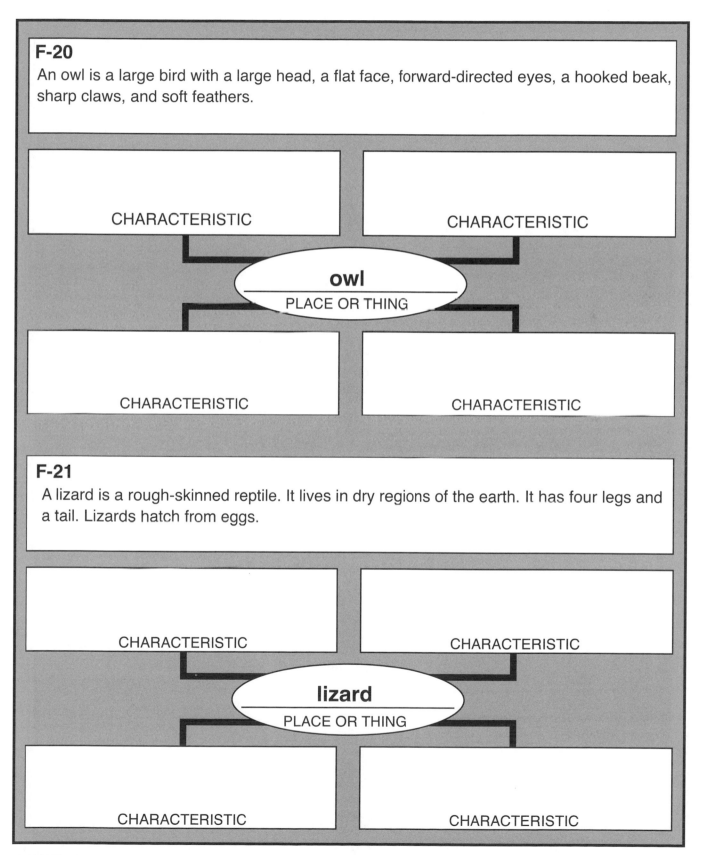

F-20

An owl is a large bird with a large head, a flat face, forward-directed eyes, a hooked beak, sharp claws, and soft feathers.

CHARACTERISTIC

CHARACTERISTIC

owl
PLACE OR THING

CHARACTERISTIC

CHARACTERISTIC

F-21

A lizard is a rough-skinned reptile. It lives in dry regions of the earth. It has four legs and a tail. Lizards hatch from eggs.

CHARACTERISTIC

CHARACTERISTIC

lizard
PLACE OR THING

CHARACTERISTIC

CHARACTERISTIC

IDENTIFYING CHARACTERISTICS OF VEHICLES

DIRECTIONS: Read each passage about a vehicle. Identify the characteristics of the vehicle and write them in the blanks.

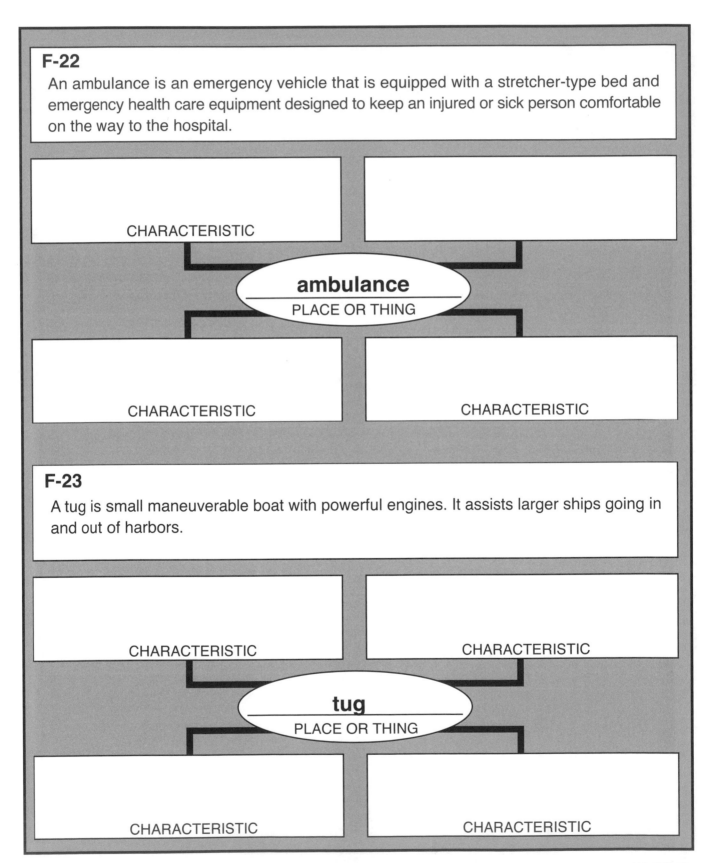

F-22

An ambulance is an emergency vehicle that is equipped with a stretcher-type bed and emergency health care equipment designed to keep an injured or sick person comfortable on the way to the hospital.

CHARACTERISTIC

CHARACTERISTIC

ambulance
PLACE OR THING

CHARACTERISTIC

CHARACTERISTIC

F-23

A tug is small maneuverable boat with powerful engines. It assists larger ships going in and out of harbors.

CHARACTERISTIC

CHARACTERISTIC

tug
PLACE OR THING

CHARACTERISTIC

CHARACTERISTIC

IDENTIFYING CHARACTERISTICS OF EARTH FEATURES

DIRECTIONS: Read each passage about an earth landform. Identify the characteristics of the land form and write them in the blanks.

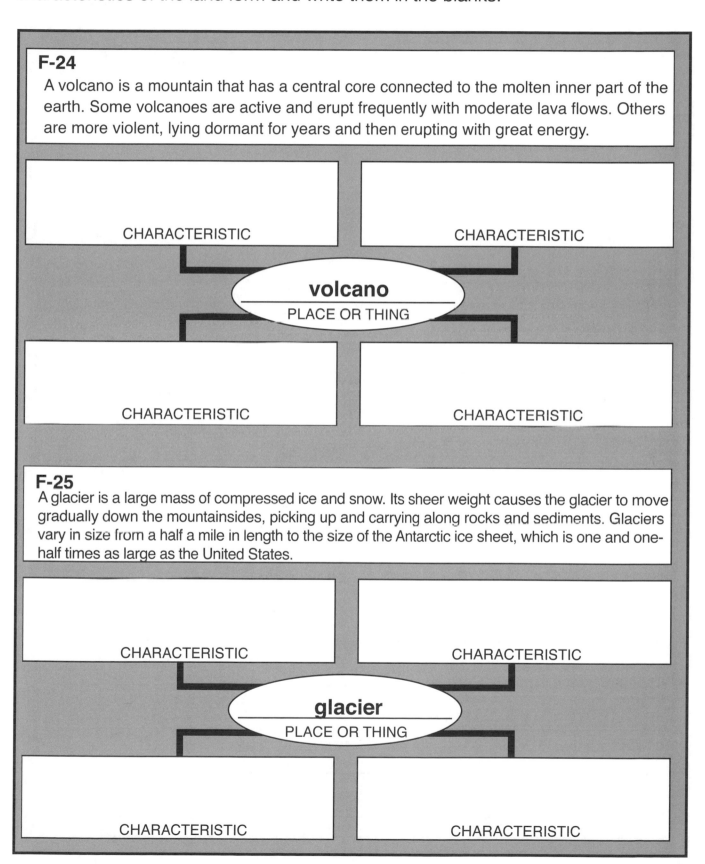

F-24

A volcano is a mountain that has a central core connected to the molten inner part of the earth. Some volcanoes are active and erupt frequently with moderate lava flows. Others are more violent, lying dormant for years and then erupting with great energy.

CHARACTERISTIC

CHARACTERISTIC

volcano
PLACE OR THING

CHARACTERISTIC

CHARACTERISTIC

F-25

A glacier is a large mass of compressed ice and snow. Its sheer weight causes the glacier to move gradually down the mountainsides, picking up and carrying along rocks and sediments. Glaciers vary in size from a half a mile in length to the size of the Antarctic ice sheet, which is one and one-half times as large as the United States.

CHARACTERISTIC

CHARACTERISTIC

glacier
PLACE OR THING

CHARACTERISTIC

CHARACTERISTIC

DESCRIBING FOODS—EXPLAIN

DIRECTIONS: In each box, describe the food that is named. Give specific characteristics.

F-26 rice

_____

_____

_____

_____

F-27 lettuce

_____

_____

_____

_____

F-28 strawberry

_____

_____

_____

_____

DESCRIBING ANIMALS—EXPLAIN

DIRECTIONS: In each box, describe the animal that is named. Give specific characteristics.

F-29 turtle

_____

_____

_____

_____

F-30 clam

_____

_____

_____

_____

F-31 hamster

_____

_____

_____

_____

DESCRIBING VEHICLES—EXPLAIN

DIRECTIONS: In each box, describe the vehicle that is named. Give specific characteristics.

F-32 pickup truck

_____

_____

_____

_____

F-33 ferry boat

_____

_____

_____

_____

F-34 helicopter

_____

_____

_____

_____

DESCRIBING PLACES ON EARTH—EXPLAIN

DIRECTIONS: In each box, describe the place or geographic feature that is named. Give specific characteristics.

F-35 tributary

_____

_____

_____

_____

F-36 plateau

_____

_____

_____

_____

F-37 equator

_____

_____

_____

DESCRIBING OCCUPATIONS—EXPLAIN

DIRECTIONS: In each box, describe the occupation that is named. Give specific characteristics.

F-38 pilot

_____

_____

_____

_____

_____

F-39 physician

_____

_____

_____

_____

_____

F-40 architect

_____

_____

_____

_____

_____

NAME THE ANIMAL—SUPPLY

DIRECTIONS: Each exercise contains a description of an animal. Read each description, then decide what is being described. Write the answer on the line.

F-41 This animal is the offspring of a male donkey and a female horse. It is much like the horse in size and body shape but has the shorter, thicker head, long ears, and braying voice of the donkey. The male of this breed is not fertile.

_____

F-42 This land-dwelling, tailless, rough-skinned amphibian is often confused with a frog. It wards off enemies by secreting poison from its skin. Since it has warts on its skin, some people mistakenly believe that, if you handle one, you will get warts.

_____

F-43 This great ape is the largest of the living primates. A male can weigh about 600 pounds. It lives in family groups. It is found only in Africa and is being threatened with extinction.

_____

F-44 This long, smooth-skinned reptile has no arms or legs. It has a special jaw that opens very wide, allowing it to swallow large food items whole. Some varieties feed on mice and rats, making this reptile an asset in reducing the rodent population.

_____

F-45 This large, rough-skined, amphibious reptile has short arms and legs and a long tail. It is distinguished from an alligator by the notch at the side of its snout, which exposes the teeth of its lower jaw.

_____

F-46 This largest living bird can grow up to 8 feet tall but cannot fly. It runs with 12-foot strides at speeds up to 40 miles per hour. It lives in dry countries and feeds on plants, fruits, grasses, and leaves, as well as insects, lizards, birds, and mice.

_____

NAME THE PLANT—SUPPLY

DIRECTIONS: Each exercise contains a description of a plant. Read each description, then decide what is being described. Write the answer on the line.

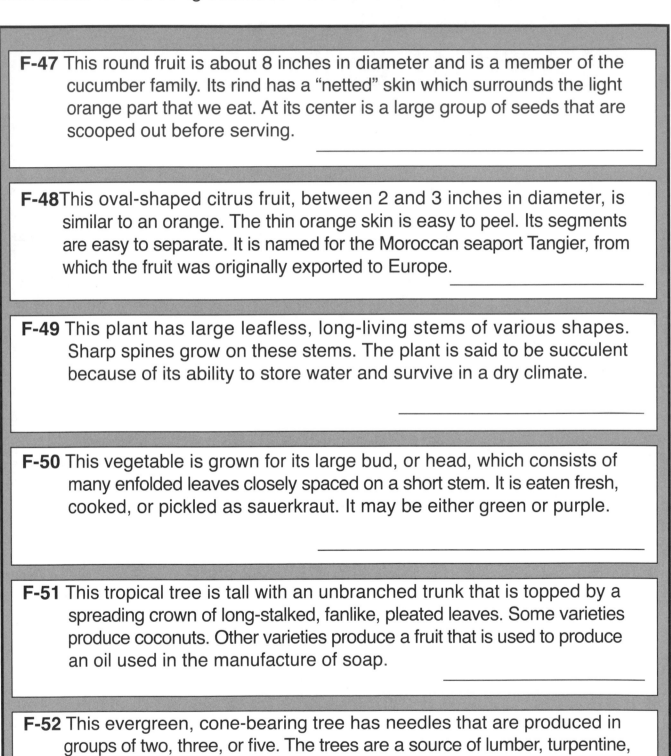

F-47 This round fruit is about 8 inches in diameter and is a member of the cucumber family. Its rind has a "netted" skin which surrounds the light orange part that we eat. At its center is a large group of seeds that are scooped out before serving. _____

F-48 This oval-shaped citrus fruit, between 2 and 3 inches in diameter, is similar to an orange. The thin orange skin is easy to peel. Its segments are easy to separate. It is named for the Moroccan seaport Tangier, from which the fruit was originally exported to Europe. _____

F-49 This plant has large leafless, long-living stems of various shapes. Sharp spines grow on these stems. The plant is said to be succulent because of its ability to store water and survive in a dry climate. _____

F-50 This vegetable is grown for its large bud, or head, which consists of many enfolded leaves closely spaced on a short stem. It is eaten fresh, cooked, or pickled as sauerkraut. It may be either green or purple. _____

F-51 This tropical tree is tall with an unbranched trunk that is topped by a spreading crown of long-stalked, fanlike, pleated leaves. Some varieties produce coconuts. Other varieties produce a fruit that is used to produce an oil used in the manufacture of soap. _____

F-52 This evergreen, cone-bearing tree has needles that are produced in groups of two, three, or five. The trees are a source of lumber, turpentine, resin, pitch, and tar. Many of these trees are grown as ornamentals for use at Christmas. _____

NAME THE VEHICLE/PLACE—SUPPLY

DIRECTIONS: Each exercise contains a description of a vehicle or a place. Read each description, then decide what is being described. Write the answer on the line.

F-53 This vehicle is a railroad car supported by one rail. There are two types, saddlebag and suspended. The saddlebag type straddles a large rail or beamway, and is powered by vertical wheels on top of the beamway. The suspended type hangs from overhead rails.

_____

F-54 This aircraft is lifted by rotating blades set on top of the vehicle. It is capable of lifting vertically and hovering in one place. This vehicle has been used for military maneuvers, agricultural purposes, and fire and rescue operations.

_____

F-55 This many-wheeled, motor vehicle is used to transport people along a fixed route within a city. It makes many stops along its route to pick up and discharge passengers. People pay a fare to ride this vehicle.

_____

F-56 This landform is very wet and usually near a larger body of water such as an ocean or a lake. This area supports grassy vegetation and is the breeding ground for many forms of aquatic life.

_____

F-57 A land mass that is completely surrounded by water is called a/an _____. A body of water completely surrounded by land is called a/an

_____.

F-58 This landform occurs at the mouth of a river. When a river enters an ocean or lake, the sediments that have been carried along are dropped. These sediments pile up to form a triangular-shaped area named for the Greek letter that has a triangular shape.

_____

WRITING DESCRIPTIONS

DIRECTIONS: Follow the directions given in the example.

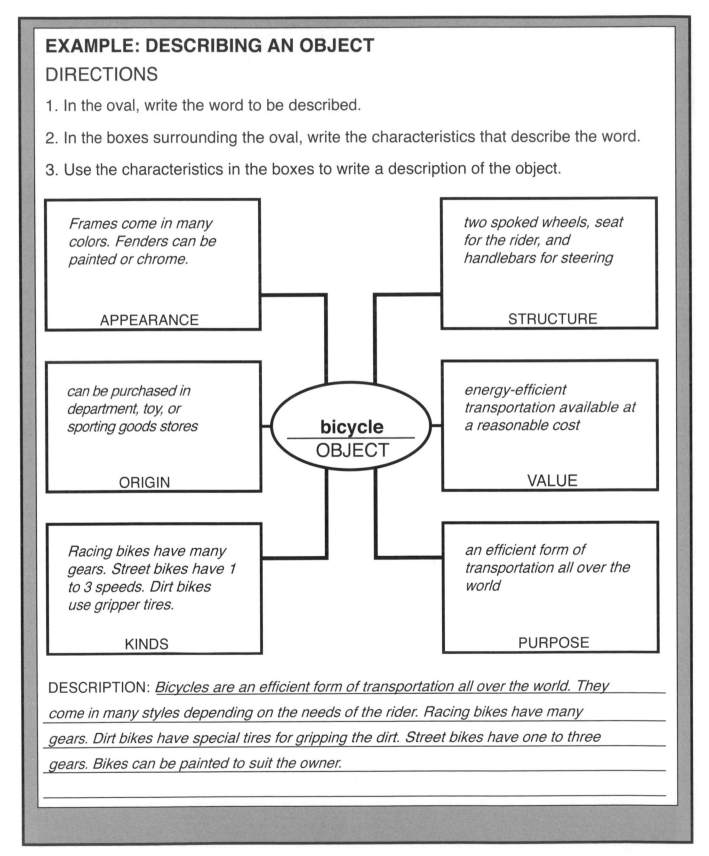

EXAMPLE: DESCRIBING AN OBJECT

DIRECTIONS

1. In the oval, write the word to be described.

2. In the boxes surrounding the oval, write the characteristics that describe the word.

3. Use the characteristics in the boxes to write a description of the object.

Frames come in many colors. Fenders can be painted or chrome.

APPEARANCE

two spoked wheels, seat for the rider, and handlebars for steering

STRUCTURE

can be purchased in department, toy, or sporting goods stores

ORIGIN

bicycle
OBJECT

energy-efficient transportation available at a reasonable cost

VALUE

Racing bikes have many gears. Street bikes have 1 to 3 speeds. Dirt bikes use gripper tires.

KINDS

an efficient form of transportation all over the world

PURPOSE

DESCRIPTION: *Bicycles are an efficient form of transportation all over the world. They come in many styles depending on the needs of the rider. Racing bikes have many gears. Dirt bikes have special tires for gripping the dirt. Street bikes have one to three gears. Bikes can be painted to suit the owner.*

WRITING DESCRIPTIONS

DIRECTIONS: Follow the directions given. Use the diagram at the bottom of the page to help you write a description of beans.

F-59

DIRECTIONS

1. Look at the word to be described.

2. In the boxes surrounding the oval, write the characteristics that describe the word.

3. Use the characteristics in the boxes to write a description of the object.

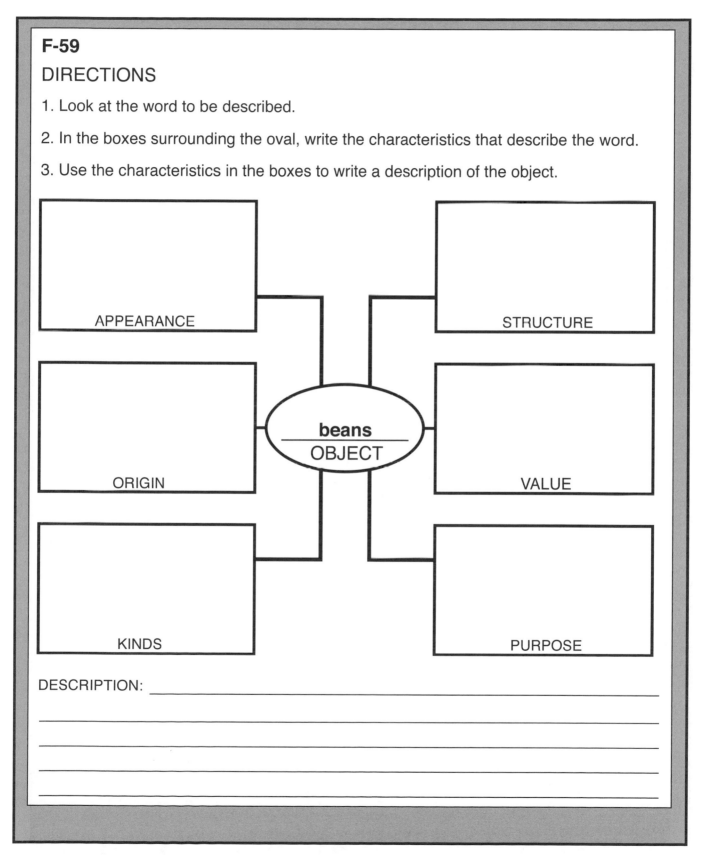

APPEARANCE

STRUCTURE

ORIGIN

beans
OBJECT

VALUE

KINDS

PURPOSE

DESCRIPTION: _____

_____

_____

_____

_____

WRITING DESCRIPTIONS

DIRECTIONS: Follow the directions given. Use the diagram below to help you write a descriptions of a computer.

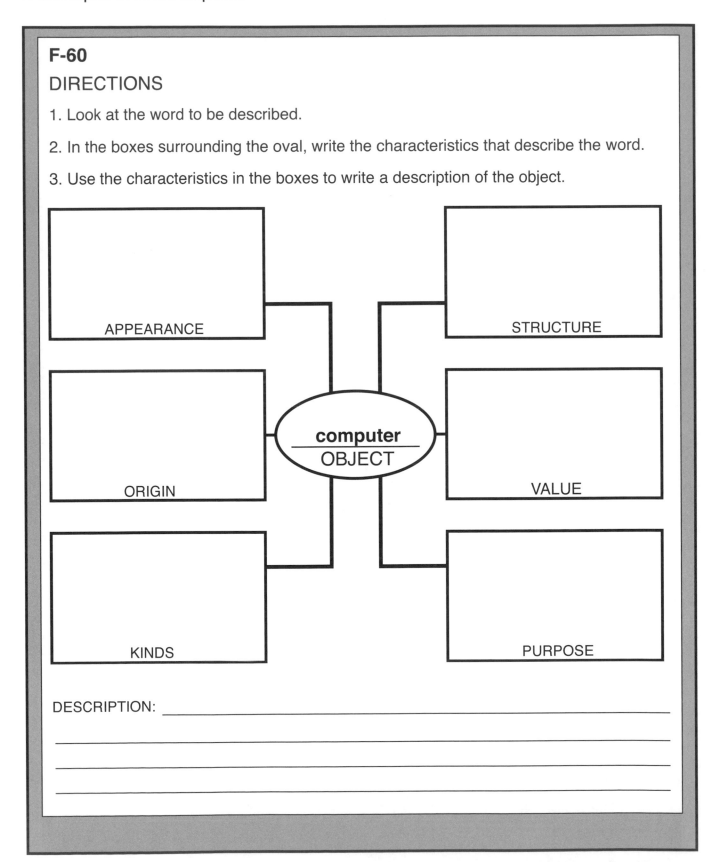

F-60

DIRECTIONS

1. Look at the word to be described.

2. In the boxes surrounding the oval, write the characteristics that describe the word.

3. Use the characteristics in the boxes to write a description of the object.

APPEARANCE

STRUCTURE

ORIGIN

computer
OBJECT

VALUE

KINDS

PURPOSE

DESCRIPTION: _____

_____

_____

_____

WRITING DESCRIPTIONS

DIRECTIONS: Follow the directions given. Use the diagram below to help you write description of a school.

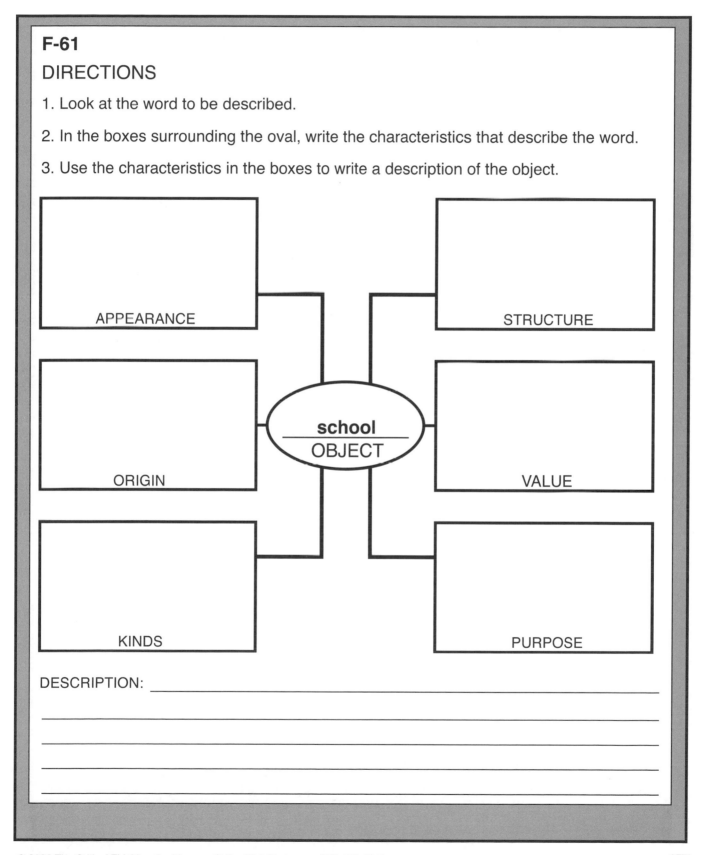

F-61

DIRECTIONS

1. Look at the word to be described.

2. In the boxes surrounding the oval, write the characteristics that describe the word.

3. Use the characteristics in the boxes to write a description of the object.

APPEARANCE

STRUCTURE

ORIGIN

school
OBJECT

VALUE

KINDS

PURPOSE

DESCRIPTION: _____

_____

_____

_____

_____

WRITING DESCRIPTIONS

DIRECTIONS: Follow the directions given in the example.

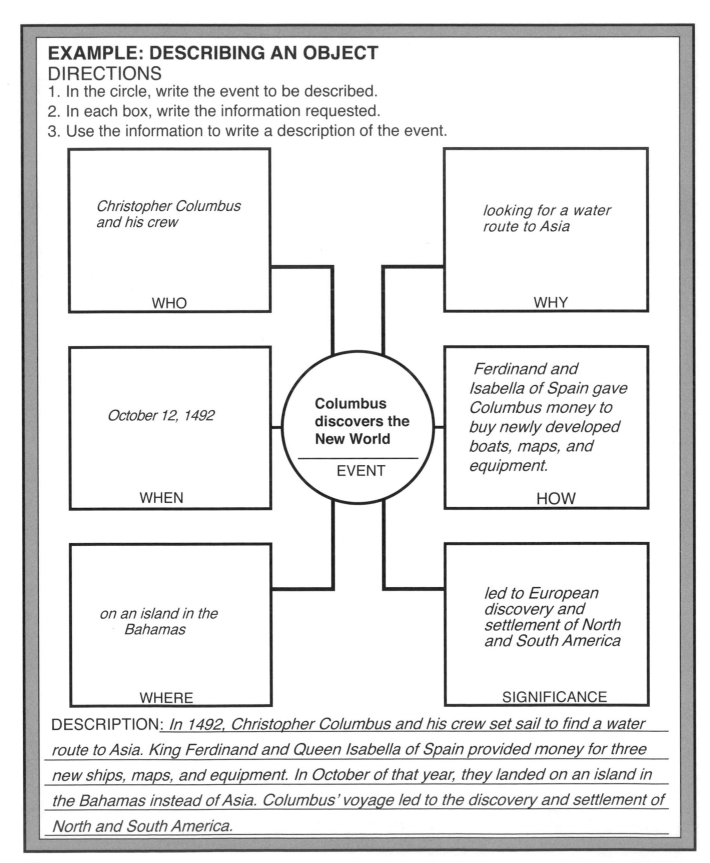

EXAMPLE: DESCRIBING AN OBJECT
DIRECTIONS
1. In the circle, write the event to be described.
2. In each box, write the information requested.
3. Use the information to write a description of the event.

Christopher Columbus and his crew

WHO

looking for a water route to Asia

WHY

October 12, 1492

WHEN

Columbus discovers the New World

EVENT

Ferdinand and Isabella of Spain gave Columbus money to buy newly developed boats, maps, and equipment.

HOW

on an island in the Bahamas

WHERE

led to European discovery and settlement of North and South America

SIGNIFICANCE

DESCRIPTION: *In 1492, Christopher Columbus and his crew set sail to find a water route to Asia. King Ferdinand and Queen Isabella of Spain provided money for three new ships, maps, and equipment. In October of that year, they landed on an island in the Bahamas instead of Asia. Columbus' voyage led to the discovery and settlement of North and South America.*

WRITING DESCRIPTIONS

DIRECTIONS: Use the diagram at the bottom of the page to help you write a description of the voyage of the *Mayflower*.

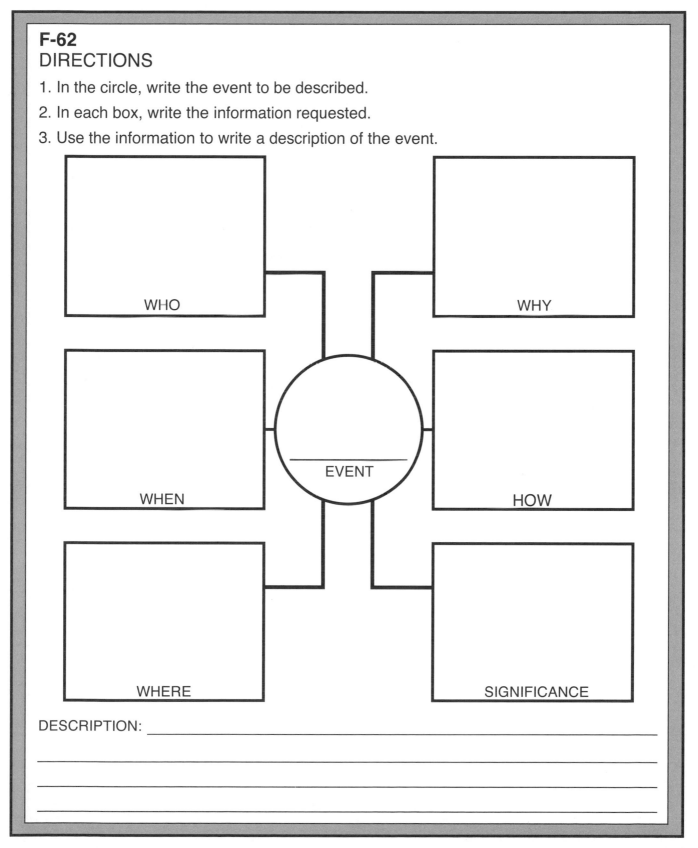

F-62
DIRECTIONS

1. In the circle, write the event to be described.

2. In each box, write the information requested.

3. Use the information to write a description of the event.

WHO

WHY

WHEN

EVENT

HOW

WHERE

SIGNIFICANCE

DESCRIPTION: _____

_____

_____

_____

WRITING DESCRIPTIONS

DIRECTIONS: Use the diagram below to help you write a description of the signing of the Declaration of Independence.

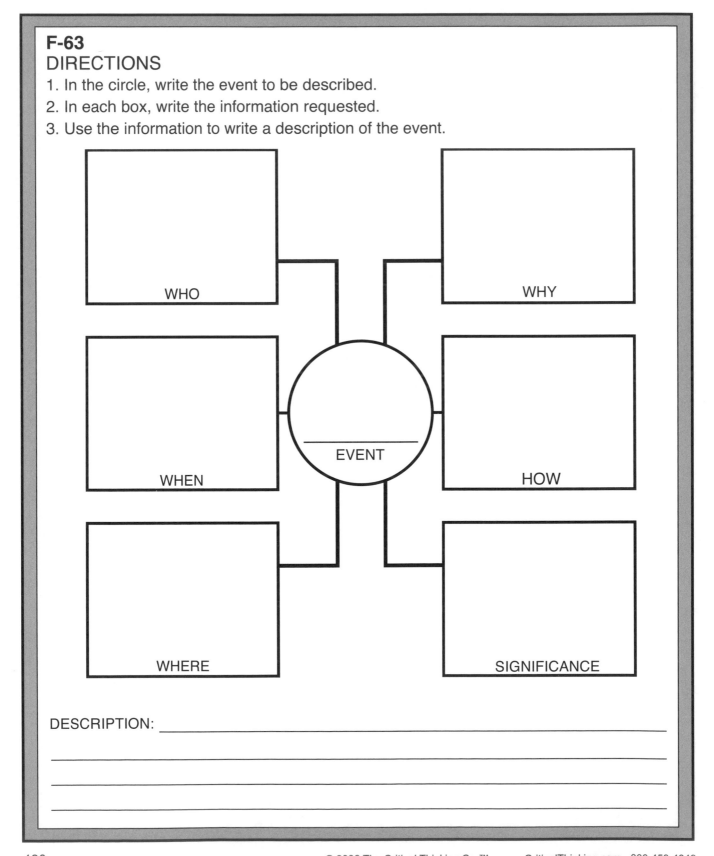

F-63
DIRECTIONS
1. In the circle, write the event to be described.
2. In each box, write the information requested.
3. Use the information to write a description of the event.

WHO

WHY

WHEN

EVENT

HOW

WHERE

SIGNIFICANCE

DESCRIPTION: _____

_____

_____

_____

WRITING DESCRIPTIONS

DIRECTIONS: Use the diagram below to help you write a description of the Civil War in the United States.

F-64
DIRECTIONS

1. In the circle, write the event to be described.

2. In each box, write the information requested.

3. Use the information to write a description of the event.

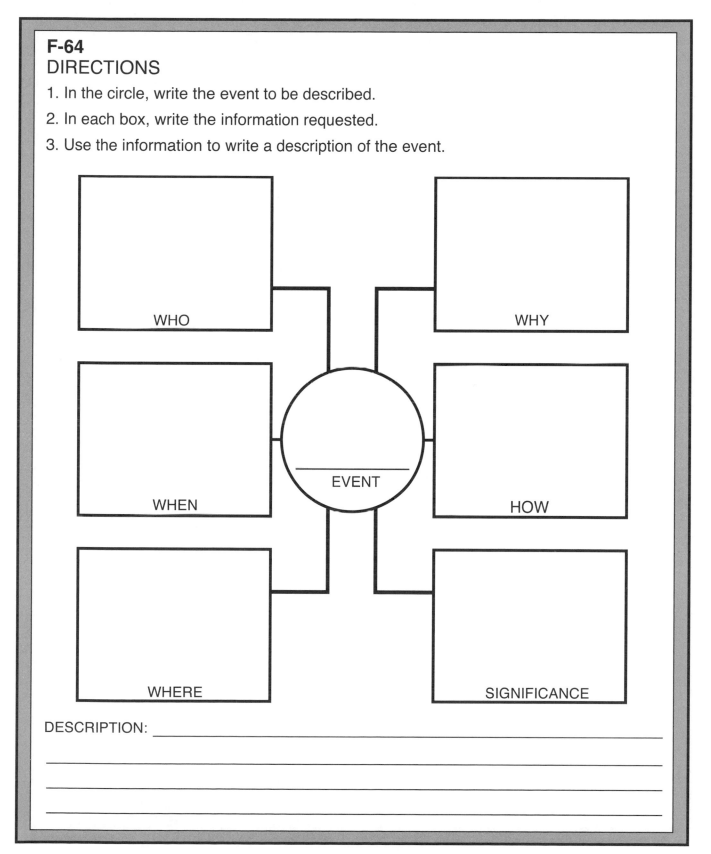

WHO

WHY

WHEN

EVENT

HOW

WHERE

SIGNIFICANCE

DESCRIPTION: _____

_____

_____

_____

WRITING DESCRIPTIONS

DIRECTIONS: Select an interesting and important object in your home, school, or neighborhood. Use the three diagrams to record details and information about the object that would help you describe it to someone who had never seen it. Then use all three diagrams to write your description in the box at the bottom of the next page.

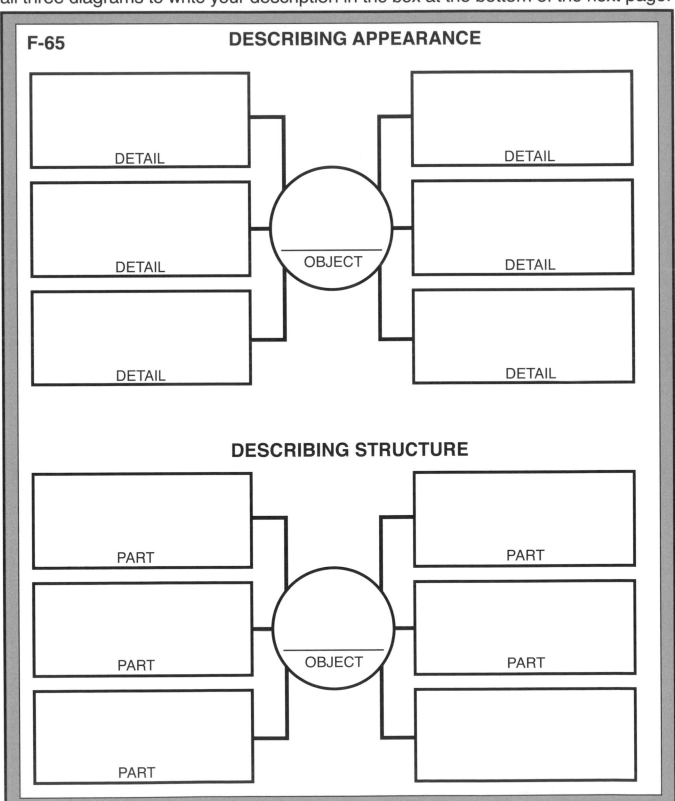

F-65

DESCRIBING APPEARANCE

DETAIL

DETAIL

DETAIL

OBJECT

DETAIL

DETAIL

DETAIL

DESCRIBING STRUCTURE

PART

PART

PART

OBJECT

PART

PART

PART

WRITING DESCRIPTIONS

DIRECTIONS: This is the second page of this lesson. Use this diagram and the two diagrams on the previous page to write your description in the box at the bottom of the page.

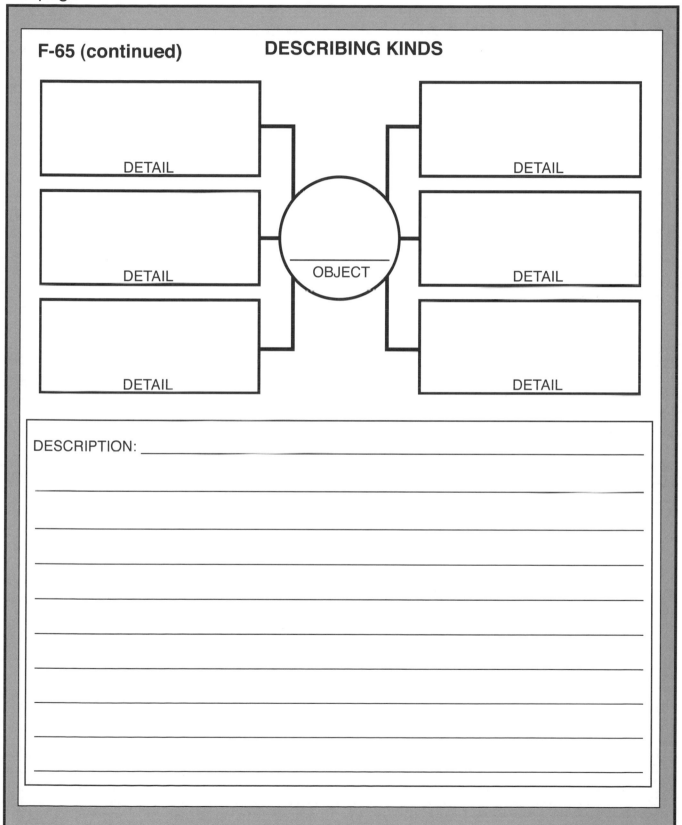

F-65 (continued)　　　DESCRIBING KINDS

DETAIL

DETAIL

DETAIL

OBJECT

DETAIL

DETAIL

DETAIL

DESCRIPTION: _____

_____

_____

_____

_____

_____

_____

_____

_____

CHAPTER SEVEN

Describing Shapes	**Describing Things**
Figural Similarities and Differences	**Verbal Similarities and Differences**
Figural Sequences	**Verbal Sequences**
Figural Classifications	**Verbal Classifications**
Figural Analogies	**Verbal Analogies**

OPPOSITES—SELECT

DIRECTIONS: Each line contains four verbs. Read the first verb and think about what it means. One of the next three verbs will mean the opposite of the first verb. Circle the one that is the opposite of the first verb.

G-1	**play**	**a.** amuse	**b.** entertain	**c.** work
G-2	**allow**	**a.** deny	**b.** let	**c.** permit
G-3	**mend**	**a.** break	**b.** correct	**c.** patch
G-4	**save**	**a.** collect	**b.** store	**c.** spend
G-5	**harm**	**a.** damage	**b.** hurt	**c.** benefit
G-6	**doubt**	**a.** believe	**b.** challenge	**c.** question
G-7	**reduce**	**a.** cut	**b.** diminish	**c.** increase
G-8	**conclude**	**a.** close	**b.** finish	**c.** open
G-9	**approach**	**a.** arrive	**b.** leave	**c.** reach
G-10	**escape**	**a.** depart	**b.** flee	**c.** return
G-11	**reject**	**a.** accept	**b.** dismiss	**c.** overlook
G-12	**overlook**	**a.** miss	**b.** ignore	**c.** choose

OPPOSITES—SELECT

DIRECTIONS: Each line contains four adjectives. Read the first adjective and think about what it means. One of the next three adjectives will mean the opposite of the first objective. Circle the one that is the opposite of the first adjective.

G-13	neat	**a.** clean	**b.** messy	**c.** orderly
G-14	tight	**a.** close	**b.** firm	**c.** loose
G-15	rude	**a.** discourteous	**b.** polite	**c.** vulgar
G-16	timid	**a.** bashful	**b.** bold	**c.** shy
G-17	familiar	**a.** common	**b.** known	**c.** strange
G-18	plain	**a.** fancy	**b.** ordinary	**c.** simple
G-19	public	**a.** free	**b.** open	**c.** private
G-20	sharp	**a.** alert	**b.** bright	**c.** slow
G-21	honest	**a.** unethical	**b.** lawful	**c.** truthful
G-22	diverse	**a.** different	**b.** identical	**c.** varied
G-23	lively	**a.** alert	**b.** bright	**c.** sluggish
G-24	worthless	**a.** useless	**b.** trivial	**c.** valuable

OPPOSITES—SELECT

DIRECTIONS: Each line contains four adverbs. Read the first adverb and think about what it means. One of the next three adverbs will mean the opposite of the first adverb. Circle the one that is the opposite of the first adverb.

G-25	**accidentally**	a. randomly	b. incidentally	c. purposefully
G-26	**afterward**	a. before	b. later	c. next
G-27	**barely**	a. amply	b. hardly	c. scarcely
G-28	**maybe**	a. perhaps	b. possibly	c. surely
G-29	**deeply**	a. intensely	b. hardly	c. greatly
G-30	**concisely**	a. accurately	b. briefly	c. wordily
G-31	**gradually**	a. slowly	b. eventually	c. suddenly
G-32	**capably**	a. incompetently	b. exceptionally	c. superbly
G-33	**eternally**	a. always	b. forever	c. seldom
G-34	**onward**	a. ahead	b. backward	c. forward
G-35	**mightily**	a. forcefully	b. strongly	c. weakly
G-36	**rarely**	a. infrequently	b. often	c. seldom

OPPOSITES—SUPPLY

DIRECTIONS: Each line contains a verb. Read the verb and think about what it means. Think of another verb (or verbs) that means the opposite of the given verb. Write the verb(s) in the box.

G-37	add

G-38	reject

G-39	excite

G-40	decrease

G-41	multiply

G-42	approve

G-43	capture

G-44	melt

G-45	deny

G-46	emphasize

G-47	depart

G-48	separate

OPPOSITES—SUPPLY

DIRECTIONS: Each line contains a noun. Read the noun and think about what it means. Think of another noun (or nouns) that means the opposite of the given noun. Write the noun(s) in the box.

G-49	dawn

G-50	sorrow

G-51	debt

G-52	question

G-53	youth

G-54	plenty

G-55	success

G-56	native

G-57	interior

G-58	basement

G-59	introduction

G-60	shortage

OPPOSITES—SUPPLY

DIRECTIONS: Each line contains an adjective. Read the adjective and think about what it means. Think of another adjective (or adjectives) that means the opposite of the given adjective. Write the adjective(s) in the box.

G-61	still
G-62	ancient
G-63	positive
G-64	ordinary
G-65	glad
G-66	excellent
G-67	partial
G-68	past
G-69	difficult
G-70	popular
G-71	impatient
G-72	valuable

SIMILARITIES—SELECT

DIRECTIONS: Each line contains four verbs. Read the first verb and think about what it means. One of the next three verbs means almost the same thing. Circle the one that is most like the first verb in meaning.

G-73	break	**a.** crack	**b.** mend	**c.** repair
G-74	lead	**a.** attempt	**b.** direct	**c.** follow
G-75	seem	**a.** appear	**b.** have	**c.** need
G-76	begin	**a.** make	**b.** start	**c.** try
G-77	jog	**a.** hike	**b.** pace	**c.** run
G-78	manage	**a.** control	**b.** start	**c.** stop
G-79	continue	**a.** expect	**b.** prevent	**c.** proceed
G-80	desire	**a.** have	**b.** try	**c.** want
G-81	clear	**a.** plant	**b.** remove	**c.** set
G-82	care	**a.** ignore	**b.** neglect	**c.** tend
G-83	produce	**a.** break	**b.** manufacture	**c.** reduce
G-84	survive	**a.** die	**b.** perish	**c.** recover

SIMILARITIES—SELECT

DIRECTIONS: Each line contains four adjectives. Read the first adjective and think about what it means. One of the next three adjectives means almost the same thing. Circle the one that is most like the first adjective in meaning.

G-85	**active**	**a.** busy	**b.** quiet	**c.** still
G-86	**tired**	**a.** calm	**b.** rested	**c.** weary
G-87	**curious**	**a.** familiar	**b.** peculiar	**c.** similar
G-88	**personal**	**a.** open	**b.** private	**c.** public
G-89	**initial**	**a.** first	**b.** last	**c.** middle
G-90	**former**	**a.** current	**b.** earlier	**c.** present
G-91	**novel**	**a.** different	**b.** familiar	**c.** old
G-92	**earnest**	**a.** serious	**b.** casual	**c.** careless
G-93	**temporary**	**a.** continuous	**b.** brief	**c.** permanent
G-94	**favorable**	**a.** critical	**b.** friendly	**c.** negative
G-95	**clever**	**a.** average	**b.** dull	**c.** sharp
G-96	**mobile**	**a.** fixed	**b.** movable	**c.** stationary

SIMILARITIES—SELECT

DIRECTIONS: Each line contains four adjectives. Sometimes the same word can have several different meanings. Read the first adjective in each row and think about what it means. Circle the one that is most like the first adjective in meaning.

G-97	**dull**	**a.** boring	**b.** exciting	**c.** loud
G-98	**dull**	**a.** blunt	**b.** even	**c.** sharp

G-99	**hard**	**a.** difficult	**b.** simple	**c.** smooth
G-100	**hard**	**a.** easy	**b.** firm	**c.** loose
G-101	**hard**	**a.** fantastic	**b.** idealistic	**c.** realistic

G-102	**clear**	**a.** bright	**b.** gloomy	**c.** hazy
G-103	**clear**	**a.** blurred	**b.** certain	**c.** vague
G-104	**clear**	**a.** bare	**b.** clogged	**c.** occupied

G-105	**fine**	**a.** awful	**b.** excellent	**c.** poor
G-106	**fine**	**a.** coarse	**b.** rough	**c.** delicate
G-107	**fine**	**a.** broad	**b.** thin	**c.** wide
G-108	**fine**	**a.** clear	**b.** cloudy	**c.** gloomy

SIMILARITIES—SELECT

DIRECTIONS: Each line contains four verbs. Sometimes the same word can have several different meanings. Read the first verb in each row and think about what it means. Circle another verb that is most like the first one in meaning.

G-109	**raise**	**a.** lower	**b.** lift	**c.** slide
G-110	**raise**	**a.** increase	**b.** reduce	**c.** use
G-111	**raise**	**a.** destroy	**b.** grow	**c.** maintain

G-112	**cut**	**a.** peel	**b.** slice	**c.** tear
G-113	**cut**	**a.** hire	**b.** increase	**c.** reduce
G-114	**cut**	**a.** comb	**b.** dry	**c.** shave
G-115	**cut**	**a.** concentrate	**b.** dilute	**c.** thicken

G-116	**fail**	**a.** cure	**b.** decline	**c.** heal
G-117	**fail**	**a.** flunk	**b.** pass	**c.** win
G-118	**fail**	**a.** dwindle	**b.** grow	**c.** supply

G-119	**drop**	**a.** fall	**b.** rise	**c.** soar
G-120	**drop**	**a.** decline	**b.** grow	**c.** hold

SIMILARITIES—SUPPLY

DIRECTIONS: Each line contains a verb. Read the verb and think about what it means. Think of another verb (or verbs) that means almost the same. Write the verb(s) in the box.

G-121	capture
G-122	select
G-123	ruin
G-124	require
G-125	complete
G-126	consider
G-127	contain
G-128	shut
G-129	create
G-130	proceed
G-131	nourish
G-132	strike

SIMILARITIES—SUPPLY

DIRECTIONS: Each line contains an adjective. Read the adjective and think about what it means. Think of another adjective (or adjectives) that means almost the same. Write the adjective(s) in the box.

G-133	whole

G-134	most

G-135	extra

G-136	single

G-137	annual

G-138	brilliant

G-139	cautious

G-140	artificial

G-141	polite

G-142	minor

G-143	substantial

G-144	handy

SIMILARITIES—SUPPLY

DIRECTIONS: Each line contains a noun. Read the noun and think about what it means. Think of a noun (or nouns) that means almost the same. Write the noun(s) in the box.

G-145	instructor

G-146	opportunity

G-147	explanation

G-148	power

G-149	delight

G-150	achievement

G-151	boundary

G-152	career

G-153	section

G-154	announcement

G-155	device

G-156	supplement

HOW ALIKE?—SELECT

DIRECTIONS: Each line contains two words related to social studies. Think about the ways the two words are alike. Circle the sentence(s) that is true of both words.

G-157 postage stamps
coins

   a. Both can be collected as a hobby.
   b. Both are produced by the government.
   c. Both have a monetary value printed on them.

G-158 king
president

   a. Both are elected.
   b. Both are national leaders.
   c. Both participate in national ceremonies.

G-159 goods
services

   a. Both are objects.
   b. Both can be purchased.
   c. Both require workers.

G-160 globe
map

   a. Both are drawings of all or part of the earth.
   b. Both are flat.
   c. Both can be used to estimate distances between places.

G-161 lake
ocean

   a. Both are bodies of water.
   b. Both can be located on maps.
   c. Both contain drinkable water.

G-162 checks
money

   a. Both can be obtained at a bank.
   b. Both can be used to buy things.
   c. Both need to be endorsed.

HOW ALIKE?—SELECT

DIRECTIONS: Each line contains two words related to communication. Think about the ways the two words are alike. Circle the sentence(s) that is true of both words.

G-163 magazine
newspaper

a. Both are usually published daily.
b. Both have editors.
c. Both can have reporters.

G-164 radio
telephone

a. Both deliver sounds.
b. Both can be dialed or tuned.
c. Both broadcast programs.

G-165 fax
letter

a. Both are delivered by the postal service.
b. Both require special sending and receiving equipment.
c. Both convey information.

G-166 debate
political speech

a. Both present opposing points of view.
b. Both involve speaking.
c. Both concern the speakers' opinions.

G-167 television news
historical documentary

a. Both are based on fact.
b. Both discuss current issues.
c. Both are informative.

G-168 conversation
lecture

a. Both convey information
b. Both involve speaking.
c. Both are spoken by teachers or visiting experts.

HOW ALIKE?—SELECT

DIRECTIONS: Each line contains two words related to science. Think about the ways the two words are alike. Circle the sentence(s) that is true of both words.

G-169 noise
sound

   a. Both are caused by vibrations.
   b. Both can be heard.
   c. Both are never pleasant.

G-170 root
stem

   a. Both are parts of a plant.
   b. Both are above ground.
   c. Some kinds of each can be eaten.

G-171 lever
pulley

   a. Both are simple machines.
   b. Both need ropes or strings.
   c. Both can make work easier.

G-172 frog
snake

   a. Both have backbones.
   b. Both are reptiles.
   c. Both are amphibians.

G-173 corn
wheat

   a. Both are grasses.
   b. Both are grains.
   c. Both can be eaten.

G-174 ice
cloud

   a. Both are solid.
   b. Both are forms of water.
   c. Both take up space.

HOW ALIKE?—SELECT

DIRECTIONS: Each line contains two words related to art or music. Think about the ways the two words are alike. Circle the sentence(s) that is true of both words.

G-175 painting
photograph

   a. Both are pictures.
   b. Both can be sold in art galleries.
   c. Both must represent real objects.

G-176 piano
xylophone

   a. Both are musical instruments.
   b. Both have keys.
   c. Both are played by hitting with a stick.

G-177 marching band
orchestra

   a. Both have horn players.
   b. Both have violin players.
   c. Both produce music.

G-178 artist
composer

   a. Both are talented people.
   b. Both are involved in the arts.
   c. Both write music.

G-179 paints
musical instruments

   a. Both are used by musicians.
   b. Both can be used by talented people.
   c. Both can be held in the hand.

G-180 canvas
music staff paper

   a. Both can be used to produce a creative work.
   b. Both have paint applied to them.
   c. Both are used to write music.

HOW ALIKE AND HOW DIFFERENT?

DIRECTIONS: Each line contains two words related to social studies. Describe how the words are alike and how they are different.

| **G-181** neighborhood community | HOW ALIKE? |
| | HOW DIFFERENT? |

| **G-182** mayor governor | HOW ALIKE? |
| | HOW DIFFERENT? |

| **G-183** country continent | HOW ALIKE? |
| | HOW DIFFERENT? |

| **G-184** weather climate | HOW ALIKE? |
| | HOW DIFFERENT? |

| **G-185** dictatorship democracy | HOW ALIKE? |
| | HOW DIFFERENT? |

HOW ALIKE AND HOW DIFFERENT?

DIRECTIONS: Each line contains two words related to science. Describe how the words are alike and how they are different.

| **G-186**
light
sound | HOW ALIKE? |
| | HOW DIFFERENT? |

| **G-187**
amphibian
reptile | HOW ALIKE? |
| | HOW DIFFERENT? |

| **G-188**
fruit
seed | HOW ALIKE? |
| | HOW DIFFERENT? |

| **G-189**
machine
work | HOW ALIKE? |
| | HOW DIFFERENT? |

| **G-190**
planet
star | HOW ALIKE? |
| | HOW DIFFERENT? |

HOW ALIKE AND HOW DIFFERENT?

DIRECTIONS: Each line contains two words related to mathematics. Describe how the words are alike and how they are different.

| **G-191** square rectangle | HOW ALIKE? |
| | HOW DIFFERENT? |

| **G-192** rectangle parallelogram | HOW ALIKE? |
| | HOW DIFFERENT? |

| **G-193** parallelogram rhombus | HOW ALIKE? |
| | HOW DIFFERENT? |

| **G-194** parallelogram trapezoid | HOW ALIKE? |
| | HOW DIFFERENT? |

| **G-195** square rhombus | HOW ALIKE? |
| | HOW DIFFERENT? |

WORD WEB—SELECT AND SUPPLY

DIRECTIONS: Sometimes common words have more than one meaning. In each blank box below, write a word from the choice box that has almost the same meaning as the synonym next to the blank.

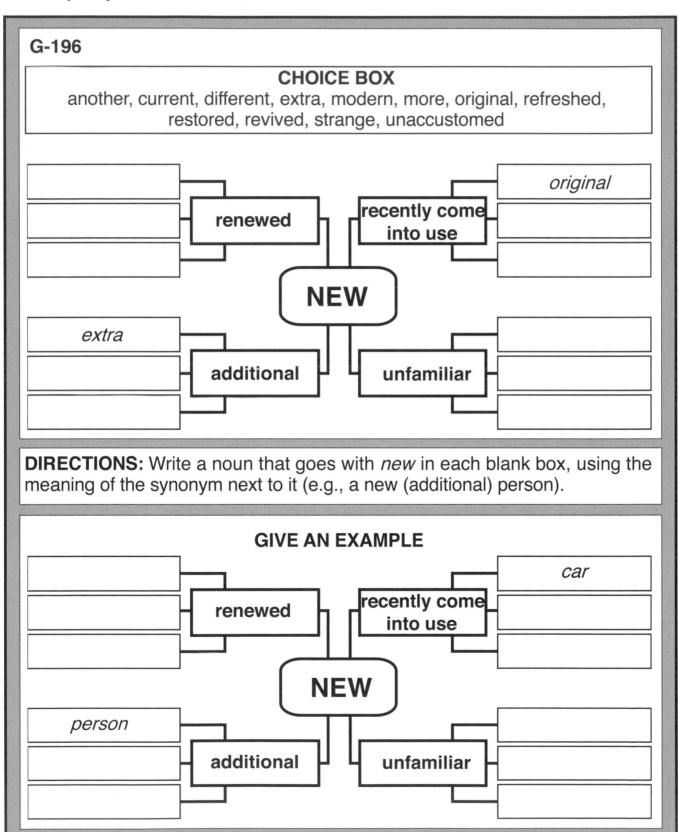

G-196

CHOICE BOX
another, current, different, extra, modern, more, original, refreshed, restored, revived, strange, unaccustomed

renewed

recently come into use — *original*

NEW

extra — additional

unfamiliar

DIRECTIONS: Write a noun that goes with *new* in each blank box, using the meaning of the synonym next to it (e.g., a new (additional) person).

GIVE AN EXAMPLE

renewed

recently come into use — *car*

NEW

person — additional

unfamiliar

WORD WEB—SELECT AND SUPPLY

DIRECTIONS: Sometimes common words have more than one meaning. In each blank box below, write a word from the choice box that has almost the same meaning as the synonym next to the blank.

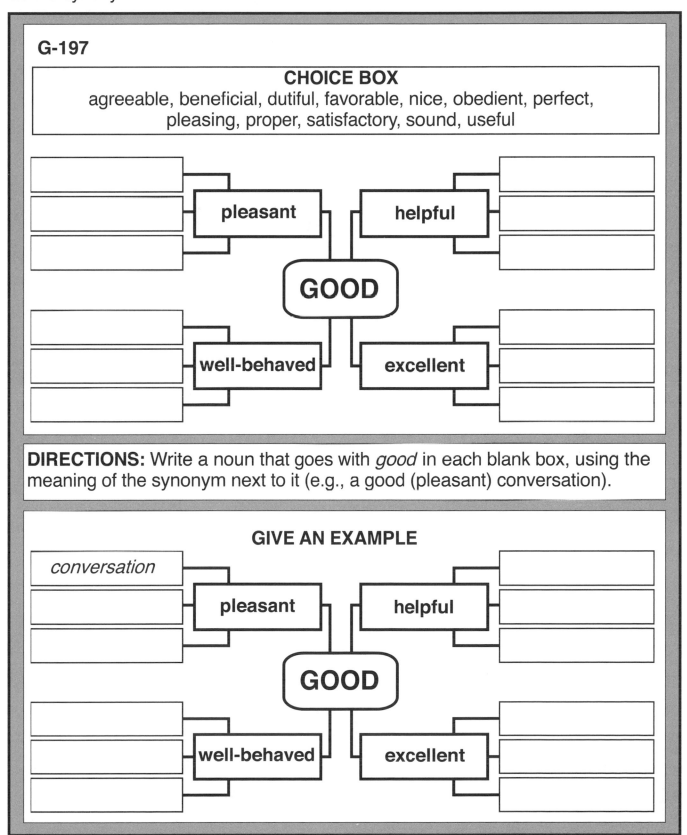

G-197

CHOICE BOX
agreeable, beneficial, dutiful, favorable, nice, obedient, perfect, pleasing, proper, satisfactory, sound, useful

pleasant

helpful

GOOD

well-behaved

excellent

DIRECTIONS: Write a noun that goes with *good* in each blank box, using the meaning of the synonym next to it (e.g., a good (pleasant) conversation).

GIVE AN EXAMPLE

conversation

pleasant

helpful

GOOD

well-behaved

excellent

WORD WEB—SELECT AND SUPPLY

DIRECTIONS: Sometimes common words have more than one meaning. In each blank box below, write a word from the choice box that has almost the same meaning as the synonym next to the blank.

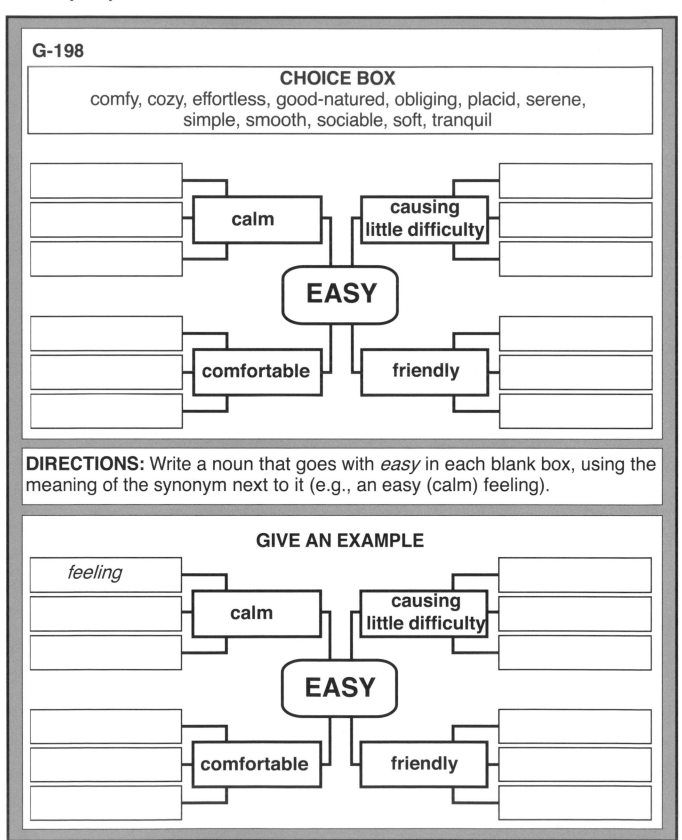

G-198

CHOICE BOX
comfy, cozy, effortless, good-natured, obliging, placid, serene, simple, smooth, sociable, soft, tranquil

calm

causing little difficulty

EASY

comfortable

friendly

DIRECTIONS: Write a noun that goes with *easy* in each blank box, using the meaning of the synonym next to it (e.g., an easy (calm) feeling).

GIVE AN EXAMPLE

feeling

calm

causing little difficulty

EASY

comfortable

friendly

WORD WEB—SELECT AND SUPPLY

DIRECTIONS: Sometimes common words have more than one meaning. In each blank box below, write a word from the choice box that has almost the same meaning as the synonym next to the blank.

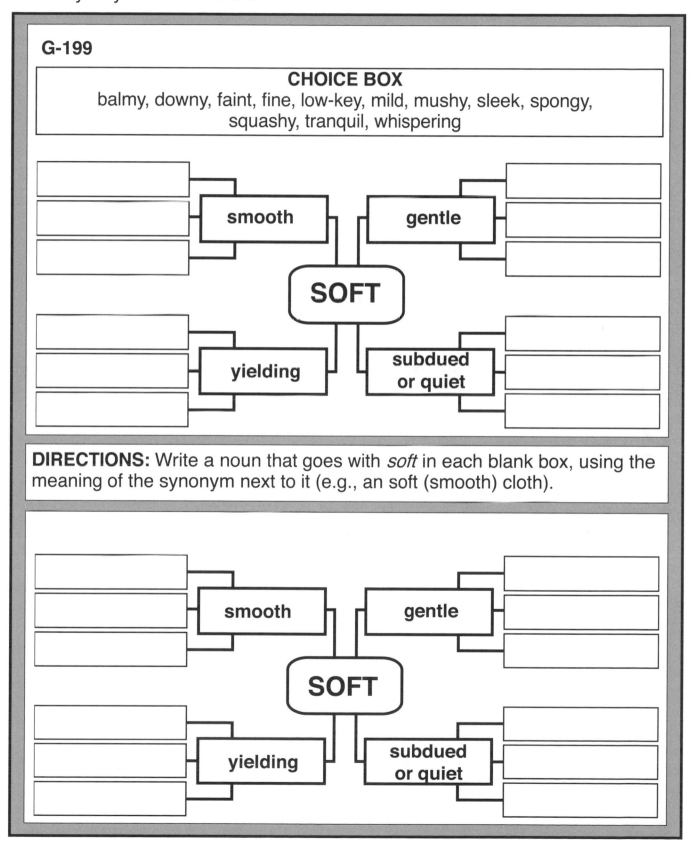

G-199

CHOICE BOX
balmy, downy, faint, fine, low-key, mild, mushy, sleek, spongy, squashy, tranquil, whispering

smooth

gentle

SOFT

yielding

subdued or quiet

DIRECTIONS: Write a noun that goes with *soft* in each blank box, using the meaning of the synonym next to it (e.g., an soft (smooth) cloth).

smooth

gentle

SOFT

yielding

subdued or quiet

209

WORD WEB—SELECT AND SUPPLY

DIRECTIONS: Sometimes common words have more than one meaning. In each blank box below, write a word from the choice box that has almost the same meaning as the synonym next to the blank.

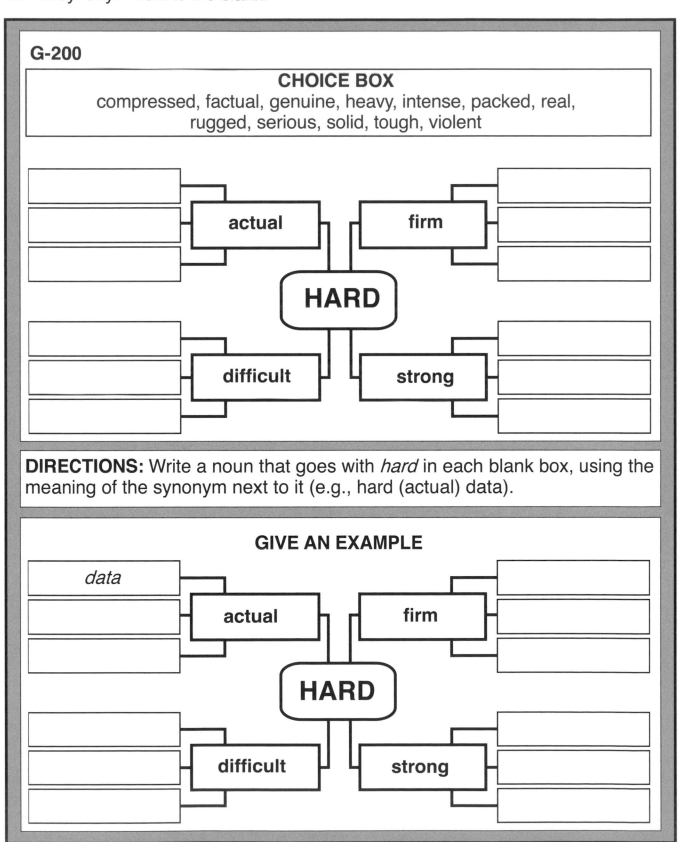

G-200

CHOICE BOX
compressed, factual, genuine, heavy, intense, packed, real, rugged, serious, solid, tough, violent

actual

firm

HARD

difficult

strong

DIRECTIONS: Write a noun that goes with *hard* in each blank box, using the meaning of the synonym next to it (e.g., hard (actual) data).

GIVE AN EXAMPLE

data

actual

firm

HARD

difficult

strong

WORD WEB—SELECT AND SUPPLY

DIRECTIONS: Sometimes common words have more than one meaning. In each blank box below, write a word from the choice box that has almost the same meaning as the synonym next to the blank.

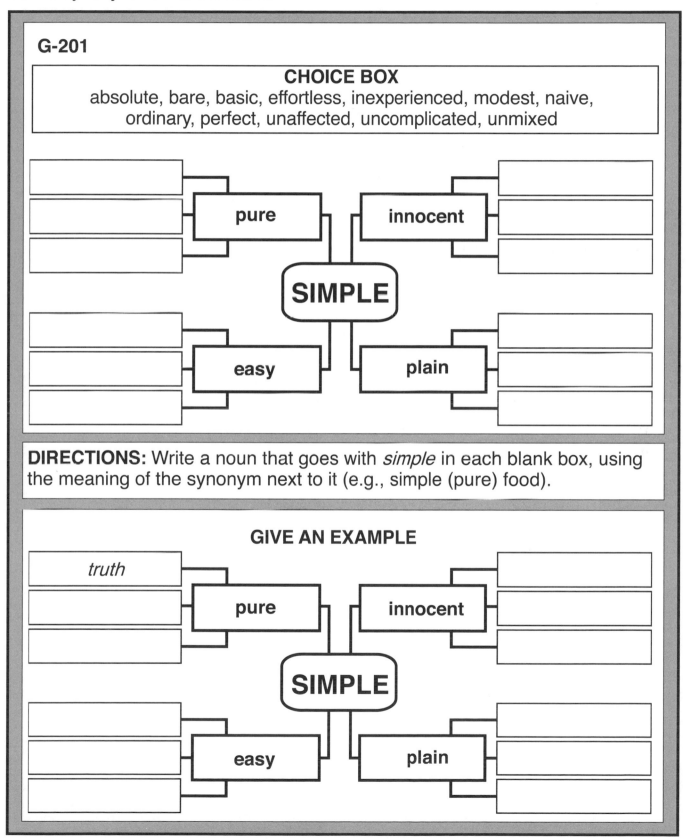

G-201

CHOICE BOX
absolute, bare, basic, effortless, inexperienced, modest, naive, ordinary, perfect, unaffected, uncomplicated, unmixed

pure

innocent

SIMPLE

easy

plain

DIRECTIONS: Write a noun that goes with *simple* in each blank box, using the meaning of the synonym next to it (e.g., simple (pure) food).

GIVE AN EXAMPLE

truth

pure

innocent

SIMPLE

easy

plain

COMPARE AND CONTRAST—GRAPHIC ORGANIZER

DIRECTIONS: Read the following information about spiders and insects. Use this information to compare and contrast spiders and insects in the graphic organizer on the next page.

INSECTS AND SPIDERS

Insects and spiders have jointed appendages, segmented bodies, and exoskeletons. Insects have three pairs of walking legs and spiders have four pairs. Their jointed legs bend to allow quick movement. Insects have segmented bodies with three parts: the head, the thorax, and the abdomen. Spiders have two major body parts, the cephalothorax and the abdomen. Both types of animal have an exoskeleton. This is an external skeleton that protects the body and is molted as the animal grows. Insects have antennae. Antennae are sense organs found on the head that can detect odors. Spiders do not have antennae. They do, however, have spinnerets which produce the fine silk used for their webs.

Spiders are predators that feed primarily on other insects. Spiders can swallow only liquids, so digestive juices are pumped onto the prey, it is digested externally, and the spider swallows the resulting liquid. Insects obtain food by a variety of methods, including biting, lapping, and sucking. Butterflies suck nectar from a flower through their proboscis (feeding tube). Honeybees lap nectar with their tongues. Beetles, wasps, and ants use their powerful biting jaws.

COMPARE AND CONTRAST—GRAPHIC ORGANIZER

DIRECTIONS: Use the graphic organizer below to compare and contrast insects and spiders.

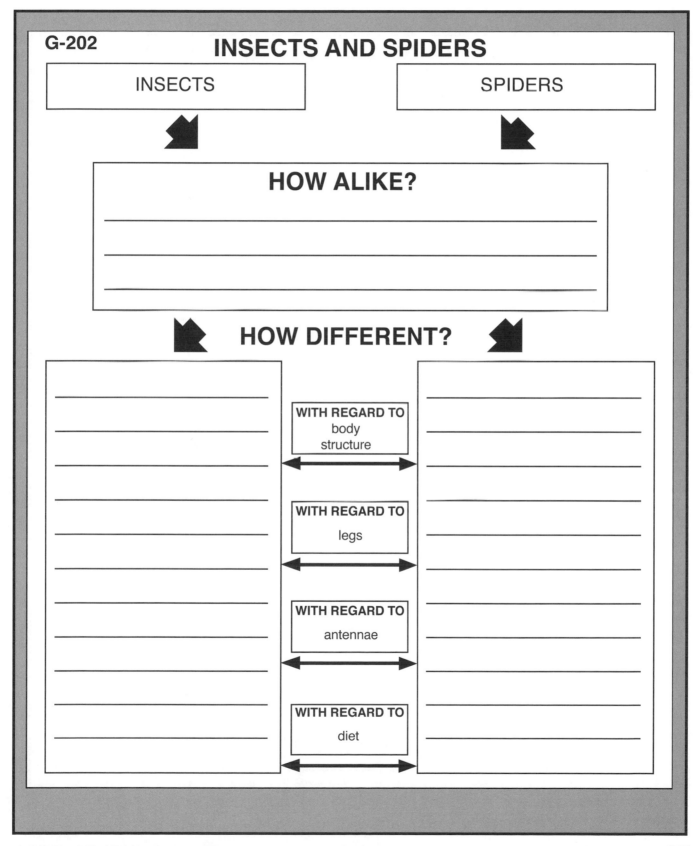

COMPARE AND CONTRAST—GRAPHIC ORGANIZER

DIRECTIONS: Use the graphic organizer below to compare and contrast a parallelogram and an isosceles trapezoid.

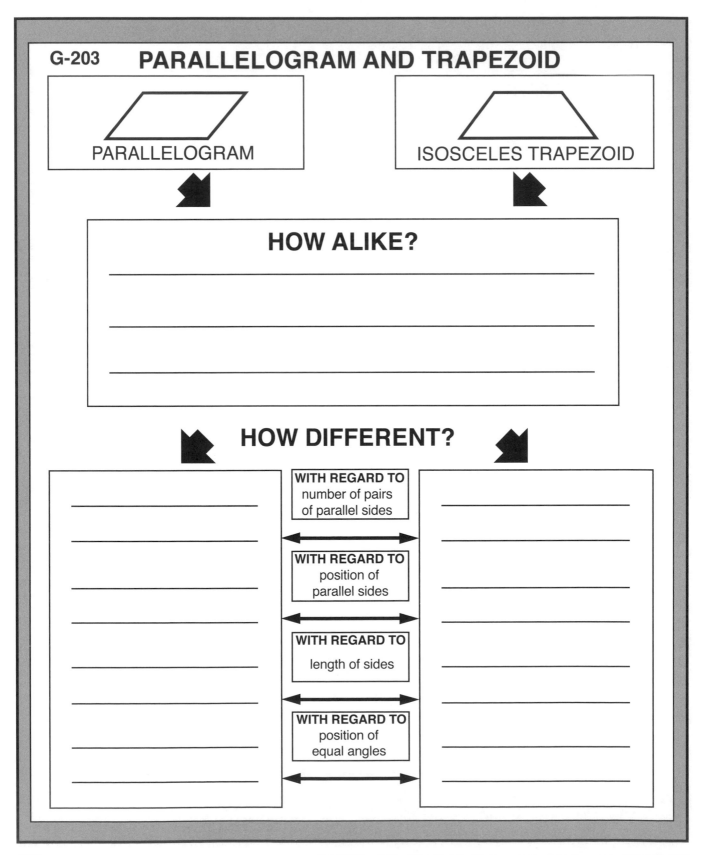

COMPARE AND CONTRAST—GRAPHIC ORGANIZER

DIRECTIONS: Use the graphic organizer below to compare and contrast democracy and dictatorship.

G-204 COMPARING AND CONTRASTING TWO IDEAS

DEMOCRACY	DICTATORSHIP

HOW ALIKE?

_____

_____

_____

HOW DIFFERENT?

DEMOCRACY	WITH REGARD TO	DICTATORSHIP
_____	who controls the government	_____
_____	←→	_____
_____	WITH REGARD TO how control is determined	_____
_____	←→	_____
_____	WITH REGARD TO freedoms	_____
_____	←→	_____
_____	WITH REGARD TO succession of leaders	_____
_____	←→	_____

CHAPTER EIGHT

Describing Shapes	→	Describing Things	←
Figural Similarities and Differences	→	Verbal Similarities and Differences	
Figural Sequences	→	Verbal Sequences	
Figural Classifications	→	Verbal Classifications	
Figural Analogies	→	Verbal Analogies	

FOLLOWING DIRECTIONS—SELECT

DIRECTIONS: For each set of directions below, circle the figure that correctly represents the directions.

EXAMPLE
DIRECTIONS: Draw a triangle with two long, equal sides. Use the shortest side of the triangle as one side of a square.

A.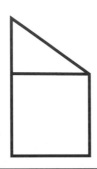

B.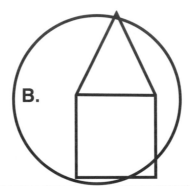

C.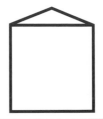

H-1 DIRECTIONS: Draw a rectangle. Draw a diamond inside the rectangle that touches the rectangle at four points.

A.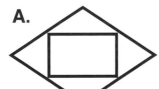

B.

C.

H-2 DIRECTIONS: Draw a square. Use the top of the square as the bottom of a triangle. Draw a circle inside the square that touches all sides of the square.

A.

B.

C.

FOLLOWING DIRECTIONS—SELECT

DIRECTIONS: For each set of directions below, circle the figure that correctly represents the directions.

H-3 DIRECTIONS: Draw a right triangle with the base and height the same length. Draw a rectangle using the height of the triangle as the long side of the rectangle. Inside the triangle, draw a circle that touches all sides of the triangle.

A. 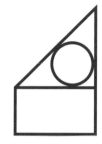   **B.**    **C.**

H-4 DIRECTIONS: Draw two squares, one above the other. Draw a triangle inside the upper square. Draw a circle inside the lower square.

A.    **B.**    **C.**

H-5 DIRECTIONS: Draw a square. Divide the square into two equal parts by drawing a line from the upper left corner to the lower right corner. Draw a rectangle using the bottom of the square as the top of the rectangle.

A. 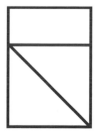   **B.** 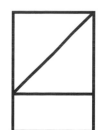   **C.**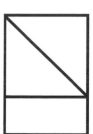

FOLLOWING DIRECTIONS—SUPPLY

DIRECTIONS: For each set of directions below, draw a figure that correctly represents the directions.

H-6 DIRECTIONS: Using the grid of dots below, draw a circle near the center of the grid. Directly above the circle, draw a square. To the right of the square, draw a triangle.

H-7 DIRECTIONS: Using the grid of dots below, draw a square near the lower left corner. Near the upper right corner, draw a circle. Directly below the circle, draw a triangle.

FOLLOWING DIRECTIONS—SUPPLY

DIRECTIONS: For each set of directions below, draw a figure that correctly represents the directions.

H-8 DIRECTIONS: Using the grid of dots below, draw a circle near the center of the grid. To the right of the circle, draw a triangle that is taller than the circle. To the left of the circle, draw a square that is shorter than the circle.

H-9 DIRECTIONS: Using the grid of dots below, draw a large rectangle. Inside the rectangle, draw a white circle and a black square. The square should be to the right of the circle.

FOLLOWING DIRECTIONS—SUPPLY

INSTRUCTIONS: Each problem should be drawn on a whole sheet of paper. Follow the directions exactly.

H-10 DIRECTIONS

a. Find the midpoint of the left side of the paper and draw a small square (the midpoint is halfway down the paper).

b. Find the midpoint of the right side of the paper and draw a small square.

c. Draw a line across the paper that touches each square but does not go into either square.

H-11 DIRECTIONS

a. Write an "X" in each of the four corners of the paper.

b. Draw an arrow from the top left corner to the bottom left corner.

c. Draw an arrow from the bottom left corner to the bottom right corner.

d. What large letter did you form?

H-12 DIRECTIONS

a. Draw a line from the middle of the top of the paper to the middle of the bottom of the paper.

b. Draw a line from the middle of the left edge of the paper to the middle of the right edge of the paper.

c. Using the point where the lines cross as the center of a circle, draw the biggest circle you can.

H-13 DIRECTIONS

a. Draw a line up and down the paper and keep the line about an inch from the left edge of the paper.

b. Draw a line across the page and keep it about an inch below the top of the paper.

c. Darken the square that is formed in the upper left corner.

WRITING DIRECTIONS

INSTRUCTIONS: Look at the figure on the left very carefully. Write directions for drawing the figure so that a classmate could draw the figure without seeing it.

H-14

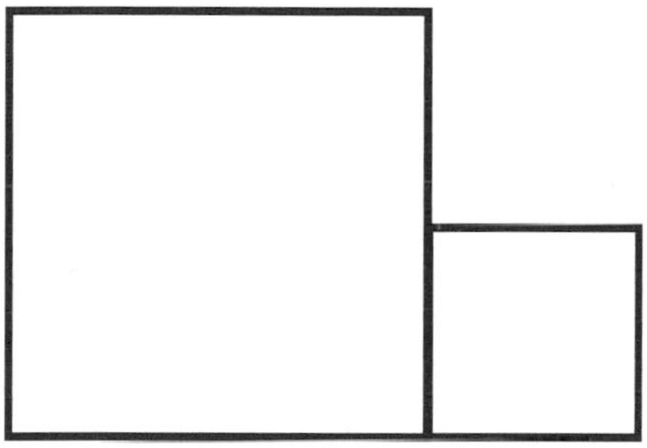

_____

_____

_____

_____

_____

_____

_____

H-15

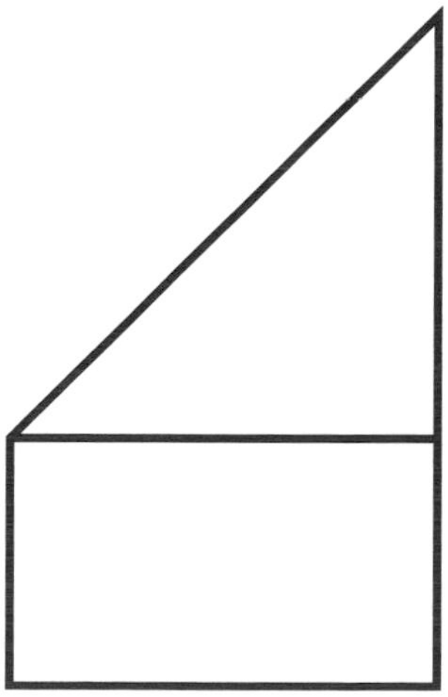

_____

_____

_____

_____

_____

_____

_____

WRITING DIRECTIONS

INSTRUCTIONS: Look at the figure on the left very carefully. Write directions for drawing the figure so that a classmate could draw the figure without seeing it.

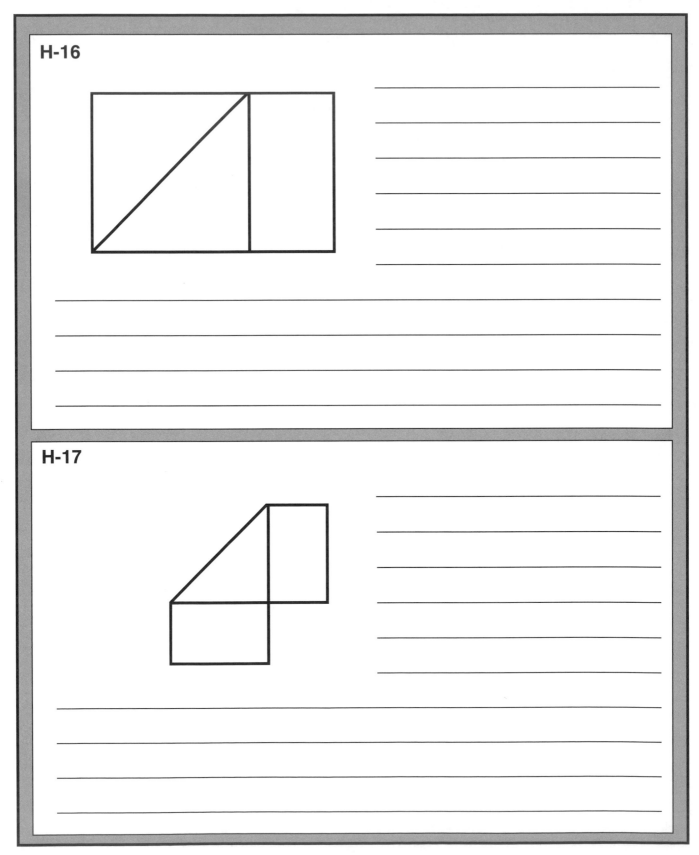

H-16

_____

_____

_____

_____

_____

_____

_____

_____

_____

_____

H-17

_____

_____

_____

_____

_____

_____

_____

_____

_____

_____

RECOGNIZING DIRECTION—A

DIRECTIONS: Imagine that you are standing in the circle, facing the direction of the arrow. The square is straight ahead. Fill in the blanks below to describe the shapes that are to your left, to your right, or behind you.

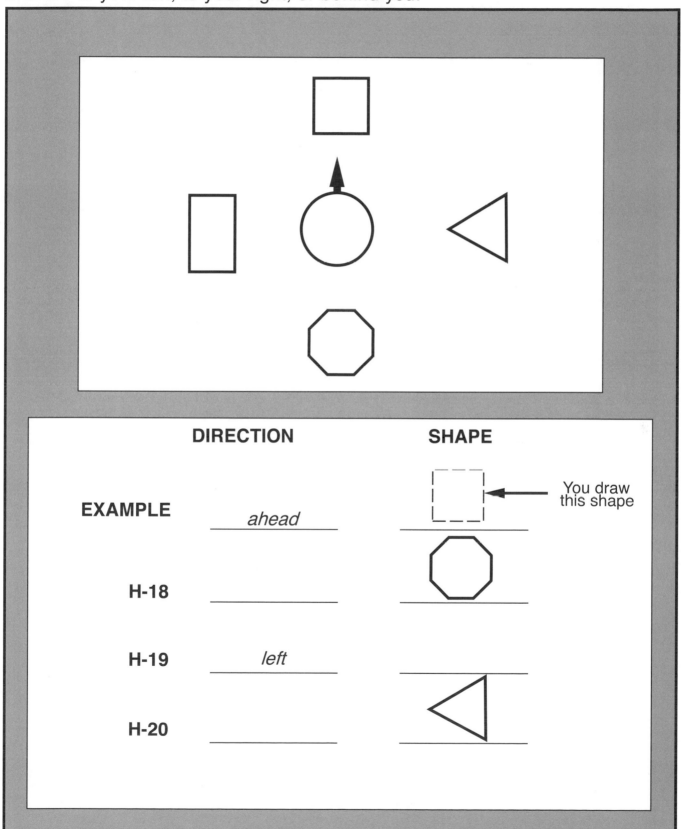

	DIRECTION	**SHAPE**
EXAMPLE	*ahead*	You draw this shape
H-18	_____	
H-19	*left*	
H-20	_____	

RECOGNIZING DIRECTION—A

DIRECTIONS: Imagine that you are standing in the circle, facing the direction of the arrow. The hexagon is straight ahead. Fill in the blanks below to describe the shapes that are to your left, to your right, or behind you.

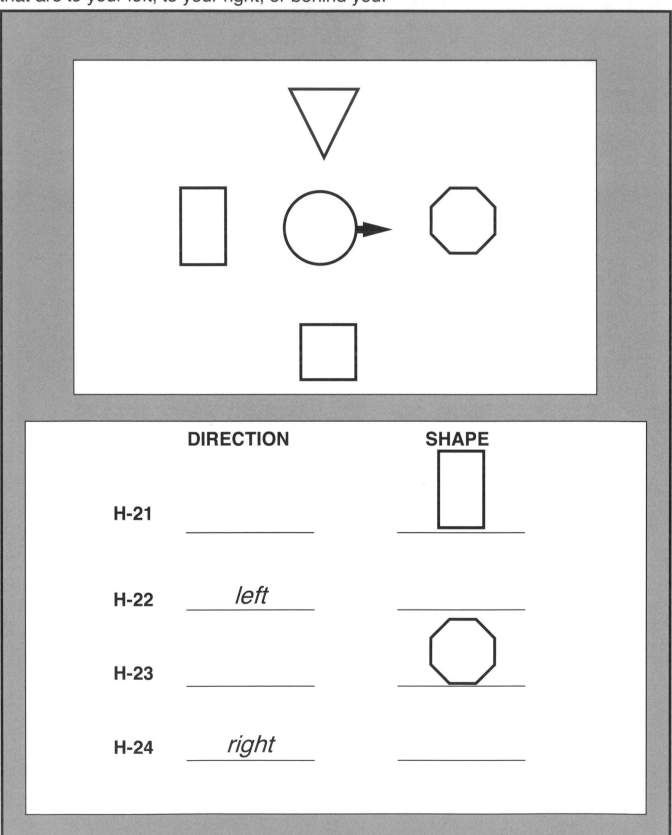

	DIRECTION	SHAPE
H-21	_____	_____
H-22	*left*	_____
H-23	_____	_____
H-24	*right*	_____

RECOGNIZING DIRECTION—B

DIRECTIONS: Imagine that you are standing in the circle below, facing north (N), west (W), south (S), or east (E). Draw the shape you are facing or the shape on your right. For example, if you are facing north (N), as shown in the example, then the rectangle is straight ahead and the triangle is on your right. Trace the triangle in the blank in the first row. Next, imagine that you are facing west (W); draw the missing shape in the blank in the second row.

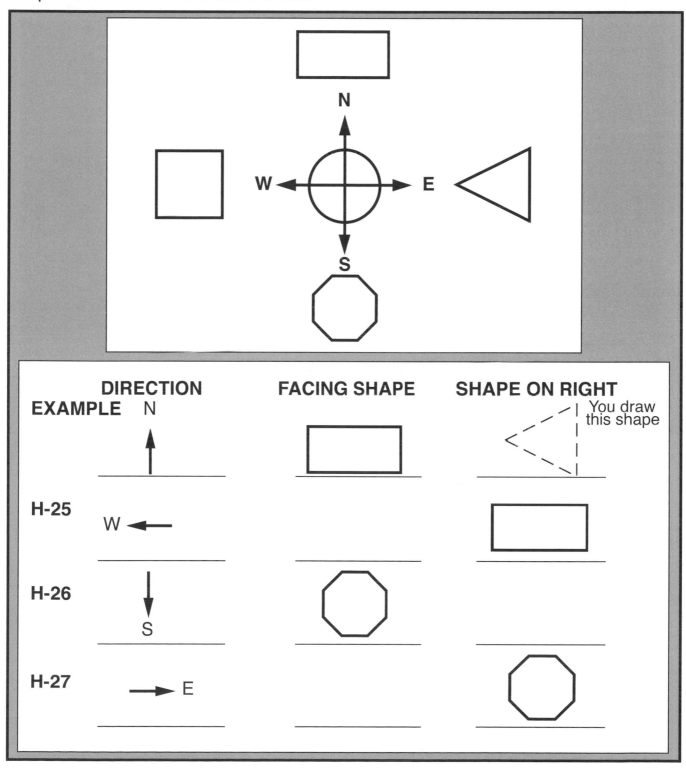

RECOGNIZING DIRECTION—B

DIRECTIONS: Imagine that you are standing in the circle below, facing either north (N), west (W), south (S), or east (E). By knowing the positions of two or more shapes, determine the direction you are facing and draw any missing shapes. For example, if the rectangle is on your right and the octagon is on your left, then you will be facing the square. (Draw the square.) If you are facing the square, you are facing west. (Draw the letter and arrow.)

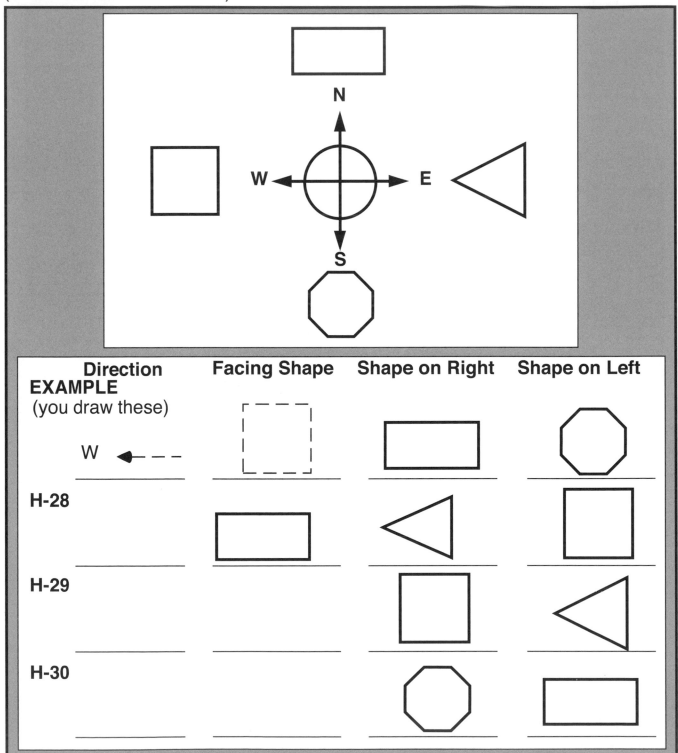

RECOGNIZING DIRECTION—B

DIRECTIONS: Imagine that you are standing in the circle below, facing either north (N), west (W), south (S), or east (E). By knowing the positions of two or more shapes, determine the direction you are facing. Draw the missing shapes and directions.

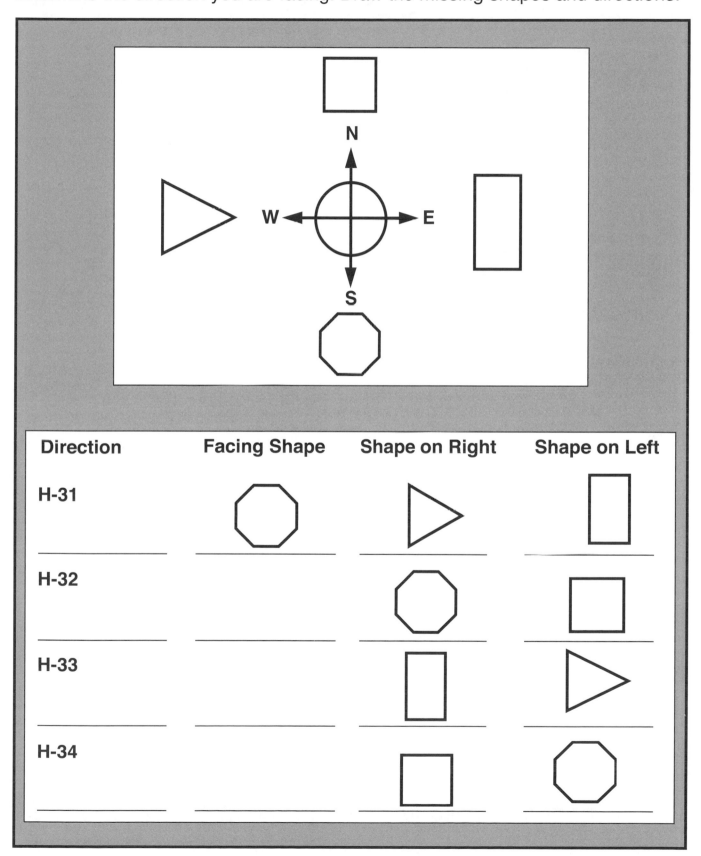

Direction	Facing Shape	Shape on Right	Shape on Left
H-31	octagon	triangle	rectangle
H-32		octagon	square
H-33		rectangle	triangle
H-34		square	octagon

DESCRIBING LOCATIONS

DIRECTIONS: Locate the parts of Midville described in the exercises. Read the instructions for each exercise and mark the map accordingly.

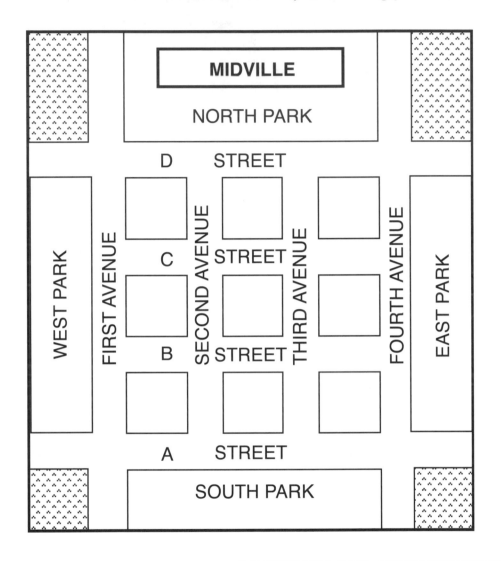

H-35 Print a "P" where Second Avenue and C Street cross.

H-36 Print a "Q" where Third Avenue and A Street cross.

H-37 Print an "R" where First Avenue and D Street cross.

H-38 Which letter (P, Q, or R) is closest to West Park?   Answer:_____

H-39 Which letter is in the northern part of Midville?   Answer:_____

H-40 Which street or avenue is closest to East Park?   Answer: _____

DESCRIBING LOCATIONS

DIRECTIONS: Locate the parts of Midville described in the exercises. Read the instructions for each exercise and answer the questions.

```
                        ┌─────────────────────┐
                        │     MIDVILLE        │
                        └─────────────────────┘
                          NORTH PARK

                    D        STREET

              FIRST AVENUE  SECOND AVENUE  THIRD AVENUE  FOURTH AVENUE
  WEST PARK                                                              EAST PARK
                    C        STREET

                    B        STREET

                    A        STREET

                          SOUTH PARK
```

H-41 You are facing West Park. Third Avenue is one block behind you. C Street is one block to your right. You are located where _____ Street meets _____ Avenue.

What street or avenue is one block to your left?   Answer: _____
How far are you from North Park?   Answer: _____ blocks

H-42 You have moved and are now facing south. C Street is one block behind you. Third Avenue is now two blocks to your left. You are now located where _____ Street meets _____ Avenue.

What street or avenue is one block ahead of you? Answer: _____
How far are you from East Park?   Answer: _____ blocks

DESCRIBING DIRECTIONS

DIRECTIONS: Locate the parts of Midville described in the exercises. Read the instructions for each exercise and answer the questions.

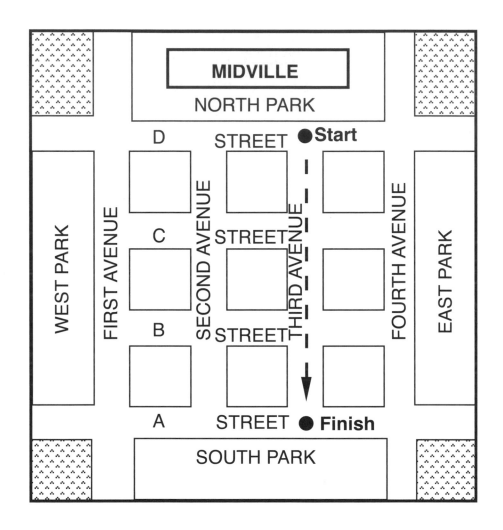

EXAMPLE: If you start at Third Avenue and D Street and travel three blocks south, you will be at the corner of Third Avenue and A Street. (Follow the arrows from Start to Finish.)

H-43 If you start at Fourth Avenue and C Street and travel three blocks west, where will you be?
Answer: Where _____ Street meets _____ Avenue.

H-44 If you start at Second Avenue and D Street and travel in a straight line to Fourth Avenue and D Street, how far have you traveled?
Answer: _____ blocks.

In what direction did you travel? Answer: _____

DESCRIBING DIRECTIONS

DIRECTIONS: Locate the parts of Midville described in the exercises. Read the instructions for each exercise and answer the questions.

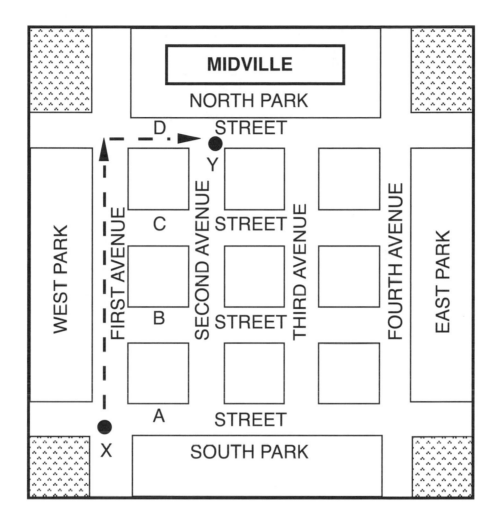

H-45 Describe the path shown by the arrows between points X and Y.

Go _____ blocks to the _____ and _____ blocks to the _____.
    (number)   (direction)   (number)   (direction)

H-46 Draw and describe another path having one turn which will go from point X to point Y.

Go _____ blocks to the _____ and _____ blocks to the _____.
    (number)   (direction)   (number)   (direction)

How many total blocks are traveled in each path? Answer: Each path is _____ blocks long.
    (number)

DESCRIBING DIRECTIONS

DIRECTIONS: Locate the parts of Midville described in the exercises. Read the instructions for each exercise and answer the questions.

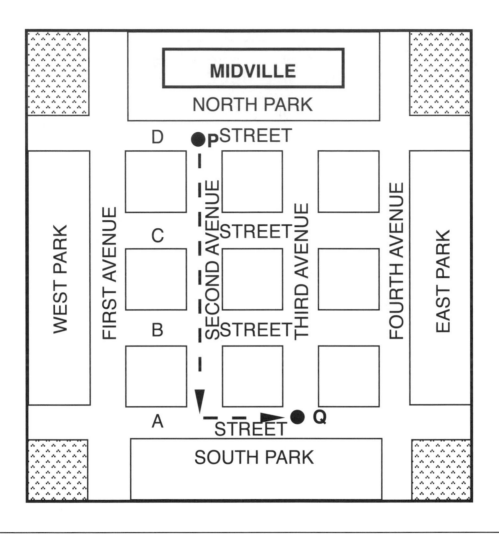

H-47 Describe the path shown by the arrows between points P and Q.

Go_____ blocks to the _____ and _____ blocks to the _____ .
    (number)   (direction)   (number)   (direction)

H-48 Draw and describe another path having one turn which will go from point P to point Q.

Go_____ blocks to the _____ and _____ blocks to the _____.
    (number)   (direction)   (number)   (direction)

How many total blocks are traveled in each path?
Answer: Each path is _____ blocks long.
                              (number)

DESCRIBING DIRECTIONS

DIRECTIONS: Locate the parts of Midville described in the exercises. Read the instructions for each exercise and answer the questions.

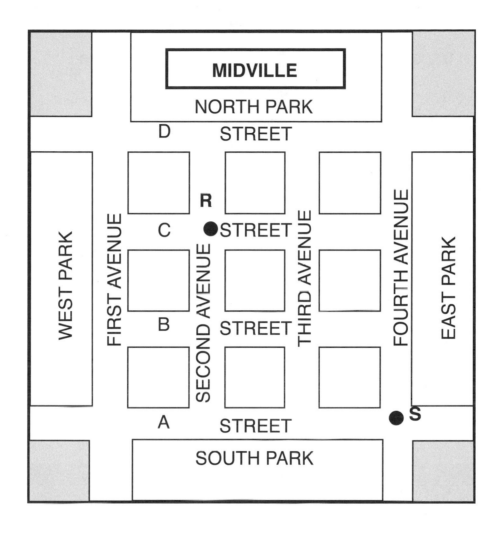

H-49 Use a dotted line (…..) to draw a path from point R to point S that is four blocks long and has two turns. Describe the path.

Go_____blocks to the _____ and _____ blocks to the _____
   (number)   (direction)   (number)   (direction)

and _____ blocks to the _____ .
     (number)   (direction)

H-50 Use a dashed line (---) to draw another path from point R to point S that is four blocks long and has two turns. Describe the path.

Go_____ blocks to the_____and_____blocks to the_____
   (number)   (direction)   (number)   (direction)

and _____ blocks to the _____ .
     (number)   (direction)

TIME SEQUENCE—SELECT

DIRECTIONS: The first two words in each group suggest an order of occurrence. On the blank, write the word from the column on the right that will continue the time sequence.

H-51 leave, travel, _____

arrive
depart
drive

H-52

earn, save, _____

gain
receive
spend

H-53 plan, build, _____

construct
design
occupy

H-54 cause, event, _____

chance
reason
result

H-55 early, prompt, _____

late
now
soon

H-56 measure, mark, _____

cut
line
rule

H-57 sleep, waken, _____

rise
slumber
stir

TIME SEQUENCE—RANK

DIRECTIONS: On the lines below, rewrite each group of words in order of occurrence from earliest to latest.

H-58   clean, cook, eat

_____, _____, _____

H-59   dial, hang up, talk

_____, _____, _____

H-60   buy, shop, use

_____, _____, _____

H-61   attack, battle, defeat

_____, _____, _____

H-62   lesson, performance, practice

_____, _____, _____

H-63   continue, finish, start

_____, _____, _____

H-64   dry, rinse, wash

_____, _____, _____

TIME SEQUENCE—SUPPLY

DIRECTIONS: The words or phrases in each group suggest an order of occurrence. Think of a word that will continue the time sequence and write it in the blank. You may need to use a dictionary.

H-65 born, live, _____

H-66 plow, plant, _____

H-67 begin, continue, _____

H-68 past, present, _____

H-69 dawn, morning, _____

H-70 hurt, treat, _____

H-71 inhale, hold breath, _____

H-72 read catalog, select product, _____

H-73 enroll, attend, _____

DEGREE OF MEANING—SELECT

DIRECTIONS: The words in each group suggest a sequence of rank, degree, size, or order. In the blank, write the word from the column on the right that will come next in the sequence.

H-74 chilly, frosty, _____

brisk
cool
freezing

H-75 ahead, beside, _____

behind
beneath
between

H-76 hint, ask, _____

demand
request
suggest

H-77 sad, depressed, _____

hopeless
sorry
unhappy

H-78 scarce, adequate, _____

enough
few
plenty

H-79 satisfactory, admirable, _____

average
ordinary
excellent

H-80 mist, light rain, _____

downpour
drizzle
fog

DEGREE OF MEANING—SELECT

DIRECTIONS: The words in each group suggest a sequence of rank, degree, size, or order. In the blank, write the word from the column on the right that will come next in the sequence.

H-81 gentle, firm, _____

harsh
mild
tender

H-82 exact, similar, _____

alike
different
identical

H-83 asleep, calm, active, _____

excited
quiet
resting

H-84 incomplete, poor, _____

careless
average
worthless

H-85 shy, fearful, _____

bashful
coy
terrified

H-86 fatigued, weary, _____

drained
exhausted
tired

H-87 bothered, displeased,_____

annoyed
disappointed
disgusted

DEGREE OF MEANING—RANK

DIRECTIONS: On the lines below, rewrite each group of words in order from least or smallest to greatest or largest in degree, rank, size, or order.

H-88   delighted, pleased, thrilled

_____ , _____ , _____

H-89   danger, safety, threat

_____ , _____ , _____

H-90   doze, nap, sleep

_____ , _____ , _____

H-91   bright, dark, dim

_____ , _____ , _____

H-92   desert, jungle, prairie

_____ , _____ , _____

H-93   lake, ocean, pond

_____ , _____ , _____

H-94   continent, country, state

_____ , _____ , _____

DEGREE OF MEANING—RANK

DIRECTIONS: On the lines below, rewrite each group of words in order from lowest or smallest to highest or largest in degree, rank, size, or order.

H-95 class, pupil, school

_____, _____, _____

H-96 painful, sore, tender

_____, _____, _____

H-97 burst, full, swell

_____, _____, _____

H-98 empty, overflowing, full

_____, _____, _____

H-99 full, hungry, starving

_____, _____, _____

H-100 gallon, pint, quart

_____, _____, _____

H-101 foot, inch, yard

_____, _____, _____

DEGREE OF MEANING—SUPPLY

DIRECTIONS: The words in each group suggest a sequence of degree, rank, size, or order. Think of a word that will continue the sequence and write it in the blank. You may need to use a dictionary.

H-102 mayor, governor, _____

H-103 front, side, _____

H-104 few, many, _____

H-105 far, farther, _____

H-106 more, some, _____

H-107 word, sentence, _____

H-108 same, similar, _____

H-109 good, better, _____

H-110 cool, warm, _____

DEGREE OF MEANING—SUPPLY

DIRECTIONS: On the lines below, rewrite each group of words in order from lowest or smallest to highest or largest in degree, rank, size, or order.

H-111 short, average, _____

H-112 dark, dawn, _____

H-113 day, week, _____

H-114 caterpillar, cocoon, _____

H-115 scene, act, _____

H-116 home, neighborhood, _____

H-117 foal, colt, _____

H-118 duet, trio, _____

H-119 tenor, baritone, _____

TRANSITIVITY—COMPARISON

DIRECTIONS: In these sentences, animals or objects are being compared according to some characteristic they have in common. Read the sentences and use the diagrams to figure out the order. Then list the items in order.

H-120 The adult fox terrier is about four inches taller than the West Highland terrier (Westie). The Airedale is the largest dog in the terrier breed. List the terriers in descending order beginning with the largest.

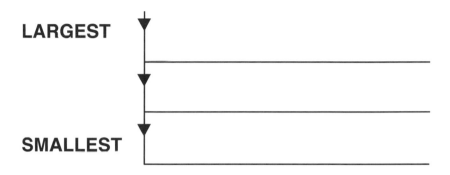

H-121 A bus is faster than a bicycle. Subway trains are faster than buses but slower than monorail trains. List the vehicles in descending order beginning with the fastest.

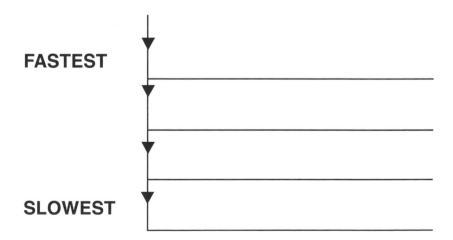

245

TRANSITIVITY—COMPARISON

DIRECTIONS: In these sentences, people or objects are being compared according to some characteristic they have in common (age, size, or position). Read the sentences and use the diagrams to figure out the order. List the items in order.

H-122   Mary is older than Gloria. Gloria is younger than Elizabeth. Michelle is older than Elizabeth but younger than Mary. Writer the four names in order, starting with the name of the oldest person.

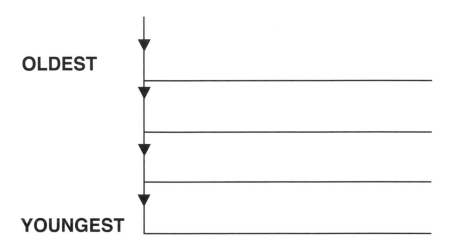

OLDEST

YOUNGEST

H-123   Three houses are in a row. One is modern, one is colonial, and one is Victorian. The colonial house is north of the modern house and south of the Victorian house. List the houses in order from north to south.

NORTH _____, _____, _____, **SOUTH**

H-124   Christine, Eric, Jesse, John, and Taryn are in line at the movie. Taryn is in front of Eric but behind John. Christine is behind Eric but in front of Jesse. List the children in order from front to rear.

FRONT   **REAR**

_____, _____, _____, _____, _____,

TRANSITIVITY—COMPARISON

DIRECTIONS: In these sentences, events are being compared according to their occurrence. Arrange the events in order of occurrence from earliest to latest.

H-125   John Quincy Adams, the sixth president of the United States, was the son of John Adams, the second president. John Adams became president after two terms as vice president during the presidency of George Washington. Thomas Jefferson followed John Adams as president.

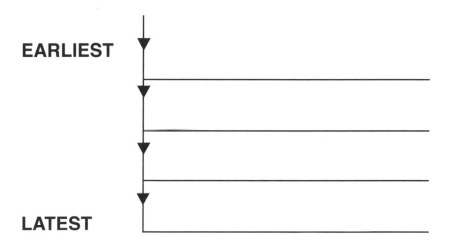

H-126   The oldest permanent European settlement in the United States is St. Augustine, Florida. Plymouth, Massachusetts, was settled thirteen years after the Jamestown, Virginia, colony. List these historic cities in the order they were settled.

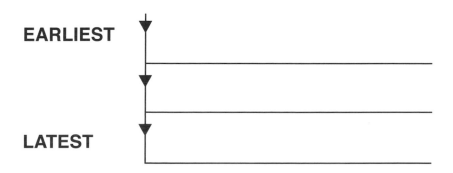

TRANSITIVITY—COMPARISON

DIRECTIONS: In these sentences, events are being compared according to their occurrence. Arrange the events in order of occurrence from earliest to latest.

H-127 Number these sentences in order of occurrence from the earliest to the latest. Use the time line to keep track of the time order.

_____ a. Between eighteen months and two years, a baby begins to speak in sentences.

_____ b. One of a newborn baby's first skills is grasping objects or toys.

_____ c. The infant begins to crawl when it is about six months old.

_____ d. Soon after a baby's first birthday, the child begins to use words.

EVENTS IN INFANT'S LIFE

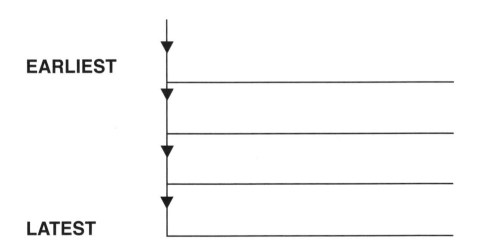

EARLIEST

LATEST

TRANSITIVITY—COMPARISON

DIRECTIONS: In these sentences, events are being compared according to their occurrence. Arrange the events in order of occurrence from earliest to latest.

H-128   Number these sentences in order of occurrence from the earliest to the latest. Use the time line to keep track of the time order.

_____   a. Bob Keeshan played Captain Kangaroo on the *Captain Kangaroo Show.*

_____   b. Before playing Captain Kangaroo, Bob Keeshan played Clarabelle the Clown on the *Howdy Doody Show.*

_____   c. After the success of *Sesame Street*, Children's Television Workshop developed *The Electric Company*.

_____   d. Recognizing the educational benefits of the *Captain Kangaroo Show*, Children's Television Workshop produced *Sesame Street* to emphasize learning concepts for young children.

List these children's television shows from the earliest to the latest.

CHILDREN'S TELEVISION SHOWS

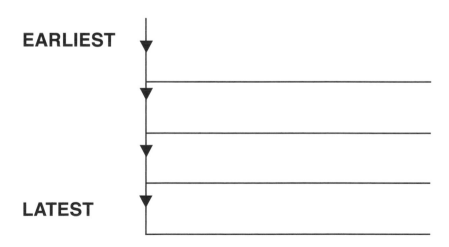

EARLIEST

LATEST

COMMON SEQUENCES

DIRECTIONS: Many things you do must be done in order. List the phrases in the order they should occur.

H-129   Steps in Taking a Photograph

Click the shutter
Focus the camera
Find the subject in the lens
Print the picture
Turn the camera on

1. _____

2. _____

3. _____

4. _____

5. _____

H-130   Steps in Making a Phone Call

Dial area code
Dial seven digit number
Hang up
Look up number
Talk

1. _____

2. _____

3. _____

4. _____

5. _____

COMMON SEQUENCES

DIRECTIONS: Many things you do must be done in order. List the phrases in the order they should occur.

H-131   Steps in Planning a Candy Sale

Buy the materials to make candy
Cook the candy
Decide on the type of candy you will make
Find a recipe for the candy
Package the candy
Sell the candy

1. _____

2. _____

3. _____

4. _____

5. _____

6. _____

H-132   Steps in Adopting a Dog

Ask your parents if you can have a dog
Go to the animal shelter with your family
Pay for the license and adoption fee
Pick out the dog
Take the dog home
Talk with your family about the kind of dog that is best for the family

1. _____

2. _____

3. _____

4. _____

5. _____

6. _____

TRANSITIVITY—FAMILY TREE

Family tree diagrams are used to show relationships between generations in a family. By using symbols, the diagram helps you organize relationships between

husband and wife

parent and child

sister and brother

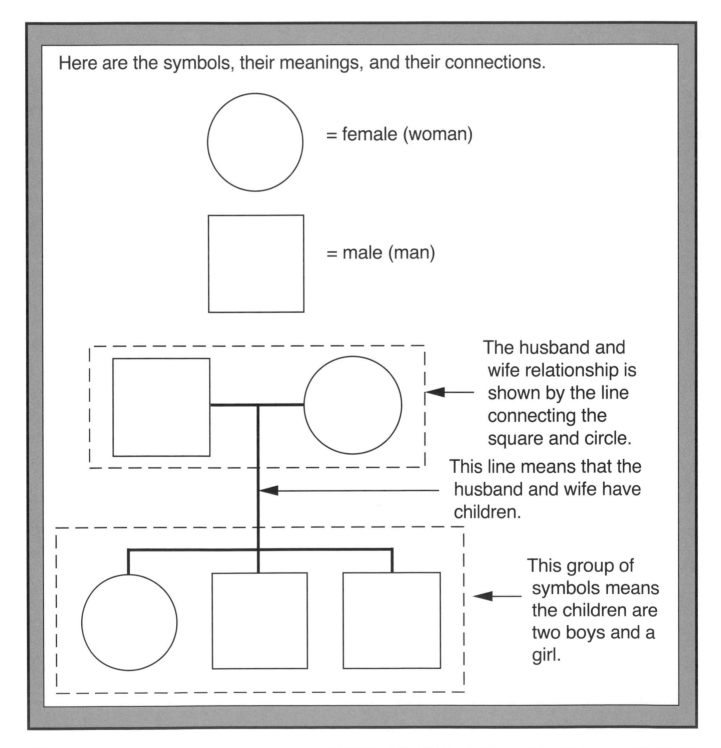

Here are the symbols, their meanings, and their connections.

= female (woman)

= male (man)

The husband and wife relationship is shown by the line connecting the square and circle.

This line means that the husband and wife have children.

This group of symbols means the children are two boys and a girl.

TRANSITIVITY—FAMILY TREE

DIRECTIONS: In the family tree diagram below, circles represent females and squares represent males. Use the clues fo fill in the diagram.

CLUES

Juan and Rosita have the same names as their grandparents. Marie has the same name as her mother.

One of Jose's daughters has the same name as Jose's mother.

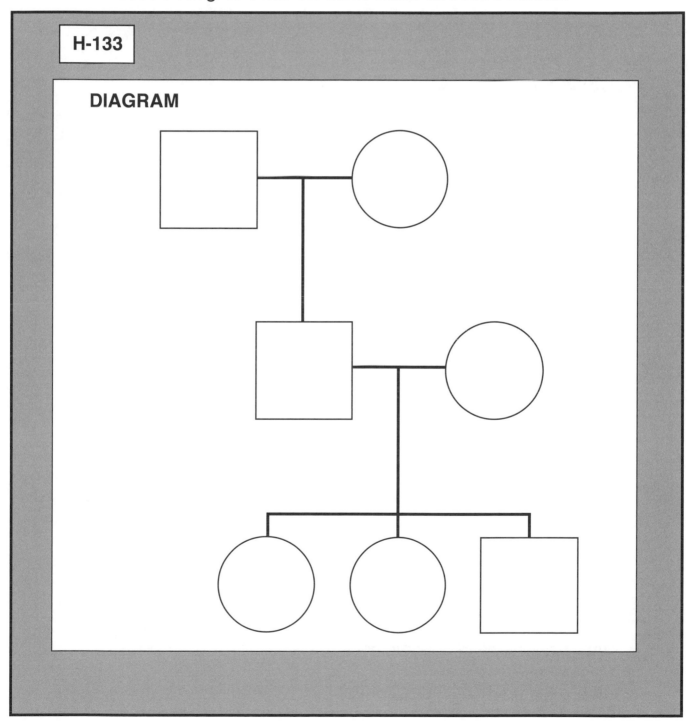

H-133

DIAGRAM

TRANSITIVITY—FAMILY TREE

DIRECTIONS: In the family tree diagram below, circles represent females and squares represent males. Use the clues fo fill in the diagram.

CLUES

Jim is the father of Bill and Mary.

Jane is Mary's sister.

Helen is Mary's mother.

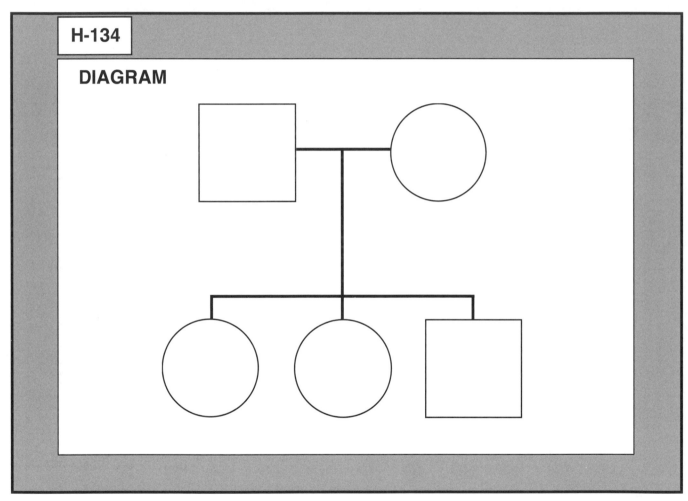

H-134

DIAGRAM

QUESTIONS

1. What is the name of Jim's wife? _____

2. What is the name of Jane's brother? _____

3. What is the name of Bill's mother? _____

4. What is the name of Jane's father? _____

TRANSITIVITY—FAMILY TREE

DIRECTIONS: In the family tree diagram below, circles represent females and squares represent males. Use the clues fo fill in the diagram.

CLUES
Michael and Irene Cooper have two children.
The children are named for Michael's father and Irene's mother.
The grandparents are Frank and Ruth Brown, and John and Bonnie Cooper.

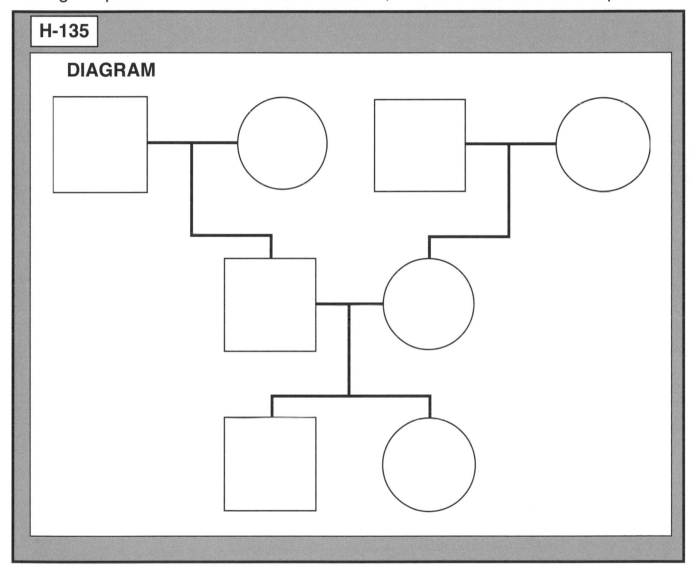

H-135

DIAGRAM

QUESTIONS

1. What was Irene's name before she got married?

_____

2. What are the names of Michael and Irene's children?

_____

255

YOUR FAMILY TREE

DIRECTIONS: Write the first and last names of a member of your family in each square or circle. If all your sisters and brothers won't fit on the row beside your name, add their names to the row below.

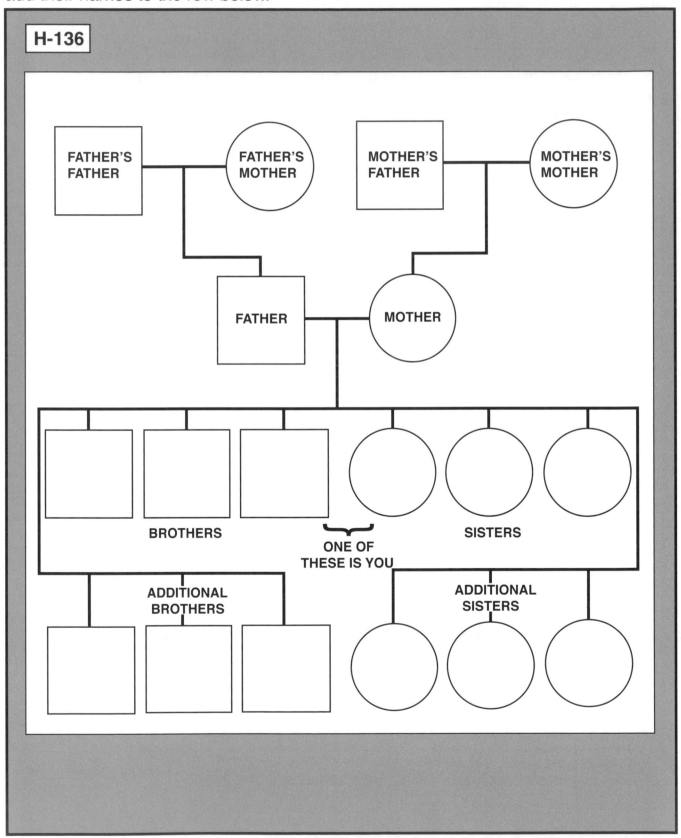

DEDUCTIVE REASONING—INSTRUCTIONS

A Mind Benders® problem asks you to match items with their characteristics. Making a matrix helps you work the problem. Here is a *Mind Benders®* problem involving three people and their pets.

EXAMPLE

Michael, Sarah, and Tina own a cat, a goldfish, and a parakeet. From the clues below, match the pet owner's names with the pets.

> **a.** Tina is allergic to animal fur.
>
> **b.** Michael's pet does not use kitty litter or live in a cage.

STEP 1   From the clue "Tina is allergic to animal fur," you can figure out that Tina does not own the cat. Find the row marked T for Tina and write "NO" in the column marked *C* for cat.

	C	G	P
M			
S			
T	NO		

STEP 2   The second clue, "Michael's pet does not use kitty litter or live in a cage," tells you that Michael does not own a cat or a bird. Find the row marked *M* for Michael and write "NO" in both the *C* column for cat and the *P* column for parakeet.

	C	G	P
M	NO		NO
S			
T	NO		

STEP 3   You know that each person owns a pet. Since neither Michael nor Tina owns the cat, Sarah must be the cat owner. Write "YES" in the *S* row for Sarah and the *C* column for cat.

	C	G	P
M	NO		NO
S	YES		
T	NO		

DEDUCTIVE REASONING—INSTRUCTIONS

STEP 4   Since Sarah owns the cat, Sarah does not own the goldfish or the parakeet. Write "NO" in the *S* row in both the *G* column for goldfish and the *P* column for parakeet.

	C	G	P
M	NO		NO
S	YES	NO	NO
T	NO		

STEP 5   By the same kind of reasoning, you see that the only vacancy in the *M* row is in the *G* column (for goldfish). From this, you figure out (deduce) that Michael is the goldfish owner. Write a "YES" in this position.

	C	G	P
M	NO	YES	NO
S	YES	NO	NO
T	NO		

STEP 6   Since Michael owns the goldfish, then neither Sarah nor Tina own the goldfish. You have already figured out (deduced) that Sarah doesn't own the goldfish. Now you know that Tina doesn't either. Mark "NO" in the *T* row and the *G* column.

	C	G	P
M	NO	YES	NO
S	YES	NO	NO
T	NO	NO	

STEP 7   The only vacancy remaining on the chart is in the T row and the P column. You now know that Tina is the parakeet owner. You are now ready to fill in the answers:

Sarah is the cat owner.

Michael is the goldfish owner.

Tina is the parakeet owner.

DEDUCTIVE REASONING

H-137 In looking up her family tree, Mrs. Bradford found that members of her family had been born in Bourne, Dartmouth, and Salem. Her ancestors' names were Abraham, James, and Nathaniel. From the clues below, match the names with the places of birth.

a. Nathaniel was older than James.

b. Abraham's mother and father came from Europe and settled in Salem just before he was born.

c. The youngest Bradford was born in Dartmouth.

	Abraham	James	Nathaniel
Bourne			
Dartmouth			
Salem			

Abraham was born in

_____ .

James was born in

_____ .

Nathaniel was born in

_____ .

H-138 Onju, Pedro, and Richard are all in different grades at school. The children are either in the third, fourth, or fifth grade. From the clues below, match the children with their grade.

a. Pedro and Onju are not in the third grade.

b. Onju is in a higher grade than Pedro.

	3rd	4th	5th
Onju			
Pedro			
Richard			

Onju is in _____ grade.

Pedro is in _____ grade.

Richard is in _____ grade.

DEDUCTIVE REASONING

H-139   A mouse, a rabbit, and a tiger are called Cicero, Ego, and Fred. From the clues below, match the name with the animal.

    a. Ego is larger than a mouse.

    b. Cicero is older than the rabbit but younger than the tiger.

    c. Fred is older than Cicero.

	Mouse	Rabbit	Tiger
Cicero			
Ego			
Fred			

Cicero is the _____.

Ego is the _____.

Fred is the _____.

H-140   David, Hector, and Maria are on different teams. They are each either on the baseball team, the football team, or the swimming team. From the clues below, match the students with their teams.

    a. Maria can't swim.

    b. David is better at swimming than Hector.

    c. Hector is the quarterback on his team.

	Baseball	Football	Swimming
D			
H			
M			

David is on the _____ team.

Hector is on the _____ team.

Maria is on the _____ team.

DEDUCTIVE REASONING

H-141   Anita, Beth, and Juan are a cook, a nurse, and a typist. From the clues below, match each person with their job.

a. Juan cannot type.

b. Anita is neither the nurse nor the typist.

	Cook	Nurse	Typist
A			
B			
J			

Anita is the _____.

Beth is the _____.

Juan is the _____.

H-142   Mr. Allen, Mr. Franklin, Ms. Smith, and Mrs. Townsend teach either first grade, second grade, third grade, or art. From the clues below, match each teacher with his or her class.

a. Mr. Allen does not teach reading or arithmetic.

b. Mr. Smith teaches a lower grade than Mrs. Townsend but a higher grade than Mr. Franklin.

	1st	2nd	3rd	Art
A				
F				
S				
T				

Mr. Allen is the _____ teacher.

Mr. Franklin is the _____ teacher.

Ms. Smith is the _____ teacher.

Mrs. Townsend is the _____ teacher.

DEDUCTIVE REASONING

H-143   George, Nancy, and Shannon are an astronaut, a computer programmer, and a mathematics teacher. From the clues below, match the people with their professions.

a. George is neither the astronaut nor the computer programmer.

b. Nancy is not the astronaut.

	George	Nancy	Shannon
A			
CP			
MT			

George is the _____ .

Nancy is the _____ .

Shannon is the _____ .

H-144   Three race car drivers named Graham, Mario, and Pancho entered cars in a 24-hour race, and each won a prize. From the clues below, determine who drove each car and what prize was won by each driver.

a. The coupe won a higher prize than Mario's car.

b. Mario did not drive the Spyder.

c. A hatchback won a prize.

d. Graham's car won first prize.

e. The Spyder came in second.

	Coupe	Hatch-back	Spyder
Graham			
Mario			
Pancho			

Place	Car	Driver
First		
Second		
Third		

DEDUCTIVE REASONING

H-145   Bob, Chris, Nancy, and Pat have different colored bikes. The bikes are red, blue, green, and white. From the clues below, match the bikes with the owners.

    a. Bob and Chris have ten-speed bikes.

    b. Chris's friend has a blue bike.

    c. Nancy has a three-speed and is a friend of the owner of the white bike.

    d. Nancy sometimes rides her brother's blue ten-speed bike.

    e. Pat does not like his friend's green bike.

    f. The red bike has one speed.

	Bob	Chris	Nancy	Pat
Red				
Blue				
Green				
White				

	Axe	Hammer	Pliers	Saw
Bill				
Jane				
Kim				
Tom				

Diagram for problem **H-146** below.

H-146   Bill, Jane, Kim, and Tom brought an axe, a hammer, a pair of pliers, and a saw to build a project at school. From the clues below, match the students with the tools. (Use the diagram above on the right.)

    a. Neither Bill nor the girl with the pliers brought the hammer.

    b. Jane couldn't find a cutting tool.

    c. Kim brought her mom's hammer.

    d. Bill lost his axe after the project started.

DEDUCTIVE REASONING

H-147   In science class, students learn the eating habits of several types of animals. Some animals eat meat and others eat plants. Some animals eat both plants and animals. Some animals eat plankton. For her science project, Marisa picked four animals of different sizes and studied their eating habits. From the clues below, match the eating habits with the sizes of the four animals. The animal sizes can be described as small, medium, large, and very large.

a. The large animal is neither a meat eater nor a plankton eater.

b. The medium-sized animal is larger than the plankton eater.

c. The meat eater is larger than the plant eater.

d. The plant eater is the largest animal.

	Meat	Plant	Meat & Plant	Plankton
Small				
Medium				
Large				
Very Large				

FOLLOWING YES—NO RULES—A

DIRECTIONS: Darken the correct circles along the path from START to FINISH by following the YES-NO rule.

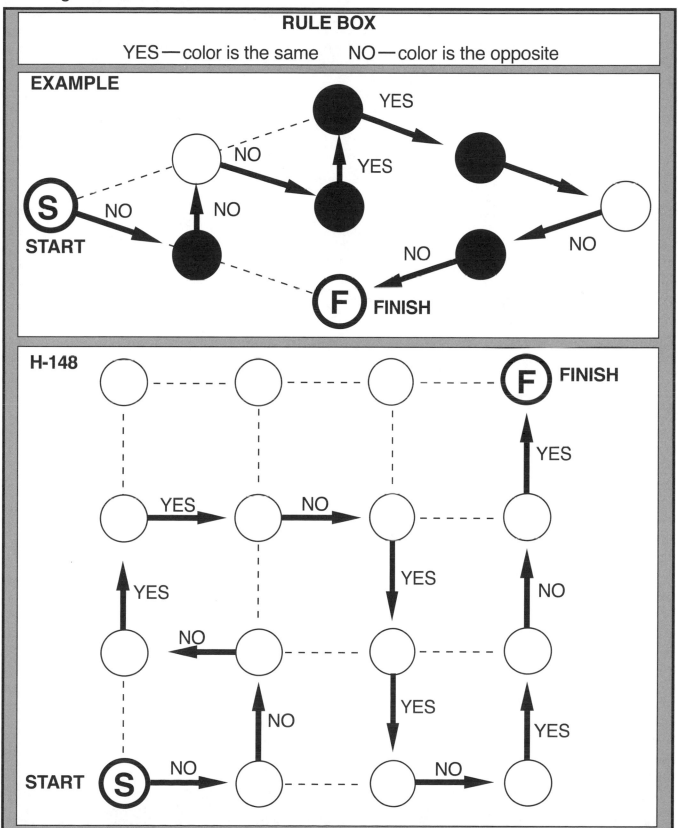

RULE BOX

YES—color is the same   NO—color is the opposite

EXAMPLE

H-148

FOLLOWING YES—NO RULES—A

DIRECTIONS: Darken the correct circles along the path from START to FINISH by following the YES-NO rule.

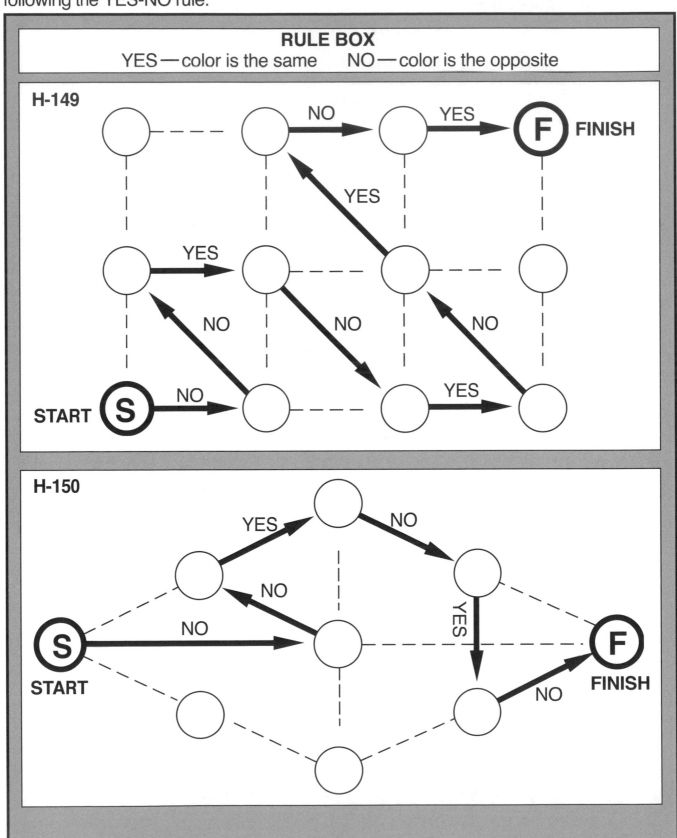

FOLLOWING YES—NO RULES—B

DIRECTIONS: Follow the arrows from START to FINISH. In the box near each arrow, write "YES" or "NO" according to the YES-NO rule.

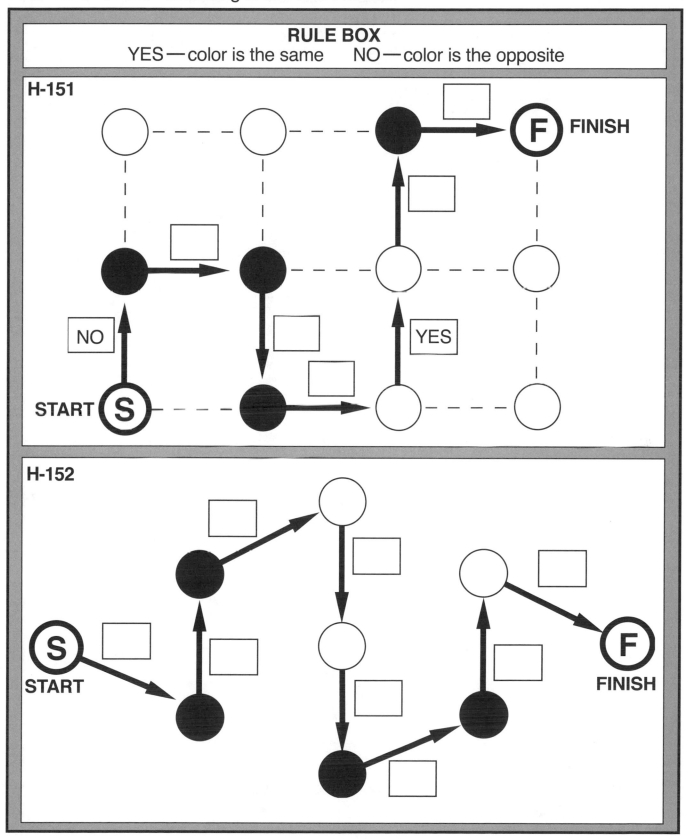

RULE BOX
YES — color is the same   NO — color is the opposite

FOLLOWING YES—NO RULES—B

DIRECTIONS: Follow the arrows from START to FINISH. In the box near each arrow write "YES" or "NO" according to the YES-NO rule.

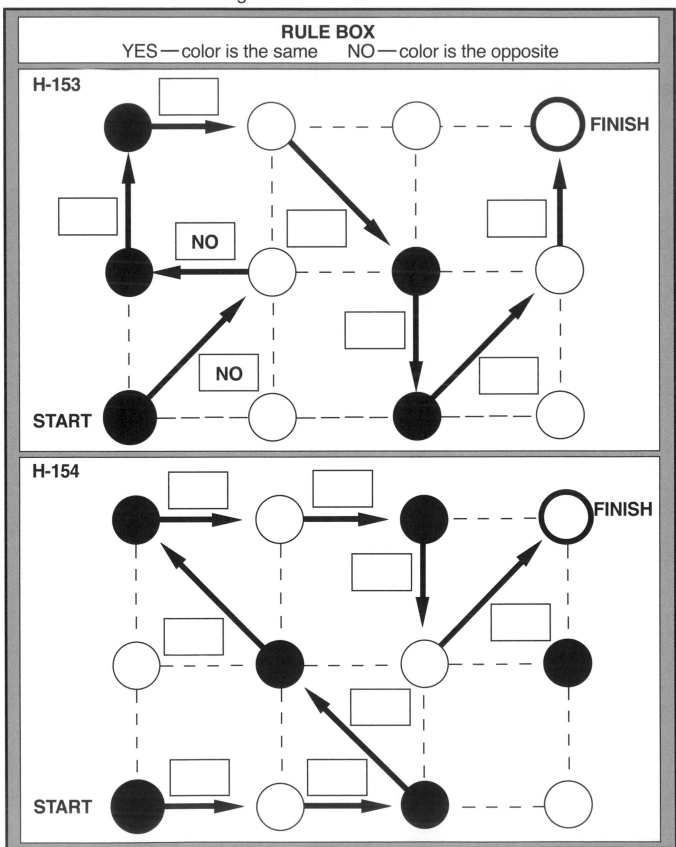

WRITING YES—NO RULES

DIRECTIONS: In each exercise below, there are three paths from START to FINISH. One path is dotted ○○○, one path is solid ——— , and one path is dashed — — — . Supply the rule for each path.

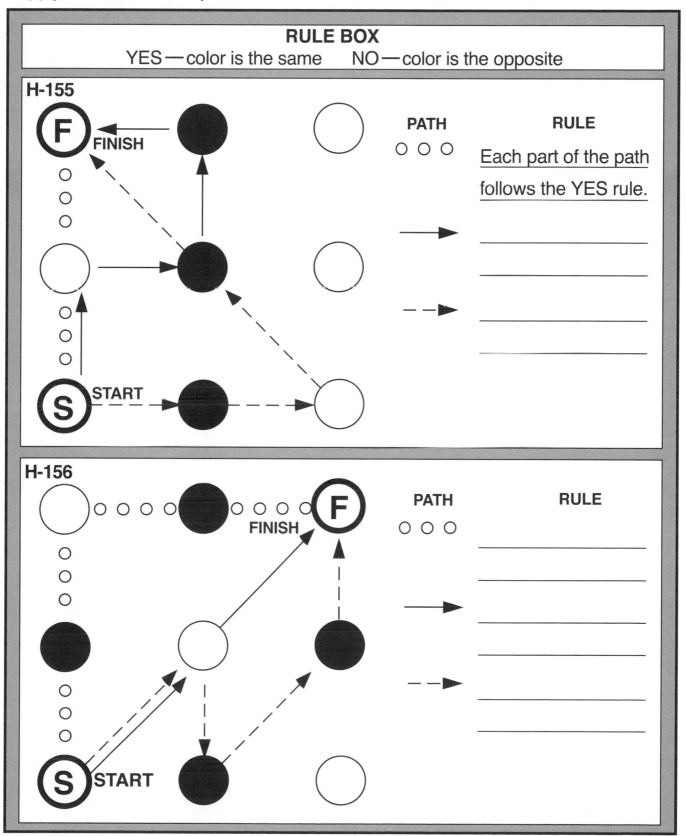

RULE BOX

YES—color is the same   NO—color is the opposite

H-155

PATH   ○ ○ ○

RULE

Each part of the path follows the YES rule.

H-156

PATH   ○ ○ ○

RULE

FOLLOWING YES—NO RULES—SUPPLY

DIRECTIONS: Two blank grids are provided for you to make up your own YES-NO exercises. Trade your exercises with a classmate.

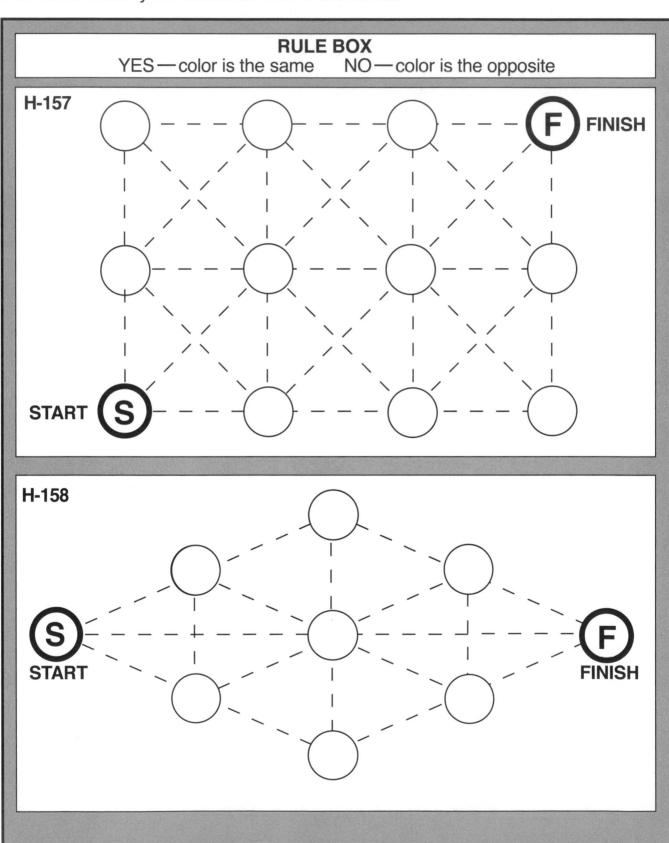

COMPLETING TRUE—FALSE TABLES

DIRECTIONS: After reading the example, complete the TRUE-FALSE table below.

This group of shapes will be used to produce TRUE-FALSE tables.

EXAMPLE of a completed TRUE-FALSE table.

	IT IS STRIPED	IT IS CHECKED	IT IS SQUARE
(striped square)	TRUE	FALSE	TRUE
(checked square)	FALSE	TRUE	TRUE
(checked circle)	FALSE	TRUE	FALSE

H-159 Complete the following table.

	IT IS BLACK	IT IS STRIPED	IT IS CHECKED	IT IS SQUARE
(black square)	TRUE	FALSE	FALSE	TRUE
(striped square)				
(checked square)				
(black circle)				
(striped circle)				
(checked circle)				

COMPLETING TRUE—FALSE TABLES

DIRECTIONS: Complete the TRUE-FALSE tables below.

This group of shapes will be used to produce TRUE-FALSE tables.

H-160 Complete the following table.

	IT IS BLACK	IT IS STRIPED	IT IS NOT BLACK
△	FALSE	FALSE	TRUE
⊘ (striped circle)			
■ (black square)			

H-161 Complete the following table.

	IT IS BLACK	IT IS STRIPED	IT IS NOT BLACK	IT IS NOT STRIPED
△	FALSE	FALSE	TRUE	TRUE
⊘ (striped circle)		TRUE		
▨ (striped square)	FALSE			
● (black circle)			FALSE	
■ (black square)				TRUE
△				TRUE

FOLLOWING IF—THEN RULES

DIRECTIONS: From the group of shapes, circle the shapes that follow the rule.

EXAMPLE
RULE: If the shape is a square, then it is white.

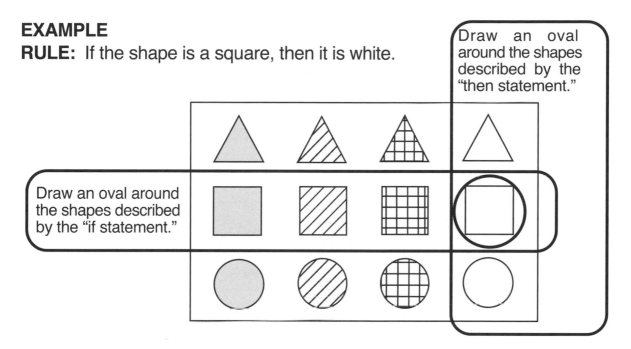

The phrase "if the shape is a square" means that only squares are being considered by the rule. Draw an oval around the row of squares.

The phrase "then it is white" means that only white shapes follow the rule. Draw an oval around the column of white shapes. There is only one shape, the white square, that follows the rule. Notice that it is enclosed by both the "if-oval" and the "then-oval."

Draw a circle around the white square to show that it follows the rule. It follows the "if" part of the rule because it is a square, and it follows the "then" part because it is white.

H-162 RULE: If the shape is a circle, then it is gray.

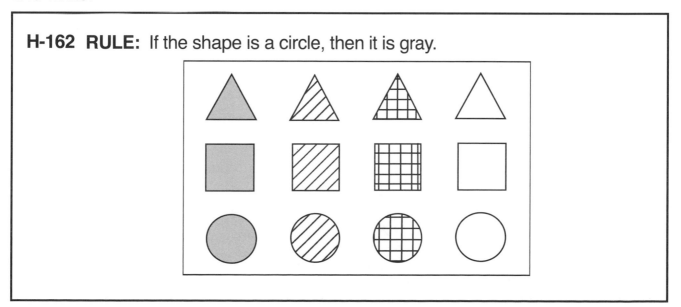

273

FOLLOWING IF—THEN RULES—A

DIRECTIONS: From the group of shapes, circle the shapes that follow the rule.

H-163 RULE: If the shape is white, then it is a square.

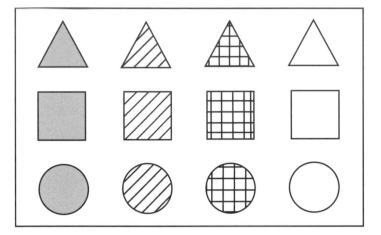

H-164 RULE: If the shape is striped, then it is a triangle.

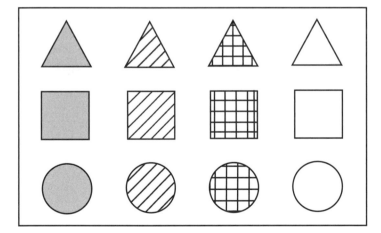

H-165 RULE: If the shape is checked, then it is a circle.

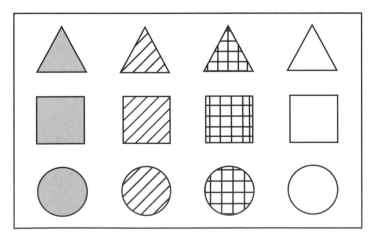

FOLLOWING IF—THEN RULES—A

DIRECTIONS: From the group of shapes, circle the shapes that follow the rule.

H-166 RULE: If the shape is a triangle, then it is striped.

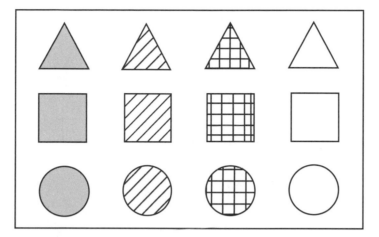

H-167 RULE: If the shape is striped, then it is a square.

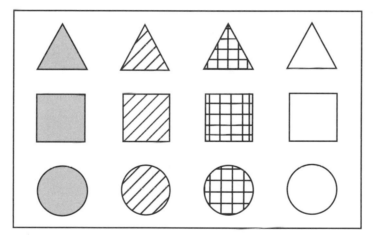

H-168 RULE: If the shape is not striped, then it is a circle.

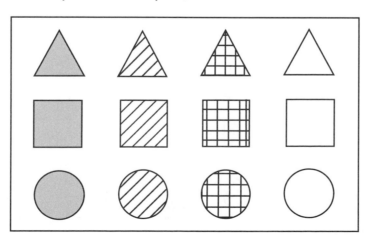

275

FOLLOWING IF—THEN RULES—A

DIRECTIONS: From the group of shapes, circle the shapes that follow the rule.

H-169 RULE: If the shape is a square, then it is checked.

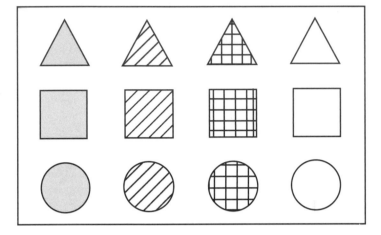

H-170 RULE: If the shape is not a square, then it is striped.

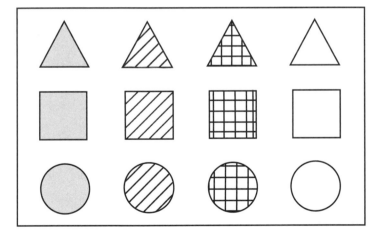

H-171 RULE: If the shape is not a square, then it is not white.

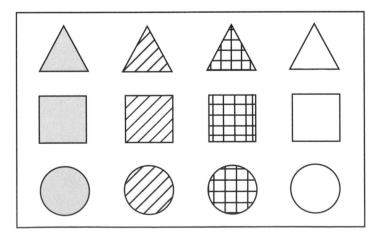

FOLLOWING IF—THEN RULES—B

DIRECTIONS: Decide which groups of shapes (1, 2, 3, 4) fit the rule.

H-172
RULE: If the shape is checked, then it is a square.

1.
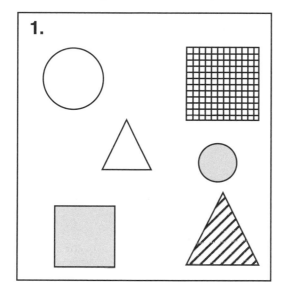

2.
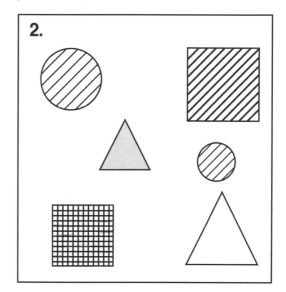

3.
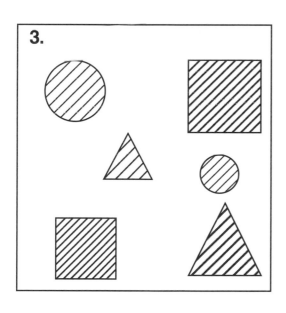

4.
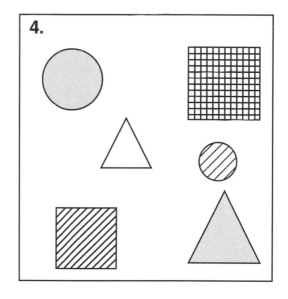

Shapes in groups _____ fit the rule.

REASONS _____

_____

FOLLOWING IF—THEN RULES—B

DIRECTIONS: Decide which groups of shapes (1, 2, 3, 4) fit the rule.

H-173
RULE: If the shape is a circle, then it is striped.

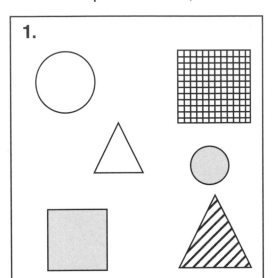

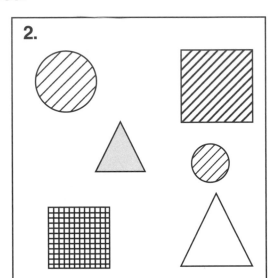

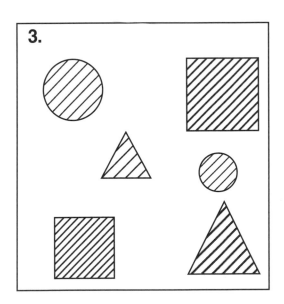

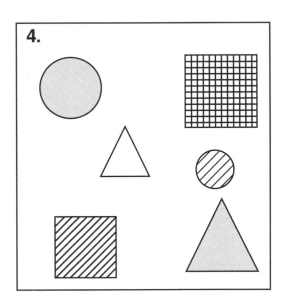

Shapes in groups _____ fit the rule.

REASONS _____

_____

FOLLOWING IF—THEN RULES—B

DIRECTIONS: Mark the unshaded shapes so that each group fits the rule.

H-174 RULE: If the shape is a triangle, then it is striped.

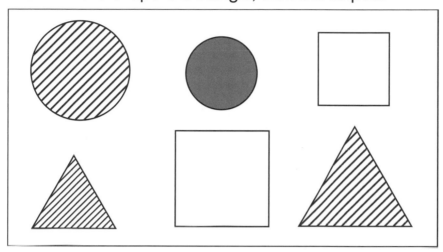

H-175 RULE: If the shape is striped, then it is a triangle.

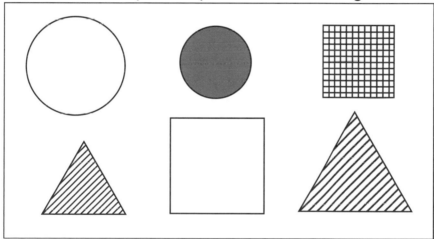

H-176 In exercise **H-174**, can you have
a) a striped circle? _____ or b) a checked square? _____
REASONS _____
_____

H-177 In exercise **H-175**, can you have
a) a striped circle? _____ or b) a checked square? _____
REASONS _____
_____

FOLLOWING IF—THEN RULES—B

DIRECTIONS: Mark the shapes so that all of them fit the rule.

H-178 RULE: If the shape is a square, then it is checked.

H-179 RULE: If the shape is checked, then it is a square.

H-180 In exercise **H-178,** can you have
a) a checked triangle? _____ or b) a striped square? _____

REASONS _____

_____

H-181 In exercise **H-179**, can you have
a) a checked triangle? _____ or b) a striped square? _____

REASONS _____

_____

GRAPHIC ORGANIZER—CYCLE DIAGRAM

DIRECTIONS: Many sequences in nature repeat. They are called *cycles*. Use the sentences in the choice box to show the food chain cycle. Write each step in the correct box.

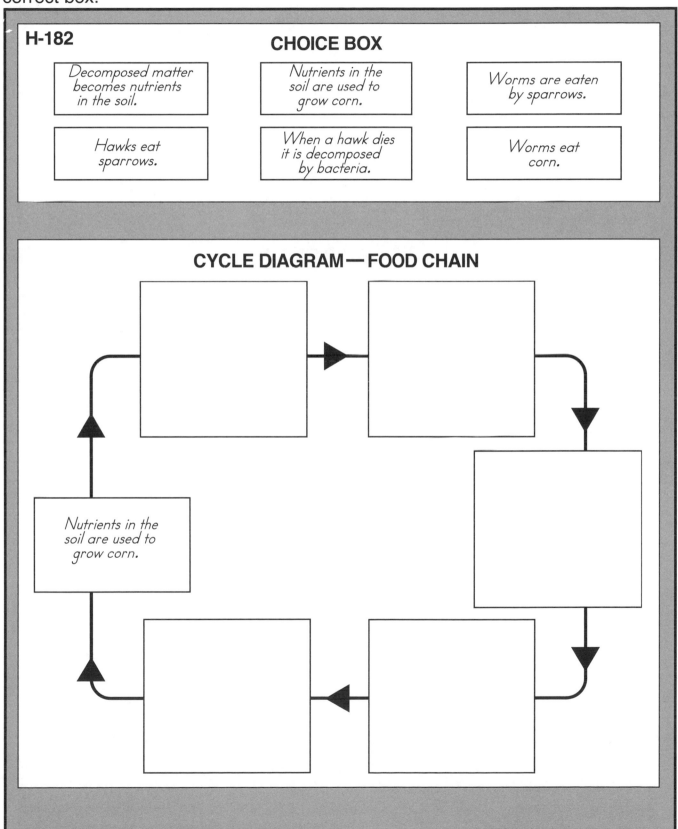

H-182

CHOICE BOX

Decomposed matter becomes nutrients in the soil.	Nutrients in the soil are used to grow corn.	Worms are eaten by sparrows.
Hawks eat sparrows.	When a hawk dies it is decomposed by bacteria.	Worms eat corn.

CYCLE DIAGRAM—FOOD CHAIN

Nutrients in the soil are used to grow corn.

GRAPHIC ORGANIZER—CYCLE DIAGRAM

DIRECTIONS: Many sequences in nature repeat. They are called *cycles*. Use the sentences in the choice box to show the water cycle. Write each step in the correct box.

H-183

CHOICE BOX

Clouds form when the water vapor reaches a sufficient amount.	Energy from the sun causes water to evaporate from bodies of water.	Runoff water collects in streams, lakes, and oceans.
Clouds grow in size until they become saturated.	Rain falls from the saturated clouds.	Water vapor rises into the atmosphere.

THE WATER CYCLE

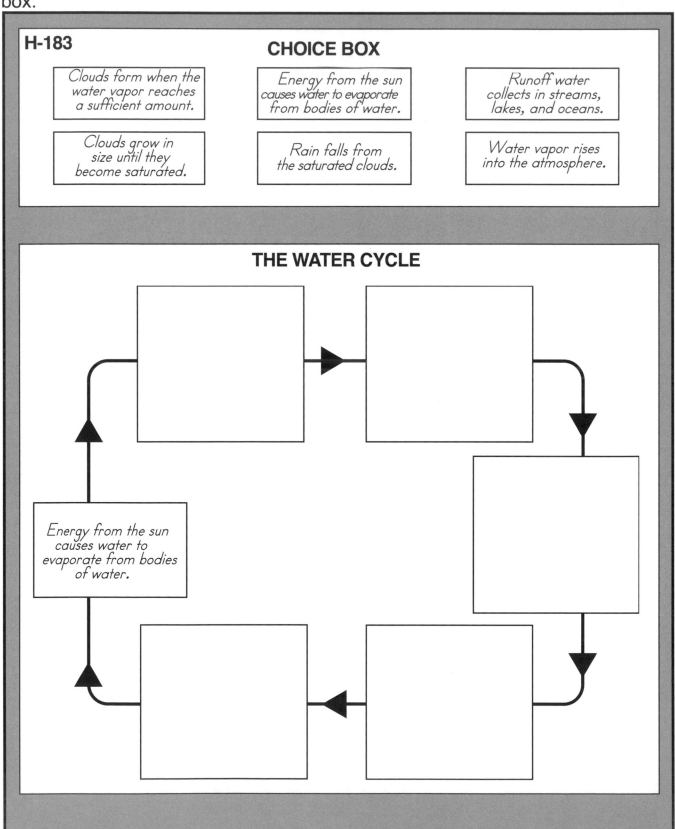

Energy from the sun causes water to evaporate from bodies of water.

GRAPHIC ORGANIZER—CYCLE DIAGRAM

DIRECTIONS: Many sequences in nature repeat. They are called *cycles*. Use the sentences in the choice box to show the flow of blood in the human body. Write each step in the correct box.

H-184

CHOICE BOX

Arteries deliver blood to the organs of the body.	Oxygen−poor blood is enriched with oxygen in the lungs.	The heart pumps blood out a major artery.
Organs of the body take food and/or oxygen from the blood.	Oxygen−rich blood is returned to the heart.	Veins return oxygen−poor blood to the lungs.

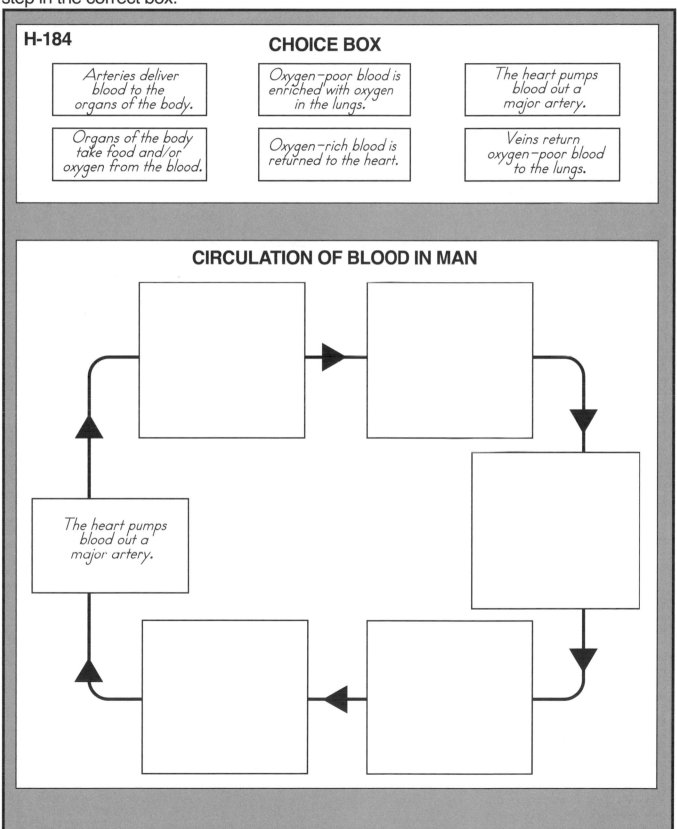

CIRCULATION OF BLOOD IN MAN

The heart pumps blood out a major artery.

GRAPHIC ORGANIZER—TIMELINE

DIRECTIONS: Using the list on the left, mark each president's term of office in its correct chronological order on the timeline at the right. Remember to count the spaces.

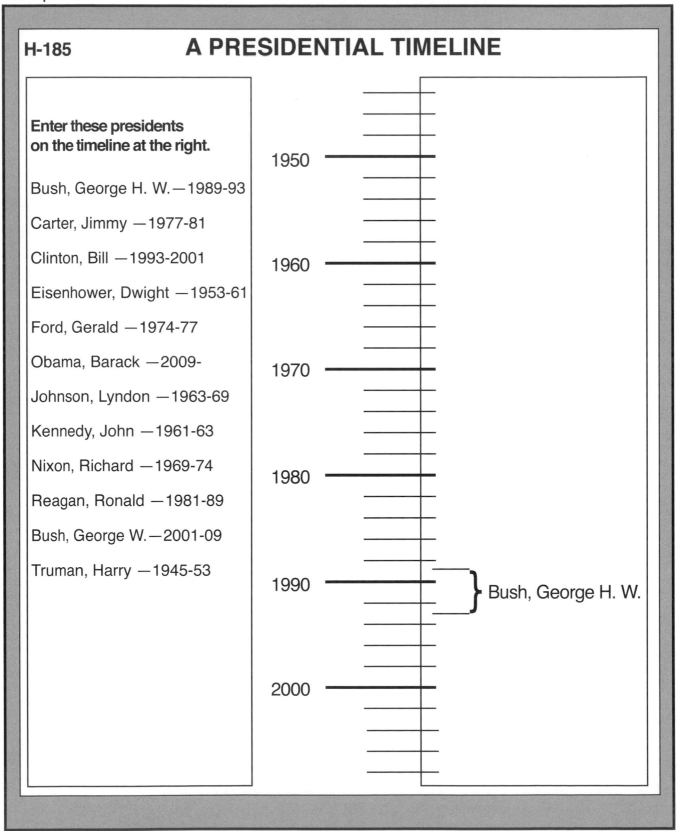

H-185

A PRESIDENTIAL TIMELINE

Enter these presidents on the timeline at the right.

Bush, George H. W.—1989-93

Carter, Jimmy —1977-81

Clinton, Bill —1993-2001

Eisenhower, Dwight —1953-61

Ford, Gerald —1974-77

Obama, Barack —2009-

Johnson, Lyndon —1963-69

Kennedy, John —1961-63

Nixon, Richard —1969-74

Reagan, Ronald —1981-89

Bush, George W.—2001-09

Truman, Harry —1945-53

1950

1960

1970

1980

1990 } Bush, George H. W.

2000

GRAPHIC ORGANIZER—TIMELINE

DIRECTIONS: Using the list on the left, mark each war in its correct chronological order on the timeline at the right. Remember to count the spaces.

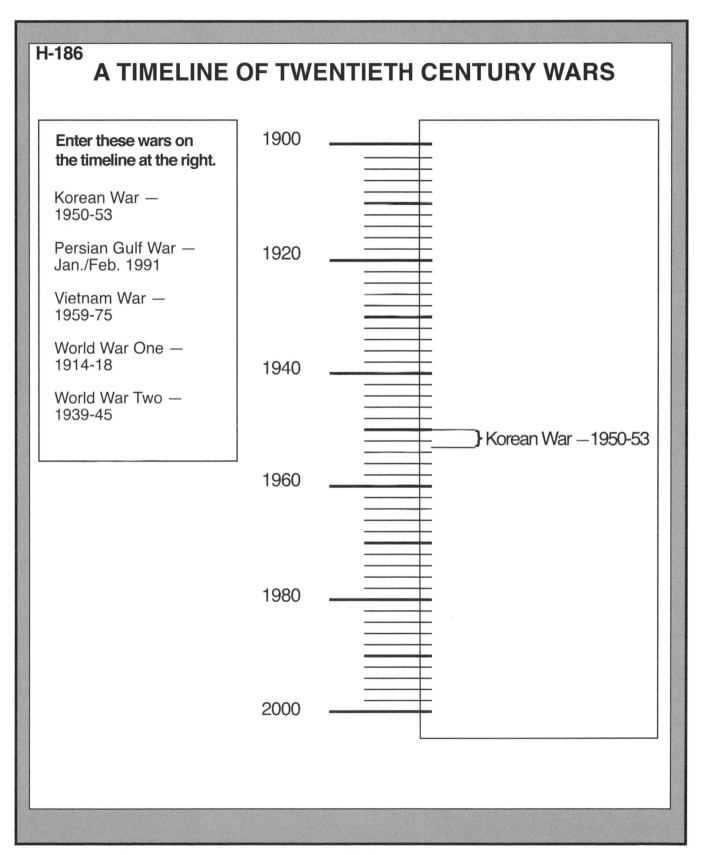

H-186

A TIMELINE OF TWENTIETH CENTURY WARS

Enter these wars on the timeline at the right.

Korean War — 1950-53

Persian Gulf War — Jan./Feb. 1991

Vietnam War — 1959-75

World War One — 1914-18

World War Two — 1939-45

1900

1920

1940

} Korean War — 1950-53

1960

1980

2000

CHAPTER NINE

Describing Shapes	→	Describing Things
Figural Similarities and Differences	→	Verbal Similarities and Differences
Figural Sequences	→	Verbal Sequences
Figural Classifications	→	Verbal Classifications
Figural Analogies	→	Verbal Analogies

PARTS OF A WHOLE—SELECT

DIRECTIONS: On each line are four words from language arts lessons. Read the words and decide which word represents a whole thing and which words are parts of the whole thing. On the lines below each group, write the word that represents the whole thing, then list the words that are its parts.

EXAMPLE: closing, greeting, letter, signature

The words represent parts of a letter that you might write to a friend. The WHOLE is the letter and the PARTS are the greeting, the closing, and the signature.

WHOLE _____*letter*_____ PARTS _____*greeting*_____ , _____*closing*_____ , _____*signature*_____

I-1 book, chapter, index, table of contents

WHOLE_____ PARTS_____ , _____ , _____

I-2 comics, editorial, newspaper, sports

WHOLE_____ PARTS_____ , _____ , _____

I-3 books, card file, library, shelves

WHOLE_____ PARTS_____ , _____ , _____

I-4 argument, debate, rebuttal, statement of proposition

WHOLE_____ PARTS_____ , _____ , _____

I-5 advertisements, articles, magazine, photographs

WHOLE_____ PARTS_____ , _____ , _____

PARTS OF A WHOLE—SELECT

DIRECTIONS: On each line are four words from social studies lessons. Read the words and decide which word represents a whole thing and which words are parts of the whole thing. On the lines below each group, write the word that represents the whole thing, then list the words that are its parts.

I-6   alleys, block, buildings, streets

WHOLE_____ PARTS_____, _____, _____

I-7   churches, homes, neighborhood, schools

WHOLE_____ PARTS_____, _____, _____

I-8   city, downtown, neighborhood, suburb

WHOLE_____ PARTS_____, _____, _____

I-9   cities, county, rural areas, towns

WHOLE_____ PARTS_____, _____, _____

I-10 cities, counties, state, townships

WHOLE_____ PARTS_____, _____, _____

I-11 forests, mountains, nation, rivers

WHOLE_____ PARTS_____, _____, _____

I-12 continents, atmosphere, Earth, oceans

WHOLE_____ PARTS_____, _____, _____

PARTS OF A WHOLE—SELECT

DIRECTIONS: On each line are four words from science lessons. Read the words and decide which word represents a whole thing and which words are parts of the whole thing. On the lines below each group first write the word that represents the whole thing, then list the words that are parts of the whole thing.

I-13 leaves, plant, root, stem

WHOLE_____ PARTS_____, _____, _____

I-14 backbone, brain, heart, mammal

WHOLE_____ PARTS_____, _____, _____

I-15 blossom, bulb, stem, tulip

WHOLE_____ PARTS_____, _____, _____

I-16 fruit, pulp, seeds, skin

WHOLE_____ PARTS_____, _____, _____

I-17 antennae, insect, jointed legs, segmented abdomen

WHOLE_____ PARTS_____, _____, _____

I-18 backbone, fish, gills, scales

WHOLE_____ PARTS_____, _____, _____

I-19 beak, bird, feathers, wings

WHOLE_____ PARTS_____, _____, _____

CLASS AND MEMBERS—SELECT

DIRECTIONS: On each line are four words from language arts lessons. Read the words and decide which word represents the class to which the other words belong. On the lines below each group, write the word that represents the class, then list the words that are members of that class.

I-20   drama, fiction, novel, short story

CLASS _____ MEMBERS_____, _____, _____

I-21   autobiographies, diaries, journals, personal histories

CLASS _____ MEMBERS_____, _____, _____

I-22   a, an, articles, the

CLASS _____ MEMBERS_____, _____, _____

I-23   exclamations, questions, sentences, statements

CLASS _____ MEMBERS_____, _____, _____

I-24   figures of speech, metaphors, personification, similes

CLASS_____ MEMBERS_____, _____, _____

I-25   adjectives, adverbs, nouns, parts of speech

CLASS _____ MEMBERS_____, _____, _____

I-26   almanac, atlas, dictionary, reference book

CLASS _____ MEMBERS_____, _____, _____

CLASS AND MEMBERS—SELECT

DIRECTIONS: On each line are four words from social studies lessons. Read the words and decide which word represents the class to which the other words belong. On the lines below each group, write the word that represents the class, then list the words that are members of that class.

I-27 appliances, clothing, food, goods

CLASS _____ MEMBERS_____, _____, _____

I-28 kings, leaders, presidents, prime ministers

CLASS _____ MEMBERS_____, _____, _____

I-29 city, federal, government, state

CLASS _____ MEMBERS_____, _____, _____

I-30 economics, geography, history, social sciences

CLASS_____ MEMBERS_____, _____, _____

I-31 elementary, high, middle, school

CLASS_____ MEMBERS_____, _____, _____

I-32 cleaning, repairing, protecting, service

CLASS_____ MEMBERS_____, _____, _____

I-33 democracy, government, monarchy, republic

CLASS_____ MEMBERS_____, _____, _____

CLASS AND MEMBERS—SELECT

DIRECTIONS: On each line are four words from science lessons. Read the words and decide which word represents the class to which the other words belong. On the lines below each group, write the word that represents the class, then list the words that are members of that class.

I-34 corn, grain, oats, wheat

CLASS _____ MEMBERS_____, _____, _____

I-35 ape, mammal, man, whale

CLASS _____ MEMBERS_____, _____, _____

I-36 daisy, flower, rose, tulip

CLASS _____ MEMBERS_____, _____, _____

I-37 apple, banana, fruit, pear

CLASS _____ MEMBERS_____, _____, _____

I-38 beetle, fly, grasshopper, insect

CLASS_____ MEMBERS_____, _____, _____

I-39 fish, guppy, perch, trout

CLASS _____ MEMBERS_____, _____, _____

I-40 bird, heron, penguin, sandpiper

CLASS _____ MEMBERS_____, _____, _____

SENTENCES CONTAINING CLASSES AND SUBCLASSES

DIRECTIONS: In each sentence there are three words that name members of a class. Underline these words. Inside each box, write the words in order from most general class to the most specific class. The general class (1) will contain the less general class (2) and the most specific class (3). Write the most general class on line (1), the less general class on line (2), and the most specific class on line (3).

EXAMPLE   The <u>orange</u> is a popular <u>citrus fruit</u>. "Fruit" is the most general class and belongs on line 1. "Citrus" is a kind of fruit and belongs on line 2. "Orange" is a kind of citrus fruit and belongs on line 3.

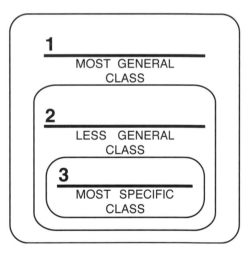

I-41   When asked to select a vegetable, Jan selected lima beans.

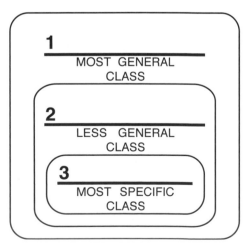

I-42   Yolanda went to the pastry shop to buy a cherry pie.

SENTENCES CONTAINING CLASSES AND SUBCLASSES

DIRECTIONS: In each sentence, underline three words that name members of a class. In each box, write the words in order from the most general class on line 1 to the most specific class on line 3.

I-43   Maria reads many kinds of books, but mysteries are her favorite kind of fiction.

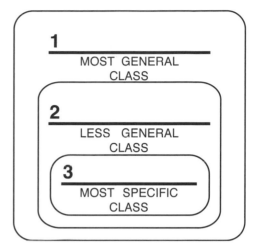

I-44   Raymond owns a camper-van recreational vehicle.

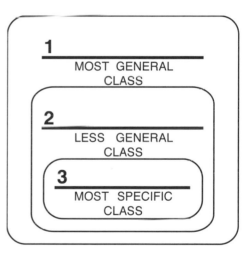

I-45   Mr. Baker went to the lumberyard and bought some pine boards.

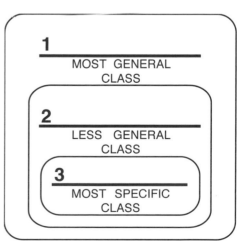

SENTENCES CONTAINING CLASSES AND SUBCLASSES

DIRECTIONS: In each sentence, underline three words that name members of a class. In each box, write the words in order from the most general class on line 1 to the most specific class on line 3.

I-46   A ladybug was the only beetle that Josh could find for his insect collection.

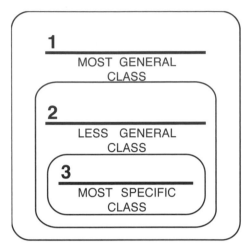

I-47   Mrs. Elledge used weed killer on her dandelion plants.

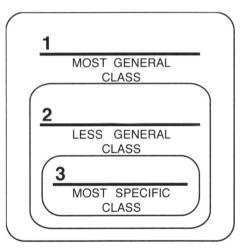

I-48   Some people think the black widow spider is an insect, but actually it is an arachnid.

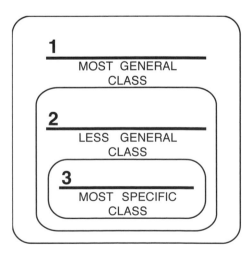

SENTENCES CONTAINING CLASSES AND SUBCLASSES

DIRECTIONS: In each sentence, underline three words that name members of a class. In each box, write the words in order from the most general class on line 1 to the most specific class on line 3.

I-49   The worker honeybee is the insect that produces honey.

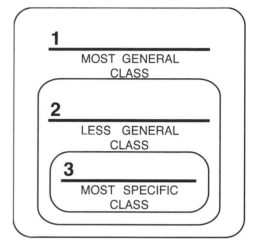

I-50   The Galapagos tortoise is a large reptile that lives on the land.

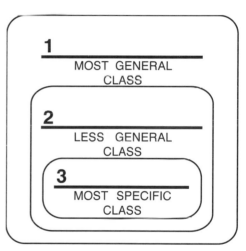

I-51   The heron is a beautiful wading bird found in the South.

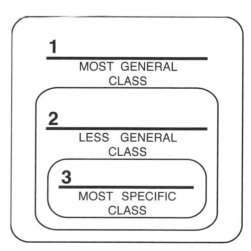

HOW ARE THESE WORDS ALIKE?—SELECT

DIRECTIONS: Circle the letter in front of the answer that **best** describes the class of words.

I-52 alarm, horn, siren

 a. bell
 b. safety
 c. warning

I-53 blotch, smear, stain

 a. blemish
 b. rip
 c. tear

I-54 different, odd, peculiar

 a. little
 b. strange
 c. weak

I-55 dollar, peso, pound

 a. coin
 b. money
 c. penny

I-56 aim, design, intend

 a. draw
 b. finish
 c. plan

I-57 grab, grasp, grip

 a. hit
 b. hold
 c. try

I-58 caution, slow, yield

 a. intersection
 b. stop light
 c. warning

HOW ARE THESE WORDS ALIKE?—SELECT

DIRECTIONS: Circle the letter in front of the answer that **best** describes the class of words.

I-59   border, hem, rim

    a. center
    b. edge
    c. part

I-60   even, level, planed

    a. rough
    b. slant
    c. smooth

I-61   fable, fairy tale, myth

    a. fact
    b. fiction
    c. history

I-62   clock, ruler, thermometer

    a. electrical devices
    b. measuring devices
    c. mechanical devices

I-63   fork, knife, spoon

    a. drawing tools
    b. kitchen tools
    c. woodworking tools

I-64   chisel, drill, saw

    a. drawing tools
    b. kitchen tools
    c. woodworking tools

I-65   compass, ruler, protractor

    a. drawing tools
    b. kitchen tools
    c. woodworking tools

HOW ARE THESE WORDS ALIKE?—SELECT

DIRECTIONS: Each exercise contains three words that belong to a common class. From the choice box, select the class that **best** describes each group of words and write it on the line. The words in the choice box may be used more than once.

CHOICE BOX
high, line, show

I-66   path, road, route,   _____

I-67   direct, guide, lead,   _____

I-68   big, soaring, tall,   _____

I-69   produce, put on, stage,   _____

I-70   business, job, work,   _____

I-71   film, movie, motion picture,   _____

I-72   piercing, sharp, shrill,   _____

I-73   disclose, discover, present,   _____

I-74   column, rank, row,   _____

I-75   costly, dear, expensive,   _____

I-76   indicate, read, register,   _____

I-77   display, offer, supply,   _____

HOW ARE THESE WORDS ALIKE?—SELECT

DIRECTIONS: Each exercise contains three words that belong to a common class. From the choice box, select the class that **best** describes each group of words and write it on the line. The words in the choice box may be used more than once.

CHOICE BOX
band, change, fair, spring

I-78   average, ordinary, plain,   _____

I-79   hop, leap, jump,   _____

I-80   swap, switch, trade,   _____

I-81   favorable, honest, just,   _____

I-82   club, team, troop,   _____

I-83   brook, season, wire coil,   _____

I-84   group, musicians, orchestra,   _____

I-85   shift, turn, vary,   _____

I-86   clear, light, sunny,   _____

I-87   belt, strip, stripe,   _____

I-88   coins, substitute, variety,   _____

I-89   display, entertainment, festival   _____

HOW ARE THESE WORDS ALIKE?—SELECT

DIRECTIONS: Each exercise contains three words that belong to a common class. From the choice box, select the class that **best** describes each group of words and write it on the line. The words in the choice box may be used more than once.

CHOICE BOX
flow, kind, party, pass

I-90   go, proceed, travel,   _____

I-91   band, crew, group,   _____

I-92   pour, spout, stream,   _____

I-93   beat, outdo, top,   _____

I-94   friendly, pleasant, tender,   _____

I-95   proceed, rise, spring,   _____

I-96   give, hand, reach,   _____

I-97   club, side, union,   _____

I-98   a throw, ticket, valley,   _____

I-99   current, flood, tide,   _____

I-100   class, sort, type,   _____

HOW ARE THESE NOUNS ALIKE?—EXPLAIN

DIRECTIONS: Each group of three nouns has a similar meaning. Explain how the nouns in each group are alike.

EXAMPLE: chalk, plaster, sugar

   These materials are all white powders.

I-101   claws, horns, tusks

_____

I-102   court, diamond, rink

_____

I-103   glare, gleam, ray

_____

I-104   cure, medication, remedy

_____

I-105   hush, quiet, still

_____

I-106   adornment, ornament, ribbon

_____

HOW ARE THESE VERBS ALIKE?—EXPLAIN

DIRECTIONS: Each group of three verbs has a similar meaning. Explain how the verbs in each group are alike.

I-107   ask, inquire, quiz

_____

I-108   float, glide, soar

_____

I-109   boil, evaporate, vaporize

_____

I-110   jog, sprint, dash

_____

I-111   mumble, murmur, whisper

_____

I-112   await, expect, hope

_____

I-113   blast, burst, explode

_____

HOW ARE THESE ADJECTIVES ALIKE?—EXPLAIN

DIRECTIONS: Each group of three adjectives has a similar meaning. Explain how the adjectives in each group are alike.

I-114   brave, fearless, gallant

_____

I-115   gentle, kind, tender

_____

I-116   gross, large, massive

_____

I-117   slender, slight, slim

_____

I-118   firm, sure, steady

_____

I-119   forceful, mighty, powerful

_____

I-120   passive, quiet, still

_____

HOW ARE THESE WEATHER WORDS ALIKE?—EXPLAIN

DIRECTIONS: Each group of three words describes a weather condition. Explain how the terms in each group are alike.

I-121   drizzle, shower, sprinkle

_____

I-122   nippy, chilly, cool

_____

I-123   bright, clear, cloudless

_____

I-124   blustery, breezy, gusty

_____

I-125   foggy, hazy, overcast

_____

I-126   damp, muggy, sticky

_____

I-127   cloudburst, downpour, thunderstorm

_____

EXPLAIN THE EXCEPTION

DIRECTIONS: Each group of four words contains one member that is an exception to the class. Explain how the similar words are alike and how the exception is different.

EXAMPLE: candle, eye, lamp, star

Candle, lamp, and star are similar because they give off light. Eye is the exception to the class "things that give off light." The eye receives light but does not give off light.

I-128   cloud, rain, snow, umbrella

_____

_____

_____

I-129   cabbage, corn, lettuce, spinach

_____

_____

_____

I-130   relax, rest, sleep, work

_____

_____

_____

I-131   hear, look, read, see

_____

_____

_____

EXPLAIN THE EXCEPTION

DIRECTIONS: Each group of four words contains one member that is an exception to the class. Explain how the similar words are alike and how the exception is different.

I-132 ice, iron, water, wood

_____

_____

_____

I-133 clams, crabs, minnows, snail

_____

_____

_____

I-134 bacon, beef, eggs, ham

_____

_____

_____

I-135   basket, bottle, can, jar

_____

_____

_____

I-136 button, pocket, snap, zipper

_____

_____

_____

EXPLAIN THE EXCEPTION

DIRECTIONS: Each group of four words contains one member that is an exception to the class. Explain how the similar words are alike and how the exception is different.

I-137 cartoons, newscast, situation comedy, soap opera

_____

_____

_____

I-138 clock, ruler, tape measure, yardstick

_____

_____

_____

I-139 flute, trumpet, tuba, violin

_____

_____

_____

I-140 automobile, bicycle, motorcycle, truck

_____

_____

_____

I-141 bottle, cup, mug, strainer

_____

_____

_____

SORTING INTO CLASSES

DIRECTIONS: Sort the following words into two classes: those which suggest happiness and those which suggest sadness.

I-142	CHOICE BOX	
	cheerless, content, delighted, discouraged, dismal, displeased, dreary, fortunate, groaning, joyous, lucky, miserable, satisfied, sorrowful, successful	
HAPPY		**SAD**

SORTING INTO CLASSES

DIRECTIONS: Sort the following words into the categories of people, places, and things.

I-143	CHOICE BOX	
actor, airport, beach, bicycle, book, captain, computer, crew, doctor, factory, friend, garden, house, newspaper, nurse, office, pilot, school, station, stove, teacher, television, vegetable, zoo		
PEOPLE	**PLACES**	**THINGS**

SORTING INTO CLASSES

DIRECTIONS: Sort the following list of words into groups of words that tell who, when, or where.

I-144	CHOICE BOX	
all, always, anybody, anyone, downstairs, downtown, early, everybody, everyone, far away, inside, in town, later, long ago, nearby, never, next door, nobody, no one, now, outside, some, somebody, someone, sometimes, sooner, today, tomorrow, upstairs, uptown, yesterday		
WHO	**WHEN**	**WHERE**

SORTING INTO CLASSES

DIRECTIONS: Sort the following animals into the categories of birds, forest animals, and water animals. Animals may belong in more than one category.

I-145	CHOICE BOX	
beaver, chipmunk, cougar, dolphin, eagle, eel, frog, heron, loon, moose, ostrich, owl, pelican, penguin, porpoise, raccoon, shark, sloth, weasel, whale		
BIRDS	**FOREST ANIMALS**	**WATER ANIMALS**
_____	_____	_____
_____	_____	_____
_____	_____	_____
_____	_____	_____
_____	_____	_____
_____	_____	_____
_____	_____	_____
_____	_____	_____
_____	_____	_____
_____	_____	_____

BRANCHING DIAGRAMS

DIRECTIONS: Use the branching diagram below to classify recreational activities into sports and games. The sports can be divided into team or individual sports. Games may be described as table games or movement games.

I-146	RECREATIONAL ACTIVITIES
	baseball, checkers, chess, football, golf, gymnastics, hockey, hopscotch, jump rope, soccer, skating, skiing, tag

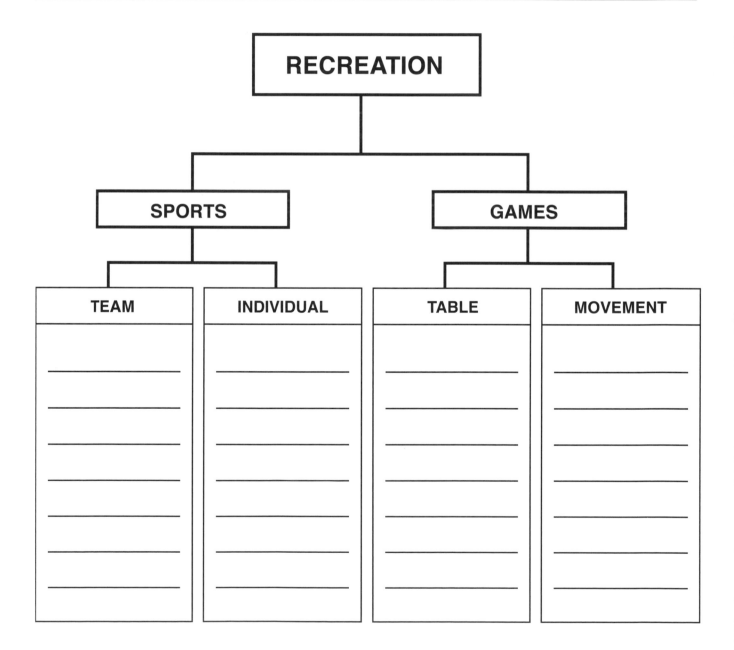

BRANCHING DIAGRAMS

DIRECTIONS: On the next page there is a branching diagram that can be used to classify living things into large subclasses of plants and animals. These subclasses can be further subdivided into smaller groups.

I-147   Use the diagram on the next page to classify the following living things.

ant	elephant	potato
bean	horse	robin
bee	maple	rose
butterfly	minnow	shark
carrot	oak	tulip
cat	ostrich	tuna
chicken	pine	violet

BRANCHING DIAGRAM FOR EXERCISE I-147

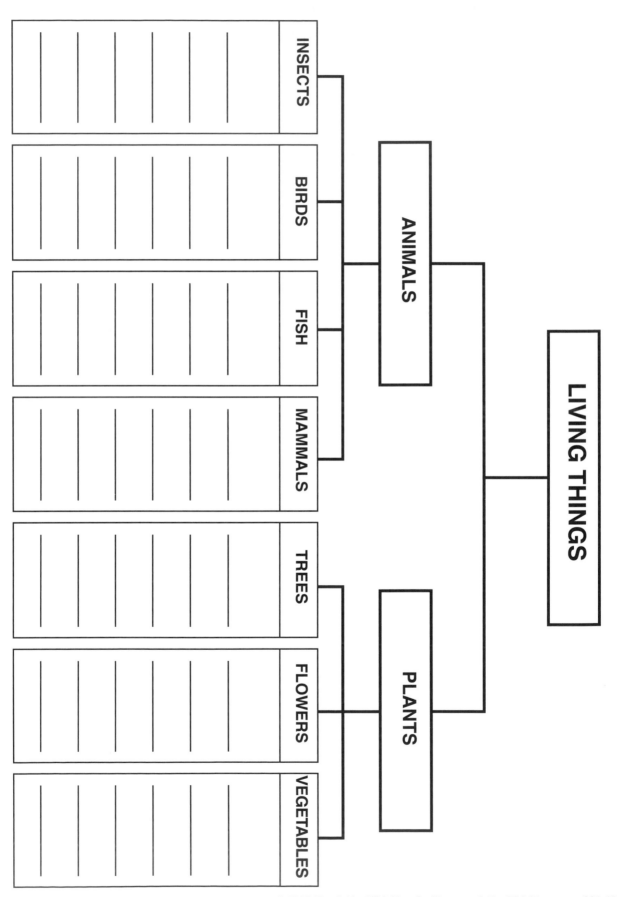

DIAGRAMMING CLASSES—THREE EXAMPLES

EXAMPLE 1: bicycles, trucks, vehicles

The first diagram pictures two distinctly different classes within a common class. The large circle represents vehicles. The smaller circles represent bicycles and trucks.

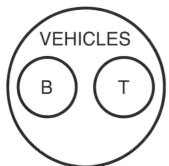

A bicycle is a kind of vehicle, and a truck is a kind of vehicle. However, no truck is a bicycle.

B = bicycles
T = trucks

EXAMPLE 2: truck, van, vehicles

The second diagram pictures a class-subclass relationship. All of the items in one class are members of a larger class.

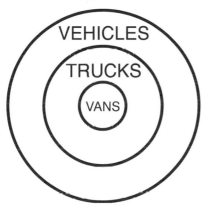

A truck is a kind of vehicle, and a van is a kind of truck. The smaller circle representing trucks is inside the large circle representing vehicles. The smallest circle representing vans is inside the circle representing trucks because all vans are trucks.

EXAMPLE 3: bicycles, mopeds, motorcycles, vehicles

Is there a form of bicycle that is also a form of motorcycle?

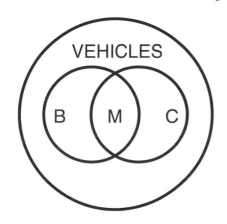

A moped can be operated by peddling like a bicycle. A moped can also be powered by its engine like a motorcycle. This relationship can be shown by an overlapping diagram like this one.

B = bicycles
C = motorcycles
M = mopeds

DIAGRAMMING CLASSES—SELECT

DIRECTIONS: Select the diagram that correctly pictures the way each word group can be classified. Put an "X" through the diagram that cannot be used for this group of words. Label the parts of the correct diagram to show the word relationship.

I-148   Word group: coins (c), coins for collecting (cc), coins for spending (cs)

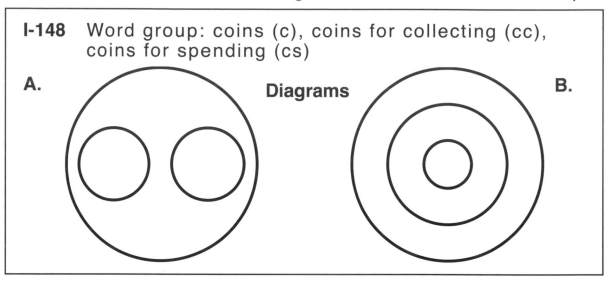

1-149   Word group: coins (c), dimes (d), money (m)

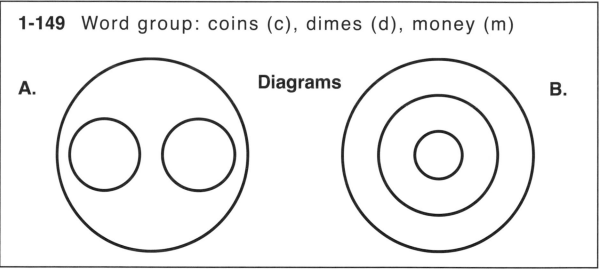

1-150   Word group: coins (c), dollar bills (db), money (m)

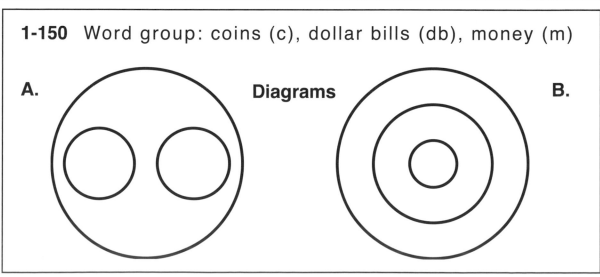

DIAGRAMMING CLASSES—SELECT

DIRECTIONS: Draw a line from the group of words to the diagram that pictures the correct relationship. Use the abbreviation in the parentheses to label the diagrams correctly.

WORD GROUPS

I-151

Food (Fo)

Food that grows on vines (Fv)

Fruit (Fr)

Fruit that grows on vines (Frv)

I-152

Food (Fo)

Fruit (Fr)

Oranges (O)

I-153

Food (Fo)

Fruit (Fr)

Vegetables (V)

DIAGRAMS

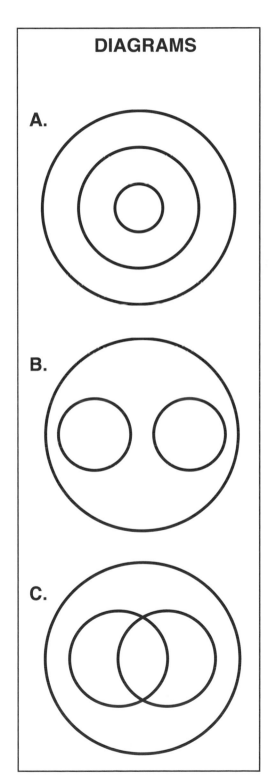

A.

B.

C.

DIAGRAMMING CLASSES—SELECT

DIRECTIONS: Draw a line from the group of words to the diagram that pictures the correct relationship. Use the abbreviation in the parentheses to label the diagrams correctly.

WORD GROUPS

I-154

Birds (B)

Chickens (C)

Ducks (D)

I-155

Birds (B)

Ducks (D)

Wild Birds (WB)

I-156

Birds (B)

Chickens (C)

Hens (H)

DIAGRAMS

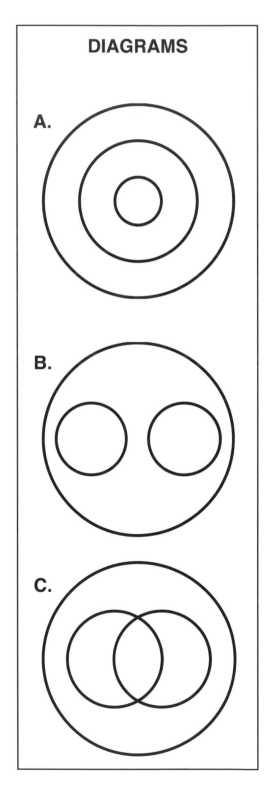

A.

B.

C.

DIAGRAMMING CLASSES—SELECT

DIRECTIONS: Draw a line from the group of words to the diagram that pictures the correct relationship. Use the abbreviation in the parentheses to label the diagrams correctly.

WORD GROUPS

I-157

Fathers (F)

Mothers (M)

Parents (P)

I-158

Female Teachers (FT)

Mothers (M)

Women (W)

I-159

Mothers (M)

People (P)

Women (W)

DIAGRAMS

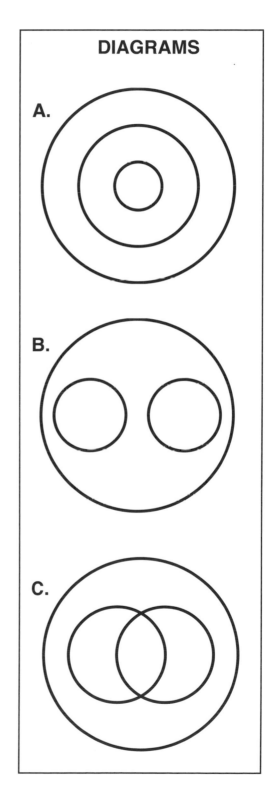

A.

B.

C.

DIAGRAMMING CLASSES—SELECT AND EXPLAIN

DIRECTIONS: In these exercises, you are to describe the relationship between two groups of household items and then pick the diagram that describes this relationship. Use the abbreviations in the parentheses to label the diagram correctly. You may use one of the following phrases to fill in the blank in the sentence describing the classes.

includes, is included in, overlaps, is separate from

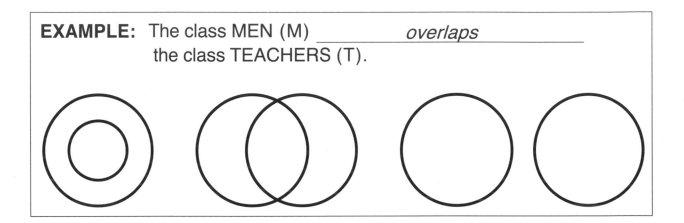

EXAMPLE: The class MEN (M) _____ *overlaps* _____
the class TEACHERS (T).

Some men are teachers and some teachers are men, thus the class MEN overlaps the class TEACHERS. This means that the second diagram fits. The overlapping part, or intersection, represents MEN TEACHERS.

If the first diagram is tried with T in the outer circle, it would mean that all men are teachers, which is not true. If the first diagram is tried with M in the outer circle, it would mean that all teachers are men, which is not true. The first diagram does not fit these classes.

If the last diagram is used with M in one circle and T in the other, it would mean that no men are teachers, which is not true. The last diagram does not fit these classes.

DIAGRAMMING CLASSES—SELECT AND EXPLAIN

DIRECTIONS: Describe the relationships between two groups of household items and then pick the diagram that describes this relationship. Use the abbreviations in the parentheses to label the diagram correctly. You may use one of the following phrases to fill in the blank in the sentence describing the classes.

includes, is included in, overlaps, or *is separate from*

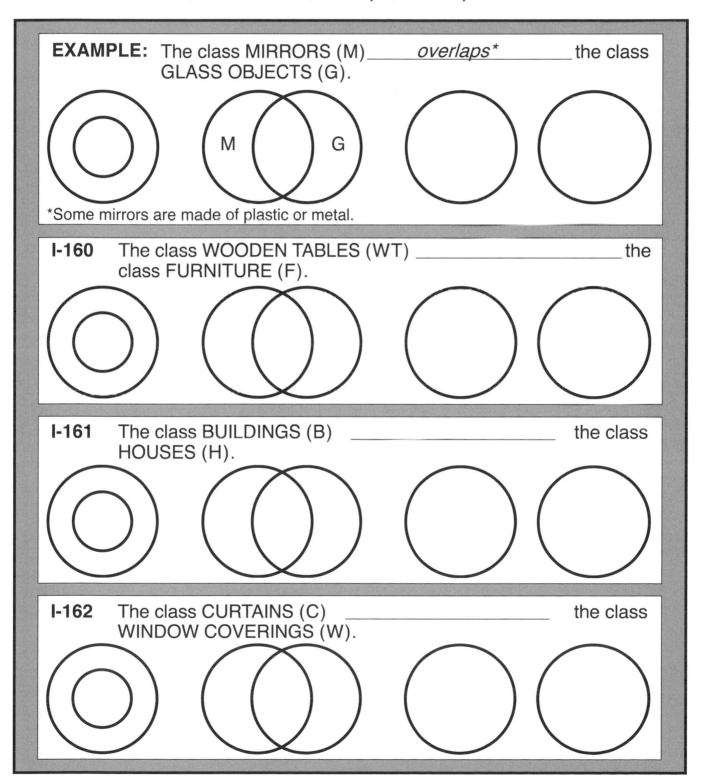

EXAMPLE: The class MIRRORS (M) _____*overlaps**_____ the class GLASS OBJECTS (G).

*Some mirrors are made of plastic or metal.

I-160 The class WOODEN TABLES (WT) _____ the class FURNITURE (F).

I-161 The class BUILDINGS (B) _____ the class HOUSES (H).

I-162 The class CURTAINS (C) _____ the class WINDOW COVERINGS (W).

DIAGRAMMING CLASSES—SELECT AND EXPLAIN

DIRECTIONS: Describe the relationship between two classes of life science terms and then pick the diagram that describes this relationship. Use the abbreviations in the parentheses to label the diagram correctly. You may use one of the following phrases to fill in the blank in the sentence describing the classes.

includes, is included in, overlaps, or *is separate from*

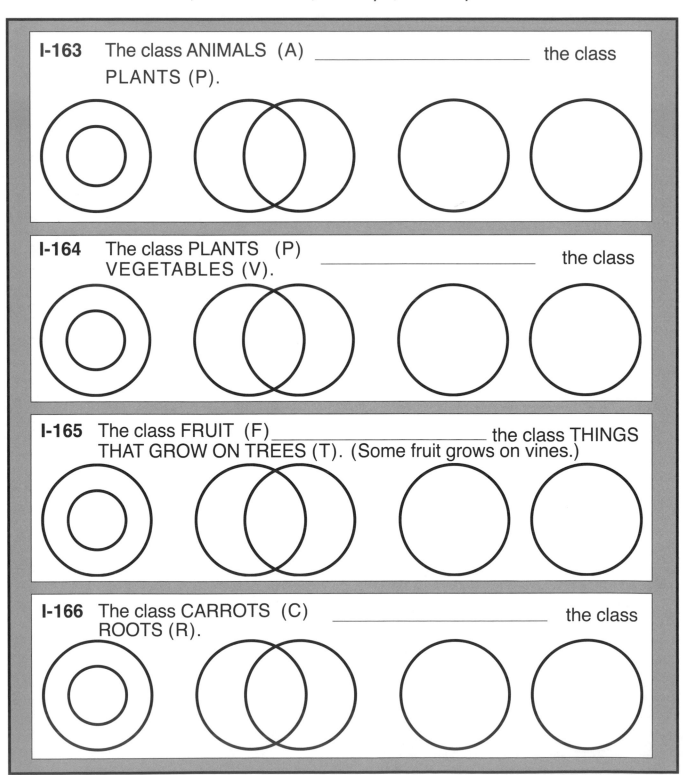

I-163   The class ANIMALS (A) _____ the class PLANTS (P).

I-164   The class PLANTS (P) _____ the class VEGETABLES (V).

I-165   The class FRUIT (F) _____ the class THINGS THAT GROW ON TREES (T). (Some fruit grows on vines.)

I-166   The class CARROTS (C) _____ the class ROOTS (R).

DIAGRAMMING CLASSES—SELECT AND EXPLAIN

DIRECTIONS: Describe the relationship between two classes of earth science terms and then pick the diagram that describes this relationship. Use the abbreviations in the parentheses to label the diagram correctly. You may use one of the following phrases to fill in the blank in the sentence describing the classes.

includes, is included in, overlaps, or *is separate from*

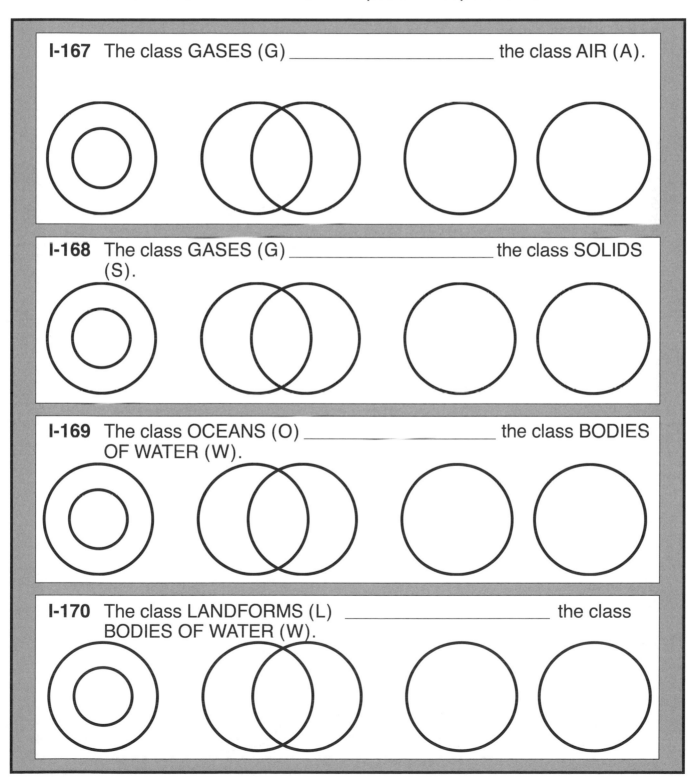

I-167   The class GASES (G) _____ the class AIR (A).

I-168   The class GASES (G) _____ the class SOLIDS (S).

I-169   The class OCEANS (O) _____ the class BODIES OF WATER (W).

I-170   The class LANDFORMS (L) _____ the class BODIES OF WATER (W).

DIAGRAMMING CLASSES—SELECT AND EXPLAIN

DIRECTIONS: Describe the relationship between two classes of geometry terms and then pick the diagram that describes this relationship. Use the abbreviations in the parentheses to label the diagram correctly. You may use one of the following phrases to fill in the blank in the sentence describing the classes.

includes, is included in, overlaps, or *is separate from*

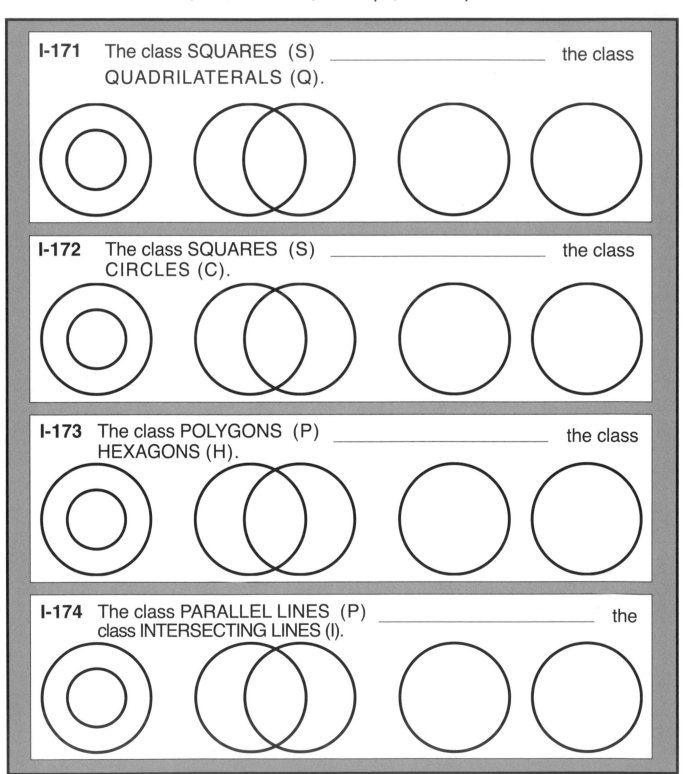

I-171   The class SQUARES (S) _____ the class QUADRILATERALS (Q).

I-172   The class SQUARES (S) _____ the class CIRCLES (C).

I-173   The class POLYGONS (P) _____ the class HEXAGONS (H).

I-174   The class PARALLEL LINES (P) _____ the class INTERSECTING LINES (I).

OVERLAPPING CLASSES—MATRIX

DIRECTIONS: If words or names can be described by two characteristics, a matrix diagram can be used to show that relationship. Each item must fit in the box that shows the characteristic of the row and the characteristic of the column.

Here is an exercise that illustrates the use of a matrix diagram.

I-175   At Wilson School, it is not possible for students to take both band and chorus, so the boys and girls in Ms. Robinson's class take either band or chorus. Fill in the following matrix diagram showing the music activities of Ms. Robinson's class.

STUDENT	ACTIVITY
Anne	Chorus
Bruce	Band
Carl	Band
Donna	Band
Harold	Chorus
Ivan	Chorus
Jane	Band
Kathy	Band
Mary	Chorus
Ruth	Chorus

EXAMPLE: Anne is in the chorus.

Anne is a girl and her name belongs in row 2. Anne is in the chorus and her name also belongs in the chorus column—column 2 on the right. Anne's name appears in the matrix as shown below.

		Column 1 **BAND**	Column 2 **CHORUS**
Row 1	**BOYS**		
Row 2	**GIRLS**		*Anne*

OVERLAPPING CLASSES—MATRIX

DIRECTIONS: Sort the following words in the choice box by their material and their use. If an item is commonly made of more than one type of material, list it in more than one row.

I-176	CHOICE BOX
button, brush, bolt, can, cotton, string, clothespin, eraser, aluminum foil, frying pan, glue, ice cream carton, jar, kettle, masking tape, mop, paint scraper, paper cup, pocket, rag, rubber band, safety pin, staple, steel wool, styrofoam sandwich box, tank, toothpaste tube, trash bag, wire, wire brush	

EXAMPLE: nail

A nail is used to fasten boards together. A nail is made of metal. Therefore, a nail can be classified as both a fastener and metal. The word *nail* should be classified in the matrix box in the fastener column and the metal row as shown below.

	FASTENERS	CLEANERS	CONTAINERS
PLASTIC			
METAL	*nail*		
OTHER			

OVERLAPPING CLASSES—MATRIX

DIRECTIONS: Sort the following words in the choice box by their taste, touch, sound, or appearance. Use the matrix to show whether the word is generally favorable, generally unfavorable, or sometimes favorable. Words may be used in more than one column.

I-177	CHOICE BOX
beautiful, bitter, blinding, bright, cool, deafening, delicious, dull, fine, furry, handsome, icy, loud, musical, noisy, plain, rough, salty, scalding, sharp, soft, soothing, sour, spoiled, sweet, ugly, warm, wet	

EXAMPLE: ripe

Ripe can be used to describe both the appearance and the taste of being ready to eat. Since readiness to eat is favorable, *ripe* fits into the matrix in the generally favorable row and in both the taste and appearance columns.

	TASTE	TOUCH	SOUND	APPEARANCE
GENERALLY FAVORABLE	*ripe*			*ripe*
GENERALLY UNFAVORABLE				
SOMETIMES FAVORABLE & SOMETIMES UNFAVORABLE				

RELATIONSHIPS—EXPLAIN

DIRECTIONS: Each word in box A is related in the same way to the word on the same line in box B. Describe how the words in box A are related to the words in box B.

I-178

A	B	Relationship
bird	robin	
book	novel	_____
dog	setter	
fruit	lemon	_____
reptile	lizard	
		_____

I-179

A	B	Relationship
bicycle	handlebar	
bird	feather	_____
chair	arm	
river	mouth	_____
tree	trunk	
		_____

I-180

A	B	Relationship
beat	rhythm	
degree	temperature	_____
foot	length	
month	time	_____
watt	electricity	
		_____

I-181

A	B	Relationship
box	lid	
building	roof	_____
hill	crest	
mountain	peak	_____
room	ceiling	
		_____

RELATIONSHIPS—EXPLAIN

DIRECTIONS: Each word in box A is related in the same way to the word on the same line in box B. Describe how the words in box A are related to the words in box B.

I-182

A
answer
ask
peak
pleased
sure

B
reply
question
top
satisfied
certain

Relationship

_____

_____

_____

I-183

A
breathe
disagree
exercise
fasten
speak

B
gasp
object
aerobics
buckle
shout

Relationship

_____

_____

_____

I-184

A
boat
building
room
shoe
statue

B
hull
basement
floor
sole
base

Relationship

_____

_____

_____

I-185

A
chef
doctor
navigator
sentry
teacher

B
cooks
treats
plots
guards
explains

Relationship

_____

_____

_____

RELATIONSHIPS—EXPLAIN

DIRECTIONS: Each word in box A is related in the same way to the word on the same line in box B. Describe how the words in box A are related to the words in box B.

I-186

A
consumer
dissatisfied
murky
free
raw

B
producer
content
clear
confined
cooked

Relationship

_____

_____

_____

I-187

A
acre
foot
gallon
pound
week

B
area
length
volume
weight
time

Relationship

_____

_____

_____

I-188

A
run
sleep
study
talk
walk

B
fast
soundly
hard
rapidly
briskly

Relationship

_____

_____

_____

I-189

A
automobile
cloth
fruit
officer
vegetable

B
sedan
silk
apple
captain
carrot

Relationship

_____

_____

_____

CLASSIFYING SHAPES WITH A BULL'S EYE DIAGRAM

DIRECTIONS: Read the definitions of these shapes, complete the diagram below, and draw a conclusion. Hint: Use *all* in your conclusion, as in "*all* fathers are men and *all* men are males."

I-190

SHAPES

DEFINITIONS

This is a **parallelogram**. It is a special quadrilateral with two pairs of parallel sides.

This is a **quadrilateral**. It is a general four-sided figure with no special properties.

This is a **rectangle**. It is a special parallelogram with four square corners.

This is a **square**. Its is a special rectangle with four sides that are the same length.

CLASSIFYING SHAPES WITH A BULL'S EYE DIAGRAM

MOST GENERAL CLASS

LESS GENERAL CLASS

MORE SPECIFIC CLASS

MOST SPECIFIC CLASS

CONCLUSION _____

_____

_____

_____

CLASSIFYING SHAPES WITH A MATRIX

DIRECTIONS: Read the definitions of these shapes and complete the matrix below. Put a check mark in the box of every geometry term that applies to each closed, four-sided shape.

I-191   DEFINITIONS

A **parallelogram** is a closed, four-sided shape with two pairs of parallel sides.
A **quadrilateral** is any closed, four-sided shape.
A **rectangle** is a special parallelogram with four square corners (right angles).
A **rhombus** is a special parallelogram with four equal sides.
A **square** is a special rectangle with four sides that are the same length.
A **trapezoid** is a quadrilateral with one pair of parallel sides.

	PARALLELOGRAM	QUADRILATERAL	RECTANGLE	RHOMBUS	SQUARE	TRAPEZOID

CLASSIFYING SHAPES WITH A BRANCHING DIAGRAM

DIRECTIONS: Name the shapes in the shape box. In each box on the branching diagram, draw the shape that belongs there and write its name.

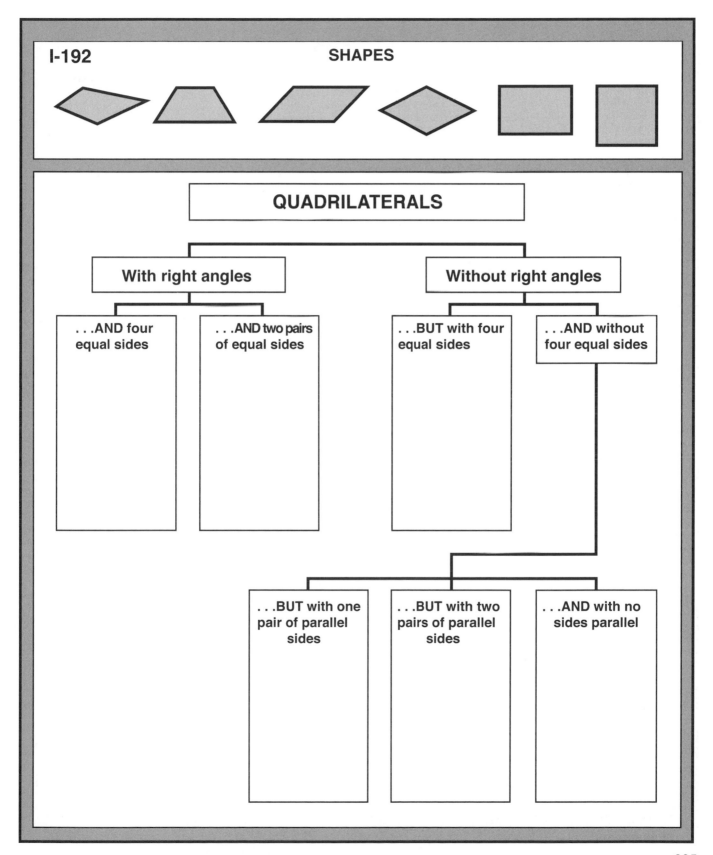

I-192

SHAPES

QUADRILATERALS

With right angles

Without right angles

. . .AND four equal sides

. . .AND two pairs of equal sides

. . .BUT with four equal sides

. . .AND without four equal sides

. . .BUT with one pair of parallel sides

. . .BUT with two pairs of parallel sides

. . .AND with no sides parallel

CLASSIFYING SHAPES WITH AN OVERLAPPING CLASSES DIAGRAM

DIRECTIONS: Name the shapes in the shape box. Draw and label each shape in the region of the diagram that best describes it.

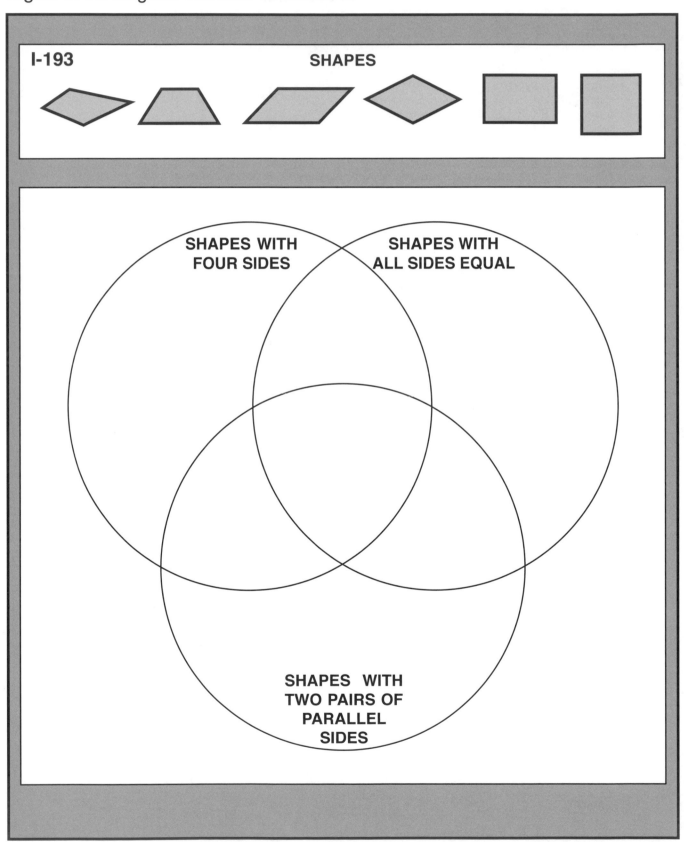

CHAPTER TEN

Describing Shapes	→	Describing Things
↓		↓
Figural Similarities and Differences	→	Verbal Similarities and Differences
↓		↓
Figural Sequences	→	Verbal Sequences
↓		↓
Figural Classifications	→	Verbal Classifications
↓		↓
Figural Analogies	→	Verbal Analogies

ANALOGIES—INSTRUCTIONS

An analogy is a relationship between two word pairs that are related in the same way.

EXAMPLE

father: man :: mother : woman

The groups of dots (: and ::) represent words.
In place of the : read "is to" or "is related to."
In place of the :: read "as."
The above analogy should be read

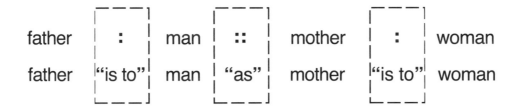

The relationship between the first pair of words **must be the same** as the relationship between the second pair of words. In the example above, the relationship is "All fathers are men just as all mothers are women."

ANALOGIES—INSTRUCTIONS

Here is an example to help you do analogy exercises.

EXAMPLE

wrist : arm :: ankle : _____

a. foot
b. joint
c. leg

1. What is the relationship between wrist and arm?
   (The wrist is the joint at the lower end of the arm.)

2. Which word is related to ankle in the same way as arm is related to wrist?

Steps in answering this question:

a. Write the relationship between the first two words as a sentence. Use the words in the order that they appear.

   The **wrist** is the joint at the lower end of the **arm**.

b. Write a second sentence below the first using the third word "ankle" and a blank line.

   The **wrist** is the joint at the lower end of the **arm**.

   The **ankle** is the joint at the lower end of the_____?

c. Look at the possible answers: a. foot, b. joint, c. leg. Try each possibility in the blank and see if it fits.

   The **ankle** is the joint at the lower end of the **foot**.

   (The ankle is at the upper, not lower, end of the foot.)

   The **ankle** is the joint at the lower end of the **joint**.

   (Joint describes the relationship but does not fit in the analogy sentence.)

   The **ankle** is the joint at the lower end of the **leg**.

   (This is a true sentence and has the **same relationship** as the first sentence.)

ANTONYM OR SYNONYM ANALOGIES—SELECT

DIRECTIONS: In each exercise, decide how the first two words are related. The words are either similar or opposite. Next, look at the third word and then write a word from the list at the right that will complete a similar relationship.

EXAMPLE

fair : just :: right: _____

correct
questionable
wrong

Fair and *just* are similar in meaning. You must pick a word from the list on the right that has about the same meaning as *right*. *Questionable* means neither right nor wrong. *Wrong* is the opposite of right. *Correct* has a meaning similar to right and is the answer. Similar words are called *synonyms;* opposite words are called *antonyms*.

J-1   speak : talk :: listen : _____

discuss
hear
learn

J-2   steal : rob :: buy : _____

get
purchase
take

J-3   absent : present :: lost : _____

found
here
missing

J-4   learn : study :: teach : _____

forget
instruct
read

J-5   right : wrong :: true : _____

correct
false
real

ASSOCIATION ANALOGIES—SELECT

DIRECTIONS: In each exercise, decide how the first two words are related. The words will be associated in some way. Next, look at the third word and then write a word from the list at the right that will complete a similar relationship.

EXAMPLE

flour : bread :: fabric : _____

cloth
clothing
material

Flour is associated with breadmaking just as fabric is associated with the making of clothing. *Cloth* and *material* are synonyms for *fabric*. So the best answer is *clothing*.

J-6   knob : door :: key : _____

bolt
hinge
lock

J-7   pie : crust :: clam : _____

crab
shell
oyster

J-8   money : wallet :: liquid : _____

bottle
drink
fluid

J-9   September : autumn :: March : _____

fall
spring
winter

J-10   bank : money :: library : _____

books
buildings
cards

J-11   paw : foot :: fur : _____

animal
beast
hair

J-12   stake : tent :: anchor : _____

boat
dock
pole

"KIND OF" ANALOGIES—SELECT

DIRECTIONS: In each exercise, decide how the first two words are related. The first word represents a "kind of " the second. Next, look at the third word and then write a word from the list at the right that will complete a similar relationship.

EXAMPLE

tea : drink :: pork : _____

beef
meat
salad

Tea is a *kind of* drink. Which of the words on the right answers the question, "Pork is a *kind of*_____?" Pork is not a *kind of* beef and pork is not a *kind of* salad. Pork is a *kind of* meat, so the best answer is *meat*.

J-13 oak : wood :: cotton : _____

cloth
nylon
velvet

J-14 water : liquid :: air : _____

gas
temperature
wind

J-15 nibble : bite :: glimpse : _____

feel
look
taste

J-16 heat : energy :: gasoline : _____

automobile
force
fuel

J-17 marble : stone :: diamond : _____

gold
jewel
money

J-18 map : chart :: photograph : _____

film
painting
picture

J-19 chick : bird :: minnow : _____

animal
fish
tadpole

"PART OF" ANALOGIES—SELECT

DIRECTIONS: In each exercise, decide how the first two words are related. The first word represents a "part of" the second. Next, look at the third word and then write a word from the list at the right that will complete a similar relationship.

EXAMPLE

scales : fish :: bark : _____

dog
skin
tree

Scales are the outer *part of* a fish. Which of the words on the right answers the question, "Bark is the outer *part of*_____?" Dog is not the answer. Dogs bark, but bark is not the outer *part of* a dog. Skin is not the answer. Bark and skin are outer parts, but bark is not the outer *part of* skin. Since bark is the outer *part of* a tree, *tree* is the best answer.

J-20 plant : garden :: tree : _____

branch
forest
pine

J-21 bulb : lamp :: flame : _____

ash
candle
heat

J-22 speech : language :: melody : _____

instrument
music
note

J-23 player : team :: student : _____

class
pupil
teacher

J-24 seat : theater :: cage : _____

animal
bars
zoo

J-25 quarter : game :: season : _____

day
month
year

"USED TO" ANALOGIES—SELECT

DIRECTIONS: In each exercise, decide how the first two words are related. The second word tells what the first word is "used to" do. Next, look at the third word and then write a word from the list at the right that will complete a similar relationship.

EXAMPLE

latch : lock :: knob : _____

bolt
open
swing

A latch is *used to* lock a door. Which of the words on the right answers the question, "Knob is *used to*_____?" *Bolt* is not the answer. A bolt is similar to a latch, but a knob is not *used to* bolt a door. *Swing* is not the answer. A knob is not *used to* swing a door; a hinge is *used to* swing a door. A knob is *used to* open a door; *open* is the best answer.

J-26 closet: hang :: trunk : _____

clean
dispose
store

J-27 typewriter : write :: calculator : _____

arrange
compute
list

J-28 note : remind :: diary : _____

inform
record
write

J-29 shield : protect :: sword : _____

attack
cover
handle

J-30 pliers : grip :: screwdriver : _____

lock
pound
turn

J-31 sponge : soak up :: towel : _____

dampen
dry
wash

ACTION ANALOGIES—SELECT

DIRECTIONS: In each exercise, decide how the first two words are related. The second word gives an action done by the first word. Next, look at the third word and then write a word from the list at the right that will complete a similar relationship.

EXAMPLE

surgeon : operates :: mechanic : _____

cuts
removes
repairs

An analogy which relates a person to what he or she does, or a thing to what it does is called an action analogy. The main task that a surgeon performs is to "operate" on a patient. The main task that a mechanic performs is to "repair" a broken machine. As part of the repair task, the mechanic may need to cut or remove a part, but neither cutting nor removing is his main task.

J-32 vein : carries :: heart : _____

protects
pumps
stores

J-33 demonstration : shows :: novel : _____

displays
opens
tells

J-34 boxer : fights :: priest : _____

builds
prays
sings

J-35 elastic : stretches :: balloon : _____

deflates
expands
shrinks

J-36 joke : amuses :: lesson : _____

entertains
informs
tests

J-37 conductor : directs :: orchestra : _____

guides
plays
sings

ANTONYM OR SYNONYM ANALOGIES—SELECT

DIRECTIONS: In each exercise, decide how the first two words are related. Next, look at the third word and then write a word from the choice box that will complete a similar relationship. Some words may be used more than once.

CHOICE BOX
few, many, much, one

J-38 pair : twin :: single : _____

J-39 many : several :: some : _____

J-40 number : many :: amount : _____

J-41 sole: only :: several : _____

J-42 few : some :: lone : _____

J-43 few : many :: some : _____

J-44 several : single :: many : _____

J-45 some : several :: few : _____

J-46 few : some :: sole : _____

ASSOCIATION ANALOGIES—SELECT

DIRECTIONS: In each exercise, decide how the first two words are associated. Next, look at the third word and then write a word from the choice box that will complete a similar relationship. Some words may be used more than once.

EXAMPLE: square inch : area :: cubic inch : _____

A square inch is a measurement of area in the same way that a cubic inch is a measurement of volume.

square inch : area :: cubic inch :   ____*volume*____

CHOICE BOX
area, length, volume, weight

J-47 gallon : volume :: pound : _____

J-48 inch : length :: square inch : _____

J-49 cube : volume :: square : _____

J-50 triangle : area :: pyramid : _____

J-51 sphere : volume :: circle : _____

J-52 acre : area :: gallon : _____

J-53 ton : weight :: cup : _____

J-54 ounce : weight :: cup : _____

J-55 cubic inch : volume :: square inch : _____

ANTONYM OR SYNONYM ANALOGIES—SELECT A PAIR

DIRECTIONS: In each exercise, read the pair of words and decide how they are related. Next, select a pair of words from the choice box that will complete the analogy. The pairs in the choice box may be used more than once.

CHOICE BOX		
all : none	have : possess	send : receive

J-56   need : require   ::   _____ : _____

J-57   sell : buy   ::   _____ : _____

J-58 everything : nothing   ::   _____ : _____

J-59   make : create   ::   _____ : _____

J-60   full : empty   ::   _____ : _____

J-61   talk : listen   ::   _____ : _____

J-62 everyone : no one   ::   _____ : _____

J-63   hold : own   ::   _____ : _____

J-64   give : get   ::   _____ : _____

ASSOCIATION ANALOGIES—SELECT TWO

DIRECTIONS: In this exercise, two members of an association analogy are supplied. Select two words from the choice box that will complete the analogy. Words in the choice box may be used more than once.

EXAMPLE: garage : _____ :: barn : _____

A garage is associated with the city, while a barn is associated with the country.

CHOICE BOX
city, country, county, nation, state

J-65   mayor : _____ :: governor : _____

J-66   city : _____ :: county : _____

J-67   road : _____ :: avenue : _____

J-68   governor : _____ :: president : _____

J-69   county : _____ :: state : _____

J-70   police chief : _____ :: sheriff : _____

J-71   acre : _____ :: block : _____

J-72   garden : _____ :: farm : _____

ANALOGIES—SELECT TWO

DIRECTIONS: In this exercise, two members of an analogy are supplied. Select two words from the choice box that will complete the analogy. These analogies are of three types— "used to," "association," and "synonyms." Words in the choice box may be used more than once.

CHOICE BOX
hear, read, see, talk

J-73   books : ———————— ::   audio tape : ————————

J-74   discuss : ———————— ::   listen : ————————

J-75   examine : ———————— ::   study : ————————

J-76   inspect : ———————— ::   converse : ————————

J-77   television : ———————— ::   stereo : ————————

J-78   blind : ———————— ::   deaf : ————————

J-79   actors : ———————— ::   editors : ————————

J-80   sounds : ———————— ::   sights : ————————

J-81   observe : ———————— ::   chatter : ————————

J-82   telescope : ———————— ::   telephone : ————————

J-83 microphone : ———————— ::   microscope : ————————

ANALOGIES—SELECT TWO

DIRECTIONS: In this exercise, two members of an analogy are supplied. Select two words from the choice box that will complete the analogy. These analogies are of three types—"action," "kind of," and "part of." Words in the choice box may be used more than once.

CHOICE BOX
bear, bird, feathers, fish, fur, robin, scales, tuna

J-84 fur : _____ :: scales : _____

J-85 eagle : feather :: _____ : _____

J-86 bear : mammal :: _____ : _____

J-87 _____ : fish :: _____ : bird

J-88 _____ : flies :: _____ : swims

J-89 lungs : _____ :: gills : _____

J-90 _____ : growls :: _____ : sings

J-91 wing : _____ :: fin : _____

J-92 hair : _____ :: feather : _____

J-93 scales : _____ :: feathers : _____

J-94 tuna : _____ :: robin : _____

ANALOGIES—EXPLAIN

DIRECTIONS: Read these analogies and decide how the words in each pair are related. On the line below each analogy, explain the relationship between the words in each pair.

Here is a list of the kinds of analogies you have practiced. Use the list to help explain these analogies.

ANTONYM	KIND OF	SYNONYM
ASSOCIATION	PART OF	USED TO

EXAMPLE: banana : fruit :: carrot : vegetable

A banana is a kind of fruit just as a carrot is a kind of vegetable.

J-95 bored : excited :: rested : weary

_____

_____

J-96 beef : hamburger :: potatoes : French fries

_____

_____

J-97 compliment : praise :: criticize : blame

_____

_____

J-98 hammer : nail :: bat : ball

_____

_____

ANALOGIES—EXPLAIN

DIRECTIONS: Read these analogies and decide how the words in each pair are related. On the line below each analogy, explain the relationship between the words in each pair.

Here is a list of the kinds of analogies you have practiced. Use the list to help explain these analogies.

ANTONYM	KIND OF	SYNONYM
ASSOCIATION	PART OF	USED TO

J-99   beetle : insect :: snake : reptile

_____

_____

J-100   teacher : instruction :: musician : entertainment

_____

_____

J-101   stare : gaze :: glance : notice

_____

_____

J-102   gusty : calm :: windy : still

_____

_____

J-103   pliers : grip :: hammer : pound

_____

_____

ANALOGIES—EXPLAIN

DIRECTIONS: Read these analogies and decide how the words in each pair are related. On the line below each analogy, explain the relationship between the words in each pair.

Here is a list of the kinds of analogies you have practiced. Use the list to help explain these analogies.

ANTONYM   KIND OF   SYNONYM
ASSOCIATION   PART OF   USED TO

J-104   wick : candle :: bulb : lamp

_____

_____

J-105   budget : money :: schedule : time

_____

_____

J-106   even : smooth :: coarse : rough

_____

_____

J-107   hook : hang :: anchor : hold

_____

_____

J-108   advance : retreat :: forward : backward

_____

_____

ANALOGIES—EXPLAIN

DIRECTIONS: Read these analogies and decide how the words in each pair are related. On the line below each analogy, explain the relationship between the words in each pair.

Here is a list of the kinds of analogies you have practiced. Use the list to help explain these analogies.

ANTONYM	KIND OF	SYNONYM
ASSOCIATION	PART OF	USED TO

J-109   dial : radio :: switch : lamp

_____

_____

J-110   cloth : wash :: towel : dry

_____

_____

J-111   fly : sky :: float : water

_____

_____

J-112   ballot : vote :: check : pay

_____

_____

J-113   yam : potato :: lima : bean

_____

_____

ANTONYM OR SYNONYM ANALOGIES—SUPPLY

DIRECTIONS: Look at the first two words. Think about how they are related. The words are either similar or opposite. Next, look at the third word and produce a word from your memory that has a similar relationship.

J-114   passenger : traveler :: guest :   _____

J-115   valley : peak :: bottom :   _____

J-116   twilight : dusk :: autumn :   _____

J-117   frequently : often :: shortly :   _____

J-118   hunt : search :: locate :   _____

J-119   stick : pole :: pit :   _____

J-120   close : distant :: near :   _____

J-121   insect : bug :: child :   _____

J-122   quiet : loud :: silent :   _____

J-123   shut : close :: unfasten :   _____

J-124   bright : dim :: shiny :   _____

J-125   dash : race :: stroll :   _____

J-126   sprinkle : rain :: snack :   _____

ASSOCIATION ANALOGIES—SUPPLY

DIRECTIONS: Look at the first two words. Think about how they are related. The words will be associated in some way. Next, look at the third word and produce a word from your memory that has a similar relationship.

J-127   father : son :: king :   _____

J-128   mouse : rat :: pebble :   _____

J-129   sheet : bed :: rug :   _____

J-130   path : road :: hill :   _____

J-131   pink : red :: gray :   _____

J-132   seal : pup :: lion :   _____

J-133   scared : tremble :: sad :   _____

J-134   salesperson : customer :: teacher :   _____

J-135   designer : pattern :: architect :   _____

J-136   actor : script :: singer :   _____

J-137   mother : father :: aunt :   _____

J-138   instructor : pupil :: doctor :   _____

J-139   cloudburst : rain :: blizzard :   _____

"KIND OF" ANALOGIES—SUPPLY

DIRECTIONS: Look at the first two words. Think about how they are related. The first word represents a "kind of" the second. Next, look at the third word and produce a word from your memory that has a similar relationship.

J-140   sedan : automobile :: pickup :   _____

J-141   refrigerator : appliance :: chair :   _____

J-142   jeans : pants :: sneakers :   _____

J-143   cherry : berry :: almond :   _____

J-144   ice : solid :: water :   _____

J-145   hamburger : sandwich :: milk shake :   _____

J-146   bean : vegetable :: orange :   _____

J-147   granite : rock :: iron :   _____

J-148   swan : bird : ant :   _____

J-149   macaroon : cookie : fudge :   _____

J-150   bunk : bed :: rocker :   _____

J-151   ten-speed : bicycle :: convertible : _____

J-152   novel : book :: ballad :   _____

"PART OF" ANALOGIES—SUPPLY

DIRECTIONS: Look at the first two words. Think about how they are related. The first word represents "part of" the second. Next, look at the third word and produce a word from your memory that has a similar relationship.

J-153 tooth : tiger :: tusk : _____

J-154 bone : skeleton :: brick : _____

J-155 leg : pants :: sleeve : _____

J-156 article : newspaper :: chapter : _____

J-157 handle bars : bicycle : steering wheel : _____

J-158 hip : leg :: shoulder : _____

J-159 intermission : play :: recess : _____

J-160 needle : pine :: blade : _____

J-161 root : plant :: foundation : _____

J-162 tuner : radio :: channel selector : _____

J-163 volume control : stereo :: thermostat : _____

J-164 flaps : airplane :: brakes : _____

J-165 needle : compass :: hands : _____

"USED TO" ANALOGIES—SUPPLY

DIRECTIONS: Look at the first two words. The second word tells what the first word is "used to" do. Next, look at the third word and produce a word from your memory that has a similar relationship.

J-166   straw : drink :: fork :   _____

J-167   pencil : write :: crayon :   _____

J-168   telephone : hear :: telescope :   _____

J-169   knife : slice :: scissors :   _____

J-170   mop : wash :: broom :   _____

J-171   pencil : mark :: ruler :   _____

J-172   paperclip : fasten :: shoelace :   _____

J-173   finger : touches :: tongue :   _____

J-174   glasses : see :: crutches :   _____

J-175   food : eat :: juice :   _____

J-176   paint : wall :: shingles :   _____

J-177   blanket : cover :: basket :   _____

J-178   ruler : line :: proctractor :   _____

ACTION ANALOGIES—SUPPLY

DIRECTIONS: Look at the first two words. The words are related by some "kind of" action. Next, look at the third word and produce a word from your memory that has a similar relationship.

J-179   teacher : teaches :: student :   _____

J-180   batter : hits :: fielder :   _____

J-181   airplane : flies :: automobile :   _____

J-182   latch : locks :: knob :   _____

J-183   seamstress : sews :: carpenter :   _____

J-184   dynamite : explodes :: candle :   _____

J-185   actor : speaks :: author :   _____

J-186   pilot : flies :: pianist :   _____

J-187   burglar : steals :: customer :   _____

J-188   water : boils :: ice :   _____

J-189   retailer : sells :: manufacture :   _____

J-190   thunder : claps :: lightning :   _____

J-191   iron : sinks :: wood :   _____

ANALOGIES—SUPPLY

DIRECTIONS: Look at the first two words. Think about how they are related. Next, look at the third word and produce a word from your memory that has a similar relationship.

J-192   idle : active :: lazy : _____

J-193   groan : moan :: laugh : _____

J-194   bird : flies :: fish : _____

J-195   mare : stallion :: hen : _____

J-196   arrival : departure :: birth : _____

J-197   hinge : door :: elbow : _____

J-198   woman : blouse :: man : _____

J-199   sand : grain :: rain : _____

J-200   ring : jewelry :: coat : _____

J-201   word : sentence :: letter : _____

J-202   tow : pull :: shove : _____

J-203   flower : seed :: chicken : _____

J-204   flavor : taste :: tone : _____

ANALOGIES—SUPPLY

DIRECTIONS: Look at the first two words. Think about how they are related. Next, look at the third word and produce a word from your memory that has a similar relationship.

J-205   fingers : grasp :: teeth :   _____

J-206   sight : vision :: touch :   _____

J-207   pass : receive :: pitch :   _____

J-208   feeble : powerful :: weak :   _____

J-209   succeed : win :: fail :   _____

J-210   brush : paint :: pencil :   _____

J-211   iron : metal :: water :   _____

J-212   flock : sheep :: herd :   _____

J-213   fake : phony :: actual :   _____

J-214   raise : lower :: lift :   _____

J-215   steal : rob :: purchase :   _____

J-216   valuable : worthless :: expensive :   _____

J-217   attorney : lawyer :: physician :   _____

ANALOGIES—EXPLAIN AND SUPPLY A PAIR

DIRECTIONS: Read the pair of words and decide how they are related. On the lines below each analogy, explain the relationship between the words. After you have explained the relationship, supply a pair of words that will complete the analogy.

EXAMPLE: gallon : volume :: _____ : _____

The gallon is associated with volume as a measurement of volume. A possible similar association might be pound as a measurement of weight. The analogy would then be:

gallon : volume :: *pound* : *weight*

J-218   soldier : army :: _____ : _____

_____

_____

_____

J-219   dirty : clean :: _____ : _____

_____

_____

_____

J-220   oats : grain :: _____ : _____

_____

_____

_____

ANALOGIES—EXPLAIN AND SUPPLY A PAIR

DIRECTIONS: Read the pair of words and decide how they are related. On the lines below each analogy, explain the relationship between the words. After you have explained the relationship, supply a pair of words that will complete the analogy.

J-221   train : track :: _____ : _____

_____

_____

_____

J-222   artist : paints :: _____ : _____

_____

_____

_____

J-223   chief : tribe :: _____ : _____

_____

_____

_____

J-224   quiet : loud :: _____ : _____

_____

_____

ANALOGIES—EXPLAIN AND SUPPLY A PAIR

DIRECTIONS: Read the pair of words and decide how they are related. On the lines below each analogy, explain the relationship between the words. After you have explained the relationship, supply a pair of words that will complete the analogy.

J-225   silly : foolish :: _____ : _____

_____

_____

_____

J-226   lemon : sour :: _____ : _____

_____

_____

_____

J-227   spots : leopard :: _____ : _____

_____

_____

_____

J-228   food : eat :: _____ : _____

_____

_____

_____

ANALOGIES—PRODUCE

DIRECTIONS: Now that you have practiced selecting and suppplying the words to complete six different kinds of analogies, you are ready to create your own. See if you can produce eight or more analogies from the words in the choice box.

CHOICE BOX
bird, fins, fish, fly, horse, land, legs, sea, sky, swim, walk, wings

J-229 _____

J-230 _____

J-231 _____

J-232 _____

J-233 _____

J-234 _____

J-235 _____

J-236 _____

ANSWER GUIDE

Describing Shapes	→	Describing Things
↓		↓
Figural Similarities and Differences	→	Verbal Similarities and Differences
↓		↓
Figural Sequences	→	Verbal Sequences
↓		↓
Figural Classifications	→	Verbal Classifications
↓		↓
Figural Analogies	→	Verbal Analogies

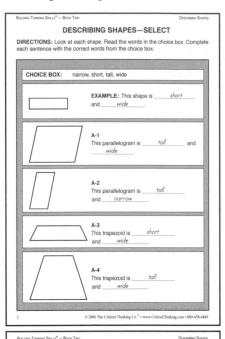

DESCRIBING SHAPES—SELECT

DIRECTIONS: Look at each shape. Read the words in the choice box. Complete each sentence with the correct words from the choice box.

CHOICE BOX: narrow, short, tall, wide

EXAMPLE: This shape is _short_ and _wide_.

A-1
This parallelogram is _tall_ and _wide_.

A-2
This parallelogram is _tall_ and _narrow_.

A-3
This trapezoid is _short_ and _wide_.

A-4
This trapezoid is _tall_ and _wide_.

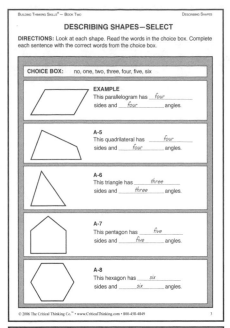

DESCRIBING SHAPES—SELECT

DIRECTIONS: Look at each shape. Read the words in the choice box. Complete each sentence with the correct words from the choice box.

CHOICE BOX: no, one, two, three, four, five, six

EXAMPLE
This parallelogram has _four_ sides and _four_ angles.

A-5
This quadrilateral has _four_ sides and _four_ angles.

A-6
This triangle has _three_ sides and _three_ angles.

A-7
This pentagon has _five_ sides and _five_ angles.

A-8
This hexagon has _six_ sides and _six_ angles.

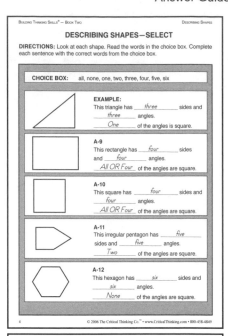

DESCRIBING SHAPES—SELECT

DIRECTIONS: Look at each shape. Read the words in the choice box. Complete each sentence with the correct words from the choice box.

CHOICE BOX: all, none, one, two, three, four, five, six

EXAMPLE:
This triangle has _three_ sides and _three_ angles. _One_ of the angles is square.

A-9
This rectangle has _four_ sides and _four_ angles. _All OR Four_ of the angles are square.

A-10
This square has _four_ sides and _four_ angles. _All OR Four_ of the angles are square.

A-11
This irregular pentagon has _five_ sides and _five_ angles. _Two_ of the angles are square.

A-12
This hexagon has _six_ sides and _six_ angles. _None_ of the angles are square.

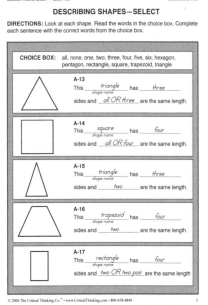

DESCRIBING SHAPES—SELECT

DIRECTIONS: Look at each shape. Read the words in the choice box. Complete each sentence with the correct words from the choice box.

CHOICE BOX: all, none, one, two, three, four, five, six, hexagon, pentagon, rectangle, square, trapezoid, triangle

A-13
This _triangle_ (shape name) has _three_ sides and _all OR three_ are the same length.

A-14
This _square_ (shape name) has _four_ sides and _all OR four_ are the same length.

A-15
This _triangle_ (shape name) has _three_ sides and _two_ are the same length.

A-16
This _trapezoid_ (shape name) has _four_ sides and _two_ are the same length.

A-17
This _rectangle_ (shape name) has _four_ sides and _two OR two pair_ are the same length.

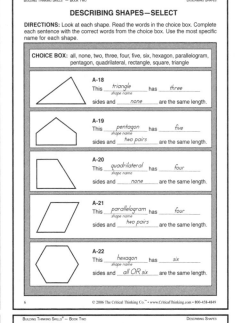

DESCRIBING SHAPES—SELECT

DIRECTIONS: Look at each shape. Read the words in the choice box. Complete each sentence with the correct words from the choice box. Use the most specific name for each shape.

CHOICE BOX: all, none, one, two, three, four, five, six, hexagon, parallelogram, pentagon, quadrilateral, rectangle, square, triangle

A-18
This _triangle_ (shape name) has _three_ sides and _none_ are the same length.

A-19
This _pentagon_ (shape name) has _five_ sides and _two pairs_ are the same length.

A-20
This _quadrilateral_ (shape name) has _four_ sides and _none_ are the same length.

A-21
This _parallelogram_ (shape name) has _four_ sides and _two pairs_ are the same length.

A-22
This _hexagon_ (shape name) has _six_ sides and _all OR six_ are the same length.

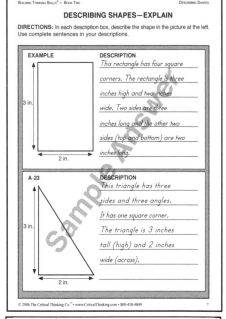

DESCRIBING SHAPES—EXPLAIN

DIRECTIONS: In each description box, describe the shape in the picture at the left. Use complete sentences in your descriptions.

EXAMPLE
3 in.
2 in.

DESCRIPTION
This rectangle has four square corners. The rectangle is three inches high and two inches wide. Two sides are three inches long and the other two sides (top and bottom) are two inches long.

A-23
3 in.
2 in.

DESCRIPTION
This triangle has three sides and three angles. It has one square corner. The triangle is 3 inches tall (high) and 2 inches wide (across).

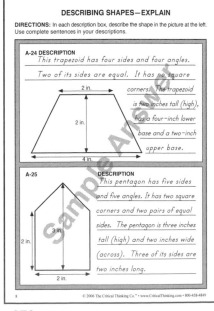

DESCRIBING SHAPES—EXPLAIN

DIRECTIONS: In each description box, describe the shape in the picture at the left. Use complete sentences in your descriptions.

A-24 DESCRIPTION
This trapezoid has four sides and four angles. Two of its sides are equal. It has no square corners. The trapezoid is two inches tall (high), has a four-inch lower base and a two-inch upper base.

2 in.
2 in.
4 in.

A-25
2 in.
3 in.
2 in.

DESCRIPTION
This pentagon has five sides and five angles. It has two square corners and two pairs of equal sides. The pentagon is three inches tall (high) and two inches wide (across). Three of its sides are two inches long.

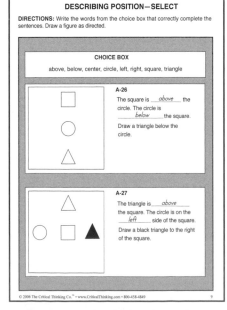

DESCRIBING POSITION—SELECT

DIRECTIONS: Write the words from the choice box that correctly complete the sentences. Draw a figure as directed.

CHOICE BOX
above, below, center, circle, left, right, square, triangle

A-26
The square is _above_ the circle. The circle is _below_ the square.
Draw a triangle below the circle.

A-27
The triangle is _above_ the square. The circle is on the _left_ side of the square.
Draw a black triangle to the right of the square.

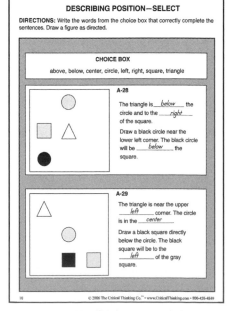

DESCRIBING POSITION—SELECT

DIRECTIONS: Write the words from the choice box that correctly complete the sentences. Draw a figure as directed.

CHOICE BOX
above, below, center, circle, left, right, square, triangle

A-28
The triangle is _below_ the circle and to the _right_ of the square.
Draw a black circle near the lower left corner. The black circle will be _below_ the square.

A-29
The triangle is near the upper _left_ corner. The circle is in the _center_.
Draw a black square directly below the circle. The black square will be to the _left_ of the gray square.

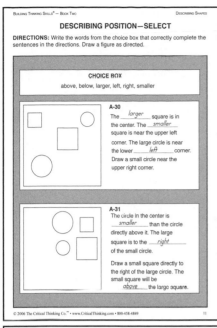

DESCRIBING POSITION—SELECT

DIRECTIONS: Write the words from the choice box that correctly complete the sentences in the directions. Draw a figure as directed.

CHOICE BOX
above, below, larger, left, right, smaller

A-30
The _larger_ square is in the center. The _smaller_ square is near the upper left corner. The large circle is near the lower _left_ corner. Draw a small circle near the upper right corner.

A-31
The circle in the center is _smaller_ than the circle directly above it. The large square is to the _right_ of the small circle. Draw a small square directly to the right of the large circle. The small square will be _above_ the large square.

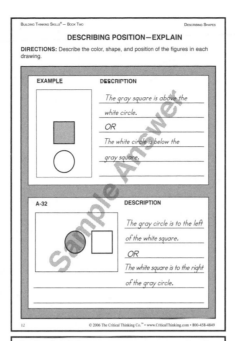

DESCRIBING POSITION—EXPLAIN

DIRECTIONS: Describe the color, shape, and position of the figures in each drawing.

EXAMPLE — DESCRIPTION
The gray square is above the white circle.
OR
The white circle is below the gray square.

A-32 — DESCRIPTION
The gray circle is to the left of the white square.
OR
The white square is to the right of the gray circle.

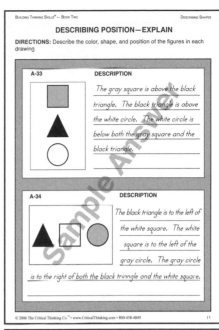

DESCRIBING POSITION—EXPLAIN

DIRECTIONS: Describe the color, shape, and position of the figures in each drawing

A-33 — DESCRIPTION
The gray square is above the black triangle. The black triangle is above the white circle. The white circle is below both the gray square and the black triangle.

A-34 — DESCRIPTION
The black triangle is to the left of the white square. The white square is to the left of the gray circle. The gray circle is to the right of both the black triangle and the white square.

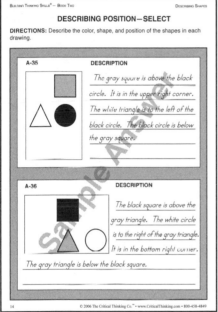

DESCRIBING POSITION—SELECT

DIRECTIONS: Describe the color, shape, and position of the shapes in each drawing.

A-35 — DESCRIPTION
The gray square is above the black circle. It is in the upper right corner. The white triangle is to the left of the black circle. The black circle is below the gray square.

A-36 — DESCRIPTION
The black square is above the gray triangle. The white circle is to the right of the gray triangle. It is in the bottom right corner. The gray triangle is below the black square.

CHARACTERISTICS OF A SHAPE

DIRECTIONS: Look at the pentagon in the center of the diagram. Write a different characteristic of the pentagon in each of the four boxes. Use these characteristics to write a description of the pentagon in the description box.

A-37
CHARACTERISTIC — gray in color
CHARACTERISTIC — five sides (pentagon)
CHARACTERISTIC — two one-inch sides that make a square corner
CHARACTERISTIC — four angles that are larger than a square corner (obtuse angles)

DESCRIPTION BOX
This gray pentagon has one square corner formed by sides that are each one inch long. The three remaining sides form four angles that are each larger than a square corner (obtuse angles).

CHARACTERISTICS OF A SHAPE

DIRECTIONS: Look at the hexagon in the center of the diagram. Write a different characteristic of the hexagon in each of the four boxes. Use these characteristics to write a description of the hexagon in the description box.

A-38
CHARACTERISTIC — gray in color
CHARACTERISTIC — six sides (hexagon)
CHARACTERISTIC — two vertical one-inch sides opposite one another (parallel)
CHARACTERISTIC — all angles are larger than a square corner (obtuse)

DESCRIPTION BOX
This gray hexagon has two vertical sides that are one inch long. All the angles are larger than a square corner.

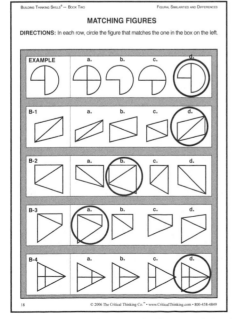

MATCHING FIGURES

DIRECTIONS: In each row, circle the figure that matches the one in the box on the left.

EXAMPLE, B-1, B-2, B-3, B-4

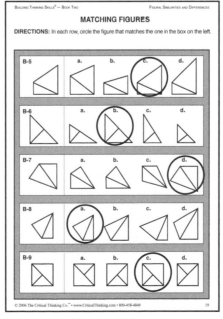

MATCHING FIGURES

DIRECTIONS: In each row, circle the figure that matches the one in the box on the left.

B-5, B-6, B-7, B-8, B-9

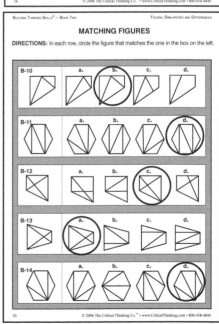

MATCHING FIGURES

DIRECTIONS: In each row, circle the figure that matches the one in the box on the left.

B-10, B-11, B-12, B-13, B-14

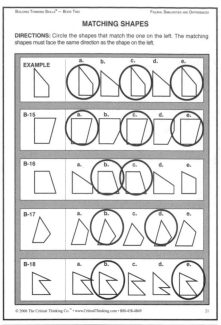

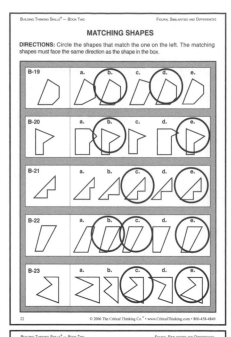

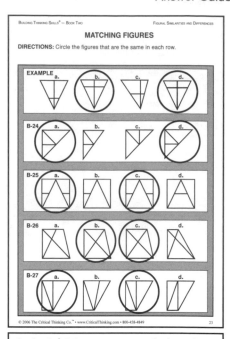

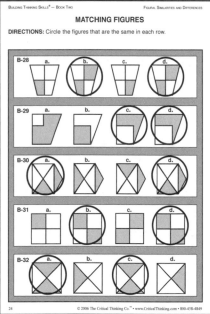

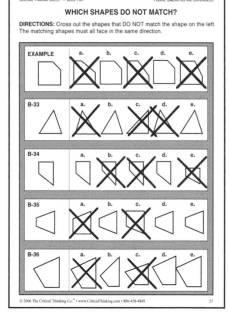

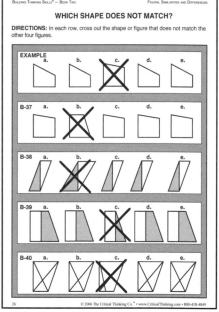

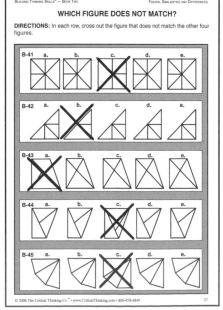

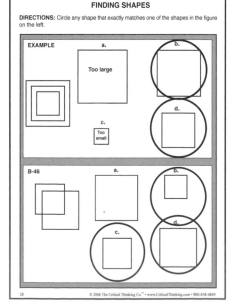

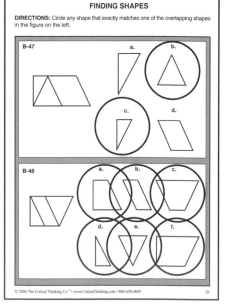

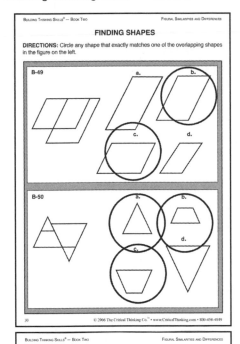

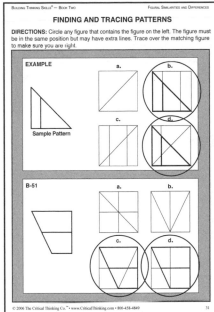

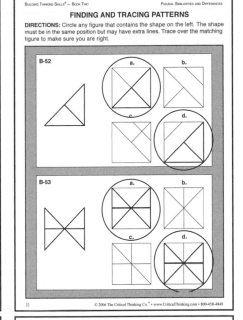

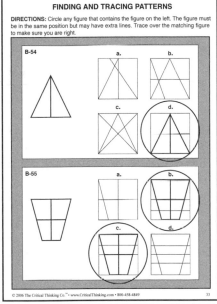

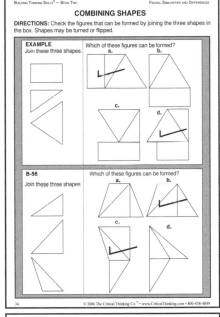

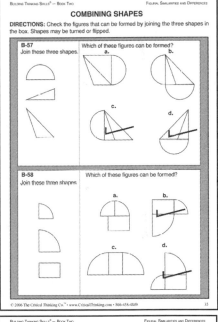

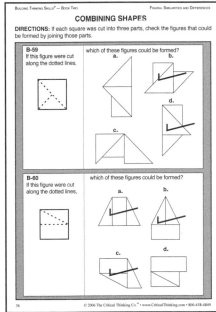

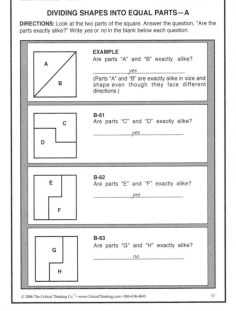

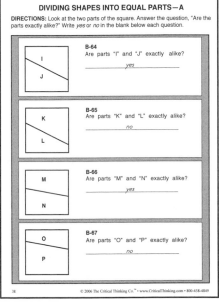

DIVIDING SHAPES INTO EQUAL PARTS—A

DIRECTIONS: Look at the two parts of the square. Answer the question, "Are the parts exactly alike?" Write *yes* or *no* in the blank below each question.

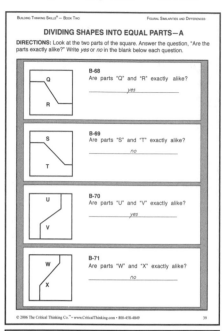

B-68 Are parts "Q" and "R" exactly alike?
yes

B-69 Are parts "S" and "T" exactly alike?
no

B-70 Are parts "U" and "V" exactly alike?
yes

B-71 Are parts "W" and "X" exactly alike?
no

DIVIDING SHAPES INTO EQUAL PARTS—B

DIRECTIONS: Divide each shape into equal parts as directed below.

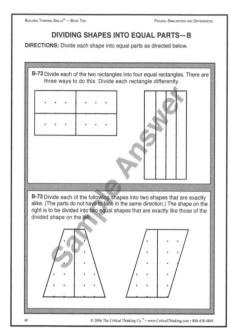

B-72 Divide each of the two rectangles into four equal rectangles. There are three ways to do this. Divide each rectangle differently.

B-73 Divide each of the following shapes into two shapes that are exactly alike. (The parts do not have to face in the same direction.) The shape on the right is to be divided into two equal shapes that are exactly like those of the divided shape on the left.

DIVIDING SHAPES INTO EQUAL PARTS—B

DIRECTIONS: Divide each of the rectangles into two equal parts. Do not draw squares or rectangles. Divide each rectangle differently.

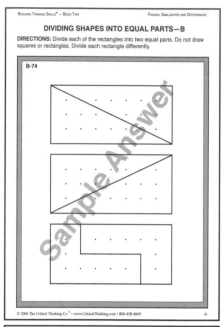

B-74

DIVIDING SHAPES INTO EQUAL PARTS—B

DIRECTIONS: Divide each of the triangles into equal parts as directed below.

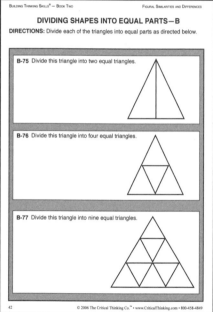

B-75 Divide this triangle into two equal triangles.

B-76 Divide this triangle into four equal triangles.

B-77 Divide this triangle into nine equal triangles.

PAPER FOLDING—SELECT

DIRECTIONS: The left side of each exercise shows an unfolded sheet of paper with holes punched in it. One of the drawings in the choice box shows how the paper will look when folded. Circle the correct answer.

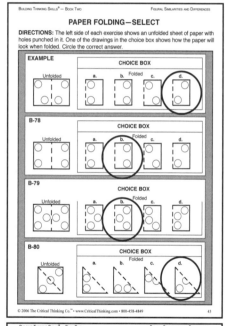

EXAMPLE

B-78

B-79

B-80

PAPER FOLDING—SELECT

DIRECTIONS: The left side of each exercise shows a folded sheet of paper with holes punched in it. One of the drawings in the choice box shows how the paper will look when unfolded. Circle the correct answer.

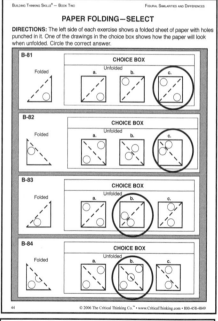

B-81

B-82

B-83

B-84

PAPER FOLDING—SUPPLY

DIRECTIONS: Here are four sheets of paper with holes punched in them. They are to be folded along the dotted line. Draw how each sheet will look after it is folded.

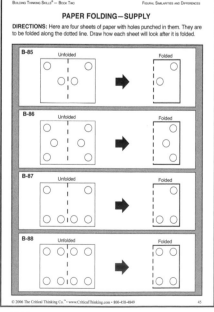

B-85

B-86

B-87

B-88

PAPER FOLDING—SUPPLY

DIRECTIONS: Here are four sheets of paper with holes punched in them. They are folded along the dotted line. Draw how each sheet will look when unfolded.

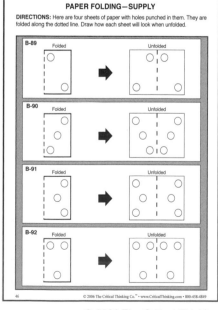

B-89

B-90

B-91

B-92

SYMMETRICAL PATTERNS—SUPPLY

DIRECTIONS: Here are four symmetrical patterns. They are to be folded along the dotted line of symmetry. Draw how each pattern will look when folded.

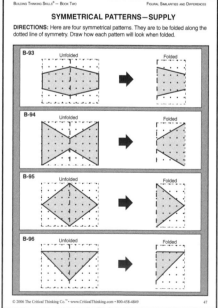

B-93

B-94

B-95

B-96

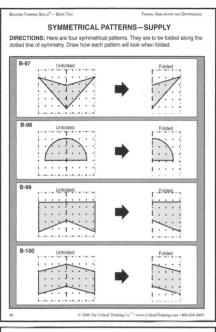

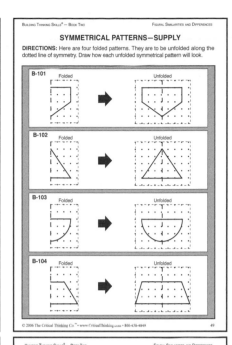

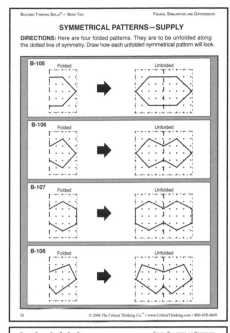

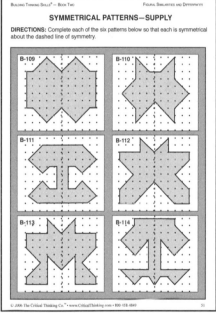

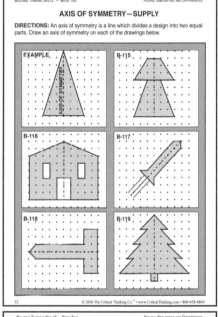

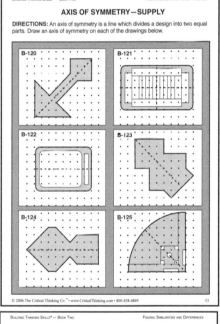

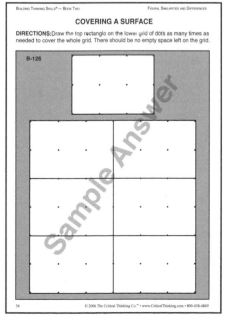

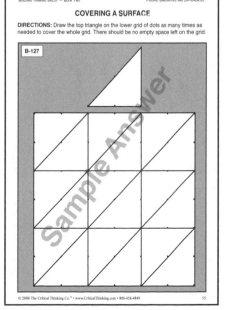

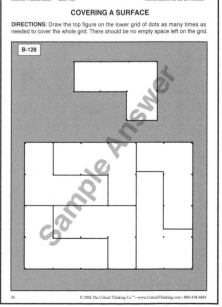

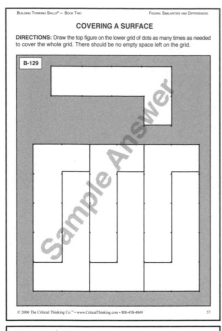

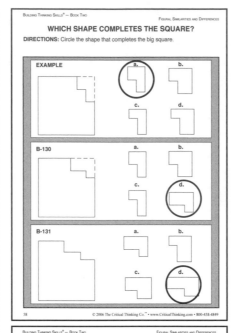

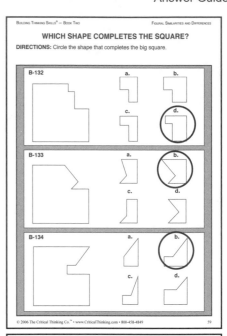

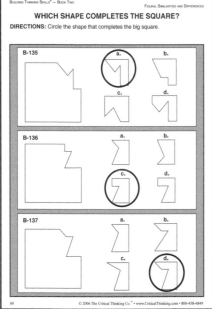

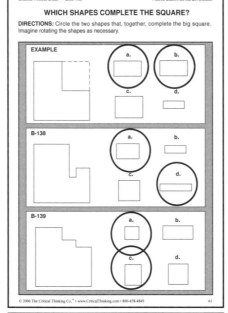

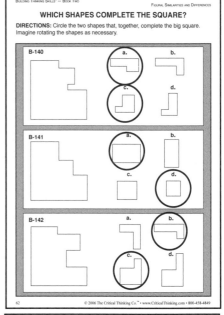

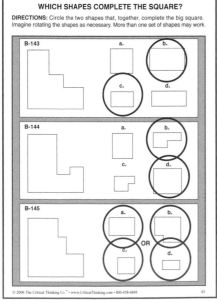

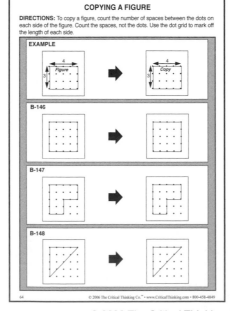

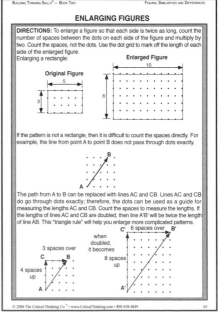

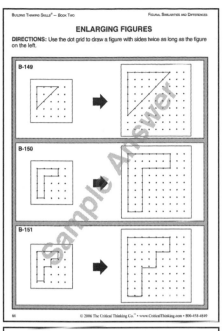

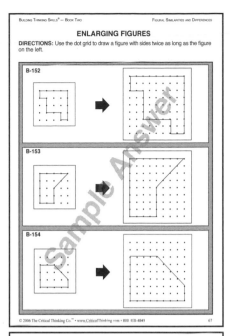

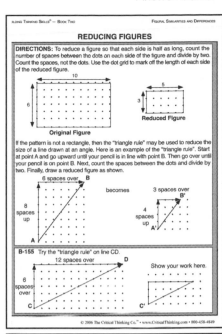

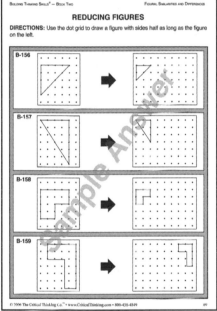

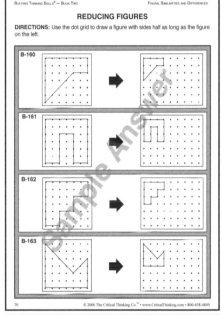

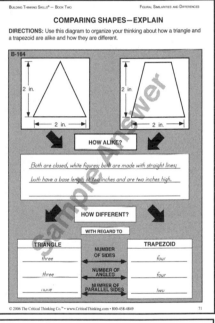

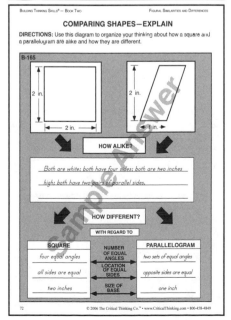

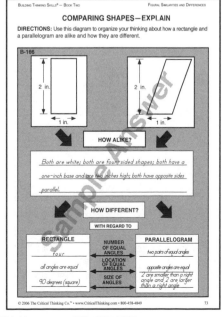

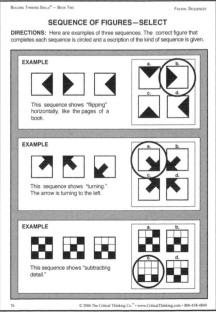

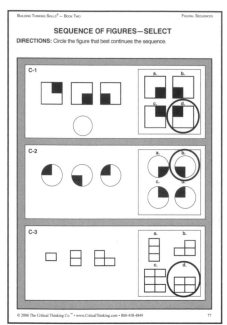

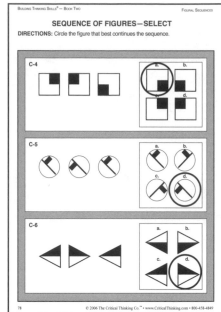

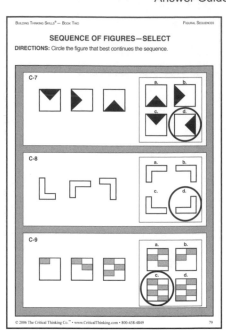

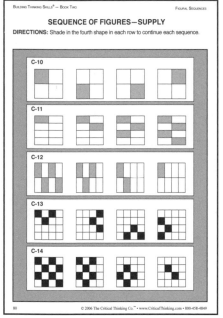

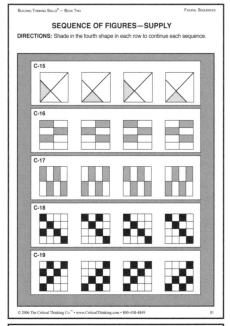

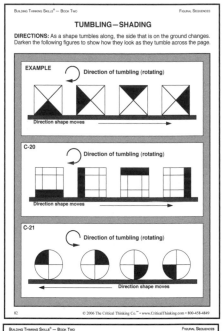

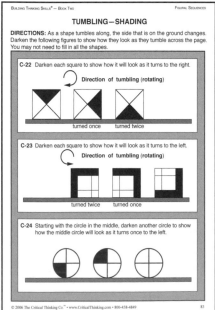

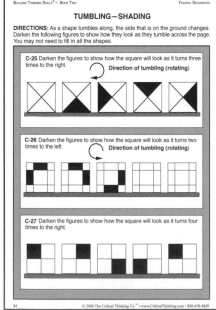

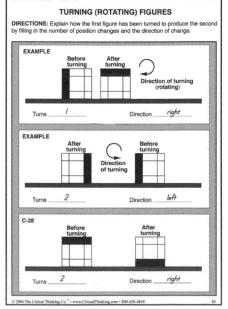

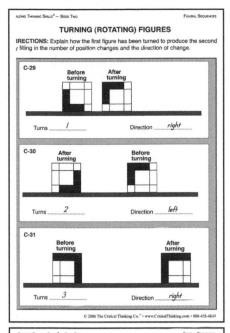

TURNING (ROTATING) FIGURES

DIRECTIONS: Explain how the first figure has been turned to produce the second by filling in the number of position changes and the direction of change.

C-29
Turns _1_   Direction _right_

C-30
Turns _2_   Direction _left_

C-31
Turns _3_   Direction _right_

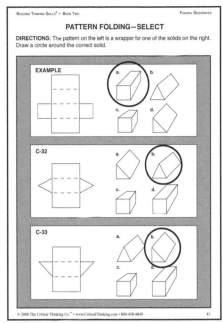

PATTERN FOLDING—SELECT

DIRECTIONS: The pattern on the left is a wrapper for one of the solids on the right. Draw a circle around the correct solid.

EXAMPLE

C-32

C-33

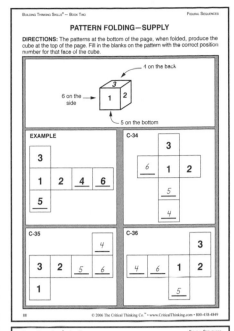

PATTERN FOLDING—SUPPLY

DIRECTIONS: The patterns at the bottom of the page, when folded, produce the cube at the top of the page. Fill in the blanks on the pattern with the correct position number for that face of the cube.

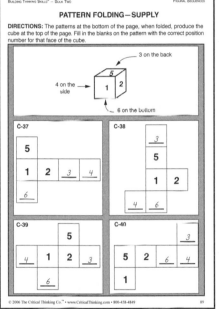

PATTERN FOLDING—SUPPLY

DIRECTIONS: The patterns at the bottom of the page, when folded, produce the cube at the top of the page. Fill in the blanks on the pattern with the correct position number for that face of the cube.

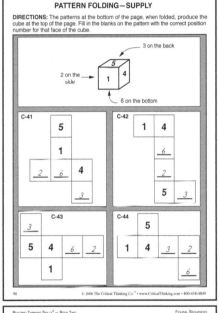

PATTERN FOLDING—SUPPLY

DIRECTIONS: The patterns at the bottom of the page, when folded, produce the cube at the top of the page. Fill in the blanks on the pattern with the correct position number for that face of the cube.

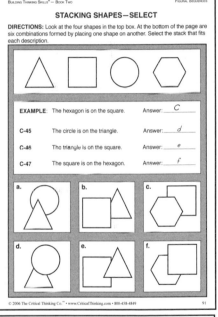

STACKING SHAPES—SELECT

DIRECTIONS: Look at the four shapes in the top box. At the bottom of the page are six combinations formed by placing one shape on another. Select the stack that fits each description.

EXAMPLE:	The hexagon is on the square.	Answer: _C_
C-45	The circle is on the triangle.	Answer: _d_
C-46	The triangle is on the square.	Answer: _e_
C-47	The square is on the hexagon.	Answer: _f_

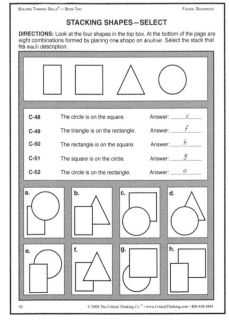

STACKING SHAPES—SELECT

DIRECTIONS: Look at the four shapes in the top box. At the bottom of the page are eight combinations formed by placing one shape on another. Select the stack that fits each description.

C-48	The circle is on the square.	Answer: _c_
C-49	The triangle is on the rectangle.	Answer: _f_
C-50	The rectangle is on the square.	Answer: _h_
C-51	The square is on the circle.	Answer: _g_
C-52	The circle is on the rectangle.	Answer: _a_

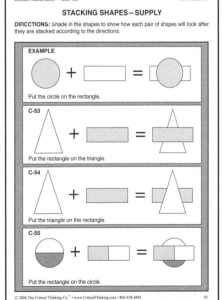

STACKING SHAPES—SUPPLY

DIRECTIONS: Shade in the shapes to show how each pair of shapes will look after they are stacked according to the directions.

EXAMPLE
Put the circle on the rectangle.

C-53
Put the rectangle on the triangle.

C-54
Put the triangle on the rectangle.

C-55
Put the rectangle on the circle.

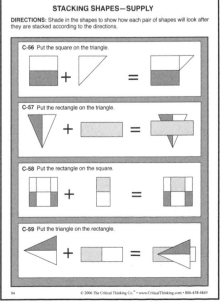

STACKING SHAPES—SUPPLY

DIRECTIONS: Shade in the shapes to show how each pair of shapes will look after they are stacked according to the directions.

C-56 Put the square on the triangle.

C-57 Put the rectangle on the triangle.

C-58 Put the rectangle on the square.

C-59 Put the triangle on the rectangle.

Building Thinking Skills® — Level 2

Answer Guide

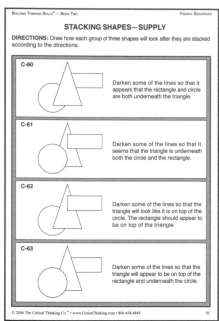

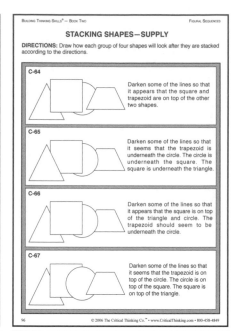

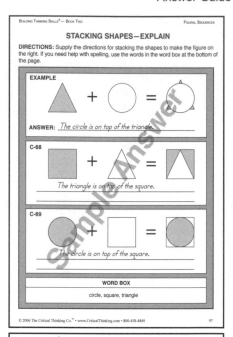

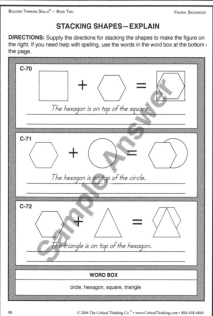

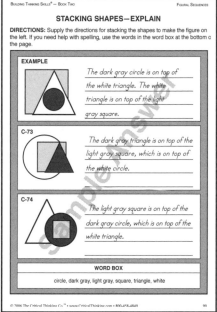

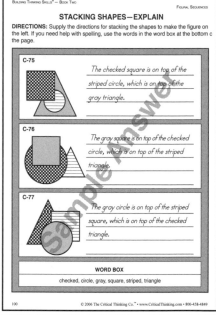

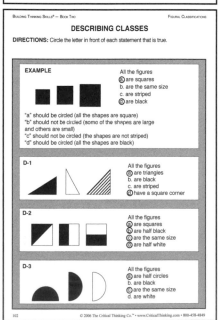

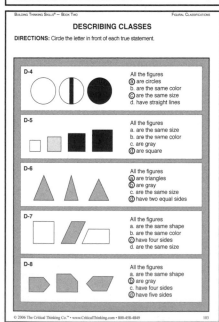

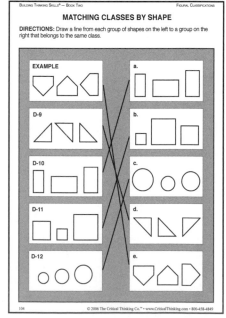

380

© 2006 The Critical Thinking Co.™ • www.CriticalThinking.com • 800-458-4849

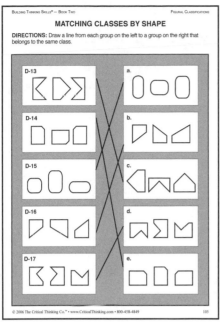

BUILDING THINKING SKILLS® — BOOK TWO — FIGURAL CLASSIFICATIONS

MATCHING CLASSES BY SHAPE

DIRECTIONS: Draw a line from each group on the left to a group on the right that belongs to the same class.

© 2006 The Critical Thinking Co.™ • www.CriticalThinking.com • 800-458-4849   105

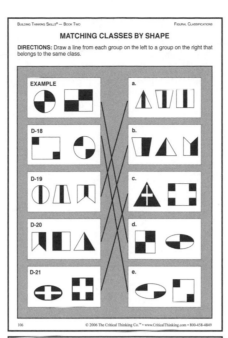

BUILDING THINKING SKILLS® — BOOK TWO — FIGURAL CLASSIFICATIONS

MATCHING CLASSES BY SHAPE

DIRECTIONS: Draw a line from each group on the left to a group on the right that belongs to the same class.

106   © 2006 The Critical Thinking Co.™ • www.CriticalThinking.com • 800-458-4849

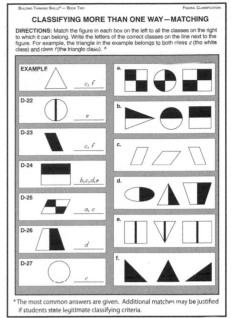

BUILDING THINKING SKILLS® — BOOK TWO — FIGURAL CLASSIFICATION

CLASSIFYING MORE THAN ONE WAY—MATCHING

DIRECTIONS: Match the figure in each box on the left to all the classes on the right to which it can belong. Write the letters of the correct classes on the line next to the figure. For example, the triangle in the example belongs to both class *c* (the white class) and class *f* (the triangle class). *

* The most common answers are given. Additional matches may be justified if students state legitimate classifying criteria.

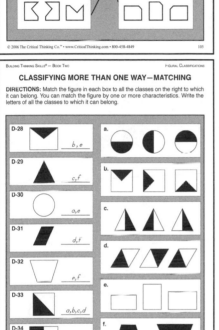

BUILDING THINKING SKILLS® — BOOK TWO — FIGURAL CLASSIFICATIONS

CLASSIFYING MORE THAN ONE WAY—MATCHING

DIRECTIONS: Match the figure in each box on the right to all the classes on the right to which it can belong. You can match the figure by one or more characteristics. Write the letters of all the classes to which it can belong.

108   © 2006 The Critical Thinking Co.™ • www.CriticalThinking.com • 800-458-4849

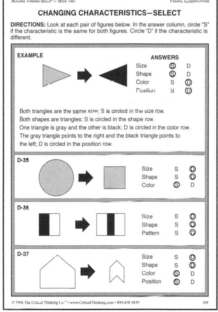

BUILDING THINKING SKILLS® — BOOK TWO — FIGURAL CLASSIFICATIONS

CHANGING CHARACTERISTICS—SELECT

DIRECTIONS: Look at each pair of figures below. In the answer column, circle "S" if the characteristic is the same for both figures. Circle "D" if the characteristic is different.

Both triangles are the same size; S is circled in the size row.
Both shapes are triangles; S is circled in the shape row.
One triangle is gray and the other is black; D is circled in the color row.
The gray triangle points to the right and the black triangle points to the left; D is circled in the position row.

© 2006 The Critical Thinking Co.™ • www.CriticalThinking.com • 800-458-4849   109

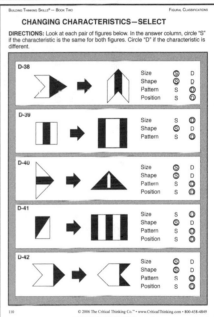

BUILDING THINKING SKILLS® — BOOK TWO — FIGURAL CLASSIFICATIONS

CHANGING CHARACTERISTICS—SELECT

DIRECTIONS: Look at each pair of figures below. In the answer column, circle "S" if the characteristic is the same for both figures. Circle "D" if the characteristic is different.

110   © 2006 The Critical Thinking Co.™ • www.CriticalThinking.com • 800-458-4849

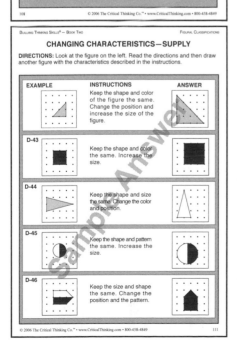

BUILDING THINKING SKILLS® — BOOK TWO — FIGURAL CLASSIFICATIONS

CHANGING CHARACTERISTICS—SUPPLY

DIRECTIONS: Look at the figure on the left. Read the directions and then draw another figure with the characteristics described in the instructions.

© 2006 The Critical Thinking Co.™ • www.CriticalThinking.com • 800-458-4849   111

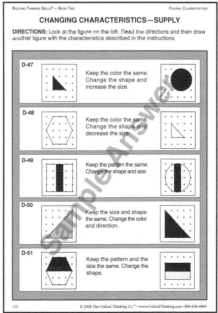

BUILDING THINKING SKILLS® — BOOK TWO — FIGURAL CLASSIFICATIONS

CHANGING CHARACTERISTICS—SUPPLY

DIRECTIONS: Look at the figure on the left. Read the directions and then draw another figure with the characteristics described in the instructions.

112   © 2006 The Critical Thinking Co.™ • www.CriticalThinking.com • 800-458-4849

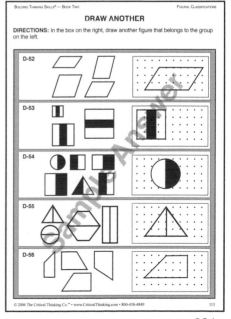

BUILDING THINKING SKILLS® — BOOK TWO — FIGURAL CLASSIFICATIONS

DRAW ANOTHER

DIRECTIONS: In the box on the right, draw another figure that belongs to the group on the left.

© 2006 The Critical Thinking Co.™ • www.CriticalThinking.com • 800-458-4849   113

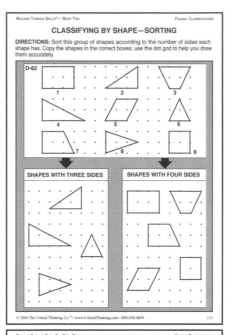

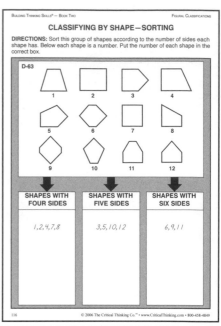

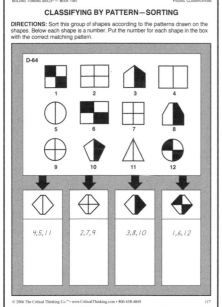

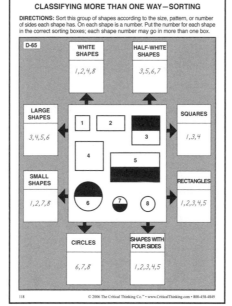

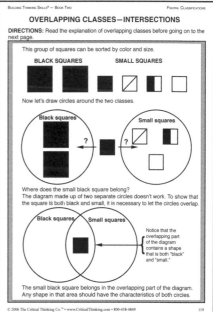

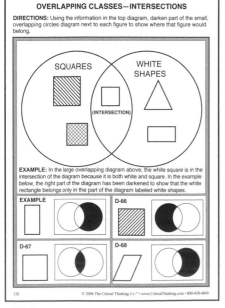

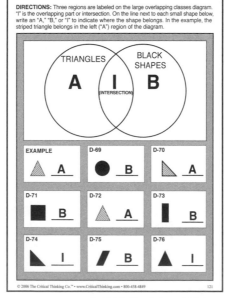

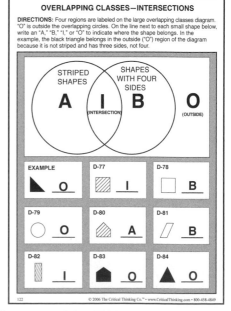

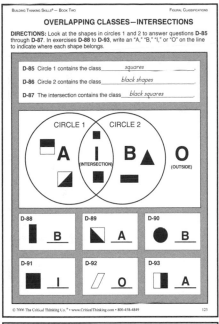

OVERLAPPING CLASSES—INTERSECTIONS

DIRECTIONS: Look at the shapes in circles 1 and 2 to answer questions D-85 through D-87. In exercises D-88 to D-93, write an "A," "B," "I," or "O" on the line to indicate where each shape belongs.

D-85 Circle 1 contains the class _squares_.
D-86 Circle 2 contains the class _black shapes_.
D-87 The intersection contains the class _black squares_.

D-88 **B**   D-89 **A**   D-90 **B**
D-91 **I**   D-92 **O**   D-93 **A**

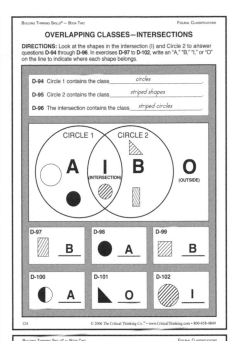

OVERLAPPING CLASSES—INTERSECTIONS

DIRECTIONS: Look at the shapes in the intersection (I) and Circle 2 to answer questions D-94 through D-96. In exercises D-97 to D-102, write an "A," "B," "I," or "O" on the line to indicate where each shape belongs.

D-94 Circle 1 contains the class _circles_.
D-95 Circle 2 contains the class _striped shapes_.
D-96 The intersection contains the class _striped circles_.

D-97 **B**   D-98 **A**   D-99 **B**
D-100 **A**   D-101 **O**   D-102 **I**

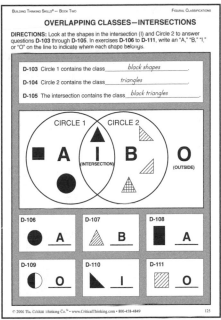

OVERLAPPING CLASSES—INTERSECTIONS

DIRECTIONS: Look at the shapes in the intersection (I) and Circle 2 to answer questions D-103 through D-105. In exercises D-106 to D-111, write an "A," "B," "I," or "O" on the line to indicate where each shape belongs.

D-103 Circle 1 contains the class _black shapes_.
D-104 Circle 2 contains the class _triangles_.
D-105 The intersection contains the class _black triangles_.

D-106 **A**   D-107 **B**   D-108 **A**
D-109 **O**   D-110 **I**   D-111 **O**

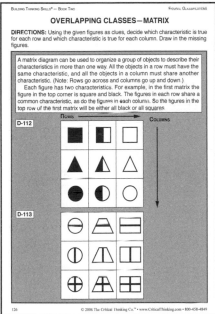

OVERLAPPING CLASSES—MATRIX

DIRECTIONS: Using the given figures as clues, decide which characteristic is true for each row and which characteristic is true for each column. Draw in the missing figures.

A matrix diagram can be used to organize a group of objects to describe their characteristics in more than one way. All the objects in a row must have the same characteristic, and all the objects in a column must share another characteristic. (Note: Rows go across and columns go up and down.)

Each figure has two characteristics. For example, in the first matrix the figure in the top corner is square and black. The figures in each row share a common characteristic, as do the figures in each column. So the figures in the top row of the first matrix will be either all black or all squares.

D-112   D-113

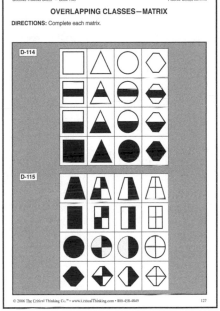

OVERLAPPING CLASSES—MATRIX

DIRECTIONS: Complete each matrix.

D-114

D-115

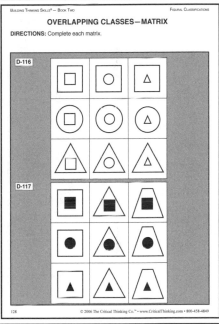

OVERLAPPING CLASSES—MATRIX

DIRECTIONS: Complete each matrix.

D-116

D-117

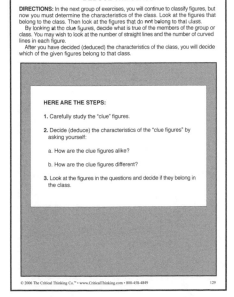

DEDUCE THE CLASS

DIRECTIONS: In the next group of exercises, you will continue to classify figures, but now you must determine the characteristics of the class. Look at the figures that belong to the class. Then look at the figures that do not belong to that class.

By looking at the clue figures, decide what is true of the members of the group or class. You may wish to look at the number of straight lines and the number of curved lines in each figure.

After you have decided (deduced) the characteristics of the class, you will decide which of the given figures belong to that class.

HERE ARE THE STEPS:

1. Carefully study the "clue" figures.

2. Decide (deduce) the characteristics of the "clue figures" by asking yourself:

   a. How are the clue figures alike?

   b. How are the clue figures different?

3. Look at the figures in the questions and decide if they belong in the class.

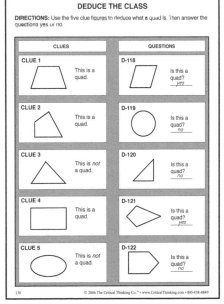

DEDUCE THE CLASS

DIRECTIONS: Use the five clue figures to deduce what a quad is. Then answer the questions yes or no.

CLUES	QUESTIONS
CLUE 1 — This is a quad.	D-118 Is this a quad? _yes_
CLUE 2 — This is a quad.	D-119 Is this a quad? _no_
CLUE 3 — This is not a quad.	D-120 Is this a quad? _no_
CLUE 4 — This is a quad.	D-121 Is this a quad? _yes_
CLUE 5 — This is not a quad.	D-122 Is this a quad? _no_

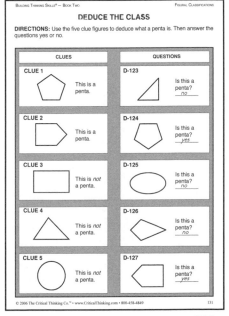

DEDUCE THE CLASS

DIRECTIONS: Use the five clue figures to deduce what a penta is. Then answer the questions yes or no.

CLUES	QUESTIONS
CLUE 1 — This is a penta.	D-123 Is this a penta? _no_
CLUE 2 — This is a penta.	D-124 Is this a penta? _yes_
CLUE 3 — This is not a penta.	D-125 Is this a penta? _no_
CLUE 4 — This is not a penta.	D-126 Is this a penta? _no_
CLUE 5 — This is not a penta.	D-127 Is this a penta? _yes_

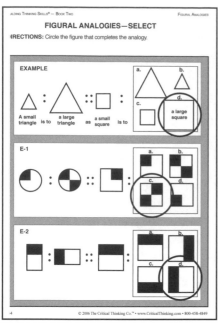

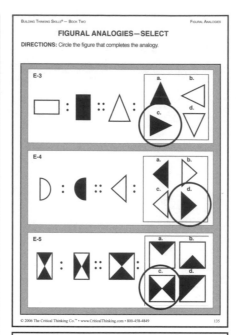

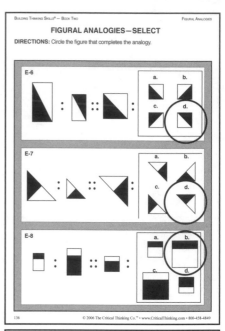

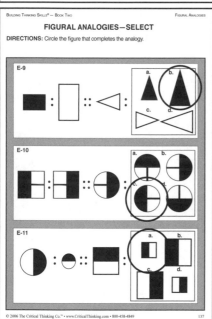

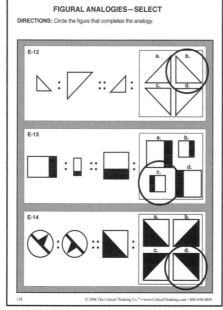

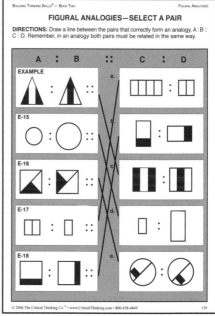

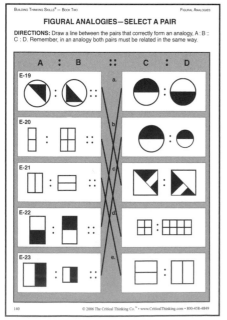

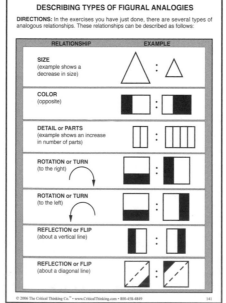

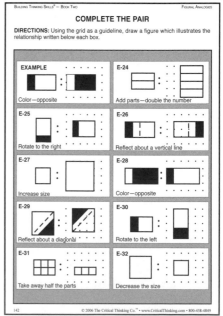

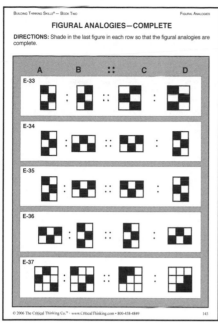

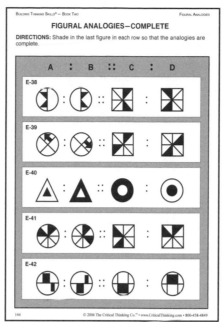

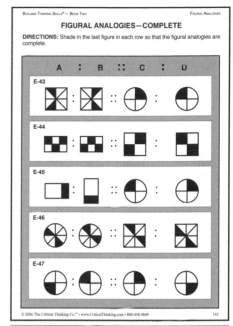

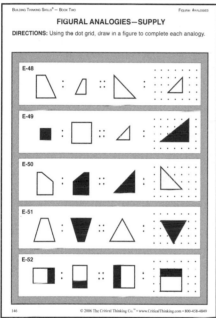

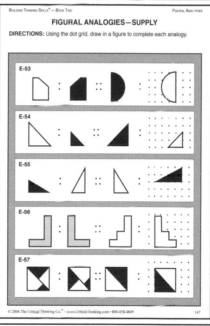

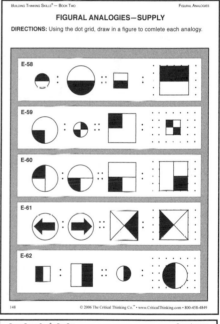

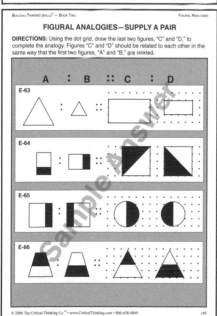

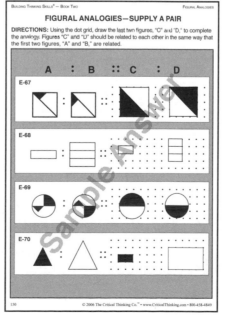

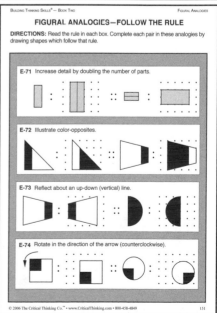

FIGURAL ANALOGIES—FOLLOW THE RULE

DIRECTIONS: Read the rule in each box. Complete each pair in these analogies by drawing shapes which follow that rule.

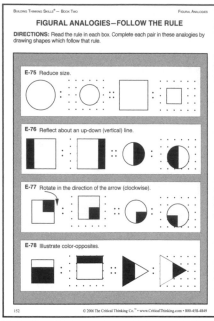

E-75 Reduce size.

E-76 Reflect about an up-down (vertical) line.

E-77 Rotate in the direction of the arrow (clockwise).

E-78 Illustrate color-opposites.

FIGURAL ANALOGIES—FOLLOW THE RULE

DIRECTIONS: Read the rule in each box. Complete each pair in these analogies by drawing shapes which follow that rule.

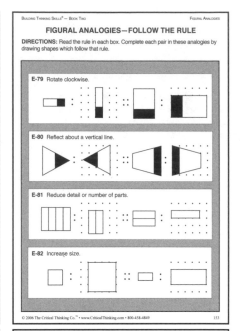

E-79 Rotate clockwise.

E-80 Reflect about a vertical line.

E-81 Reduce detail or number of parts.

E-82 Increase size.

DESCRIBING FOODS—SELECT

DIRECTIONS: Each exercise contains the names of three foods, followed by descriptions of two of the words. Choose the word that fits each description and write it in the blank.

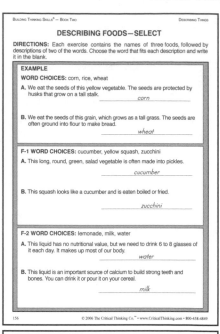

EXAMPLE

WORD CHOICES: corn, rice, wheat

A. We eat the seeds of this yellow vegetable. The seeds are protected by husks that grow on a tall stalk. _corn_

B. We eat the seeds of this grain, which grows as a tall grass. The seeds are often ground into flour to make bread. _wheat_

F-1 WORD CHOICES: cucumber, yellow squash, zucchini

A. This long, round, green, salad vegetable is often made into pickles. _cucumber_

B. This squash looks like a cucumber and is eaten boiled or fried. _zucchini_

F-2 WORD CHOICES: lemonade, milk, water

A. This liquid has no nutritional value, but we need to drink 6 to 8 glasses of it each day. It makes up most of our body. _water_

B. This liquid is an important source of calcium to build strong teeth and bones. You can drink it or pour it on your cereal. _milk_

DESCRIBING ANIMALS—SELECT

DIRECTIONS: Each exercise contains the names of three animals, followed by descriptions of two of the words. Choose the word that fits each description and write it in the blank.

F-3 WORD CHOICES: deer, elk, moose

A. The largest member of the deer family, this animal has a very large head and a long flap of skin, called a bell, that hangs under its throat. The males have large, broad, spoon-shaped antlers. _moose_

B. A medium-sized member of the deer family, this animal's coat is grayish brown with a white patch on its rump. In the United States, it is only found in the Rocky Mountains and in the Central Valley of California. _elk_

F-4 WORD CHOICES: butterfly, moth, wasp

A. This insect is dull in color, has large wings, and flies at night. _moth_

B. Groups of these stinging insects build large, paperlike, "woven" nests. _wasp_

F-5 WORD CHOICES: seal, sea lion, walrus

A. This member of the seal family has ears and flippers that are larger than those of true seals. Its long, tapered body has short, coarse hair. This animal can turn its hind flippers forward to move about on land. _sea lion_

B. This large marine mammal lives in the open water at the edge of the Arctic ice pack. It lacks external ears, has long tusks and thick, nearly hairless, skin, except for long bristles on the cheek pads. It has reversible hind flippers for moving over ice. _walrus_

DESCRIBING VEHICLES—SELECT

DIRECTIONS: Each exercise contains the names of three vehicles followed by descriptions of two of the words. Choose the word that fits each description and write it in the blank.

F-6 WORD CHOICES: bicycle, moped, motorcycle

A. This two-wheeled vehicle can be pedaled or driven by a small engine. Its top speed is about 30 miles per hour. _moped_

B. This two-wheeled vehicle is powered by a gasoline engine that can propel it at speeds up to 100 miles per hour. Because it is often driven at high speeds, it is a very dangerous vehicle, and accidents on it often result in injuries or death. _motorcycle_

F-7 WORD CHOICES: backhoe, bulldozer, crane

A. This very large vehicle moves short distances on rolling tracks. A motor-driven cable runs over the end of a long, necklike boom. A hook at the end of the cable is used to lift heavy objects. _crane_

B. This large vehicle has a large, movable scoop shovel on the back that is used to dig ditches and trenches. _backhoe_

F-8 WORD CHOICES: all-terrain vehicle, motocross bicycle, snowmobile

A. This vehicle has large, fat tires that allow it to move over almost any land or marshy area. _all-terrain vehicle_

B. This two-wheeled vehicle is small and tough. It is built to fly over dirt jumps and race around tracks. It has special tires and a rugged frame. _motocross bicycle_

DESCRIBING GEOGRAPHIC TERMS—SELECT

DIRECTIONS: Each exercise contains the names of three landforms or bodies of water, followed by descriptions of two of the words. Choose the word that fits each description and write it in the blank.

F-9 WORD CHOICES: canal, channel, stream

A. A natural, narrow waterway connecting two bodies of water. _channel_

B. A manmade, narrow waterway connecting two bodies of water. _canal_

F-10 WORD CHOICES: basin, canyon, mesa

A. A flat-topped hill with steep sides, common in deserts. _mesa_

B. A broad flat area surrounded by hills or mountains. _basin_

F-11 WORD CHOICES: island, isthmus, peninsula

A. A narrow strip of land connecting two larger land areas. _isthmus_

B. Land surrounded by water on three sides. _peninsula_

DESCRIBING OCCUPATIONS—SELECT

DIRECTIONS: Each exercise contains the names of three occupations, followed by descriptions of two of the jobs. Choose the word that fits each description and write it in the blank.

F-12 WORD CHOICES: dental hygienist, dental assistant, dentist

A. This person gives dental examinations and cleans patients' teeth but does not fill or cap teeth. _dental hygienist_

B. This person prepares a patient to see the dentist. He or she hands instruments and materials to the dentist during dental procedures, takes X-rays, takes impressions of the teeth, and performs other dental tasks. _dental assistant_

F-13 WORD CHOICES: inhalation therapist, nurse, physical therapist

A. This person helps hospitalized patients regain their ability to breathe. _inhalation therapist_

B. This person helps injured people learn to walk and/or use their arms and hands again. _physical therapist_

F-14 WORD CHOICES: computer engineer, data clerk, programmer

A. This person is responsible for entering the correct information into a computer. _data clerk_

B. This person is responsible for designing and building computers. _computer engineer_

DESCRIBING COMPUTER DEVICES—SELECT

DIRECTIONS: Each exercise contains three computer terms, followed by descriptions of two of the terms. Choose the word that fits each description and write it in the blank.

F-15 WORD CHOICES: computer processing unit, computer memory, compact disk

A. This computer component allows processed data to be stored within the computer. _computer memory_

B. This computer component allows the operator to perform complex tasks such as calculations, word processing, drawing, and bookkeeping. _computer processing unit_

F-16 WORD CHOICES: e-mail, Internet, modem

A. This device connects a computer to the World Wide Web. _modem_

B. This system of interconnections between computers allows a computer operator to send and receive information (drawings, messages, or files) from other computer users. _Internet_

F-17 WORD CHOICES: CD ROM, Random Access Memory (RAM), Read Only Memory (ROM)

A. This integrated circuit allows a computer to access (find) and use the instructions (programs) stored or fed into a computer. _Random Access Memory (RAM)_

B. This computer component allows a computer to read and store (remember) the calculations, written documents, and drawings produced by the computer operator. _Read Only Memory (ROM)_

IDENTIFYING CHARACTERISTICS OF FOOD

DIRECTIONS: Read each passage about a food. Identify the characteristics of the food and write them in the blanks.

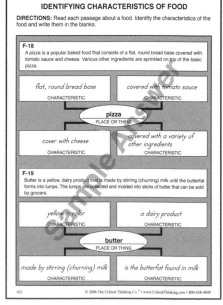

F-18
A pizza is a popular baked food that consists of a flat, round bread base covered with tomato sauce and cheese. Various other ingredients are sprinkled on top of the basic pizza.

flat, round bread base CHARACTERISTIC	covered with tomato sauce CHARACTERISTIC

pizza
PLACE OR THING

cover with cheese CHARACTERISTIC	covered with a variety of other ingredients CHARACTERISTIC

F-19
Butter is a yellow, dairy product that is made by stirring (churning) milk until the butterfat forms into lumps. The lumps are collected and molded into sticks of butter that can be sold by grocers.

yellow in color CHARACTERISTIC	a dairy product CHARACTERISTIC

butter
PLACE OR THING

made by stirring (churning) milk CHARACTERISTIC	is the butterfat found in milk CHARACTERISTIC

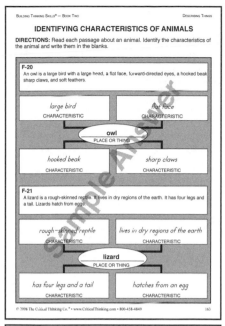

IDENTIFYING CHARACTERISTICS OF ANIMALS

DIRECTIONS: Read each passage about an animal. Identify the characteristics of the animal and write them in the blanks.

F-20
An owl is a large bird with a large head, a flat face, forward-directed eyes, a hooked beak, sharp claws, and soft feathers.

large bird CHARACTERISTIC	flat face CHARACTERISTIC

owl — PLACE OR THING

hooked beak CHARACTERISTIC	sharp claws CHARACTERISTIC

F-21
A lizard is a rough-skinned reptile. It lives in dry regions of the earth. It has four legs and a tail. Lizards hatch from eggs.

rough-skinned reptile CHARACTERISTIC	lives in dry regions of the earth CHARACTERISTIC

lizard — PLACE OR THING

has four legs and a tail CHARACTERISTIC	hatches from an egg CHARACTERISTIC

© 2006 The Critical Thinking Co.™ • www.CriticalThinking.com • 800-458-4849   163

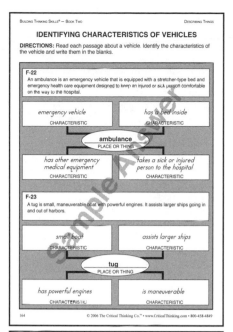

IDENTIFYING CHARACTERISTICS OF VEHICLES

DIRECTIONS: Read each passage about a vehicle. Identify the characteristics of the vehicle and write them in the blanks.

F-22
An ambulance is an emergency vehicle that is equipped with a stretcher-type bed and emergency health care equipment designed to keep an injured or sick person comfortable on the way to the hospital.

emergency vehicle CHARACTERISTIC	has a bed inside CHARACTERISTIC

ambulance — PLACE OR THING

has other emergency medical equipment CHARACTERISTIC	takes a sick or injured person to the hospital CHARACTERISTIC

F-23
A tug is small, maneuverable boat with powerful engines. It assists larger ships going in and out of harbors.

small boat CHARACTERISTIC	assists larger ships CHARACTERISTIC

tug — PLACE OR THING

has powerful engines CHARACTERISTIC	is maneuverable CHARACTERISTIC

164

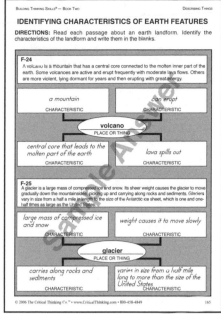

IDENTIFYING CHARACTERISTICS OF EARTH FEATURES

DIRECTIONS: Read each passage about an earth landform. Identify the characteristics of the landform and write them in the blanks.

F-24
A volcano is a mountain that has a central core connected to the molten inner part of the earth. Some volcanoes are active and erupt frequently with moderate lava flows. Others are more violent, lying dormant for years and then erupting with great energy.

a mountain CHARACTERISTIC	can erupt CHARACTERISTIC

volcano — PLACE OR THING

central core that leads to the molten part of the earth CHARACTERISTIC	lava spills out CHARACTERISTIC

F-25
A glacier is a large mass of compressed ice and snow. Its sheer weight causes the glacier to move gradually down the mountainsides, picking up and carrying along rocks and sediments. Glaciers vary in size from a half a mile in length to the size of the Antarctic ice sheet, which is one and one-half times as large as the United States.

large mass of compressed ice and snow CHARACTERISTIC	weight causes it to move slowly CHARACTERISTIC

glacier — PLACE OR THING

carries along rocks and sediments CHARACTERISTIC	varies in size from a half mile long to more than the size of the United States CHARACTERISTIC

© 2006 The Critical Thinking Co.™ • www.CriticalThinking.com • 800-458-4849   165

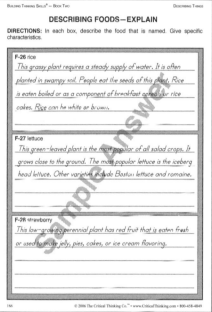

DESCRIBING FOODS—EXPLAIN

DIRECTIONS: In each box, describe the food that is named. Give specific characteristics.

F-26 rice
This grassy plant requires a steady supply of water. It is often planted in swampy soil. People eat the seeds of this plant. Rice is eaten boiled or as a component of breakfast cereals or rice cakes. Rice can be white or brown.

F-27 lettuce
This green-leaved plant is the most popular of all salad crops. It grows close to the ground. The most popular lettuce is the iceberg head lettuce. Other varieties include Boston lettuce and romaine.

F-28 strawberry
This low-growing perennial plant has red fruit that is eaten fresh or used to make jelly, pies, cakes, or ice cream flavoring.

166

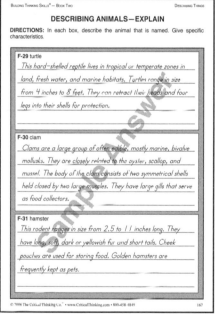

DESCRIBING ANIMALS—EXPLAIN

DIRECTIONS: In each box, describe the animal that is named. Give specific characteristics.

F-29 turtle
This hard-shelled reptile lives in tropical or temperate zones in land, fresh water, and marine habitats. Turtles range in size from 4 inches to 8 feet. They can retract their heads and four legs into their shells for protection.

F-30 clam
Clams are a large group of often edible, mostly marine, bivalve mollusks. They are closely related to the oyster, scallop, and mussel. The body of the clam consists of two symmetrical shells held closed by two large muscles. They have large gills that serve as food collectors.

F-31 hamster
This rodent ranges in size from 2.5 to 11 inches long. They have long, soft, dark or yellowish fur and short tails. Cheek pouches are used for storing food. Golden hamsters are frequently kept as pets.

167

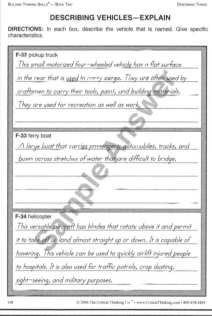

DESCRIBING VEHICLES—EXPLAIN

DIRECTIONS: In each box, describe the vehicle that is named. Give specific characteristics.

F-32 pickup truck
This small motorized four-wheeled vehicle has a flat surface in the rear that is used to carry cargo. They are often used by craftsmen to carry their tools, paint, and building materials. They are used for recreation as well as work.

F-33 ferry boat
A large boat that carries passengers, automobiles, trucks, and buses across stretches of water that are difficult to bridge.

F-34 helicopter
This versatile aircraft has blades that rotate above it and permit it to take off or land almost straight up or down. It is capable of hovering. This vehicle can be used to quickly airlift injured people to hospitals. It is also used for traffic patrols, crop dusting, sight-seeing, and military purposes.

168

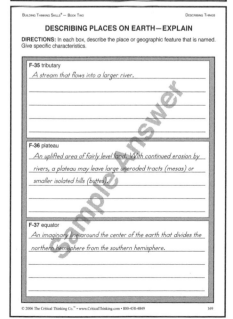

DESCRIBING PLACES ON EARTH—EXPLAIN

DIRECTIONS: In each box, describe the place or geographic feature that is named. Give specific characteristics.

F-35 tributary
A stream that flows into a larger river.

F-36 plateau
An uplifted area of fairly level land. With continued erosion by rivers, a plateau may leave large uneroded tracts (mesas) or smaller isolated hills (buttes).

F-37 equator
An imaginary line around the center of the earth that divides the northern hemisphere from the southern hemisphere.

169

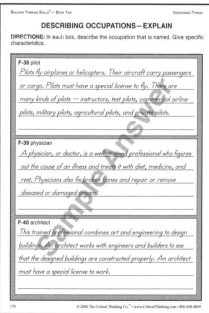

DESCRIBING OCCUPATIONS—EXPLAIN

DIRECTIONS: In each box, describe the occupation that is named. Give specific characteristics.

F-38 pilot
Pilots fly airplanes or helicopters. Their aircraft carry passengers or cargo. Pilots must have a special license to fly. There are many kinds of pilots — instructors, test pilots, commercial airline pilots, military pilots, agricultural pilots, and private pilots.

F-39 physician
A physician, or doctor, is a well-trained professional who figures out the cause of an illness and treats it with diet, medicine, and rest. Physicians also fix broken bones and repair or remove diseased or damaged organs.

F-40 architect
This trained professional combines art and engineering to design buildings. An architect works with engineers and builders to see that the designed buildings are constructed properly. An architect must have a special license to work.

170

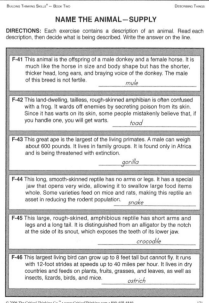

NAME THE ANIMAL—SUPPLY

DIRECTIONS: Each exercise contains a description of an animal. Read each description, then decide what is being described. Write the answer on the line.

F-41 This animal is the offspring of a male donkey and a female horse. It is much like the horse in size and body shape but has the shorter, thicker head, long ears, and braying voice of the donkey. The male of this breed is not fertile.
mule

F-42 This land-dwelling, tailless, rough-skinned amphibian is often confused with a frog. It wards off enemies by secreting poison from its skin. Since it has warts on its skin, some people mistakenly believe that, if you handle one, you will get warts.
toad

F-43 This great ape is the largest of the living primates. A male can weigh about 600 pounds. It lives in family groups. It is found only in Africa and is being threatened with extinction.
gorilla

F-44 This long, smooth-skinned reptile has no arms or legs. It has a special jaw that opens very wide, allowing it to swallow large food items whole. Some varieties feed on mice and rats, making this reptile an asset in reducing the rodent population.
snake

F-45 This large, rough-skinned, amphibious reptile has short arms and legs and a long tail. It is distinguished from an alligator by the notch at the side of its snout, which exposes the teeth of its lower jaw.
crocodile

F-46 This largest living bird can grow up to 8 feet tall but cannot fly. It runs with 12-foot strides at speeds up to 40 miles per hour. It lives in dry countries and feeds on plants, fruits, grasses, and leaves, as well as insects, lizards, birds, and mice.
ostrich

171

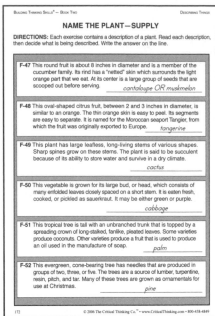

NAME THE PLANT—SUPPLY

DIRECTIONS: Each exercise contains a description of a plant. Read each description, then decide what is being described. Write the answer on the line.

F-47 This round fruit is about 8 inches in diameter and is a member of the cucumber family. Its rind has a "netted" skin which surrounds the light orange part that we eat. At its center is a large group of seeds that are scooped out before serving. _cantaloupe OR muskmelon_

F-48 This oval-shaped citrus fruit, between 2 and 3 inches in diameter, is similar to an orange. The thin orange skin is easy to peel. Its segments are easy to separate. It is named for the Moroccan seaport Tangier, from which the fruit was originally exported to Europe. _tangerine_

F-49 This plant has large leafless, long-living stems of various shapes. Sharp spines grow on these stems. The plant is said to be succulent because of its ability to store water and survive in a dry climate. _cactus_

F-50 This vegetable is grown for its large bud, or head, which consists of many enfolded leaves closely spaced on a short stem. It is eaten fresh, cooked, or pickled as sauerkraut. It may be either green or purple. _cabbage_

F-51 This tropical tree is tall with an unbranched trunk that is topped by a spreading crown of long-stalked, fanlike, pleated leaves. Some varieties produce coconuts. Other varieties produce a fruit that is used to produce an oil used in the manufacture of soap. _palm_

F-52 This evergreen, cone-bearing tree has needles that are produced in groups of two, three, or five. The trees are a source of lumber, turpentine, resin, pitch, and tar. Many of these trees are grown as ornamentals for use at Christmas. _pine_

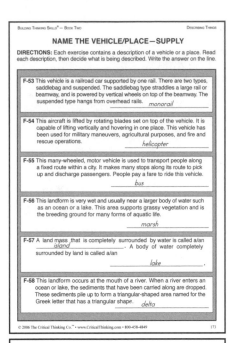

NAME THE VEHICLE/PLACE—SUPPLY

DIRECTIONS: Each exercise contains a description of a vehicle or a place. Read each description, then decide what is being described. Write the answer on the line.

F-53 This vehicle is a railroad car supported by one rail. There are two types, saddlebag and suspended. The saddlebag type straddles a single rail or beamway, and is powered by vertical wheels on top of the beamway. The suspended type hangs from overhead rails. _monorail_

F-54 This aircraft is lifted by rotating blades set on top of the vehicle. It is capable of lifting vertically and hovering in one place. This vehicle has been used for military maneuvers, agricultural purposes, and fire and rescue operations. _helicopter_

F-55 This many-wheeled, motor vehicle is used to transport people along a fixed route within a city. It makes many stops along its route to pick up and discharge passengers. People pay a fare to ride this vehicle. _bus_

F-56 This landform is very wet and usually near a larger body of water such as an ocean or a lake. This area supports grassy vegetation and is the breeding ground for many forms of aquatic life. _marsh_

F-57 A land mass that is completely surrounded by water is called a/an _island_. A body of water completely surrounded by land is called a/an _lake_.

F-58 This landform occurs at the mouth of a river. When a river enters an ocean or lake, the sediments that have been carried along are dropped. These sediments pile up to form a triangular-shaped area named for the Greek letter that has a triangular shape. _delta_

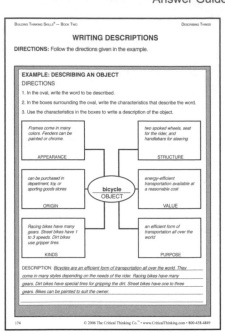

WRITING DESCRIPTIONS

DIRECTIONS: Follow the directions given in the example.

EXAMPLE: DESCRIBING AN OBJECT
DIRECTIONS
1. In the oval, write the word to be described.
2. In the boxes surrounding the oval, write the characteristics that describe the word.
3. Use the characteristics in the boxes to write a description of the object.

Frames come in many colors. Fenders can be painted or chrome. — APPEARANCE

two spoked wheels, seat for the rider, and handlebars for steering — STRUCTURE

can be purchased in department, toy, or sporting goods stores — ORIGIN

energy-efficient transportation available at a reasonable cost — VALUE

Racing bikes have many speeds. Dirt bikes have 1 to 3 speeds. Dirt bikes use gripper tires. — KINDS

an efficient form of transportation all over the world — PURPOSE

bicycle OBJECT

DESCRIPTION: _Bicycles are an efficient form of transportation all over the world. They come in many styles depending on the needs of the rider. Racing bikes have many gears. Dirt bikes have special tires for gripping the dirt. Street bikes have one to three gears. Bikes can be painted to suit the owner._

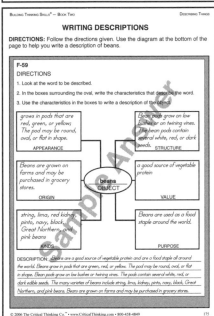

WRITING DESCRIPTIONS

DIRECTIONS: Follow the directions given. Use the diagram at the bottom of the page to help you write a description of beans.

F-59
DIRECTIONS
1. Look at the word to be described.
2. In the boxes surrounding the oval, write the characteristics that describe the word.
3. Use the characteristics in the boxes to write a description of the object.

grows in pods that are red, green, or yellow; The pod may be round, oval, or flat in shape. — APPEARANCE

Bean pods grow on low bushes or on twining vines. The bean pods contain several white, red, or dark seeds. — STRUCTURE

Beans are grown on farms and may be purchased in grocery stores. — ORIGIN

a good source of vegetable protein — VALUE

string, lima, red kidney, pinto, navy, black, Great Northern, and pink beans — KINDS

Beans are used as a food staple around the world. — PURPOSE

beans OBJECT

DESCRIPTION: _Beans are a good source of vegetable protein and are a food staple all around the world. Beans grow in pods that are green, red, or yellow. The pod may be round, oval, or flat in shape. Bean pods grow on low bushes or twining vines. The pods contain several white, red, or dark edible beans. The many varieties of beans include string, lima, kidney, pinto, navy, black, Great Northern, and pink beans. Beans are grown on farms and may be purchased in grocery stores._

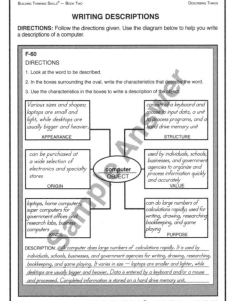

WRITING DESCRIPTIONS

DIRECTIONS: Follow the directions given. Use the diagram below to help you write a descriptions of a computer.

F-60
DIRECTIONS
1. Look at the word to be described.
2. In the boxes surrounding the oval, write the characteristics that describe the word.
3. Use the characteristics in the boxes to write a description of the object.

Various sizes and shapes; laptops are small and light, while desktops are usually bigger and heavier. — APPEARANCE

consists of a keyboard and mouse to input data, a unit to process programs, and a hard drive memory unit — STRUCTURE

can be purchased at a wide selection of electronics and specialty stores — ORIGIN

used by individuals, schools, businesses, and government agencies to organize and process information quickly and accurately — VALUE

laptops, home computers, super computers for government offices and research labs, business computers — KINDS

can do large numbers of calculations rapidly; used for writing, drawing, researching bookkeeping, and game playing — PURPOSE

computer OBJECT

DESCRIPTION: _A computer does large numbers of calculations rapidly. It is used by individuals, schools, businesses, and government agencies for writing, drawing, researching, bookkeeping, and game playing. It varies in size — laptops are smaller and lighter, while desktops are usually bigger and heavier. Data is entered by a keyboard and/or a mouse and processed. Completed information is stored on a hard drive memory unit._

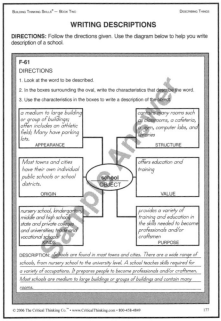

WRITING DESCRIPTIONS

DIRECTIONS: Follow the directions given. Use the diagram below to help you write description of a school.

F-61
DIRECTIONS
1. Look at the word to be described.
2. In the boxes surrounding the oval, write the characteristics that describe the word.
3. Use the characteristics in the boxes to write a description of the object.

a medium to large building or group of buildings; often includes an athletic field; Many have parking lots. — APPEARANCE

contains many rooms such as classrooms, a cafeteria, a gym, computer labs, and libraries — STRUCTURE

Most towns and cities have their own individual public schools or school districts. — ORIGIN

offers education and training — VALUE

nursery school, kindergarten, middle and high schools, state and private colleges and universities; trade and vocational schools — KINDS

provides a variety of training and education in the skills needed to become professionals and/or craftsmen — PURPOSE

school OBJECT

DESCRIPTION: _Schools are found in most towns and cities. There are a wide range of schools, from nursery school to the university level. A school teaches skills required for a variety of occupations. It prepares people to become professionals and/or craftsmen. Most schools are medium to large buildings or groups of buildings and contain many rooms._

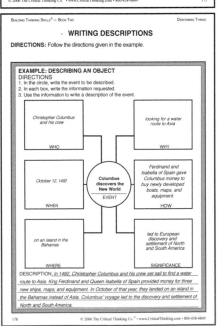

WRITING DESCRIPTIONS

DIRECTIONS: Follow the directions given in the example.

EXAMPLE: DESCRIBING AN OBJECT
DIRECTIONS
1. In the circle, write the event to be described.
2. In each box, write the information requested.
3. Use the information to write a description of the event.

Christopher Columbus and his crew — WHO

looking for a water route to Asia — WHY

October 12, 1492 — WHEN

Ferdinand and Isabella of Spain gave Columbus money to buy newly developed boats, maps, and equipment. — HOW

on an island in the Bahamas — WHERE

led to European discovery and settlement of North and South America — SIGNIFICANCE

Columbus discovers the New World EVENT

DESCRIPTION: _In 1492, Christopher Columbus and his crew set sail to find a water route to Asia. King Ferdinand and Queen Isabella of Spain provided money for three new ships, maps, and equipment. In October of that year, they landed on an island in the Bahamas instead of Asia. Columbus' voyage led to the discovery and settlement of North and South America._

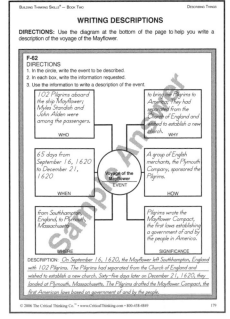

WRITING DESCRIPTIONS

DIRECTIONS: Use the diagram at the bottom of the page to help you write a description of the voyage of the Mayflower.

F-62
DIRECTIONS
1. In the circle, write the event to be described.
2. In each box, write the information requested.
3. Use the information to write a description of the event.

102 Pilgrims aboard the ship Mayflower; Myles Standish and John Alden were among the passengers. — WHO

to bring the Pilgrims to America; They had separated from the Church of England and wished to establish a new church. — WHY

65 days from September 16, 1620 to December 21, 1620 — WHEN

A group of English merchants, the Plymouth Company, sponsored the Pilgrims. — HOW

from Southampton, England, to Plymouth, Massachusetts — WHERE

Pilgrims wrote the Mayflower Compact, the first laws establishing a government of and by the people in America. — SIGNIFICANCE

Voyage of the Mayflower EVENT

DESCRIPTION: _On September 16, 1620, the Mayflower left Southampton, England with 102 Pilgrims. The Pilgrims had separated from the Church of England and wished to establish a new church. Sixty-five days later on December 21, 1620, they landed at Plymouth, Massachusetts. The Pilgrims drafted the Mayflower Compact, the first American laws based on government of and by the people._

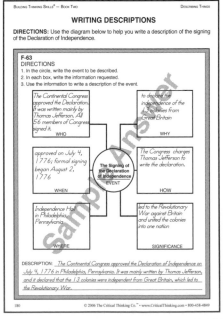

WRITING DESCRIPTIONS

DIRECTIONS: Use the diagram below to help you write a description of the signing of the Declaration of Independence.

F-63
DIRECTIONS
1. In the circle, write the event to be described.
2. In each box, write the information requested.
3. Use the information to write a description of the event.

The Continental Congress approved the Declaration. It was written mainly by Thomas Jefferson. All 56 members of Congress signed it. — WHO

to declare the independence of the 13 colonies from Great Britain — WHY

approved on July 4, 1776; formal signing began August 2, 1776 — WHEN

The Congress charges Thomas Jefferson to write the declaration. — HOW

Independence Hall in Philadelphia, Pennsylvania. — WHERE

led to the Revolutionary War against Britain and united the colonies into one nation — SIGNIFICANCE

The Signing of the Declaration of Independence EVENT

DESCRIPTION: _The Continental Congress approved the Declaration of Independence on July 4, 1776 in Philadelphia, Pennsylvania. It was mainly written by Thomas Jefferson, and it declared that the 13 colonies were independent from Great Britain, which led to the Revolutionary War._

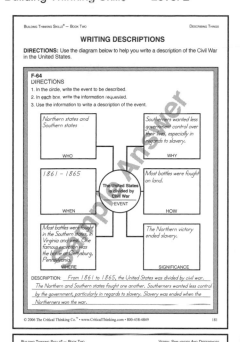
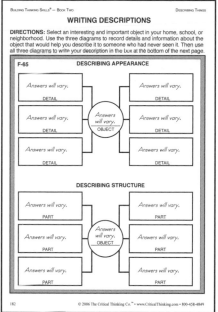
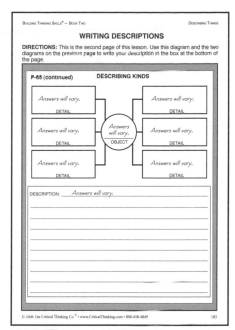
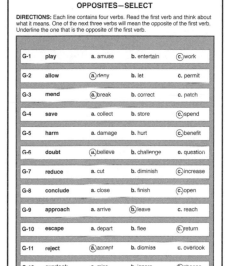
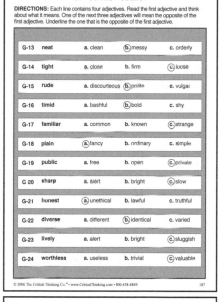
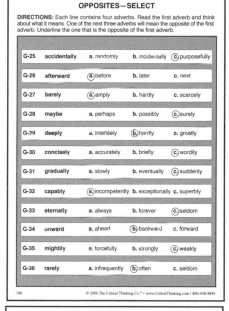
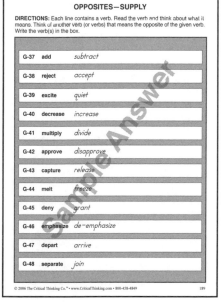
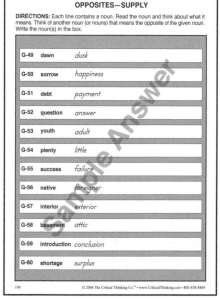
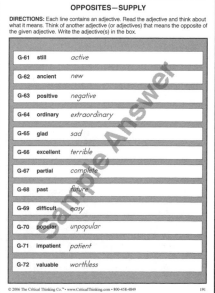

WRITING DESCRIPTIONS

F-64 — DESCRIPTION: From 1861 to 1865, the United States was divided by civil war. The Northern and Southern states fought one another. Southerners wanted less control by the government, particularly in regards to slavery. Slavery was ended when the Northerners won the war.

OPPOSITES—SELECT

G-1	play	c. work
G-2	allow	a. deny
G-3	mend	a. break
G-4	save	c. spend
G-5	harm	c. benefit
G-6	doubt	a. believe
G-7	reduce	c. increase
G-8	conclude	c. open
G-9	approach	b. leave
G-10	escape	c. return
G-11	reject	a. accept
G-12	overlook	c. choose

G-13	neat	b. messy
G-14	tight	c. loose
G-15	rude	b. polite
G-16	timid	b. bold
G-17	familiar	c. strange
G-18	plain	a. fancy
G-19	public	c. private
G-20	sharp	c. slow
G-21	honest	a. unethical
G-22	diverse	b. identical
G-23	lively	c. sluggish
G-24	worthless	c. valuable

G-25	accidentally	c. purposefully
G-26	afterward	a. before
G-27	barely	a. amply
G-28	maybe	c. surely
G-29	deeply	b. hardly
G-30	concisely	c. wordily
G-31	gradually	c. suddenly
G-32	capably	a. incompetently
G-33	eternally	c. seldom
G-34	onward	b. backward
G-35	mightily	c. weakly
G-36	rarely	b. often

OPPOSITES—SUPPLY

G-37	add	subtract
G-38	reject	accept
G-39	excite	quiet
G-40	decrease	increase
G-41	multiply	divide
G-42	approve	disapprove
G-43	capture	release
G-44	melt	freeze
G-45	deny	grant
G-46	emphasize	de-emphasize
G-47	depart	arrive
G-48	separate	join

G-49	dawn	dusk
G-50	sorrow	happiness
G-51	debt	payment
G-52	question	answer
G-53	youth	adult
G-54	plenty	little
G-55	success	failure
G-56	native	foreigner
G-57	interior	exterior
G-58	basement	attic
G-59	introduction	conclusion
G-60	shortage	surplus

G-61	still	active
G-62	ancient	new
G-63	positive	negative
G-64	ordinary	extraordinary
G-65	glad	sad
G-66	excellent	terrible
G-67	partial	complete
G-68	past	future
G-69	difficult	easy
G-70	popular	unpopular
G-71	impatient	patient
G-72	valuable	worthless

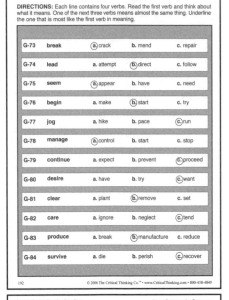

SIMILARITIES—SELECT (panel 1)

DIRECTIONS: Each line contains four verbs. Read the first verb and think about what it means. One of the next three verbs means almost the same thing. Underline the one that is most like the first verb in meaning.

G-73	break	a. crack	b. mend	c. repair
G-74	lead	a. attempt	b. direct	c. follow
G-75	seem	a. appear	b. have	c. need
G-76	begin	a. make	b. start	c. try
G-77	jog	a. hike	b. pace	c. run
G-78	manage	a. control	b. start	c. stop
G-79	continue	a. expect	b. prevent	c. proceed
G-80	desire	a. have	b. try	c. want
G-81	clear	a. plant	b. remove	c. set
G-82	care	a. ignore	b. neglect	c. tend
G-83	produce	a. break	b. manufacture	c. reduce
G-84	survive	a. die	b. perish	c. recover

(answers: G-73 a; G-74 b; G-75 a; G-76 b; G-77 c; G-78 a; G-79 c; G-80 c; G-81 b; G-82 c; G-83 b; G-84 c)

SIMILARITIES—SELECT (panel 2)

DIRECTIONS: Each line contains four adjectives. Read the first adjective and think about what it means. One of the next three adjectives means almost the same thing. Underline the one that is most like the first adjective in meaning.

G-85	active	a. busy	b. quiet	c. still
G-86	tired	a. calm	b. rested	c. weary
G-87	curious	a. familiar	b. peculiar	c. similar
G-88	personal	a. open	b. private	c. public
G-89	initial	a. first	b. last	c. middle
G-90	former	a. current	b. earlier	c. present
G-91	novel	a. different	b. familiar	c. old
G-92	earnest	a. serious	b. casual	c. careless
G-93	temporary	a. continuous	b. brief	c. permanent
G-94	favorable	a. critical	b. friendly	c. negative
G-95	clever	a. average	b. dull	c. sharp
G-96	mobile	a. fixed	b. movable	c. stationary

(answers: G-85 a; G-86 c; G-87 b; G-88 b; G-89 a; G-90 b; G-91 a; G-92 a; G-93 b; G-94 b; G-95 c; G-96 b)

SIMILARITIES—SELECT (panel 3)

DIRECTIONS: Each line contains four adjectives. Sometimes the same word can have several different meanings. Read the first adjective in each row and think about what it means. Underline the one that is most like the first adjective in meaning.

G-97	dull	a. boring	b. exciting	c. loud
G-98	dull	a. blunt	b. even	c. sharp
G-99	hard	a. difficult	b. simple	c. smooth
G-100	hard	a. easy	b. firm	c. loose
G-101	hard	a. fantastic	b. idealistic	c. realistic
G-102	clear	a. bright	b. gloomy	c. hazy
G-103	clear	a. blurred	b. certain	c. vague
G-104	clear	a. bare	b. clogged	c. occupied
G-105	fine	a. awful	b. excellent	c. poor
G-106	fine	a. coarse	b. rough	c. delicate
G-107	fine	a. broad	b. thin	c. wide
G-108	fine	a. clear	b. cloudy	c. gloomy

(answers: G-97 a; G-98 a; G-99 a; G-100 b; G-101 c; G-102 a; G-103 b; G-104 a; G-105 b; G-106 c; G-107 b; G-108 a)

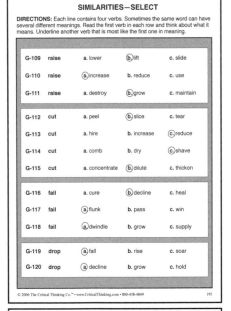

SIMILARITIES—SELECT (panel 4)

DIRECTIONS: Each line contains four verbs. Sometimes the same word can have several different meanings. Read the first verb in each row and think about what it means. Underline another verb that is most like the first one in meaning.

G-109	raise	a. lower	b. lift	c. slide
G-110	raise	a. increase	b. reduce	c. use
G-111	raise	a. destroy	b. grow	c. maintain
G-112	cut	a. peel	b. slice	c. tear
G-113	cut	a. hire	b. increase	c. reduce
G-114	cut	a. comb	b. dry	c. shave
G-115	cut	a. concentrate	b. dilute	c. thicken
G-116	fail	a. cure	b. decline	c. heal
G-117	fail	a. flunk	b. pass	c. win
G-118	fail	a. dwindle	b. grow	c. supply
G-119	drop	a. fall	b. rise	c. soar
G-120	drop	a. decline	b. grow	c. hold

(answers: G-109 b; G-110 a; G-111 b; G-112 b; G-113 c; G-114 c; G-115 b; G-116 b; G-117 a; G-118 a; G-119 a; G-120 a)

SIMILARITIES—SUPPLY (panel 5)

DIRECTIONS: Each line contains a verb. Read the verb and think about what it means. Think of another verb (or verbs) that means almost the same. Write the verb(s) in the box.

G-121	capture	hold, grab, catch
G-122	select	pick, choose, decide
G-123	ruin	destroy, wreck, demolish, bankrupt
G-124	require	demand, want, crave, request
G-125	complete	finish, fill out
G-126	consider	examine, wonder, regard, contemplate
G-127	contain	hold, include, enclose OR control, repress
G-128	shut	close, seal, block
G-129	create	make, invent, develop, build
G-130	proceed	march, move, journey, pass, progress, advance
G-131	nourish	nurse, cherish, nurture, foster, cultivate
G-132	strike	hit, swat, slap, beat, poke

SIMILARITIES—SUPPLY (panel 6)

DIRECTIONS: Each line contains an adjective. Read the adjective and think about what it means. Think of another adjective (or adjectives) that means almost the same. Write the adjective(s) in the box.

G-133	whole	all, complete, total, entire
G-134	most	greatest, largest
G-135	extra	more, additional, spare
G-136	single	one, only, sole, unmarried
G-137	annual	yearly
G-138	brilliant	beaming, radiant OR smart, clever, sharp
G-139	cautious	careful, vigilant, considerate, guarded
G-140	artificial	man-made, false, synthetic, fake, unreal
G-141	polite	courteous, mannerly, civil, thoughtful
G-142	minor	little, petty, trivial, small, unimportant
G-143	substantial	material, gross OR big, weighty OR prosperous, comfortable
G-144	handy	convenient, nearby OR practical, useful, functional

SIMILARITIES—SUPPLY (panel 7)

DIRECTIONS: Each line contains a noun. Read the noun and think about what it means. Think of a noun (or nouns) that means almost the same. Write the noun(s) in the box.

G-145	instructor	teacher, tutor, coach, educator
G-146	opportunity	chance, opening, occasion
G-147	explanation	description, answer, reason
G-148	power	skill, capacity OR might, force, vigor OR energy, electricity
G-149	delight	joy, pleasure, happiness, amusement
G-150	achievement	feat, deed, exploit, accomplishment
G-151	boundary	edge, perimeter, bounds, limits, confines
G-152	career	profession, calling, trade, vocation, craft
G-153	section	part, division, parcel, piece, portion, segment, zone, region
G-154	announcement	declaration, proclamation, statement
G-155	device	appliance, instrument, tool, utensil, machine
G-156	supplement	addition, complement, additive, appendix

HOW ALIKE?—SELECT (panel 8)

DIRECTIONS: Each line contains two words related to social studies. Think about the ways the two words are alike. Underline the sentence(s) that is true of both words.

G-157	postage stamps coins	a. Both can be collected as a hobby. b. Both are produced by the government. c. Both have a monetary value printed on them.
G-158	king president	a. Both are elected. b. Both are national leaders. c. Both participate in national ceremonies.
G-159	goods services	a. Both are objects. b. Both can be purchased. c. Both require workers.
G-160	globe map	a. Both are drawings of all or part of the earth. b. Both are flat. c. Both can be used to estimate distances between places.
G-161	lake ocean	a. Both are bodies of water. b. Both can be located on maps. c. Both contain drinkable water.
G-162	checks money	a. Both can be obtained at a bank. b. Both can be used to buy things. c. Both need to be endorsed.

(answers: G-157 a, b; G-158 b, c; G-159 b, c; G-160 a, c; G-161 a, b; G-162 a, b)

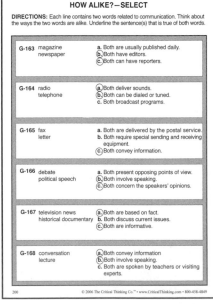

HOW ALIKE?—SELECT (panel 9)

DIRECTIONS: Each line contains two words related to communication. Think about the ways the two words are alike. Underline the sentence(s) that is true of both words.

G-163	magazine newspaper	a. Both are usually published daily. b. Both have editors. c. Both can have reporters.
G-164	radio telephone	a. Both deliver sounds. b. Both can be dialed or tuned. c. Both broadcast programs.
G-165	fax letter	a. Both are delivered by the postal service. b. Both require special sending and receiving equipment. c. Both convey information.
G-166	debate political speech	a. Both present opposing points of view. b. Both involve speaking. c. Both concern the speakers' opinions.
G-167	television news historical documentary	a. Both are based on fact. b. Both discuss current issues. c. Both are informative.
G-168	conversation lecture	a. Both convey information. b. Both involve speaking. c. Both are spoken by teachers or visiting experts.

(answers: G-163 b, c; G-164 a, b; G-165 c; G-166 b, c; G-167 a, c; G-168 a, b)

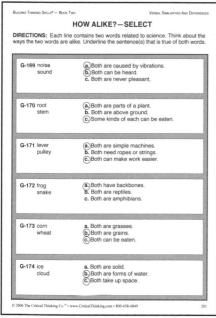

HOW ALIKE?—SELECT

DIRECTIONS: Each line contains two words related to science. Think about the ways the two words are alike. Underline the sentence(s) that is true of both words.

G-169	noise / sound	**a.** Both are caused by vibrations. **b.** Both can be heard. c. Both are never pleasant.
G-170	root / stem	**a.** Both are parts of a plant. b. Both are above ground. **c.** Some kinds of each can be eaten.
G-171	lever / pulley	**a.** Both are simple machines. b. Both need ropes or strings. **c.** Both can make work easier.
G-172	frog / snake	**a.** Both have backbones. b. Both are reptiles. c. Both are amphibians.
G-173	corn / wheat	a. Both are grasses. **b.** Both are grains. **c.** Both can be eaten.
G-174	ice / cloud	a. Both are solid. **b.** Both are forms of water. **c.** Both take up space.

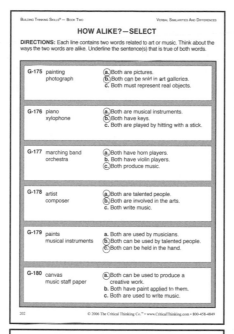

HOW ALIKE?—SELECT

DIRECTIONS: Each line contains two words related to art or music. Think about the ways the two words are alike. Underline the sentence(s) that is true of both words.

G-175	painting / photograph	**a.** Both are pictures. **b.** Both can be sold in art galleries. c. Both must represent real objects.
G-176	piano / xylophone	**a.** Both are musical instruments. b. Both have keys. **c.** Both are played by hitting with a stick.
G-177	marching band / orchestra	**a.** Both have horn players. b. Both have violin players. **c.** Both produce music.
G-178	artist / composer	**a.** Both are talented people. **b.** Both are involved in the arts. c. Both write music.
G-179	paints / musical instruments	**a.** Both are used by musicians. **b.** Both can be used by talented people. **c.** Both can be held in the hand.
G-180	canvas / music staff paper	**a.** Both can be used to produce a creative work. b. Both have paint applied to them. c. Both are used to write music.

HOW ALIKE AND HOW DIFFERENT?

DIRECTIONS: Each line contains two words related to social studies. Describe how the words are alike and how they are different.

G-181	neighborhood / community	**HOW ALIKE?** *Both are geographic divisions.* **HOW DIFFERENT?** *A neighborhood is a small area of homes, stores, churches, and schools. A community is a collection of neighborhoods.*
G-182	mayor / governor	**HOW ALIKE?** *Both are elected officials.* **HOW DIFFERENT?** *A mayor is the chief executive of a city. A governor is the chief executive of a state.*
G-183	country / continent	**HOW ALIKE?** *Both are geographic regions.* **HOW DIFFERENT?** *A continent is one of seven very large bodies of land making up the earth. A country is smaller than a continent, with one exception — the country of Australia is also its own continent.*
G-184	weather / climate	**HOW ALIKE?** *Both refer to weather conditions.* **HOW DIFFERENT?** *Weather is a daily occurrence. Climate describes the long-term average weather of a region.*
G-185	dictatorship / democracy	**HOW ALIKE?** *Both are forms of government.* **HOW DIFFERENT?** *The leader of a dictatorship is appointed by a group that seizes power of the government. The leader of a democracy is chosen by open elections.*

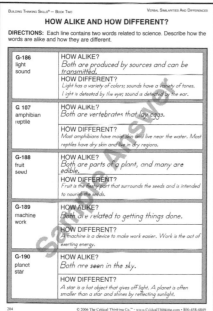

HOW ALIKE AND HOW DIFFERENT?

DIRECTIONS: Each line contains two words related to science. Describe how the words are alike and how they are different.

G-186	light / sound	**HOW ALIKE?** *Both are produced by sources and can be transmitted.* **HOW DIFFERENT?** *Light has a variety of colors; sounds have a variety of tones. Light is detected by the eye; sound is detected by the ear.*
G-187	amphibian / reptile	**HOW ALIKE?** *Both are vertebrates that lay eggs.* **HOW DIFFERENT?** *Most amphibians have moist skin and live near the water. Most reptiles have dry skin and live in dry regions.*
G-188	fruit / seed	**HOW ALIKE?** *Both are parts of a plant, and many are edible.* **HOW DIFFERENT?** *Fruit is the fleshy part that surrounds the seeds and is intended to nourish the seeds.*
G-189	machine / work	**HOW ALIKE?** *Both are related to getting things done.* **HOW DIFFERENT?** *A machine is a device to make work easier. Work is the act of exerting energy.*
G-190	planet / star	**HOW ALIKE?** *Both are seen in the sky.* **HOW DIFFERENT?** *A star is a hot object that gives off light. A planet is often smaller than a star and shines by reflecting sunlight.*

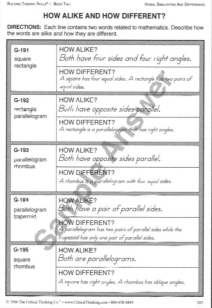

HOW ALIKE AND HOW DIFFERENT?

DIRECTIONS: Each line contains two words related to mathematics. Describe how the words are alike and how they are different.

G-191	square / rectangle	**HOW ALIKE?** *Both have four sides and four right angles.* **HOW DIFFERENT?** *A square has four equal sides. A rectangle has two pairs of equal sides.*
G-192	rectangle / parallelogram	**HOW ALIKE?** *Both have opposite sides parallel.* **HOW DIFFERENT?** *A rectangle is a parallelogram that has right angles.*
G-193	parallelogram / rhombus	**HOW ALIKE?** *Both have opposite sides parallel.* **HOW DIFFERENT?** *A rhombus is a parallelogram with four equal sides.*
G-194	parallelogram / trapezoid	**HOW ALIKE?** *Both have a pair of parallel sides.* **HOW DIFFERENT?** *A parallelogram has two pairs of parallel sides while the trapezoid has only one pair of parallel sides.*
G-195	square / rhombus	**HOW ALIKE?** *Both are parallelograms.* **HOW DIFFERENT?** *A square has right angles. A rhombus has oblique angles.*

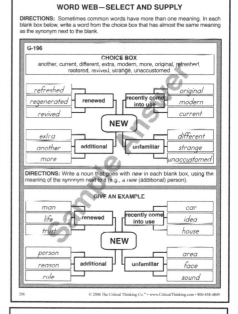

WORD WEB—SELECT AND SUPPLY

DIRECTIONS: Sometimes common words have more than one meaning. In each blank box below, write a word from the choice box that has almost the same meaning as the synonym next to the blank.

G-196

CHOICE BOX
another, current, different, extra, modern, more, original, refreshed, restored, revived, strange, unaccustomed

refreshed, *regenerated*, *revived* — **renewed** — **recently come into use** — *original*, *modern*, *current*

NEW

extra, *another*, *more* — **additional** — **unfamiliar** — *different*, *strange*, *unaccustomed*

DIRECTIONS: Write a noun that goes with *new* in each blank box, using the meaning of the synonym next to it (e.g., a new (additional) person).

GIVE AN EXAMPLE

man, *life*, *trust* — **renewed** — **recently come into use**

NEW

car, *idea*, *house*

person, *reason*, *rule* — **additional** — **unfamiliar** — *area*, *face*, *sound*

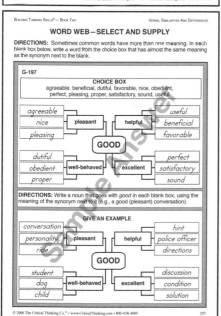

WORD WEB—SELECT AND SUPPLY

DIRECTIONS: Sometimes common words have more than one meaning. In each blank box below, write a word from the choice box that has almost the same meaning as the synonym next to the blank.

G-197

CHOICE BOX
agreeable, beneficial, dutiful, favorable, nice, obedient, perfect, pleasing, proper, satisfactory, sound, useful

agreeable, *nice*, *pleasing* — **pleasant** — **helpful** — *useful*, *beneficial*, *favorable*

GOOD

dutiful, *obedient*, *proper* — **well-behaved** — **excellent** — *perfect*, *satisfactory*, *sound*

DIRECTIONS: Write a noun that goes with *good* in each blank box, using the meaning of the synonym next to it (e.g., a good (pleasant) conversation).

GIVE AN EXAMPLE

conversation, *personality*, *ride* — **pleasant** — **helpful** — *hint*, *police officer*, *directions*

GOOD

student, *dog*, *child* — **well-behaved** — **excellent** — *discussion*, *condition*, *solution*

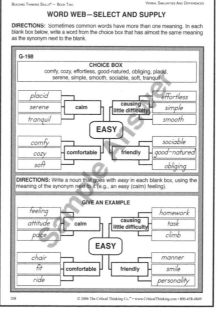

WORD WEB—SELECT AND SUPPLY

DIRECTIONS: Sometimes common words have more than one meaning. In each blank box below, write a word from the choice box that has almost the same meaning as the synonym next to the blank.

G-198

CHOICE BOX
comfy, cozy, effortless, good-natured, obliging, placid, serene, simple, smooth, sociable, soft, tranquil

placid, *serene*, *tranquil* — **calm** — **causing little difficulty** — *effortless*, *simple*, *smooth*

EASY

comfy, *cozy*, *soft* — **comfortable** — **friendly** — *sociable*, *good-natured*, *obliging*

DIRECTIONS: Write a noun that goes with *easy* in each blank box, using the meaning of the synonym next to it (e.g., an easy (calm) feeling).

GIVE AN EXAMPLE

feeling, *attitude*, *pace* — **calm** — **causing little difficulty** — *homework*, *task*, *climb*

EASY

chair, *fit*, *ride* — **comfortable** — **friendly** — *manner*, *smile*, *personality*

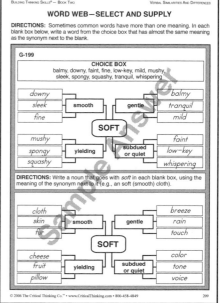

WORD WEB—SELECT AND SUPPLY

DIRECTIONS: Sometimes common words have more than one meaning. In each blank box below, write a word from the choice box that has almost the same meaning as the synonym next to the blank.

G-199

CHOICE BOX
balmy, downy, faint, fine, low-key, mild, mushy, sleek, spongy, squashy, tranquil, whispering

downy, *sleek*, *fine* — **smooth** — **gentle** — *balmy*, *tranquil*, *mild*

SOFT

mushy, *spongy*, *squashy* — **yielding** — **subdued or quiet** — *faint*, *low-key*, *whispering*

DIRECTIONS: Write a noun that goes with *soft* in each blank box, using the meaning of the synonym next to it (e.g., an soft (smooth) cloth).

GIVE AN EXAMPLE

cloth, *skin*, *fur* — **smooth** — **gentle** — *breeze*, *rain*, *touch*

SOFT

cheese, *fruit*, *pillow* — **yielding** — **subdued or quiet** — *color*, *tone*, *voice*

WORD WEB—SELECT AND SUPPLY

DIRECTIONS: Sometimes common words have more than one meaning. In each blank box, write a word from the choice box that has almost the same meaning as the synonym next to the blank.

G-200

CHOICE BOX
compressed, factual, genuine, heavy, intense, packed, real, rugged, serious, solid, tough, violent

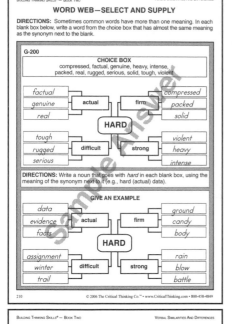

DIRECTIONS: Write a noun that goes with *hard* in each blank box, using the meaning of the synonym next to it (e.g., hard (actual) data).

WORD WEB—SELECT AND SUPPLY

DIRECTIONS: Sometimes common words have more than one meaning. In each blank box, write a word from the choice box that has almost the same meaning as the synonym next to the blank.

G-201

CHOICE BOX
absolute, bare, basic, effortless, inexperienced, modest, naive, ordinary, perfect, unaffected, uncomplicated, unmixed

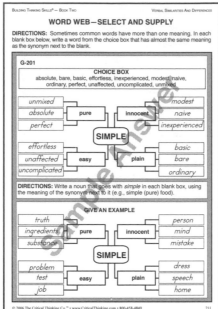

DIRECTIONS: Write a noun that goes with *simple* in each blank box, using the meaning of the synonym next to it (e.g., simple (pure) food).

COMPARE AND CONTRAST—GRAPHIC ORGANIZER

DIRECTIONS: Read the following information about spiders and insects. Use this information to compare and contrast spiders and insects in the graphic organizer on the next page.

INSECTS AND SPIDERS

Insects and spiders have jointed appendages, segmented bodies, and exoskeletons. Insects have three pairs of walking legs and spiders have four pairs. Their jointed legs bend to allow quick movement. Insects have segmented bodies with three parts: the head, the thorax, and the abdomen. Spiders have two major body parts, the cephalothorax and the abdomen. Both types of animal have an exoskeleton. This is an external skeleton that protects the body and is molted as the animal grows. Insects have antennae. Antennae are sense organs found on the head that can detect odors. Spiders do not have antennae. They do, however, have spinnerets which produce the fine silk used for their webs.

Spiders are predators that feed primarily on other insects. Spiders can swallow only liquids, so digestive juices are pumped onto the prey, it is digested externally, and the spider swallows the resulting liquid. Insects obtain food by a variety of methods, including biting, lapping, and sucking. Butterflies suck nectar from a flower through their proboscis (feeding tube). Honeybees lap nectar with their tongues. Beetles, wasps, and ants use their powerful biting jaws.

COMPARE AND CONTRAST—GRAPHIC ORGANIZER

DIRECTIONS: Use the graphic organizer below to compare and contrast insects and spiders.

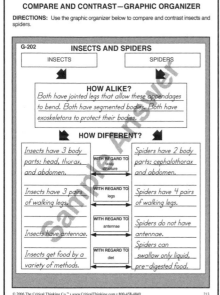

COMPARE AND CONTRAST—GRAPHIC ORGANIZER

DIRECTIONS: Use the graphic organizer below to compare and contrast a parallelogram and an isosceles trapezoid.

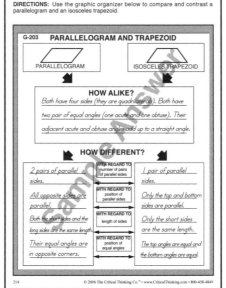

COMPARE AND CONTRAST—GRAPHIC ORGANIZER

DIRECTIONS: Use the graphic organizer below to compare and contrast democracy and dictatorship.

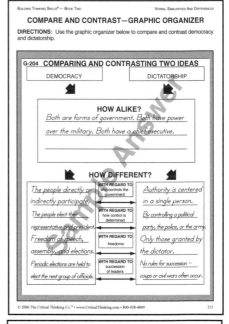

FOLLOWING DIRECTIONS—SELECT

DIRECTIONS: For each set of directions below, circle the figure that correctly represents the directions.

EXAMPLE
DIRECTIONS: Draw a triangle with two long, equal sides. Use the shortest side of the triangle as one side of a square.

H-1 DIRECTIONS: Draw a rectangle. Draw a diamond inside the rectangle that touches the rectangle at four points.

H-2 DIRECTIONS: Draw a square. Use the top of the square as the bottom of a triangle. Draw a circle inside the square that touches all sides of the square.

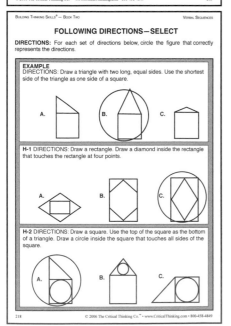

FOLLOWING DIRECTIONS—SELECT

DIRECTIONS: For each set of directions below, circle the figure that correctly represents the directions.

H-3 DIRECTIONS: Draw a right triangle with the base and height the same length. Draw a rectangle using the height of the triangle as the long side of the rectangle. Inside the triangle, draw a circle that touches all sides of the triangle.

H-4 DIRECTIONS: Draw two squares, one above the other. Draw a triangle inside the upper square. Draw a circle inside the lower square.

H-5 DIRECTIONS: Draw a square. Divide the square into two equal parts by drawing a line from the upper left corner to the lower right corner. Draw a rectangle using the bottom of the square as the top of the rectangle.

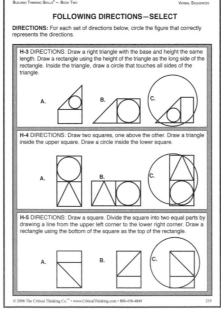

FOLLOWING DIRECTIONS—SUPPLY

DIRECTIONS: For each set of directions below, draw a figure that correctly represents the directions.

H-6 DIRECTIONS: Using the grid of dots below, draw a circle near the center of the grid. Directly above the circle, draw a square. To the right of the square, draw a triangle.

H-7 DIRECTIONS: Using the grid of dots below, draw a square near the lower left corner. Near the upper right corner, draw a circle. Directly below the circle, draw a triangle.

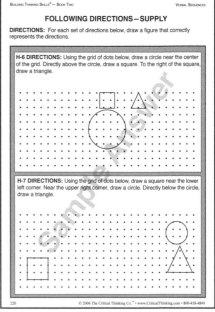

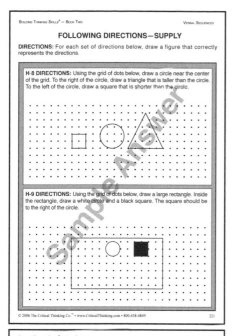

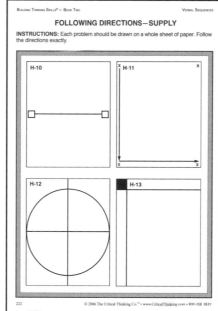

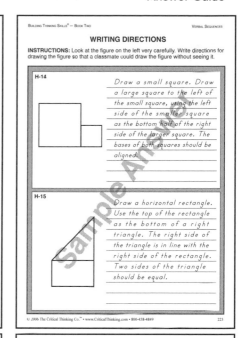

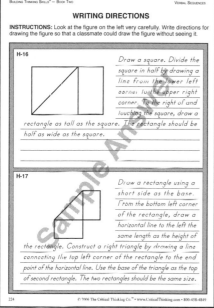

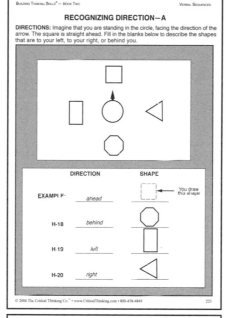

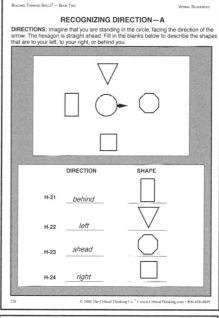

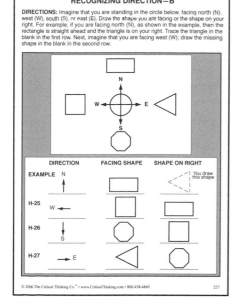

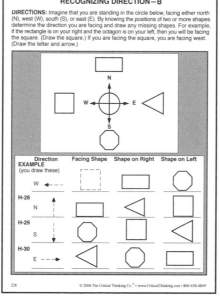

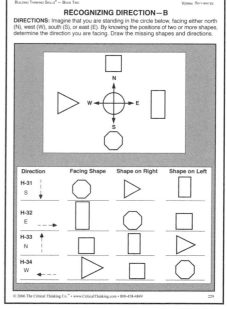

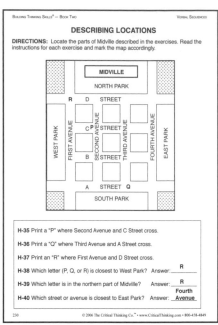

BUILDING THINKING SKILLS® — BOOK TWO   VERBAL SEQUENCES

DESCRIBING LOCATIONS

DIRECTIONS: Locate the parts of Midville described in the exercises. Read the instructions for each exercise and mark the map accordingly.

H-35 Print a "P" where Second Avenue and C Street cross.

H-36 Print a "Q" where Third Avenue and A Street cross.

H-37 Print an "R" where First Avenue and D Street cross.

H-38 Which letter (P, Q, or R) is closest to West Park?   Answer: **R**

H-39 Which letter is in the northern part of Midville?   Answer: **R**

H-40 Which street or avenue is closest to East Park?   Answer: **Fourth Avenue**

© 2006 The Critical Thinking Co.™ • www.CriticalThinking.com • 800-458-4849   230

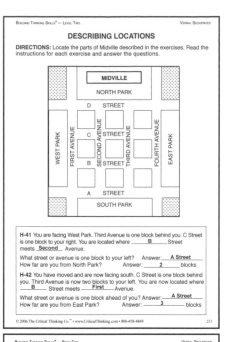

BUILDING THINKING SKILLS® — LEVEL TWO   VERBAL SEQUENCES

DESCRIBING LOCATIONS

DIRECTIONS: Locate the parts of Midville described in the exercises. Read the instructions for each exercise and answer the questions.

H-41 You are facing West Park. Third Avenue is one block behind you. C Street is one block to your right. You are located where **B** Street meets **Second** Avenue.

What street or avenue is one block to your left?   Answer: **A Street**
How far are you from North Park?   Answer: **2** blocks

H-42 You have moved and are now facing south. C Street is one block behind you. Third Avenue is now two blocks to your left. You are now located where **B** Street meets **First** Avenue.

What street or avenue is one block ahead of you?   Answer: **A Street**
How far are you from East Park?   Answer: **3** blocks

© 2006 The Critical Thinking Co.™ • www.CriticalThinking.com • 800-458-4849   231

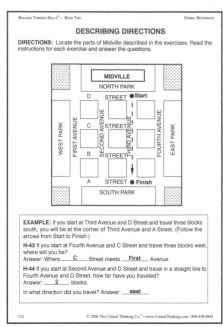

BUILDING THINKING SKILLS® — BOOK TWO   VERBAL SEQUENCES

DESCRIBING DIRECTIONS

DIRECTIONS: Locate the parts of Midville described in the exercises. Read the instructions for each exercise and answer the questions.

EXAMPLE: If you start at Third Avenue and D Street and travel three blocks south, you will be at the corner of Third Avenue and A Street. (Follow the arrows from Start to Finish.)

H-43 If you start at Fourth Avenue and C Street and travel three blocks west, where will you be?
Answer: **C** Street meets **First** Avenue.

H-44 If you start at Second Avenue and D Street and travel in a straight line to Fourth Avenue and D Street, how far have you traveled?
Answer: **2** blocks.

In what direction did you travel? Answer: **east**

232   © 2006 The Critical Thinking Co.™ • www.CriticalThinking.com • 800-458-4849

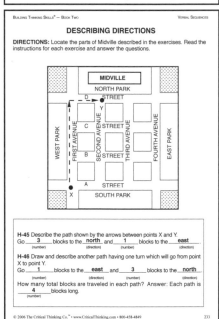

BUILDING THINKING SKILLS® — BOOK TWO   VERBAL SEQUENCES

DESCRIBING DIRECTIONS

DIRECTIONS: Locate the parts of Midville described in the exercises. Read the instructions for each exercise and answer the questions.

H-45 Describe the path shown by the arrows between points X and Y.
Go **3** blocks to the **north** and **1** blocks to the **east**.
        (number)   (direction)   (number)   (direction)

H-46 Draw and describe another path having one turn which will go from point X to point Y.
Go **1** blocks to the **east** and **3** blocks to the **north**.
        (number)   (direction)   (number)   (direction)

How many total blocks are traveled in each path? Answer: Each path is **4** blocks long.
                                                                                      (number)

© 2006 The Critical Thinking Co.™ • www.CriticalThinking.com • 800-458-4849   233

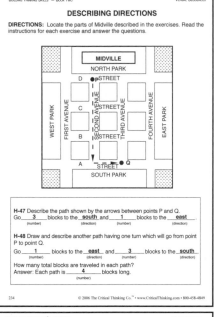

BUILDING THINKING SKILLS® — BOOK TWO   VERBAL SEQUENCES

DESCRIBING DIRECTIONS

DIRECTIONS: Locate the parts of Midville described in the exercises. Read the instructions for each exercise and answer the questions.

H-47 Describe the path shown by the arrows between points P and Q.
Go **3** blocks to the **south** and **1** blocks to the **east**.
        (number)   (direction)   (number)   (direction)

H-48 Draw and describe another path having one turn which will go from point P to point Q.
Go **1** blocks to the **east** and **3** blocks to the **south**.
        (number)   (direction)   (number)   (direction)

How many total blocks are traveled in each path?
Answer: Each path is **4** blocks long.
                          (number)

234   © 2006 The Critical Thinking Co.™ • www.CriticalThinking.com • 800-458-4849

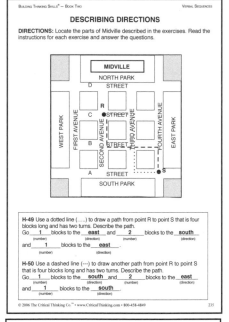

BUILDING THINKING SKILLS® — BOOK TWO   VERBAL SEQUENCES

DESCRIBING DIRECTIONS

DIRECTIONS: Locate the parts of Midville described in the exercises. Read the instructions for each exercise and answer the questions.

H-49 Use a dotted line (.....) to draw a path from point R to point S that is four blocks long and has two turns. Describe the path.
Go **1** blocks to the **east** and **2** blocks to the **south**
        (number)   (direction)   (number)   (direction)
and **1** blocks to the **east**.
        (number)   (direction)

H-50 Use a dashed line (---) to draw another path from point R to point S that is four blocks long and has two turns. Describe the path.
Go **1** blocks to the **south** and **2** blocks to the **east**
        (number)   (direction)   (number)   (direction)
and **1** blocks to the **south**.
        (number)   (direction)

© 2006 The Critical Thinking Co.™ • www.CriticalThinking.com • 800-458-4849   235

BUILDING THINKING SKILLS® — BOOK TWO   VERBAL SEQUENCES

TIME SEQUENCE—SELECT

DIRECTIONS: The first words in each group suggest an order of occurrence. On the blank, write the word from the column on the right that will continue the time sequence.

H-51 leave, travel, _arrive_   arrive / depart / drive

H-52 earn, save, _spend_   gain / receive / spend

H-53 plan, build, _occupy_   construct / design / occupy

H-54 cause, event, _result_   chance / reason / result

H-55 early, prompt, _late_   late / now / soon

H-56 measure, mark, _cut_   cut / line / rule

H-57 sleep, waken, _rise_   rise / slumber / stir

236   © 2006 The Critical Thinking Co.™ • www.CriticalThinking.com • 800-458-4849

BUILDING THINKING SKILLS® — BOOK TWO   VERBAL SEQUENCES

TIME SEQUENCE—RANK

DIRECTIONS: On the lines below, rewrite each group of words in order of occurrence from earliest to latest.

H-58 clean, cook, eat
cook, _eat_, _clean_

H-59 dial, hang up, talk
dial, _talk_, _hang up_

H-60 buy, shop, use
shop, _buy_, _use_

H-61 attack, battle, defeat
attack, _battle_, _defeat_

H-62 lesson, performance, practice
lesson, _practice_, _performance_

H-63 continue, finish, start
start, _continue_, _finish_

H-64 dry, rinse, wash
wash, _rinse_, _dry_

© 2006 The Critical Thinking Co.™ • www.CriticalThinking.com • 800-458-4849   237

BUILDING THINKING SKILLS® — BOOK TWO   VERBAL SEQUENCES

TIME SEQUENCE—SUPPLY

DIRECTIONS: The words or phrases in each group suggest an order of occurrence. Think of a word that will continue the time sequence and write it in the blank. You may need to use a dictionary.

H-65 born, live, _die_

H-66 plow, plant, _harvest_

H-67 begin, continue, _end_

H-68 past, present, _future_

H-69 dawn, morning, _noon_

H-70 hurt, treat, _heal_

H-71 inhale, hold breath, _exhale_

H-72 read catalog, select product, _buy_

H-73 enroll, attend, _graduate_

238   © 2006 The Critical Thinking Co.™ • www.CriticalThinking.com • 800-458-4849

Sample Answer

DEGREE OF MEANING—SELECT (page 239)

DIRECTIONS: The words in each group suggest a sequence of rank, degree, size, or order. In the blank, write the word from the column on the right that will come next in the sequence.

H-74	chilly, frosty, _freezing_	brisk / cool / freezing
H-75	ahead, beside, _behind_	behind / beneath / between
H-76	hint, ask, _demand_	demand / request / suggest
H-77	sad, depressed, _hopeless_	hopeless / sorry / unhappy
H-78	scarce, adequate, _plenty_	enough / few / plenty
H-79	satisfactory, admirable, _excellent_	average / ordinary / excellent
H-80	mist, light rain, _downpour_	downpour / drizzle / fog

DEGREE OF MEANING—SELECT (page 240)

DIRECTIONS: The words in each group suggest a sequence of rank, degree, size, or order. In the blank, write the word from the column on the right that will come next in the sequence.

H-81	gentle, firm, _harsh_	harsh / mild / tender
H-82	exact, similar, _different_	alike / different / identical
H-83	asleep, calm, active, _excited_	excited / quiet / resting
H-84	incomplete, poor, _average_	careless / average / worthless
H-85	shy, fearful, _terrified_	bashful / coy / terrified
H-86	fatigued, weary, _exhausted_	drained / exhausted / tired
H-87	bothered, displeased, _disgusted_	annoyed / disappointed / disgusted

DEGREE OF MEANING—RANK (page 241)

DIRECTIONS: On the lines below, rewrite each group of words in order from least or smallest to greatest or largest in degree, rank, size, or order.

H-88	delighted, pleased, thrilled	pleased / delighted / thrilled	
H-89	danger, safety, threat	safety / threat / danger	
H-90	doze, nap, sleep	doze / nap / sleep	
H-91	bright, dark, dim	dark / dim / bright	
H-92	desert, jungle, prairie	desert / prairie / jungle	
H-93	lake, ocean, pond	pond / lake / ocean	
H-94	continent, country, state	state / country / continent	

DEGREE OF MEANING—RANK (page 242)

DIRECTIONS: On the lines below, rewrite each group of words in order from lowest or smallest to highest or largest in degree, rank, size, or order.

H-95	class, pupil, school	pupil / class / school	
H-96	painful, sore, tender	tender / sore / painful	
H-97	burst, full, swell	swell / full / burst	
H-98	empty, overflowing, full	empty / full / overflowing	
H-99	full, hungry, starving	starving / hungry / full	
H-100	gallon, pint, quart	pint / quart / gallon	
H-101	foot, inch, yard	inch / foot / yard	

DEGREE OF MEANING—SUPPLY (page 243)

DIRECTIONS: The words in each group suggest a sequence of degree, rank, size, or order. Think of a word that will continue the sequence and write it in the blank. You may need to use a dictionary.

H-102	mayor, governor, _president_
H-103	front, side, _back_
H-104	few, many, _most_
H-105	far, farther, _furthest_
H-106	more, some, _none_
H-107	word, sentence, _paragraph_
H-108	same, similar, _different_
H-109	good, better, _best_
H-110	cool, warm, _hot_

Sample Answer

DEGREE OF MEANING—SUPPLY (page 244)

DIRECTIONS: The words in each group suggest a sequence of degree, rank, size, or order. Think of a word that will continue the sequence and write it in the blank. You may need to use a dictionary.

H-111	short, average, _tall_
H-112	dark, dawn, _daylight_
H-113	day, week, _month_
H-114	caterpillar, cocoon, _butterfly_
H-115	scene, act, _play_
H-116	home, neighborhood, _community_
H-117	foal, colt, _horse_
H-118	duet, trio, _quartet_
H-119	tenor, baritone, _bass_

Sample Answer

TRANSITIVITY—COMPARISON (page 245)

DIRECTIONS: In these sentences, animals or objects are being compared according to some characteristic they have in common. Read the sentences and use the diagrams to figure out the order. Then list the items in order.

H-120 The adult fox terrier is about four inches taller than the West Highland terrier (Westie). The Airedale is the largest dog in the terrier breed. List the terriers in descending order beginning with the largest.

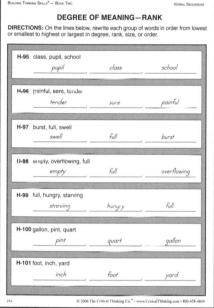

LARGEST — Airedale / fox terrier / West Highland (Westie) — SMALLEST

H-121 A bus is faster than a bicycle. Subway trains are faster than buses but slower than monorail trains. List the vehicles in descending order beginning with the fastest.

FASTEST — monorail / subway / bus / bicycle — SLOWEST

TRANSITIVITY—COMPARISON (page 246)

DIRECTIONS: In these sentences, people or objects are being compared according to some characteristic they have in common (age, size, or position). Read the sentences and use the diagrams to figure out the order. List the items in order.

H-122 Mary is older than Gloria. Gloria is younger than Elizabeth. Michelle is older than Elizabeth but younger than Mary. Write the four names in order, starting with the name of the oldest person.

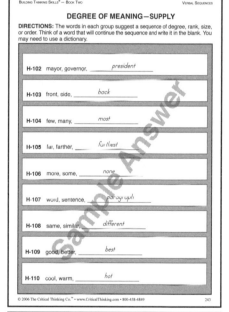

OLDEST — Mary / Michelle / Elizabeth / Gloria — YOUNGEST

H-123 Three houses are in a row. One is modern, one is colonial, and one is Victorian. The colonial house is north of the modern house and south of the Victorian house. List the houses in order from north to south.

NORTH — Victorian / colonial / modern — SOUTH

H-124 Christine, Eric, Jesse, John, and Taryn are in line at the movie. Taryn is in front of Eric but behind John. Christine is behind Eric but in front of Jesse. List the children in order from front to rear.

FRONT — John / Taryn / Eric / Christine / Jesse — REAR

TRANSITIVITY—COMPARISON (page 247)

DIRECTIONS: In these sentences, events are being compared according to their occurrence. Arrange the events in order of occurrence from earliest to latest.

H-125 John Quincy Adams, the sixth president of the United States, was the son of John Adams, the second president. John Adams became president after two terms as vice president during the presidency of George Washington. Thomas Jefferson followed John Adams as president.

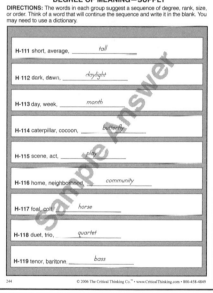

EARLIEST — George Washington / John Adams / Thomas Jefferson / John Quincy Adams — LATEST

H-126 The oldest permanent European settlement in the United States is St. Augustine, Florida. Plymouth, Massachusetts, was settled thirteen years after the Jamestown, Virginia, colony. List these historic cities in the order they were settled.

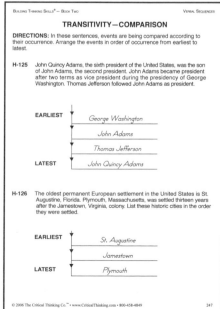

EARLIEST — St. Augustine / Jamestown / Plymouth — LATEST

Panel 1 (p. 248)

TRANSITIVITY—COMPARISON

DIRECTIONS: In these sentences, events are being compared according to their occurrence. Arrange the events in order of occurrence from earliest to latest.

H-127 Number these sentences in order of occurrence from the earliest to the latest. Use the time line to keep track of the time order.

4 a. Between eighteen months and two years, a baby begins to speak in sentences.

1 b. One of a newborn baby's first skills is grasping objects or toys.

2 c. The infant begins to crawl when it is about six months old.

3 d. Soon after a baby's first birthday, the child begins to use words.

EVENTS IN INFANT'S LIFE

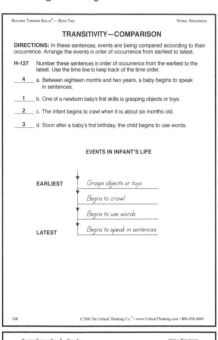

EARLIEST — Grasps objects or toys
Begins to crawl
Begins to use words
LATEST — Begins to speak in sentences

Panel 2 (p. 249)

TRANSITIVITY—COMPARISON

DIRECTIONS: In these sentences, events are being compared according to their occurrence. Arrange the events in order of occurrence from earliest to latest.

H-128 Number these sentences in order of occurrence from the earliest to the latest. Use the time line to keep track of the time order.

2 a. Bob Keeshan played Captain Kangaroo on the *Captain Kangaroo Show*.

1 b. Before playing Captain Kangaroo, Bob Keeshan played Clarabelle the Clown on the *Howdy Doody Show*.

4 c. After the success of *Sesame Street*, Children's Television Workshop developed *The Electric Company*.

3 d. Recognizing the educational benefits of the *Captain Kangaroo Show*, Children's Television Workshop produced *Sesame Street* to emphasize learning concepts for young children.

List these children's television shows from the earliest to the latest.

CHILDREN'S TELEVISION SHOWS

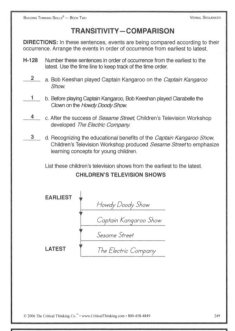

EARLIEST — Howdy Doody Show
Captain Kangaroo Show
Sesame Street
LATEST — The Electric Company

Panel 3 (p. 250)

COMMON SEQUENCES

DIRECTIONS: Many things you do must be done in order. List the phrases in the order they should occur.

H-129 Steps in Taking a Photograph

Click the shutter
Focus the camera
Find the subject in the lens
Print the picture
Turn the camera on

1. Turn the camera on
2. Find the subject in the lens
3. Focus the camera
4. Click the shutter
5. Print the picture

H-130 Steps in Making a Phone Call

Dial area code
Dial seven digit number
Hang up
Look up number
Talk

1. Look up number
2. Dial area code
3. Dial seven digit number
4. Talk
5. Hang up

Panel 4 (p. 251)

COMMON SEQUENCES

DIRECTIONS: Many things you do must be done in order. List the phrases in the order they should occur.

H-131 Steps in Planning a Candy Sale

Buy the materials to make candy
Cook the candy
Decide on the type of candy you will make
Find a recipe for the candy
Package the candy
Sell the candy

1. Decide on the type of candy you will make
2. Find a recipe for the candy
3. Buy the materials to make candy
4. Cook the candy
5. Package the candy
6. Sell the candy

H-132 Steps in Adopting a Dog

Ask your parents if you can have a dog
Go to the animal shelter with your family
Pay for the license and adoption fee
Pick out the dog
Take the dog home
Talk with your family about the kind of dog that is best for the family

1. Ask your parents if you can have a dog
2. Talk with your family about the kind of dog that is best for the family
3. Go to the animal shelter with your family
4. Pick out the dog
5. Pay for the license and adoption fee
6. Take the dog home

Panel 5 (p. 252)

TRANSITIVITY—FAMILY TREE

Family tree diagrams are used to show relationships between generations in a family. By using symbols, the diagram helps you organize relationships between

husband and wife

parent and child

sister and brother

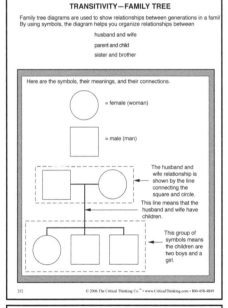

Here are the symbols, their meanings, and their connections.

◯ = female (woman)

▢ = male (man)

The husband and wife relationship is shown by the line connecting the square and circle. This line means that the husband and wife have children.

This group of symbols means the children are two boys and a girl.

Panel 6 (p. 253)

TRANSITIVITY—FAMILY TREE

DIRECTIONS: In the family tree diagram below, circles represent females and squares represent males. Use the clues to fill in the diagram.

CLUES

Juan and Rosita have the same names as their grandparents. Marie has the same name as her mother.

One of Jose's daughters has the same name as Jose's mother.

H-133

DIAGRAM

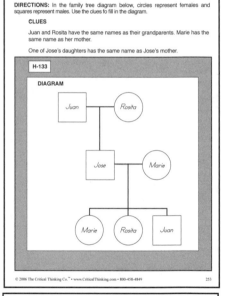

Juan — Rosita

Jose — Marie

Marie   Rosita   Juan

Panel 7 (p. 254)

TRANSITIVITY—FAMILY TREE

DIRECTIONS: In the family tree diagram below, circles represent females and squares represent males. Use the clues to fill in the diagram.

CLUES

Jim is the father of Bill and Mary.
Jane is Mary's sister.
Helen is Mary's mother.

H-134

DIAGRAM

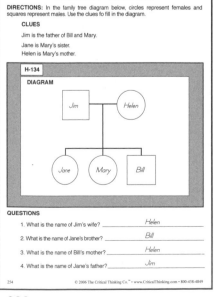

Jim — Helen

Jane   Mary   Bill

QUESTIONS

1. What is the name of Jim's wife? _____ Helen

2. What is the name of Jane's brother? _____ Bill

3. What is the name of Bill's mother? _____ Helen

4. What is the name of Jane's father? _____ Jim

Panel 8 (p. 255)

TRANSITIVITY—FAMILY TREE

DIRECTIONS: In the family tree diagram below, circles represent females and squares represent males. Use the clues to fill in the diagram.

CLUES

Michael and Irene Cooper have two children.
The children are named for Michael's father and Irene's mother.
The grandparents are Frank and Ruth Brown, and John and Bonnie Cooper.

H-135

DIAGRAM

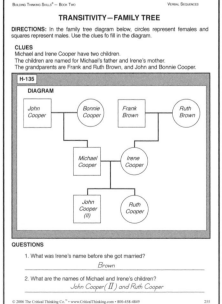

John Cooper — Bonnie Cooper   Frank Brown — Ruth Brown

Michael Cooper — Irene Cooper

John Cooper (II)   Ruth Cooper

QUESTIONS

1. What was Irene's name before she got married?
Brown

2. What are the names of Michael and Irene's children?
John Cooper (II) and Ruth Cooper

Panel 9 (p. 256)

YOUR FAMILY TREE

DIRECTIONS: Write the first and last names of a member of your family in each square or circle. If all your sisters and brothers won't fit on the row beside your name, add their names to the row below.

H-136

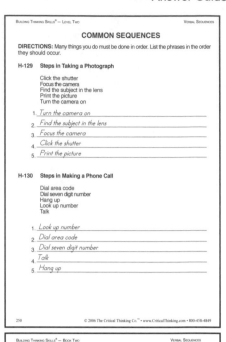

FATHER'S FATHER   FATHER'S MOTHER   MOTHER'S FATHER   MOTHER'S MOTHER

FATHER   MOTHER

BROTHERS   SISTERS

ONE OF THESE IS YOU

ADDITIONAL BROTHERS   ADDITIONAL SISTERS

(ANSWERS WILL VARY)

Panel 1 (p. 257)

DEDUCTIVE REASONING—INSTRUCTIONS

A Mind Benders® problem asks you to match items with their characteristics. Making a matrix helps you work the problem. Here is a Mind Bender® involving three people and their pets.

EXAMPLE

Michael, Sarah, and Tina own a cat, a goldfish, and a parakeet. From the clues below, match the pet owner's names with the pets.

a. Tina is allergic to animal fur.

b. Michael's pet does not use kitty litter or live in a cage.

STEP 1 From the clue "Tina is allergic to animal fur," you can figure out that Tina does not own the cat. Find the row marked T for Tina and write "NO" in the column marked C for cat.

	C	G	P
M			
S			
T	NO		

STEP 2 The second clue, "Michael's pet does not use kitty litter or live in a cage," tells you that Michael does not own a cat or a bird. Find the row marked M for Michael and write "NO" in both the C column for cat and the P column for parakeet.

	C	G	P
M	NO		NO
S			
T	NO		

STEP 3 You know that each person owns a pet. Since neither Michael nor Tina owns the cat, Sarah must be the cat owner. Write "YES" in the S row for Sarah and the C column for cat.

	C	G	P
M	NO		NO
S	YES		
T	NO		

Panel 2 (p. 258)

DEDUCTIVE REASONING—INSTRUCTIONS

STEP 4 Since Sarah owns the cat, Sarah does not own the goldfish or the parakeet. Write "NO" in the S row in both the G column for goldfish and the P column for parakeet.

	C	G	P
M	NO		NO
S	YES	NO	NO
T	NO		

STEP 5 By the same kind of reasoning, you see that the only vacancy in the M row is in the G column (for goldfish). From this, you figure out (deduce) that Michael is the goldfish owner. Write a "YES" in this position.

	C	G	P
M	NO	YES	NO
S	YES	NO	NO
T	NO		

STEP 6 Since Michael owns the goldfish, then neither Sarah nor Tina own the goldfish. You have already figured out (deduced) that Sarah doesn't own the goldfish. Now you know that Tina doesn't either. Mark "NO" in the T row and the G column.

	C	G	P
M	NO	YES	NO
S	YES	NO	NO
T	NO	NO	

STEP 7 The only vacancy remaining on the chart is in the T row and the P column. You now know that Tina is the parakeet owner. You are now ready to fill in the answers:

Sarah is the cat owner.

Michael is the goldfish owner.

Tina is the parakeet owner.

Panel 3 (p. 259)

DEDUCTIVE REASONING

H-137 In looking up her family tree, Mrs. Bradford found that members of her family had been born in Bourne, Dartmouth, and Salem. Her ancestors' names were Abraham, James, and Nathaniel. From the clues below, match the names with the places of birth.

a. Nathaniel was older than James.

b. Abraham's mother and father came from Europe and settled in Salem just before he was born.

c. The youngest Bradford was born in Dartmouth.

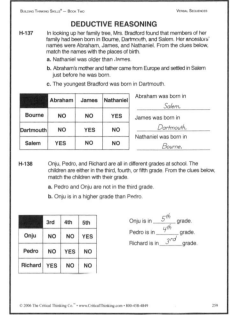

	Abraham	James	Nathaniel
Bourne	NO	NO	YES
Dartmouth	NO	YES	NO
Salem	YES	NO	NO

Abraham was born in _Salem_.

James was born in _Dartmouth_.

Nathaniel was born in _Bourne_.

H-138 Onju, Pedro, and Richard are all in different grades at school. The children are either in the third, fourth, or fifth grade. From the clues below, match the children with their grade.

a. Pedro and Onju are not in the third grade.

b. Onju is in a higher grade than Pedro.

	3rd	4th	5th
Onju	NO	NO	YES
Pedro	NO	YES	NO
Richard	YES	NO	NO

Onju is in _5th_ grade.

Pedro is in _4th_ grade.

Richard is in _3rd_ grade.

Panel 4 (p. 260)

DEDUCTIVE REASONING

H-139 A mouse, a rabbit, and a tiger are called Cicero, Ego, and Fred. From the clues below, match the name with the animal.

a. Ego is larger than a mouse.

b. Cicero is older than the rabbit but younger than the tiger.

c. Fred is older than Cicero.

	Mouse	Rabbit	Tiger
Cicero	YES	NO	NO
Ego	NO	YES	NO
Fred	NO	NO	YES

Cicero is the _mouse_.

Ego is the _rabbit_.

Fred is the _tiger_.

H-140 David, Hector, and Maria are on different teams. They are each either on the baseball team, the football team, or the swimming team. From the clues below, match the students with their teams.

a. Maria can't swim.

b. David is better at swimming than Hector.

c. Hector is the quarterback on his team.

	Baseball	Football	Swimming
D	NO	NO	YES
H	NO	YES	NO
M	YES	NO	NO

David is on the _swimming_ team.

Hector is on the _football_ team.

Maria is on the _baseball_ team.

Panel 5 (p. 261)

DEDUCTIVE REASONING

H-141 Anita, Beth, and Juan are a cook, a nurse, and a typist. From the clues below, match each person with their job.

a. Juan cannot type.

b. Anita is neither the nurse nor the typist.

	Cook	Nurse	Typist
A	YES	NO	NO
B	NO	NO	YES
J	NO	YES	NO

Anita is the _cook_.

Beth is the _typist_.

Juan is the _nurse_.

H-142 Mr. Allen, Mr. Franklin, Ms. Smith, and Mrs. Townsend teach either first grade, second grade, third grade, or art. From the clues below, match each teacher with his or her class.

a. Mr. Allen does not teach reading or arithmetic.

b. Mr. Smith teaches a lower grade than Mrs. Townsend but a higher grade than Mr. Franklin.

	1st	2nd	3rd	Art
A	NO	NO	NO	YES
F	YES	NO	NO	NO
S	NO	YES	NO	NO
T	NO	NO	YES	NO

Mr. Allen is the _art_ teacher.

Mr. Franklin is the _first grade_ teacher.

Ms. Smith is the _second grade_ teacher.

Mrs. Townsend is the _third grade_ teacher.

Panel 6 (p. 262)

DEDUCTIVE REASONING

H-143 George, Nancy, and Shannon are an astronaut, a computer programmer, and a mathematics teacher. From the clues below, match the people with their professions.

a. George is neither the astronaut nor the computer programmer.

b. Nancy is not the astronaut.

	George	Nancy	Shannon
A	NO	NO	YES
CP	NO	YES	NO
MT	YES	NO	NO

George is the _mathematics teacher_.

Nancy is the _computer programmer_.

Shannon is the _astronaut_.

H-144 Three race car drivers named Graham, Mario, and Pancho entered cars in a 24-hour race, and each won a prize. From the clues below, determine who drove each car and what prize was won by each driver.

a. The coupe won a higher prize than Mario's car.

b. Mario did not drive the Spyder.

c. A hatchback won a prize.

d. Graham's car won first prize.

e. The Spyder came in second.

	Coupe	Hatch-back	Spyder
Graham	YES	NO	NO
Mario	NO	YES	NO
Pancho	NO	NO	YES

Place	Car	Driver
First	Coupe	Graham
Second	Spyder	Pancho
Third	Hatchback	Mario

Panel 7 (p. 263)

DEDUCTIVE REASONING

H-145 Bob, Chris, Nancy, and Pat have different colored bikes. The bikes are red, blue, green, and white. From the clues below, match the bikes with the owners.

a. Bob and Chris have ten-speed bikes.

b. Chris's friend has a blue bike.

c. Nancy has a three-speed and is a friend of the owner of the white bike.

d. Nancy sometimes rides her brother's blue ten-speed bike.

e. Pat does not like his friend's green bike.

f. The red bike has one speed.

	Bob	Chris	Nancy	Pat
Red	NO	NO	NO	YES
Blue	YES	NO	NO	NO
Green	NO	NO	YES	NO
White	NO	YES	NO	NO

	Axe	Hammer	Pliers	Saw
Bill	YES	NO	NO	NO
Jane	NO	NO	YES	NO
Kim	NO	YES	NO	NO
Tom	NO	NO	NO	YES

Diagram for problem **H-146** below.

H-146 Bill, Jane, Kim, and Tom brought an axe, a hammer, a pair of pliers, and a saw to build a project at school. From the clues below, match the students with the tools. (Use the diagram above on the right.)

a. Neither Bill nor the girl with the pliers brought the hammer.

b. Jane couldn't find a cutting tool.

c. Kim brought her mom's hammer.

d. Bill lost his axe after the project started.

Panel 8 (p. 264)

DEDUCTIVE REASONING

H-147 In science class, students learn the eating habits of several types of animals. Some animals eat meat and others eat plants. Some animals eat both plants and meat. Some animals eat plankton. For her science project, Marisa picked four animals of different sizes and studied their eating habits. From the clues below, match the eating habits with the sizes of the four animals. The animal sizes can be described as small, medium, large, and very large.

a. The large animal is neither a meat eater nor a plankton eater.

b. The medium-sized animal is larger than the plankton eater.

c. The meat eater is larger than the plant eater.

d. The plant eater is not large.

	Meat	Plant	Meat & Plant	Plankton
Small	NO	NO	NO	YES
Medium	NO	NO	YES	NO
Large	NO	YES	NO	NO
Very Large	YES	NO	NO	NO

Panel 9 (p. 265)

FOLLOWING YES–NO RULES—A

DIRECTIONS: Darken the correct circles along the path from START to FINISH by following the YES-NO rule.

RULE BOX

YES—color is the same   NO—color is not the same

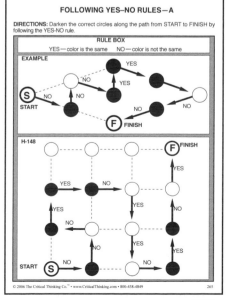

EXAMPLE

H-148

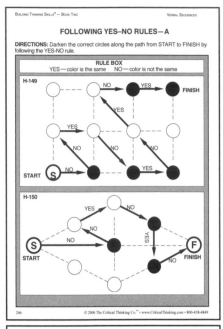

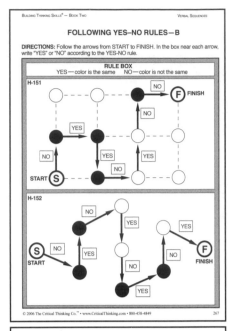

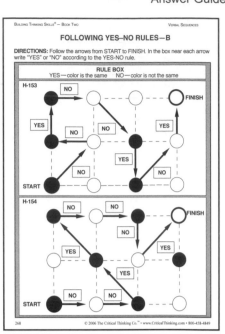

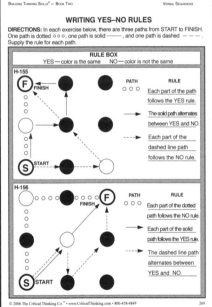

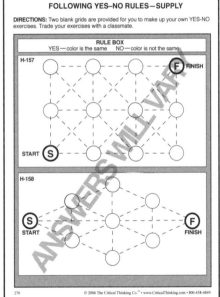

COMPLETING TRUE–FALSE TABLES

DIRECTIONS: After reading the example, complete the TRUE-FALSE table below.

This group of shapes will be used to produce TRUE-FALSE tables.

EXAMPLE of a completed TRUE-FALSE table.

	IT IS STRIPED	IT IS CHECKED	IT IS SQUARE
	TRUE	FALSE	TRUE
	FALSE	TRUE	TRUE
	FALSE	TRUE	FALSE

H-159   Complete the following table.

	IT IS BLACK	IT IS STRIPED	IT IS CHECKED	IT IS SQUARE
	TRUE	FALSE	FALSE	TRUE
	FALSE	TRUE	FALSE	TRUE
	FALSE	FALSE	TRUE	TRUE
	TRUE	FALSE	FALSE	FALSE
	FALSE	TRUE	FALSE	FALSE
	FALSE	FALSE	TRUE	FALSE

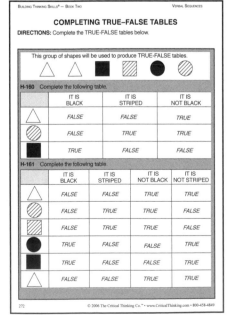

COMPLETING TRUE–FALSE TABLES

DIRECTIONS: Complete the TRUE-FALSE tables below.

This group of shapes will be used to produce TRUE-FALSE tables.

H-160   Complete the following table.

	IT IS BLACK	IT IS STRIPED	IT IS NOT BLACK
	FALSE	FALSE	TRUE
	FALSE	TRUE	TRUE
	TRUE	FALSE	FALSE

H-161   Complete the following table.

	IT IS BLACK	IT IS STRIPED	IT IS NOT BLACK	IT IS NOT STRIPED
	FALSE	FALSE	TRUE	TRUE
	FALSE	TRUE	TRUE	FALSE
	FALSE	TRUE	TRUE	FALSE
	TRUE	FALSE	FALSE	TRUE
	TRUE	FALSE	FALSE	TRUE
	FALSE	FALSE	TRUE	TRUE

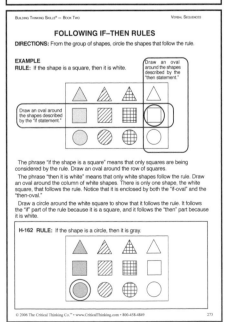

FOLLOWING IF–THEN RULES

DIRECTIONS: From the group of shapes, circle the shapes that follow the rule.

EXAMPLE
RULE: If the shape is a square, then it is white.

The phrase "if the shape is a square" means that only squares are being considered by the rule. Draw an oval around the row of squares.

The phrase "then it is white" means that only white shapes follow the rule. Draw an oval around the column of white shapes. There is only one shape, the white square, that follows the rule. Notice that it is enclosed by both the "if-oval" and the "then-oval."

Draw a circle around the white square to show that it follows the rule. It follows the "if" part of the rule because it is a square, and it follows the "then" part because it is white.

H-162 RULE: If the shape is a circle, then it is gray.

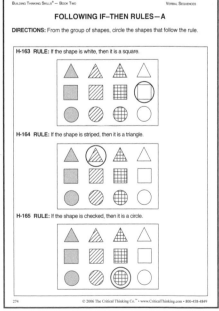

FOLLOWING IF–THEN RULES—A

DIRECTIONS: From the group of shapes, circle the shapes that follow the rule.

H-163 RULE: If the shape is white, then it is a square.

H-164 RULE: If the shape is striped, then it is a triangle.

H-165 RULE: If the shape is checked, then it is a circle.

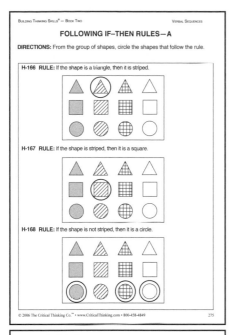

BUILDING THINKING SKILLS® — BOOK TWO   VERBAL SEQUENCES

FOLLOWING IF–THEN RULES—A

DIRECTIONS: From the group of shapes, circle the shapes that follow the rule.

H-166 RULE: If the shape is a triangle, then it is striped.

H-167 RULE: If the shape is striped, then it is a square.

H-168 RULE: If the shape is not striped, then it is a circle.

© 2006 The Critical Thinking Co.™ • www.CriticalThinking.com • 800-458-4849   275

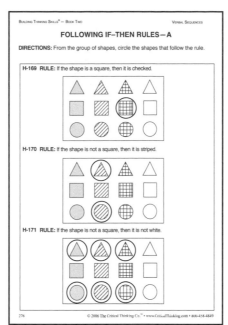

BUILDING THINKING SKILLS® — BOOK TWO   VERBAL SEQUENCES

FOLLOWING IF–THEN RULES—A

DIRECTIONS: From the group of shapes, circle the shapes that follow the rule.

H-169 RULE: If the shape is a square, then it is checked.

H-170 RULE: If the shape is not a square, then it is striped.

H-171 RULE: If the shape is not a square, then it is not white.

276   © 2006 The Critical Thinking Co.™ • www.CriticalThinking.com • 800-458-4849

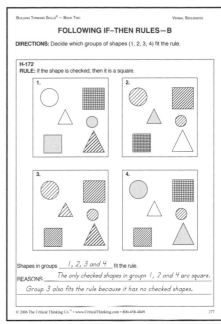

BUILDING THINKING SKILLS® — BOOK TWO   VERBAL SEQUENCES

FOLLOWING IF–THEN RULES—B

DIRECTIONS: Decide which groups of shapes (1, 2, 3, 4) fit the rule.

H-172
RULE: If the shape is checked, then it is a square.

1.   2.

3.   4.

Shapes in groups ___1, 2, 3 and 4___ fit the rule.

REASONS ___The only checked shapes in groups 1, 2 and 4 are square.___
___Group 3 also fits the rule because it has no checked shapes.___

© 2006 The Critical Thinking Co.™ • www.CriticalThinking.com • 800-458-4849   277

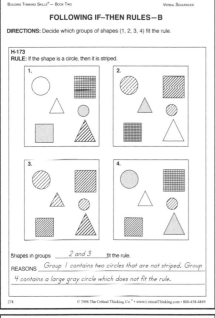

BUILDING THINKING SKILLS® — BOOK TWO   VERBAL SEQUENCES

FOLLOWING IF–THEN RULES—B

DIRECTIONS: Decide which groups of shapes (1, 2, 3, 4) fit the rule.

H-173
RULE: If the shape is a circle, then it is striped.

1.   2.

3.   4.

Shapes in groups ___2 and 3___ fit the rule.

REASONS ___Group 1 contains two circles that are not striped. Group___
___4 contains a large gray circle which does not fit the rule.___

278   © 2006 The Critical Thinking Co.™ • www.CriticalThinking.com • 800-458-4849

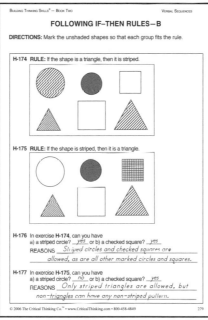

BUILDING THINKING SKILLS® — BOOK TWO   VERBAL SEQUENCES

FOLLOWING IF–THEN RULES—B

DIRECTIONS: Mark the unshaded shapes so that each group fits the rule.

H-174 RULE: If the shape is a triangle, then it is striped.

H-175 RULE: If the shape is striped, then it is a triangle.

H-176 In exercise H-174, can you have
a) a striped circle? ___yes___ or b) a checked square? ___yes___
REASONS ___Striped circles and checked squares are___
___allowed, as are all other marked circles and squares.___

H-177 In exercise H-175, can you have
a) a striped circle? ___no___ or b) a checked square? ___yes___
REASONS ___Only striped triangles are allowed, but___
___non-triangles can have any non-striped pattern.___

© 2006 The Critical Thinking Co.™ • www.CriticalThinking.com • 800-458-4849   279

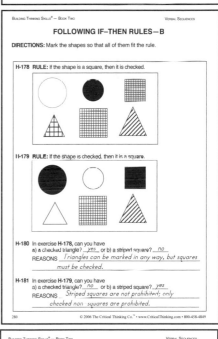

BUILDING THINKING SKILLS® — BOOK TWO   VERBAL SEQUENCES

FOLLOWING IF–THEN RULES—B

DIRECTIONS: Mark the shapes so that all of them fit the rule.

H-178 RULE: If the shape is a square, then it is checked.

H-179 RULE: If the shape is checked, then it is a square.

H-180 In exercise H-178, can you have
a) a checked triangle? ___yes___ or b) a striped square? ___no___
REASONS ___Triangles can be marked in any way, but squares___
___must be checked.___

H-181 In exercise H-179, can you have
a) a checked triangle? ___no___ or b) a striped square? ___yes___
REASONS ___Striped squares are not prohibited; only___
___checked non-squares are prohibited.___

280   © 2006 The Critical Thinking Co.™ • www.CriticalThinking.com • 800-458-4849

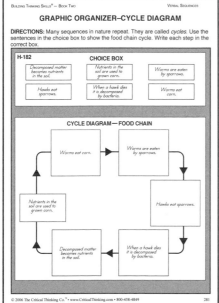

BUILDING THINKING SKILLS® — BOOK TWO   VERBAL SEQUENCES

GRAPHIC ORGANIZER–CYCLE DIAGRAM

DIRECTIONS: Many sequences in nature repeat. They are called *cycles*. Use the sentences in the choice box to show the food chain cycle. Write each step in the correct box.

H-182   **CHOICE BOX**

Decomposed matter becomes nutrients in the soil.	Nutrients in the soil are used to grow corn.	Worms are eaten by sparrows.
Hawks eat sparrows.	When a hawk dies it is decomposed by bacteria.	Worms eat corn.

CYCLE DIAGRAM—FOOD CHAIN

Worms eat corn. → Worms are eaten by sparrows.

Nutrients in the soil are used to grow corn.

Hawks eat sparrows.

Decomposed matter becomes nutrients in the soil.

When a hawk dies it is decomposed by bacteria.

281   © 2006 The Critical Thinking Co.™ • www.CriticalThinking.com • 800-458-4849

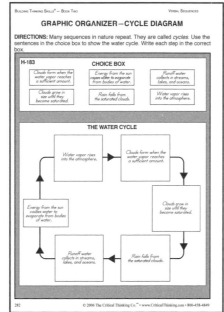

BUILDING THINKING SKILLS® — BOOK TWO   VERBAL SEQUENCES

GRAPHIC ORGANIZER–CYCLE DIAGRAM

DIRECTIONS: Many sequences in nature repeat. They are called *cycles*. Use the sentences in the choice box to show the water cycle. Write each step in the correct box.

H-183   **CHOICE BOX**

Clouds form when the water reaches a sufficient amount.	Energy from the sun causes water to evaporate from bodies of water.	Runoff water collects in streams, lakes, and oceans.
Clouds grow in size until they become saturated.	Rain falls from the saturated clouds.	Water vapor rises into the atmosphere.

THE WATER CYCLE

Water vapor rises into the atmosphere. → Clouds form when the water vapor reaches a sufficient amount.

Energy from the sun causes water to evaporate from bodies of water.

Clouds grow in size until they become saturated.

Runoff water collects in streams, lakes, and oceans.

Rain falls from the saturated clouds.

282   © 2006 The Critical Thinking Co.™ • www.CriticalThinking.com • 800-458-4849

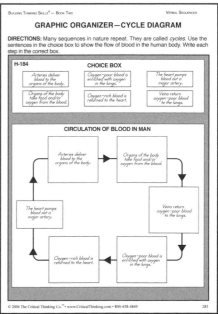

BUILDING THINKING SKILLS® — BOOK TWO   VERBAL SEQUENCES

GRAPHIC ORGANIZER–CYCLE DIAGRAM

DIRECTIONS: Many sequences in nature repeat. They are called *cycles*. Use the sentences in the choice box to show the flow of blood in the human body. Write each step in the correct box.

H-184   **CHOICE BOX**

Arteries deliver blood to the organs of the body.	Oxygen-poor blood is enriched with oxygen in the lungs.	The heart pumps blood out a major artery.
Organs of the body take food and/or oxygen from the blood.	Oxygen-rich blood is returned to the heart.	Veins return oxygen-poor blood to the lungs.

CIRCULATION OF BLOOD IN MAN

Arteries deliver blood to the organs of the body. → Organs of the body take food and/or oxygen from the blood.

The heart pumps blood out a major artery.

Veins return oxygen-poor blood to the lungs.

Oxygen-rich blood is returned to the heart.

Oxygen-poor blood is enriched with oxygen in the lungs.

© 2006 The Critical Thinking Co.™ • www.CriticalThinking.com • 800-458-4849   283

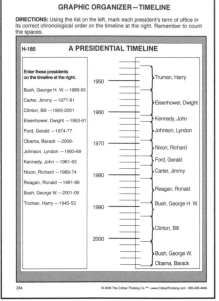

GRAPHIC ORGANIZER—TIMELINE

DIRECTIONS: Using the list on the left, mark each president's term of office in its correct chronological order on the timeline at the right. Remember to count the spaces.

H-185   A PRESIDENTIAL TIMELINE

Enter these presidents on the timeline at the right.

Bush, George H. W. —1989-93
Carter, Jimmy —1977-81
Clinton, Bill —1993-2001
Eisenhower, Dwight —1953-61
Ford, Gerald —1974-77
Obama, Barack —2009-
Johnson, Lyndon —1963-69
Kennedy, John —1961-63
Nixon, Richard —1969-74
Reagan, Ronald —1981-89
Bush, George W. —2001-09
Truman, Harry —1945-53

1950 — Truman, Harry
— Eisenhower, Dwight
1960 — Kennedy, John
— Johnson, Lyndon
1970 — Nixon, Richard
— Ford, Gerald
— Carter, Jimmy
1980 — Reagan, Ronald
— Bush, George H. W.
1990 — Clinton, Bill
2000 — Bush, George W.
— Obama, Barack

284   © 2006 The Critical Thinking Co.™ • www.CriticalThinking.com • 800-458-4849

GRAPHIC ORGANIZER—TIME LINE

DIRECTIONS: Using the list on the left, mark each war in its correct chronological order on the time line at the right. Remember to count the spaces.

H-186   A TIME LINE OF TWENTIETH CENTURY WARS

Enter these wars on the time line at the right.

Korean War — 1950-53
Persian Gulf War — Jan./Feb. 1991
Vietnam War — 1955-75
World War One — 1914-18
World War Two — 1939-45

1900
— World War One 1914-1918
1920
1940 — World War Two 1939-1945
— Korean War —1950-53
1960 — Vietnam War 1955-1975
1980
— Persian Gulf War Jan/Feb 1991
2000

285   © 2006 The Critical Thinking Co.™ • www.CriticalThinking.com • 800-458-4849

PARTS OF A WHOLE—SELECT

DIRECTIONS: On each line are four words from language arts lessons. Read the words and decide which word represents a whole thing and which words are parts of the whole thing. On the lines below each group, write the word that represents the whole thing, then list the words that are its parts.

EXAMPLE: closing, greeting, letter, signature

The words represent parts of a letter that you might write to a friend. The WHOLE is the letter and the PARTS are the greeting, the closing, and the signature.

WHOLE *letter* PARTS *greeting*, *closing*, *signature*

I-1 book, chapter, index, table of contents
WHOLE *book* PARTS *chapter*, *index*, *table of contents*

I-2 comics, editorial, newspaper, sports
WHOLE *newspaper* PARTS *comics*, *editorial*, *sports*

I-3 books, card file, library, shelves
WHOLE *library* PARTS *books*, *card file*, *shelves*

I-4 argument, debate, rebuttal, statement of proposition
WHOLE *debate* PARTS *argument*, *rebuttal*, *statement of proposition*

I-5 advertisements, articles, magazine, photographs
WHOLE *magazine* PARTS *advertisements*, *articles*, *photographs*

288   © 2006 The Critical Thinking Co.™ • www.CriticalThinking.com • 800-458-4849

PARTS OF A WHOLE—SELECT

DIRECTIONS: On each line are four words from social studies lessons. Read the words and decide which word represents a whole thing and which words are parts of the whole thing. On the lines below each group, write the word that represents the whole thing, then list the words that are its parts.

I-6 alleys, block, buildings, streets
WHOLE *block* PARTS *alleys*, *buildings*, *streets*

I-7 churches, homes, neighborhood, schools
WHOLE *neighborhood* PARTS *churches*, *homes*, *schools*

I-8 city, downtown, neighborhood, suburb
WHOLE *city* PARTS *downtown*, *neighborhood*, *suburb*

I-9 cities, county, rural areas, towns
WHOLE *county* PARTS *cities*, *rural areas*, *towns*

I-10 cities, counties, state, townships
WHOLE *state* PARTS *cities*, *counties*, *townships*

I-11 forests, mountains, nation, rivers
WHOLE *nation* PARTS *forests*, *mountains*, *rivers*

I-12 continents, atmosphere, Earth, oceans
WHOLE *Earth* PARTS *continents*, *atmosphere*, *oceans*

© 2006 The Critical Thinking Co.™ • www.CriticalThinking.com • 800-458-4849   289

PARTS OF A WHOLE—SELECT

DIRECTIONS: On each line are four words from science lessons. Read the words and decide which word represents a whole thing and which words are parts of the whole thing. On the lines below each group first write the word that represents the whole thing, then list the words that are parts of the whole thing.

I-13 leaves, plant, root, stem
WHOLE *plant* PARTS *leaves*, *root*, *stem*

I-14 backbone, brain, heart, mammal
WHOLE *mammal* PARTS *backbone*, *brain*, *heart*

I-15 blossom, bulb, stem, tulip
WHOLE *tulip* PARTS *bulb*, *stem*, *blossom*

I-16 fruit, pulp, seeds, skin
WHOLE *fruit* PARTS *pulp*, *seeds*, *skin*

I-17 antennae, insect, jointed legs, segmented abdomen
WHOLE *insect* PARTS *antennae*, *jointed legs*, *segmented abdomen*

I-18 backbone, fish, gills, scales
WHOLE *fish* PARTS *backbone*, *gills*, *scales*

I-19 beak, bird, feathers, wings
WHOLE *bird* PARTS *beak*, *feathers*, *wings*

290   © 2006 The Critical Thinking Co.™ • www.CriticalThinking.com • 800-458-4849

CLASS AND MEMBERS—SELECT

DIRECTIONS: On each line are four words from language arts lessons. Read the words and decide which word represents the class to which the other words belong. On the lines below each group, write the word that represents the class, then list the words that are members of that class.

I-20 drama, fiction, novel, short story
CLASS *fiction* MEMBERS *drama*, *novel*, *short story*

I-21 autobiographies, diaries, journals, personal histories
CLASS *personal histories* MEMBERS *diaries*, *journals*, *autobiographies*

I-22 a, an, articles, the
CLASS *articles* MEMBERS *a*, *an*, *the*

I-23 exclamations, questions, sentences, statements
CLASS *sentences* MEMBERS *exclamations*, *questions*, *statements*

I-24 figures of speech, metaphors, personification, similes
CLASS *figures of speech* MEMBERS *metaphors*, *personification*, *similes*

I-25 adjectives, adverbs, nouns, parts of speech
CLASS *parts of speech* MEMBERS *adjectives*, *adverbs*, *nouns*

I-26 almanac, atlas, dictionary, reference book
CLASS *reference book* MEMBERS *almanac*, *atlas*, *dictionary*

© 2006 The Critical Thinking Co.™ • www.CriticalThinking.com • 800-458-4849   291

CLASS AND MEMBERS—SELECT

DIRECTIONS: On each line are four words from social studies lessons. Read the words and decide which word represents the class to which the other words belong. On the lines below each group, write the word that represents the class, then list the words that are members of that class.

I-27 appliances, clothing, food, goods
CLASS *goods* MEMBERS *appliances*, *clothing*, *food*

I-28 kings, leaders, presidents, prime ministers
CLASS *leaders* MEMBERS *kings*, *presidents*, *prime ministers*

I-29 city, federal, government, state
CLASS *government* MEMBERS *city*, *federal*, *state*

I-30 economics, geography, history, social sciences
CLASS *social sciences* MEMBERS *economics*, *geography*, *history*

I-31 elementary, high, middle, school
CLASS *school* MEMBERS *elementary*, *middle*, *high*

I-32 cleaning, repairing, protecting, service
CLASS *service* MEMBERS *cleaning*, *repairing*, *protecting*

I-33 democracy, government, monarchy, republic
CLASS *government* MEMBERS *democracy*, *monarchy*, *republic*

292   © 2006 The Critical Thinking Co.™ • www.CriticalThinking.com • 800-458-4849

CLASS AND MEMBERS—SELECT

DIRECTIONS: On each line are four words from science lessons. Read the words and decide which word represents the class to which the other words belong. On the lines below each group, write the word that represents the class, then list the words that are members of that class.

I-34 corn, grain, oats, wheat
CLASS *grain* MEMBERS *corn*, *oats*, *wheat*

I-35 ape, mammal, man, whale
CLASS *mammal* MEMBERS *ape*, *man*, *whale*

I-36 daisy, flower, rose, tulip
CLASS *flower* MEMBERS *daisy*, *rose*, *tulip*

I-37 apple, banana, fruit, pear
CLASS *fruit* MEMBERS *apple*, *banana*, *pear*

I-38 beetle, fly, grasshopper, insect
CLASS *insect* MEMBERS *fly*, *grasshopper*, *beetle*

I-39 fish, guppy, perch, trout
CLASS *fish* MEMBERS *guppy*, *perch*, *trout*

I-40 bird, heron, penguin, sandpiper
CLASS *bird* MEMBERS *heron*, *penguin*, *sandpiper*

© 2006 The Critical Thinking Co.™ • www.CriticalThinking.com • 800-458-4849   293

SENTENCES CONTAINING CLASSES AND SUBCLASSES

DIRECTIONS: In each sentence there are three words that name members of a class. Underline these words. Inside each box, write the words in order from most general class to the most specific class. The general class (1) will contain the less general class (2) and the most specific class (3). Write the most general class on line (1), the less general class on line (2), and the most specific class on line (3).

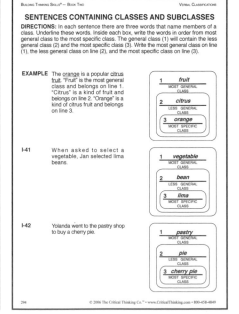

EXAMPLE The orange is a popular citrus fruit. "Fruit" is the most general class and belongs on line 1. "Citrus" is a kind of fruit and belongs on line 2. "Orange" is a kind of citrus fruit and belongs on line 3.

1 *fruit* MOST GENERAL CLASS
2 *citrus* LESS GENERAL CLASS
3 *orange* MOST SPECIFIC CLASS

I-41 When asked to select a vegetable, Jan selected lima beans.

1 *vegetable* MOST GENERAL CLASS
2 *bean* LESS GENERAL CLASS
3 *lima* MOST SPECIFIC CLASS

I-42 Yolanda went to the pastry shop to buy a cherry pie.

1 *pastry* MOST GENERAL CLASS
2 *pie* LESS GENERAL CLASS
3 *cherry pie* MOST SPECIFIC CLASS

294   © 2006 The Critical Thinking Co.™ • www.CriticalThinking.com • 800-458-4849

SENTENCES CONTAINING CLASSES AND SUBCLASSES

DIRECTIONS: In each sentence, underline three words that name members of a class. In each box, write the words in order from the most general class on line 1 to the most specific class on line 3.

I-43 Maria reads many kinds of books, but mysteries are her favorite kind of fiction.

I-44 Raymond owns a camper-van recreational vehicle.

I-45 Mr. Baker went to the lumberyard and bought some pine boards.

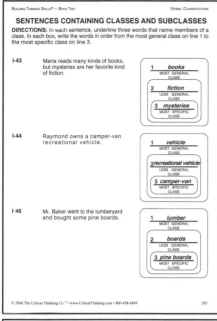

SENTENCES CONTAINING CLASSES AND SUBCLASSES

DIRECTIONS: In each sentence, underline three words that name members of a class. In each box, write the words in order from the most general class on line 1 to the most specific class on line 3.

I-46 A ladybug was the only beetle that Josh could find for his insect collection.

I-47 Mrs. Elledge used weed killer on her dandelion plants.

I-48 Some people think the black widow spider is an insect, but actually it is an arachnid.

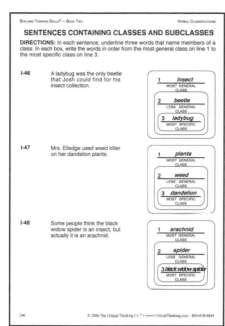

SENTENCES CONTAINING CLASSES AND SUBCLASSES

DIRECTIONS: In each sentence, underline three words that name members of a class. In each box, write the words in order from the most general class on line 1 to the most specific class on line 3.

I-49 The worker honeybee is the insect that produces honey.

I-50 The Galapagos tortoise is a large reptile that lives on the land.

I-51 The heron is a beautiful wading bird found in the South.

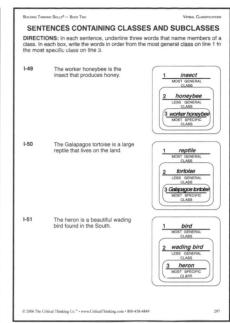

HOW ARE THESE WORDS ALIKE?—SELECT

DIRECTIONS: Circle the letter in front of the answer that best describes the class of words.

I-52	alarm, horn, siren	a. bell / b. safety / **c. warning**
I-53	blotch, smear, stain	**a. blemish** / b. rip / c. tear
I-54	different, odd, peculiar	a. little / **b. strange** / c. weak
I-55	dollar, peso, pound	a. coin / **b. money** / c. penny
I-56	aim, design, intend	a. draw / b. finish / **c. plan**
I-57	grab, grasp, grip	a. hit / **b. hold** / c. try
I-58	caution, slow, yield	a. intersection / b. stop light / **c. warning**

HOW ARE THESE WORDS ALIKE?—SELECT

DIRECTIONS: Circle the letter in front of the answer that best describes the class of words.

I-59	border, hem, rim	a. center / **b. edge** / c. part
I-60	even, level, planed	a. rough / b. slant / **c. smooth**
I-61	fable, fairy tale, myth	a. fact / **b. fiction** / c. history
I-62	clock, ruler, thermometer	a. electrical devices / **b. measuring devices** / c. mechanical devices
I-63	fork, knife, spoon	a. drawing tools / **b. kitchen tools** / c. woodworking tools
I-64	chisel, drill, saw	a. drawing tools / b. kitchen tools / **c. woodworking tools**
I-65	compass, ruler, protractor	**a. drawing tools** / b. kitchen tools / c. woodworking tools

HOW ARE THESE WORDS ALIKE?—SELECT

DIRECTIONS: Each exercise contains three words that belong to a common class. From the choice box, select the class that best describes each group of words and write it on the line. The words in the choice box may be used more than once.

CHOICE BOX
high, line, show

I-66	path, road, route,	line
I-67	direct, guide, lead,	show
I-68	big, soaring, tall,	high
I-69	produce, put on, stage,	show
I-70	business, job, work,	line
I-71	film, movie, motion picture,	show
I-72	piercing, sharp, shrill,	high
I-73	disclose, discover, present,	show
I-74	column, rank, row,	line
I-75	costly, dear, expensive,	high
I-76	indicate, read, register,	show
I-77	display, offer, supply,	show

HOW ARE THESE WORDS ALIKE?—SELECT

DIRECTIONS: Each exercise contains three words that belong to a common class. From the choice box, select the class that best describes each group of words and write it on the line. The words in the choice box may be used more than once.

CHOICE BOX
band, change, fair, spring

I-78	average, ordinary, plain,	fair
I-79	hop, leap, jump,	spring
I-80	swap, switch, trade,	change
I-81	favorable, honest, just,	fair
I-82	club, team, troop,	band
I-83	brook, season, wire coil,	spring
I-84	group, musicians, orchestra,	band
I-85	shift, turn, vary,	change
I-86	clear, light, sunny,	fair
I-87	belt, strip, stripe,	band
I-88	coins, substitute, variety,	change
I-89	display, entertainment, festival	fair

HOW ARE THESE WORDS ALIKE?—SELECT

DIRECTIONS: Each exercise contains three words that belong to a common class. From the choice box, select the class that best describes each group of words and write it on the line. The words in the choice box may be used more than once.

CHOICE BOX
flow, kind, party, pass

I-90	go, proceed, travel,	flow OR pass
I-91	band, crew, group,	party
I-92	pour, spout, stream,	flow
I-93	beat, outdo, top,	pass
I-94	friendly, pleasant, tender,	kind
I-95	proceed, rise, spring,	flow OR pass
I-96	give, hand, reach,	pass
I-97	club, side, union,	party
I-98	a throw, ticket, valley,	pass
I-99	current, flood, tide,	flow
I-100	class, sort, type,	kind

HOW ARE THESE NOUNS ALIKE?—EXPLAIN

DIRECTIONS: Each group of three nouns has a similar meaning. Explain how the nouns in each group are alike.

EXAMPLE: chalk, plaster, sugar
These materials are all white powders.

I-101 claws, horns, tusks
They are all hard and sharp parts of animals.

I-102 court, diamond, rink
They are all sports arenas.

I-103 glare, gleam, ray
They are all light beams.

I-104 cure, medication, remedy
They are all treatments of disorders.

I-105 hush, quiet, still
They are all low levels of sound.

I-106 adornment, ornament, ribbon
They are all decorations.

Building Thinking Skills® — Book Two   Verbal Classifications

HOW ARE THESE VERBS ALIKE?—EXPLAIN

DIRECTIONS: Each group of three verbs has a similar meaning. Explain how the verbs in each group are alike.

I-107 ask, inquire, quiz

They are all ways to question something or someone.

I-108 float, glide, soar

They are all things that airborne objects do.

I-109 boil, evaporate, vaporize

They are all ways to change water to steam or water vapor.

I-110 jog, sprint, dash

They are all types of running.

I-111 mumble, murmur, whisper

They are all types of soft talking.

I-112 await, expect, hope

They all relate to expectation.

I-113 blast, burst, explode

They are all loud noises.

Building Thinking Skills® — Book Two   Verbal Classifications

HOW ARE THESE ADJECTIVES ALIKE?—EXPLAIN

DIRECTIONS: Each group of three adjectives has a similar meaning. Explain how the adjectives in each group are alike.

I-114 brave, fearless, gallant

They all relate to courage.

I-115 gentle, kind, tender

They all relate to treatment, care, or pleasant ways to be.

I-116 gross, large, massive

They all relate to heaviness.

I-117 slender, slight, slim

They all relate to thinness.

I-118 firm, sure, steady

They all relate to dependability or stability.

I-119 forceful, mighty, powerful

They all relate to strength.

I-120 passive, quiet, still

They all relate to not moving or inactivity.

Building Thinking Skills® — Book Two   Verbal Classifications

HOW ARE THESE WEATHER WORDS ALIKE?—EXPLAIN

DIRECTIONS: Each group of three words describes a weather condition. Explain how the terms in each group are alike.

I-121 drizzle, shower, sprinkle

They all describe light rain.

I-122 nippy, chilly, cool

They all describe below average temperatures.

I-123 bright, clear, cloudless

They all describe a high degree of visibility.

I-124 blustery, breezy, gusty

They all describe high winds.

I-125 foggy, hazy, overcast

They all describe a low degree of visibility.

I-126 damp, muggy, sticky

They all describe high humidity.

I-127 cloudburst, downpour, thunderstorm

They all describe heavy rain.

Building Thinking Skills® — Book Two   Verbal Classifications

EXPLAIN THE EXCEPTION

DIRECTIONS: Each group of four words contains one member that is an exception to the class. Explain how the similar words are alike and how the exception is different.

EXAMPLE: candle, eye, lamp, star

Candle, lamp, and star are similar because they give off light. Eye is the exception to the class "things that give off light." The eye receives light but does not give off light.

I-128 cloud, rain, snow, umbrella

Umbrella is the exception to the class "weather terms" because it is not a type of weather.

I-129 cabbage, corn, lettuce, spinach

Corn is the exception to the class "leafy vegetables" because it is a grain.

I-130 relax, rest, sleep, work

Work is the exception to the class "quiet actions" because it usually involves at least some noise.

I-131 hear, look, read, see

Hear is the exception to the class "visual words" because it relates to sound.

Building Thinking Skills® — Book Two   Verbal Classifications

EXPLAIN THE EXCEPTION

DIRECTIONS: Each group of four words contains one member that is an exception to the class. Explain how the similar words are alike and how the exception is different.

I-132 ice, iron, water, wood

Water is the exception to the class "solids" because it is a liquid.

I-133 clams, crabs, minnows, snail

Minnows are the exception to the class "shellfish" because they do not have hard shells.

I-134 bacon, beef, eggs, ham

Eggs are the exception to the class "meat" because eggs are not a form of meat.

I-135 basket, bottle, can, jar

Basket is the exception to the class "containers with lids" because most baskets don't have lids.

I-136 button, pocket, snap, zipper

Pocket is the exception to the class "fasteners" because a pocket doesn't join two things together.

Building Thinking Skills® — Book Two   Verbal Classifications

EXPLAIN THE EXCEPTION

DIRECTIONS: Each group of four words contains one member that is an exception to the class. Explain how the similar words are alike and how the exception is different.

I-137 cartoons, newscast, situation comedy, soap opera

Newscast is the exception to the class "fictional television programs" because a newscast is about real events and people.

I-138 clock, ruler, tape measure, yardstick

Clock is the exception to the class "distance measuring devices" because it measures time.

I-139 flute, trumpet, tuba, violin

Violin is the exception to the class "wind instruments" because it is a string instrument.

I-140 automobile, bicycle, motorcycle, truck

Bicycle is the exception to the class "engine powered vehicles" because a person powers it.

I-141 bottle, cup, mug, strainer

Strainer is the exception to the class "containers for liquids" because it will not hold liquids.

Building Thinking Skills® — Book Two   Verbal Classifications

SORTING INTO CLASSES

DIRECTIONS: Sort the following words into two classes: those which suggest happiness and those which suggest sadness.

I-142   CHOICE BOX

cheerless, content, delighted, discouraged, dismal, displeased, dreary, fortunate, groaning, joyous, lucky, miserable, satisfied, sorrowful, successful

HAPPY	SAD
content	*discouraged*
delighted	*dismal*
fortunate	*displeased*
joyous	*dreary*
lucky	*groaning*
satisfied	*miserable*
successful	*sorrowful*
	cheerless

Building Thinking Skills® — Book Two   Verbal Classifications

SORTING INTO CLASSES

DIRECTIONS: Sort the following words into the categories of people, places, and things.

I-143   CHOICE BOX

actor, airport, beach, bicycle, book, captain, computer, crew, doctor, factory, friend, garden, house, newspaper, nurse, office, pilot, school, station, stove, teacher, television, vegetable, zoo

PEOPLE	PLACES	THINGS
actor	*airport*	*bicycle*
captain	*beach*	*book*
doctor	*factory*	*computer*
friend	*garden*	*stove*
nurse	*house*	*vegetable*
pilot	*office*	*television*
teacher	*school*	*newspaper*
crew	*station*	
	zoo	

Building Thinking Skills® — Book Two   Verbal Classifications

SORTING INTO CLASSES

DIRECTIONS: Sort the following list of words into groups of words that tell who, when, or where.

I-144   CHOICE BOX

all, always, anybody, anyone, downstairs, downtown, early, everybody, everyone, far away, inside, in town, later, long ago, nearby, never, next door, nobody, no one, now, outside, some, somebody, someone, sometimes, sooner, today, tomorrow, upstairs, uptown, yesterday

WHO	WHEN	WHERE
all	*always*	*downstairs*
anybody	*never*	*downtown*
anyone	*early*	*far away*
everybody	*later*	*inside*
everyone	*long ago*	*in town*
nobody	*now*	*nearby*
no one	*sometimes*	*next door*
some	*sooner*	*outside*
somebody	*today*	*upstairs*
someone	*tomorrow*	*uptown*
	yesterday	

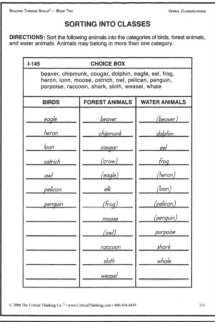

SORTING INTO CLASSES

DIRECTIONS: Sort the following animals into the categories of birds, forest animals, and water animals. Animals may belong in more than one category.

I-145	CHOICE BOX	

beaver, chipmunk, cougar, dolphin, eagle, eel, frog, heron, loon, moose, ostrich, owl, pelican, penguin, porpoise, raccoon, shark, sloth, weasel, whale

BIRDS	FOREST ANIMALS	WATER ANIMALS
eagle	beaver	(beaver)
heron	chipmunk	dolphin
loon	cougar	eel
ostrich	(crow)	frog
owl	(eagle)	(heron)
pelican	elk	(loon)
penguin	(frog)	(pelican)
	moose	(penguin)
	(owl)	porpoise
	raccoon	shark
	sloth	whale
	weasel	

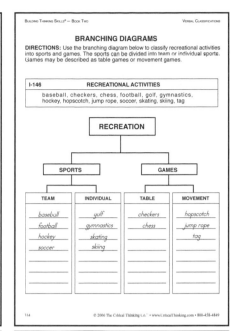

BRANCHING DIAGRAMS

DIRECTIONS: Use the branching diagram below to classify recreational activities into sports and games. The sports can be divided into team or individual sports. Games may be described as table games or movement games.

I-146	RECREATIONAL ACTIVITIES	

baseball, checkers, chess, football, golf, gymnastics, hockey, hopscotch, jump rope, soccer, skating, skiing, tag

RECREATION

SPORTS — **GAMES**

TEAM	INDIVIDUAL	TABLE	MOVEMENT
baseball	golf	checkers	hopscotch
football	gymnastics	chess	jump rope
hockey	skating		tag
soccer	skiing		

BRANCHING DIAGRAMS

DIRECTIONS: On the next page there is a branching diagram that can be used to classify living things into large subclasses of plants and animals. These subclasses can be further subdivided into smaller groups.

I-147   Use the diagram on the next page to classify the following living things.

ant	elephant	potato
bean	horse	robin
bee	maple	rose
butterfly	minnow	shark
carrot	oak	tulip
cat	ostrich	tuna
chicken	pine	violet

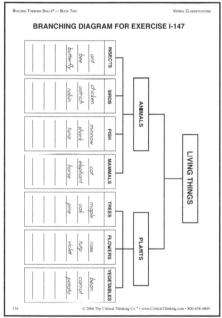

BRANCHING DIAGRAM FOR EXERCISE I-147

INSECTS: butterfly, bee, ant
BIRDS: robin, ostrich, chicken
FISH: minnow, shark, tuna
MAMMALS: horse, elephant, cat
TREES: pine, oak, maple
FLOWERS: violet, tulip, rose
VEGETABLES: potato, carrot, bean

ANIMALS / PLANTS → LIVING THINGS

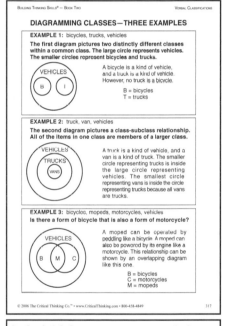

DIAGRAMMING CLASSES—THREE EXAMPLES

EXAMPLE 1: bicycles, trucks, vehicles
The first diagram pictures two distinctly different classes within a common class. The large circle represents vehicles. The smaller circle represent bicycles and trucks.

A bicycle is a kind of vehicle, and a truck is a kind of vehicle. However, no truck is a bicycle.

B = bicycles
T = trucks

EXAMPLE 2: truck, van, vehicles
The second diagram pictures a class-subclass relationship. All of the items in one class are members of a larger class.

A truck is a kind of vehicle, and a van is a kind of truck. The smaller circle representing trucks is inside the large circle representing vehicles. The smallest circle representing vans is inside the circle representing trucks because all vans are trucks.

EXAMPLE 3: bicycles, mopeds, motorcycles, vehicles
Is there a form of bicycle that is also a form of motorcycle?

A moped can be operated by peddling like a bicycle. A moped can also be powered by its engine like a motorcycle. This relationship can be shown by an overlapping diagram like this one.

B = bicycles
C = motorcycles
M = mopeds

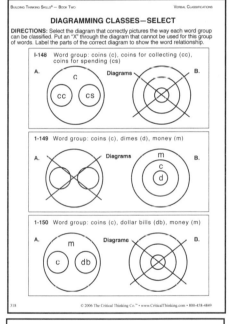

DIAGRAMMING CLASSES—SELECT

DIRECTIONS: Select the diagram that correctly pictures the way each word group can be classified. Put an "X" through the diagram that cannot be used for this group of words. Label the parts of the correct diagram to show the word relationship.

I-148   Word group: coins (c), coins for collecting (cc), coins for spending (cs)

A.   c / cc / cs   Diagrams   B. (X)

1-149   Word group: coins (c), dimes (d), money (m)

A. (X)   Diagrams   B. m / c / d

1-150   Word group: coins (c), dollar bills (db), money (m)

A. m / c / db   Diagrams   B. (X)

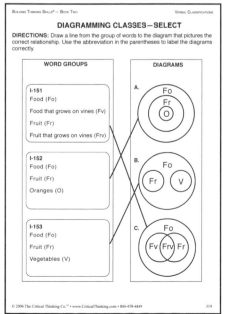

DIAGRAMMING CLASSES—SELECT

DIRECTIONS: Draw a line from the group of words to the diagram that pictures the correct relationship. Use the abbreviation in the parentheses to label the diagrams correctly.

WORD GROUPS	DIAGRAMS

I-151
Food (Fo)
Food that grows on vines (Fv)
Fruit (Fr)
Fruit that grows on vines (Frv)

A.   Fo / Fr / O

I-152
Food (Fo)
Fruit (Fr)
Oranges (O)

B.   Fo / Fr / V

I-153
Food (Fo)
Fruit (Fr)
Vegetables (V)

C.   Fo / Fv / Frv / Fr

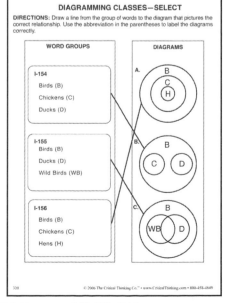

DIAGRAMMING CLASSES—SELECT

DIRECTIONS: Draw a line from the group of words to the diagram that pictures the correct relationship. Use the abbreviation in the parentheses to label the diagrams correctly.

WORD GROUPS	DIAGRAMS

I-154
Birds (B)
Chickens (C)
Ducks (D)

A.   B / C / H

I-155
Birds (B)
Ducks (D)
Wild Birds (WB)

B.   B / C / D

I-156
Birds (B)
Chickens (C)
Hens (H)

C.   B / WB / D

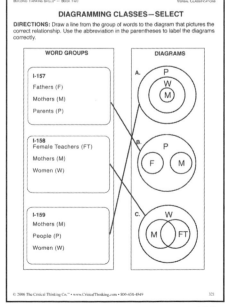

DIAGRAMMING CLASSES—SELECT

DIRECTIONS: Draw a line from the group of words to the diagram that pictures the correct relationship. Use the abbreviation in the parentheses to label the diagrams correctly.

WORD GROUPS	DIAGRAMS

I-157
Fathers (F)
Mothers (M)
Parents (P)

A.   P / W / M

I-158
Female Teachers (FT)
Mothers (M)
Women (W)

B.   P / F / M

I-159
Mothers (M)
People (P)
Women (W)

C.   W / M / FT

Panel 1 (p. 322)

Building Thinking Skills® — Book Two   Verbal Classifications

DIAGRAMMING CLASSES—SELECT AND EXPLAIN

DIRECTIONS: In these exercises, you are to describe the relationship between two groups of household items and then pick the diagram that describes this relationship. Use the abbreviations in the parentheses to label the diagram correctly. You may use one of the following phrases to fill in the blank in the sentence describing the classes.

includes, is included in, overlaps, is separate from

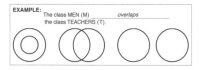

EXAMPLE:
The class MEN (M) ___overlaps___ the class TEACHERS (T).

Some men are teachers and some teachers are men, thus the class MEN overlaps the class TEACHERS. This means that the second diagram fits. The overlapping part, or intersection, represents MEN TEACHERS.

If the first diagram is tried with T in the outer circle, it would mean that all men are teachers, which is not true. If the first diagram is tried with M in the outer circle, it would mean that all teachers are men, which is not true. The first diagram does not fit these classes.

If the last diagram is used with M in one circle and T in the other, it would mean that no men are teachers, which is not true. The last diagram does not fit these classes.

322   © 2006 The Critical Thinking Co.™ • www.CriticalThinking.com • 800-458-4849

Panel 2 (p. 323)

Building Thinking Skills® — Book Two   Verbal Classifications

DIAGRAMMING CLASSES—SELECT AND EXPLAIN

DIRECTIONS: Describe the relationships between two groups of household items and then pick the diagram that describes this relationship. Use the abbreviations in the parentheses to label the diagram correctly. You may use one of the following phrases to fill in the blank in the sentence describing the classes.

includes, is included in, overlaps, or is separate from

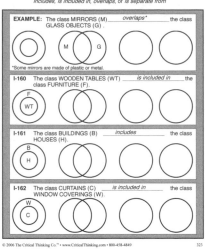

EXAMPLE: The class MIRRORS (M) ___overlaps*___ the class GLASS OBJECTS (G) .

*Some mirrors are made of plastic or metal.

I-160 The class WOODEN TABLES (WT) ___is included in___ the class FURNITURE (F).

I-161 The class BUILDINGS (B) ___includes___ the class HOUSES (H).

I-162 The class CURTAINS (C) ___is included in___ the class WINDOW COVERINGS (W).

© 2006 The Critical Thinking Co.™ • www.CriticalThinking.com • 800-458-4849   323

Panel 3 (p. 324)

Building Thinking Skills® — Book Two   Verbal Classifications

DIAGRAMMING CLASSES—SELECT AND EXPLAIN

DIRECTIONS: Describe the relationship between two classes of life science terms and then pick the diagram that describes this relationship. Use the abbreviations in the parentheses to label the diagram correctly. You may use one of the following phrases to fill in the blank in the sentence describing the classes.

includes, is included in, overlaps, or is separate from

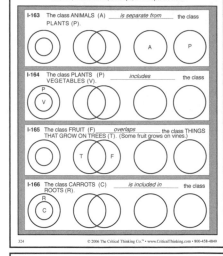

I-163 The class ANIMALS (A) ___is separate from___ the class PLANTS (P).

I-164 The class PLANTS (P) ___includes___ the class VEGETABLES (V).

I-165 The class FRUIT (F) ___overlaps___ the class THINGS THAT GROW ON TREES (T). (Some fruit grows on vines.)

I-166 The class CARROTS (C) ___is included in___ the class ROOTS (R).

324   © 2006 The Critical Thinking Co.™ • www.CriticalThinking.com • 800-458-4849

Panel 4 (p. 325)

Building Thinking Skills® — Book Two   Verbal Classifications

DIAGRAMMING CLASSES—SELECT AND EXPLAIN

DIRECTIONS: Describe the relationship between two classes of earth science terms and then pick the diagram that describes this relationship. Use the abbreviations in the parentheses to label the diagram correctly. You may use one of the following phrases to fill in the blank in the sentence describing the classes.

includes, is included in, overlaps, or is separate from

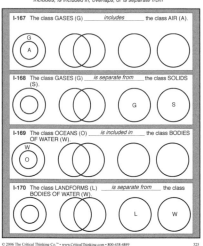

I-167 The class GASES (G) ___includes___ the class AIR (A).

I-168 The class GASES (G) ___is separate from___ the class SOLIDS (S).

I-169 The class OCEANS (O) ___is included in___ the class BODIES OF WATER (W).

I-170 The class LANDFORMS (L) ___is separate from___ the class BODIES OF WATER (W).

© 2006 The Critical Thinking Co.™ • www.CriticalThinking.com • 800-458-4849   325

Panel 5 (p. 326)

Building Thinking Skills® — Book Two   Verbal Classifications

DIAGRAMMING CLASSES—SELECT AND EXPLAIN

DIRECTIONS: Describe the relationship between two classes of geometry terms and then pick the diagram that describes this relationship. Use the abbreviations in the parentheses to label the diagram correctly. You may use one of the following phrases to fill in the blank in the sentence describing the classes.

includes, is included in, overlaps, or is separate from

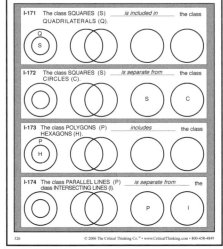

I-171 The class SQUARES (S) ___is included in___ the class QUADRILATERALS (Q).

I-172 The class SQUARES (S) ___is separate from___ the class CIRCLES (C).

I-173 The class POLYGONS (P) ___includes___ the class HEXAGONS (H).

I-174 The class PARALLEL LINES (P) ___is separate from___ the class INTERSECTING LINES (I).

326   © 2006 The Critical Thinking Co.™ • www.CriticalThinking.com • 800-458-4849

Panel 6 (p. 327)

Building Thinking Skills® — Book Two   Verbal Classifications

OVERLAPPING CLASSES—MATRIX

DIRECTIONS: If words or names can be described by two characteristics, a matrix diagram can be used to show that relationship. Each item must fit in the box that shows the characteristic of the row and the characteristic of the column. Here is an exercise that illustrates the use of a matrix diagram.

I-175 At Wilson School, it is not possible for students to take both band and chorus, so the boys and girls in Ms. Robinson's class take either band or chorus. Fill in the following matrix diagram showing the music activities of Ms. Robinson's class.

STUDENT	ACTIVITY
Anne	Chorus
Bruce	Band
Carl	Band
Donna	Band
Harold	Chorus
Ivan	Chorus
Jane	Band
Kathy	Band
Mary	Chorus
Ruth	Chorus

EXAMPLE: Anne is in the chorus.
Anne is a girl and her name belongs in row 2. Anne is in the chorus and her name also belongs in the chorus column—column 2 on the right. Anne's name appears in the matrix as shown below.

	Column 1 BAND	Column 2 CHORUS
Row 1 BOYS	Bruce Carl	Harold Ivan
Row 2 GIRLS	Donna Jane Kathy	Anne Mary Ruth

© 2006 The Critical Thinking Co.™ • www.CriticalThinking.com • 800-458-4849   327

Panel 7 (p. 328)

Building Thinking Skills® — Book Two   Verbal Classifications

OVERLAPPING CLASSES—MATRIX

DIRECTIONS: Sort the following words in the choice box by their material and their use. If an item is commonly made of more than one type of material, list it in more than one row.

I-176	CHOICE BOX
	button, brush, bolt, can, cotton, string, clothespin, eraser, aluminum foil, frying pan, glue, ice cream carton, jar, kettle, masking tape, mop, paint scraper, paper cup, pocket, rag, rubber band, safety pin, staple, steel wool, styrofoam sandwich box, tank, toothpaste tube, trash bag, wire, wire brush

EXAMPLE: nail
A nail is used to fasten boards together. A nail is made of metal. Therefore, a nail can be classified as both a fastener and metal. The word *nail* should be classified in the matrix box in the fastener column and the metal row as shown below.

	FASTENERS	CLEANERS	CONTAINERS
PLASTIC	button (bolt) clothespin	brush (mop) paint scraper	ice cream carton jar styrofoam sandwich box tank toothpaste tube trash bag
METAL	nail button bolt safety pin staple wire	paint scraper steel wool wire brush	can aluminum foil frying pan kettle tank
OTHER	(button) cotton string glue masking tape rubber band	brush eraser mop rag	ice cream carton paper cup pocket trash tank jar

328   © 2006 The Critical Thinking Co.™ • www.CriticalThinking.com • 800-458-4849

Panel 8 (p. 329)

Building Thinking Skills® — Book Two   Verbal Classifications

OVERLAPPING CLASSES—MATRIX

DIRECTIONS: Sort the following words in the choice box by their taste, touch, sound, or appearance. Use the matrix to show whether the word is generally favorable, generally unfavorable, or sometimes favorable. Words may be used in more than one column.

I-177	CHOICE BOX
	beautiful, bitter, blinding, bright, cool, deafening, delicious, dull, fine, furry, handsome, icy, loud, musical, noisy, plain, rough, salty, scalding, sharp, soft, soothing, sour, spoiled, sweet, ugly, warm, wet

EXAMPLE: ripe
Ripe can be used to describe both the appearance and the taste of being ready to eat. Since readiness to eat is favorable, *ripe* fits into the matrix in the generally favorable row and in both the taste and appearance columns.

	TASTE	TOUCH	SOUND	APPEARANCE
GENERALLY FAVORABLE	ripe delicious soothing	cool furry soft soothing	beautiful musical soft sweet soothing	fine ripe beautiful cool handsome sharp
GENERALLY UNFAVORABLE	bitter sharp spoiled	rough scalding	deafening dull sour noisy	loud blinding dull rough ugly spoiled
SOMETIMES FAVORABLE & SOMETIMES UNFAVORABLE	salty sweet sour	icy sharp warm wet	loud sharp	bright plain soft wet

© 2006 The Critical Thinking Co.™ • www.CriticalThinking.com • 800-458-4849   329

Panel 9 (p. 330)

Building Thinking Skills® — Book Two   Verbal Classifications

RELATIONSHIPS—EXPLAIN

DIRECTIONS: Each word in box A is related in the same way to the word on the same line in box B. Describe how the words in box A are related to the words in box B.

I-178

A	B	Relationship
bird	robin	*Each member of group B is*
book	novel	*a kind of its corresponding*
dog	setter	*member in group A.*
fruit	lemon	
reptile	lizard	

I-179

A	B	Relationship
bicycle	handlebar	*Each member of group B is*
bird	feather	*a part of its corresponding*
chair	arm	*member of group A.*
river	mouth	
tree	trunk	

I-180

A	B	Relationship
beat	rhythm	*Each member of group A is a*
degree	temperature	*measure of its corresponding*
foot	length	*member of group B.*
month	time	
watt	electricity	

I-181

A	B	Relationship
box	lid	*Each member of group B is the*
building	roof	*top part of its corresponding*
hill	crest	*member of group A.*
mountain	peak	
room	ceiling	

330   © 2006 The Critical Thinking Co.™ • www.CriticalThinking.com • 800-458-4849

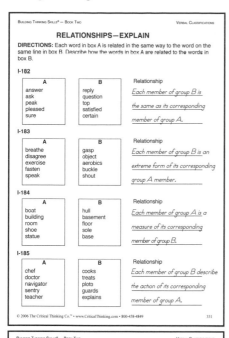

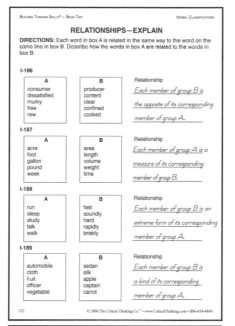

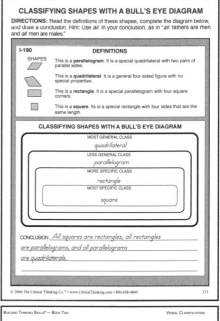

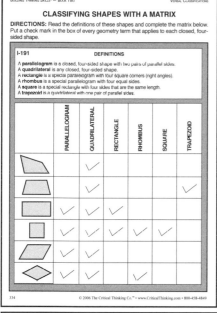

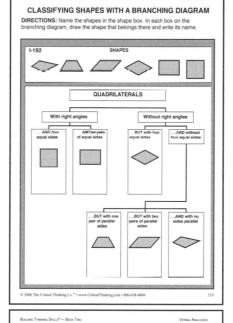

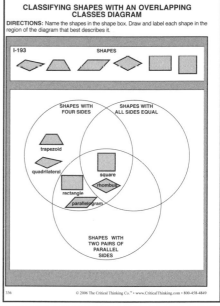

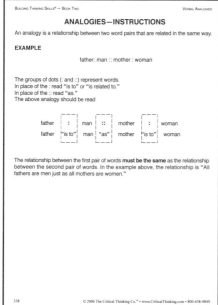

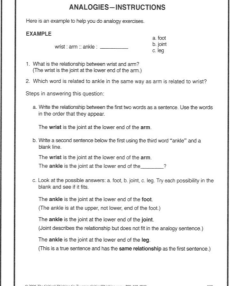

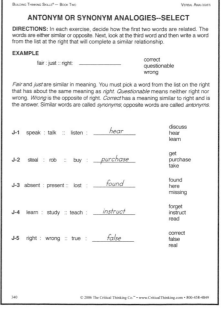

ASSOCIATION ANALOGIES—SELECT

DIRECTIONS: In each exercise, decide how the first two words are related. The words will be associated in some way. Next, look at the third word and then write a word from the list at the right that will complete a similar relationship.

EXAMPLE

flour : bread :: fabric : _____
- cloth
- clothing
- material

Flour is associated with breadmaking just as fabric is associated with the making of clothing. *Cloth* and *material* are synonyms for *fabric*. So the best answer is *clothing*.

J-6   knob : door :: key : _lock_
- bolt
- hinge
- lock

J-7   pie : crust :: clam : _shell_
- crab
- shell
- oyster

J-8   money : wallet :: liquid : _bottle_
- bottle
- drink
- fluid

J-9   September : autumn :: March : _spring_
- fall
- spring
- winter

J-10 bank : money :: library : _books_
- books
- buildings
- cards

J-11 paw : foot :: fur : _hair_
- animal
- beast
- hair

J-12 stake : tent :: anchor : _boat_
- boat
- dock
- pole

"KIND OF" ANALOGIES—SELECT

DIRECTIONS: In each exercise, decide how the first two words are related. The first word represents a "kind of " the second. Next, look at the third word and then write a word from the list at the right that will complete a similar relationship.

EXAMPLE

tea : drink :: pork : _____
- beef
- meat
- salad

Tea is a *kind of* drink. Which of the words on the right answers the question, "Pork is a *kind of* _____?" Pork is not a *kind of* beef and pork is not a *kind of* salad. Pork is a *kind of* meat, so the best answer is *meat*.

J-13 oak : wood :: cotton : _cloth_
- cloth
- nylon
- velvet

J-14 water : liquid :: air : _gas_
- gas
- temperature
- wind

J-15 nibble : bite :: glimpse : _look_
- feel
- look
- taste

J-16 heat : energy :: gasoline : _fuel_
- automobile
- force
- fuel

J-17 marble : stone :: diamond : _jewel_
- gold
- jewel
- money

J-18 map : chart :: photograph : _picture_
- film
- painting
- picture

J-19 chick : bird :: minnow : _fish_
- animal
- fish
- tadpole

"PART OF" ANALOGIES—SELECT

DIRECTIONS: In each exercise, decide how the first two words are related. The first word represents a "part of" the second. Next, look at the third word and then write a word from the list at the right that will complete a similar relationship.

EXAMPLE

scales : fish :: bark : _____
- dog
- skin
- tree

Scales are the outer *part of* a fish. Which of the words on the right answers the question, "Bark is the outer *part of* _____?" Dog is not the answer. Dogs bark, but bark is not the outer *part of* a dog. Skin is not the answer. Bark and skin are outer parts, but bark is not the outer *part of* skin. Since bark is the outer *part of* a tree, *tree* is the best answer.

J-20 plant : garden :: tree : _forest_
- branch
- forest
- pine

J-21 bulb : lamp :: flame : _candle_
- ash
- candle
- heat

J-22 speech : language :: melody : _music_
- instrument
- music
- note

J-23 player : team :: student : _class_
- class
- pupil
- teacher

J-24 seat : theater :: cage : _zoo_
- animal
- bars
- zoo

J-25 quarter : game :: season : _year_
- day
- month
- year

"USED TO" ANALOGIES—SELECT

DIRECTIONS: In each exercise, decide how the first two words are related. The second word tells what the first word is "used to" do. Next, look at the third word and then write a word from the list at the right that will complete a similar relationship.

EXAMPLE

latch : lock :: knob : _____
- bolt
- open
- swing

A latch is *used to* lock a door. Which of the words on the right answers the question, "Knob is *used to* _____?" *Bolt* is not the answer. A bolt is similar to a latch, but a knob is not *used to* bolt a door. *Swing* is not the answer. A knob is not *used to* swing a door; a hinge is *used to* swing a door. A knob is *used to* open a door; *open* is the best answer.

J-26 closet : hang :: trunk : _store_
- clean
- dispose
- store

J-27 typewriter : write :: calculator : _compute_
- arrange
- compute
- list

J-28 note : remind :: diary : _record_
- inform
- record
- write

J-29 shield : protect :: sword : _attack_
- attack
- cover
- handle

J-30 pliers : grip :: screwdriver : _turn_
- lock
- pound
- turn

J-31 sponge : soak up :: towel : _dry_
- dampen
- dry
- wash

ACTION ANALOGIES—SELECT

DIRECTIONS: In each exercise, decide how the first two words are related. The second word gives an action done by the first word. Next, look at the third word and then write a word from the list at the right that will complete a similar relationship.

EXAMPLE

surgeon : operates :: mechanic : _____
- cuts
- removes
- repairs

An analogy which relates a person to what he or she does, or a thing to what it does is called an action analogy. The main task that a surgeon performs is to "operate" on a patient. The main task that a mechanic performs is to "repair" a broken machine. As part of the repair task, the mechanic may need to cut or remove a part, but neither cutting nor removing is his main task.

J-32 vein : carries :: heart : _pumps_
- protects
- pumps
- stores

J-33 demonstration : shows :: novel : _tells_
- displays
- opens
- tells

J-34 boxer : fights :: priest : _prays_
- builds
- prays
- sings

J-35 elastic : stretches :: balloon : _expands_
- deflates
- expands
- shrinks

J-36 joke : amuses :: lesson : _informs_
- entertains
- informs
- tests

J-37 conductor : directs :: orchestra : _plays_
- guides
- plays
- sings

ANTONYM OR SYNONYM ANALOGIES—SELECT

DIRECTIONS: In each exercise, decide how the first two words are related. Next, look at the third word and then write a word from the choice box that will complete a similar relationship. Some words may be used more than once.

CHOICE BOX

few, many, much, one

J-38 pair : twin :: single : _one_

J-39 many : several :: some : _few_

J-40 number : many :: amount : _much_

J-41 sole : only :: several : _many_

J-42 few : some :: lone : _one_

J-43 few : many :: some : _much_

J-44 several : single :: many : _one_

J-45 some : several :: few : _many_

J-46 few : some :: sole : _one_

ASSOCIATION ANALOGIES—SELECT

DIRECTIONS: In each exercise, decide how the first two words are associated. Next, look at the third word and then write a word from the choice box that will complete a similar relationship. Some words may be used more than once.

EXAMPLE: square inch : area :: cubic inch : _____

A square inch is a measurement of area in the same way that a cubic inch is a measurement of volume.

square inch : area :: cubic inch : _volume_

CHOICE BOX

area, length, volume, weight

J-47 gallon : volume :: pound : _weight_

J-48 inch : length :: square inch : _area_

J-49 cube : volume :: square : _area_

J-50 triangle : area :: pyramid : _volume_

J-51 sphere : volume :: circle : _area_

J-52 acre : area :: gallon : _volume_

J-53 ton : weight :: cup : _volume_

J-54 ounce : weight :: cup : _volume_

J-55 cubic inch : volume :: square inch : _area_

ANTONYM OR SYNONYM ANALOGIES—SELECT A PAIR

DIRECTIONS: In each exercise, read the pair of words and decide how they are related. Next, select a pair of words from the choice box that will complete the analogy. The pairs in the choice box may be used more than once.

CHOICE BOX

all : none   have : possess   send : receive

J-56 need : require :: _have_ : _possess_

J-57 sell : buy :: _send_ : _receive_

J-58 everything : nothing :: _all_ : _none_

J-59 make : create :: _have_ : _possess_

J-60 full : empty :: _all_ : _none_

J-61 talk : listen :: _send_ : _receive_

J-62 everyone : no one :: _all_ : _none_

J-63 hold : own :: _have_ : _possess_

J-64 give : get :: _send_ : _receive_

ASSOCIATION ANALOGIES—SELECT

DIRECTIONS: In this exercise, two members of an association analogy are supplied. Select two words from the choice box that will complete the analogy. Words in the choice box may be used more than once.

EXAMPLE: garage : _____ :: _____ : barn

A garage is associated with the city, while a barn is associated with the country.

CHOICE BOX

city, country, county, nation, state

J-65 mayor : _city_ :: governor : _state_

J-66 city : _county_ :: county : _state_

J-67 road : _county OR country_ :: avenue : _city_

J-68 governor : _state_ :: president : _nation_

J-69 county : _state_ :: state : _nation_

J-70 police chief : _city_ :: sheriff : _county_

J-71 acre : _country_ :: block : _city_

J-72 garden : _city_ :: farm : _country_

ANALOGIES—SELECT TWO

DIRECTIONS: In this exercise, two members of an analogy are supplied. Select two words from the choice box that will complete the analogy. These analogies are of three types—"used to," "association," and "synonyms." Words in the choice box may be used more than once.

CHOICE BOX

hear, read, see, talk

J-73	books :	_read_	::	audio tape :	_hear_
J-74	discuss :	_talk_	::	listen :	_hear_
J-75	examine :	_see_	::	study :	_read_
J-76	inspect :	_see_	::	converse :	_talk_
J-77	television :	_see_	::	stereo :	_hear_
J-78	blind :	_see_	::	deaf :	_hear_
J-79	actors :	_talk_	::	editors :	_read_
J-80	sounds :	_hear_	::	sights :	_see_
J-81	observe :	_see_	::	chatter :	_talk_
J-82	telescope :	_see_	::	telephone :	_hear OR talk_
J-83	microphone :	_talk_	::	microscope :	_see_

350   © 2006 The Critical Thinking Co.™ • www.CriticalThinking.com • 800-458-4849

ANALOGIES—SELECT TWO

DIRECTIONS: In this exercise, two members of an analogy are supplied. Select two words from the choice box that will complete the analogy. These analogies are of three types—"action," "kind of," and "part of." Words in the choice box may be used more than once.

CHOICE BOX

bear, bird, feathers, fish, fur, robin, scales, tuna

J-84	fur :	_bear_	:: scales :	_fish OR tuna_	
J-85	eagle : feather ::	_bear OR tuna_ :	_fur OR scales_		
J-86	bear : mammal ::	_robin OR tuna_ :	_bird OR fish_		
J-87	_scales OR tuna_ : fish ::	_feathers OR robin_ :	bird		
J-88	_robin OR bird_ : flies ::	_tuna OR fish_ :	swims		
J-89	lungs :	_bear OR bird OR robin_ ::	gills :	_fish OR tuna_	
J-90	_bear_ :	growls ::	_robin OR_ :	sings	
J-91	wing :	_bird OR robin_ :: fin :	_fish OR tuna_		
J-92	hair :	_bear_	:: feather :	_bird OR robin_	
J-93	scales :	_fish OR tuna_ :: feathers :	_bird OR robin_		
J-94	tuna :	_fish_	:: robin :	_bird_	

351   © 2006 The Critical Thinking Co.™ • www.CriticalThinking.com • 800-458-4849

ANALOGIES—EXPLAIN

DIRECTIONS: Read these analogies and decide how the words in each pair are related. On the line below each analogy, explain the relationship between the words in each pair.

Here is a list of the kinds of analogies you have practiced. Use the list to help explain these analogies.

ANTONYM   KIND OF   SYNONYM
ASSOCIATION   PART OF   USED TO

EXAMPLE: banana : fruit :: carrot : vegetable

A banana is a kind of fruit just as a carrot is a kind of vegetable.

J-95   bored : excited :: rested : weary

Bored and excited are opposite physical feelings, and rested and weary are opposite physical feelings.

J-96   beef : hamburger :: potatoes : French fries

A hamburger is a kind of cooked beef, just as French fries are a kind of cooked potato.

J-97   compliment : praise :: criticize : blame

The words of each pair have similar meanings dealing with judgement.

J-98   hammer : nail :: bat : ball

A hammer is used to hit a nail, just as a bat is used to hit a ball.

352   © 2006 The Critical Thinking Co.™ • www.CriticalThinking.com • 800-458-4849

ANALOGIES—EXPLAIN

DIRECTIONS: Read these analogies and decide how the words in each pair are related. On the line below each analogy, explain the relationship between the words in each pair.

Here is a list of the kinds of analogies you have practiced. Use the list to help explain these analogies.

ANTONYM   KIND OF   SYNONYM
ASSOCIATION   PART OF   USED TO

J-99   beetle : insect :: snake : reptile

A beetle is a kind of insect, just as a snake is a kind of reptile.

J-100   teacher : instruction :: musician : entertainment

A teacher is associated with instruction, and a musician is associated with entertainment.

J-101   stare : gaze :: glance : notice

The words of each pair have similar meanings dealing with intensity of examination.

J-102   gusty : calm :: windy : still

The words of each pair have opposite meanings dealing with wind strength.

J-103   pliers : grip :: hammer : pound

Pliers are used to grip and a hammer is used to pound.

353   © 2006 The Critical Thinking Co.™ • www.CriticalThinking.com • 800-458-4849

ANALOGIES—EXPLAIN

DIRECTIONS: Read these analogies and decide how the words in each pair are related. On the line below each analogy, explain the relationship between the words in each pair.

Here is a list of the kinds of analogies you have practiced. Use the list to help explain these analogies.

ANTONYM   KIND OF   SYNONYM
ASSOCIATION   PART OF   USED TO

J-104   wick : candle :: bulb : lamp

A wick is part of a candle, just as a bulb is part of a lamp.

J-105   budget : money :: schedule : time

A budget is a plan for money, just as a schedule is a plan for time.

J-106   even : smooth :: coarse : rough

The words of each pair have similar meanings dealing with texture.

J-107   hook : hang :: anchor : hold

A hook is used to hang things, and an anchor is used to hold things.

J-108   advance : retreat :: forward : backward

The words of each pair have opposite meanings dealing with direction.

354   © 2006 The Critical Thinking Co.™ • www.CriticalThinking.com • 800-458-4849

ANALOGIES—EXPLAIN

DIRECTIONS: Read these analogies and decide how the words in each pair are related. On the line below each analogy, explain the relationship between the words in each pair.

Here is a list of the kinds of analogies you have practiced. Use the list to help explain these analogies.

ANTONYM   KIND OF   SYNONYM
ASSOCIATION   PART OF   USED TO

J-109   dial : radio :: switch : lamp

A dial is part of a radio, and a switch is part of a lamp.

J-110   cloth : wash :: towel : dry

A cloth is used to wash, just as a towel is used to dry.

J-111   fly : sky :: float : water

Fly is associated with sky, and float is associated with water.

J-112   ballot : vote :: check : pay

A ballot is used to vote, and a check is used to pay.

J-113   yam : potato :: lima : bean

A yam is a kind of potato, and a lima is a kind of bean.

355   © 2006 The Critical Thinking Co.™ • www.CriticalThinking.com • 800-458-4849

ANTONYM OR SYNONYM ANALOGIES—SUPPLY

DIRECTIONS: Look at the first two words. Think about how they are related. The words are either similar or opposite. Next, look at the third word and produce a word from your memory that has a similar relationship.

J-114	passenger : traveler :: guest :	_visitor_
J-115	valley : peak :: bottom :	_top_
J-116	twilight : dusk :: autumn :	_fall_
J-117	frequently : often :: shortly :	_soon_
J-118	hunt : search :: locate :	_find_
J-119	stick : pole :: pit :	_hole_
J-120	close : distant :: near :	_far_
J-121	insect : bug :: child :	_kid_
J-122	quiet : loud :: silent :	_noisy_
J-123	shut : close :: unfasten :	_open OR unlock_
J-124	bright : dim :: shiny :	_dull_
J-125	dash : race :: stroll :	_walk OR hike_
J-126	sprinkle : rain :: snack :	_meal_

Sample Answer

356   © 2006 The Critical Thinking Co.™ • www.CriticalThinking.com • 800-458-4849

ASSOCIATION ANALOGIES—SUPPLY

DIRECTIONS: Look at the first two words. Think about how they are related. The words are associated in some way. Next, look at the third word and produce a word from your memory that has a similar relationship.

J-127	father : son :: king :	_prince_
J-128	mouse : rat :: pebble :	_rock OR stone_
J-129	sheet : bed :: rug :	_floor_
J-130	path : road :: hill :	_mountain_
J-131	pink : red :: gray :	_black_
J-132	seal : pup :: lion :	_cub_
J-133	scared : tremble :: sad :	_cry OR sob_
J-134	salesperson : customer :: teacher :	_student_
J-135	designer : pattern :: architect :	_plan OR blueprint_
J-136	actor : script :: singer :	_music OR score_
J-137	mother : father :: aunt :	_uncle_
J-138	instructor : pupil :: doctor :	_patient_
J-139	cloudburst : rain :: blizzard :	_snow_

Sample Answer

357   © 2006 The Critical Thinking Co.™ • www.CriticalThinking.com • 800-458-4849

"KIND OF" ANALOGIES—SUPPLY

DIRECTIONS: Look at the first two words. Think about how they are related. The first word represents a "kind of" the second. Next, look at the third word and produce a word from your memory that has a similar relationship.

J-140	sedan : automobile :: pickup :	_truck_
J-141	refrigerator : appliance :: chair :	_furniture_
J-142	jeans : pants :: sneakers :	_shoes_
J-143	cherry : berry :: almond :	_nut_
J-144	ice : solid :: water :	_liquid_
J-145	hamburger : sandwich :: milk shake :	_drink_
J-146	bean : vegetable :: orange :	_fruit_
J-147	granite : rock :: iron :	_metal OR ore_
J-148	swan : bird :: ant :	_insect_
J-149	macaroon : cookie :: fudge :	_candy_
J-150	bunk : bed :: rocker :	_chair_
J-151	ten-speed : bicycle :: convertible :	_car OR automobile_
J-152	novel : book :: ballad :	_song OR poem_

Sample Answer

358   © 2006 The Critical Thinking Co.™ • www.CriticalThinking.com • 800-458-4849

"PART OF" ANALOGIES—SUPPLY

DIRECTIONS: Look at the first two words. Think about how they are related. The first word represents "part of" the second. Next, look at the third word and produce a word from your memory that has a similar relationship.

J-153	tooth : tiger :: tusk :	*elephant OR walrus*
J-154	bone : skeleton :: brick :	*house OR wall*
J-155	leg : pants :: sleeve :	*coat OR shirt*
J-156	article : newspaper :: chapter :	*book*
J-157	handle bars : bicycle :: steering wheel :	*car OR truck*
J-158	hip : leg :: shoulder :	*arm*
J-159	intermission : play :: recess :	*school*
J-160	needle : pine :: blade :	*grass*
J-161	root : plant :: foundation :	*building*
J-162	tuner : radio :: channel selector :	*television*
J-163	volume control : stereo :: thermostat :	*furnace OR air conditioner*
J-164	flaps : airplane :: brakes :	*car OR truck*
J-165	needle : compass :: hands :	*clock*

© 2006 The Critical Thinking Co.® • www.CriticalThinking.com • 800-458-4849   359

"USED TO" ANALOGIES—SUPPLY

DIRECTIONS: Look at the first two words. The second word tells what the first word is "used to" do. Next, look at the third word and produce a word from your memory that has a similar relationship.

J-166	straw : drink :: fork :	*eat*
J-167	pencil : write :: crayon :	*color OR draw*
J-168	telephone : hear :: telescope :	*see*
J-169	knife : slice :: scissors :	*cut*
J-170	mop : wash :: broom :	*sweep*
J-171	pencil : mark :: ruler :	*measure*
J-172	paperclip : fasten :: shoelace :	*tie*
J-173	finger : touches :: tongue :	*taste*
J-174	glasses : see :: crutches :	*walk*
J-175	food : eat :: juice :	*drink*
J-176	paint : wall :: shingles :	*roof*
J-177	blanket : cover :: basket :	*hold*
J-178	ruler : line :: proctractor :	*angle*

360   © 2006 The Critical Thinking Co.® • www.CriticalThinking.com • 800-458-4849

ACTION ANALOGIES—SUPPLY

DIRECTIONS: Look at the first two words. The words are related by some "kind of" action. Next, look at the third word and produce a word from your memory that has a similar relationship.

J-179	teacher : teaches :: student :	*learns OR studies*
J-180	batter : hits :: fielder :	*catches*
J-181	airplane : flies :: automobile :	*drives*
J-182	latch : locks :: knob :	*turns OR opens*
J-183	seamstress : sews :: carpenter :	*builds OR nails*
J-184	dynamite : explodes :: candle :	*burns*
J-185	actor : speaks :: author :	*writes*
J-186	pilot : flies :: pianist :	*plays*
J-187	burglar : steals :: customer :	*buys*
J-188	water : boils :: ice :	*melts*
J-189	retailer : sells :: manufacture :	*produces OR makes*
J-190	thunder : claps :: lightning :	*flashes*
J-191	iron : sinks :: wood :	*floats*

© 2006 The Critical Thinking Co.® • www.CriticalThinking.com • 800-458-4849   361

ANALOGIES—SUPPLY

DIRECTIONS: Look at the first two words. Think about how they are related. Next, look at the third word and produce a word from your memory that has a similar relationship.

J-192	idle : active :: lazy :	*busy*
J-193	groan : moan :: laugh :	*giggle*
J-194	bird : flies :: fish :	*swims*
J-195	mare : stallion :: hen :	*rooster*
J-196	arrival : departure :: birth :	*death*
J-197	hinge : door :: elbow :	*arm*
J-198	woman : blouse :: man :	*shirt*
J-199	sand : grain :: rain :	*drop*
J-200	ring : jewelry :: coat :	*clothing*
J-201	word : sentence :: letter :	*word*
J-202	tow : pull :: shove :	*push*
J-203	flower : seed :: chicken :	*egg*
J-204	flavor : taste :: tone :	*hear*

362   © 2006 The Critical Thinking Co.® • www.CriticalThinking.com • 800-458-4849

ANALOGIES—SUPPLY

DIRECTIONS: Look at the first two words. Think about how they are related. Next, look at the third word and produce a word from your memory that has a similar relationship.

J-205	fingers : grasp :: teeth :	*chew OR bite*
J-206	sight : vision :: touch :	*feel*
J-207	pass : receive :: pitch :	*catch*
J-208	feeble : powerful :: weak :	*strong*
J-209	succeed : win :: fail :	*lose*
J-210	brush : paint :: pencil :	*write*
J-211	iron : metal :: water :	*liquid*
J-212	flock : sheep :: herd :	*cattle*
J-213	fake : phony :: actual :	*real*
J-214	raise : lower :: lift :	*drop*
J-215	steal : rob :: purchase :	*buy*
J-216	valuable : worthless :: expensive :	*cheap*
J-217	attorney : lawyer :: physician :	*doctor*

© 2006 The Critical Thinking Co.® • www.CriticalThinking.com • 800-458-4849   363

ANALOGIES—EXPLAIN AND SUPPLY A PAIR

DIRECTIONS: Read the pair of words and decide how they are related. On the lines below each analogy, explain the relationship between the words. After you have explained the relationship, supply a pair of words that will complete the analogy.

EXAMPLE: gallon : volume :: _____ : _____

The gallon is associated with volume as a measurement of volume. A possible similar association might be pound as a measurement of weight. The analogy would then be:

gallon : volume :: *pound* : *weight*

J-218   soldier : army :: *sailor* : *navy*
A soldier is part of an army, and a sailor is part of a navy.

J-219   dirty : clean :: *illegal* : *legal*
Dirty is the opposite of clean, and illegal is the opposite of legal.

J-220   oats : grain :: *apple* : *fruit*
Oats are a kind of grain, and an apple is a kind of fruit.

364   © 2006 The Critical Thinking Co.® • www.CriticalThinking.com • 800-458-4849

ANALOGIES—EXPLAIN AND SUPPLY A PAIR

DIRECTIONS: Read the pair of words and decide how they are related. On the lines below each analogy, explain the relationship between the words. After you have explained the relationship, supply a pair of words that will complete the analogy.

J-221   train : track :: *car* : *highway*
A train runs on a track, and a car runs on a highway.

J-222   artist : paints :: *author* : *writes*
An artist paints, and an author writes.

J-223   chief : tribe :: *mayor* : *city*
A chief is the head of a tribe, and a mayor is the head of a city.

J-224   quiet : loud :: *ripe* : *rotten*
Quiet is the opposite of loud, and ripe is the opposite of rotten.

© 2006 The Critical Thinking Co.® • www.CriticalThinking.com • 800-458-4849   365

ANALOGIES—EXPLAIN AND SUPPLY A PAIR

DIRECTIONS: Read the pair of words and decide how they are related. On the lines below each analogy, explain the relationship between the words. After you have explained the relationship, supply a pair of words that will complete the analogy.

J-225   silly : foolish :: *smart* : *intelligent*
Silly and foolish mean the same thing, just as smart and intelligent mean the same thing.

J-226   lemon : sour :: *candy* : *sweet*
A lemon is sour, just as candy is sweet.

J-227   spots : leopard :: *trunk* : *elephant*
Spots are a characteristic of a leopard, just as a trunk is a characteristic of an elephant.

J-228   food : eat :: *beverage* : *drink*
Food is used to eat, just as a beverage is used to drink.

366   © 2006 The Critical Thinking Co.® • www.CriticalThinking.com • 800-458-4849

ANALOGIES—PRODUCE

DIRECTIONS: Now that you have practiced selecting and supplying the words to complete six different kinds of analogies, you are ready to create your own. See if you can produce eight or more analogies from the words in the choice box.

CHOICE BOX

bird, fins, fish, fly, horse, land, legs, sea, sky, swim, walk, wings

J-229   *fins : fish :: wings : birds*

J-230   *wings : birds :: legs : horse*

J-231   *fly : wings :: walk : legs*

J-232   *fly (insect) : wings :: horse : legs*

J-233   *fins : swim :: legs : walk*

J-234   *legs : walk :: wings : fly*

J-235   *fly : sky :: swim : sea*

J-236   *wings : sky :: legs : land*

© 2006 The Critical Thinking Co.® • www.CriticalThinking.com • 800-458-4849   367